CONSTITUTING SCOTLAND

CONSTITUTING SCOTLAND

THE SCOTTISH NATIONAL MOVEMENT
AND THE WESTMINSTER MODEL

◆ ◆ ◆

W. ELLIOT BULMER

EDINBURGH
University Press

Edinburgh University Press is one of the leading university presses
in the UK. We publish academic books and journals in our selected subject
areas across the humanities and social sciences, combining cutting-edge
scholarship with high editorial and production values to produce academic
works of lasting importance. For more information visit our website:
edinburghuniversitypress.com

Edinburgh University Press Ltd
The Tun – Holyrood Road
12 (2f) Jackson's Entry
Edinburgh EH8 8PJ

Typeset in 10/11.5 Sabon by
Servis Filmsetting Ltd, Stockport, Cheshire

A CIP record for this book is available from the British Library

ISBN 978 0 7486 9759 5 (hardback)
ISBN 978 0 7486 9760 1 (webready PDF)

CONTENTS

ACKNOWLEDGEMENTS

I wish to thank the staff of Edinburgh University Press for their patience throughout the long process of producing this book.

I would also like to thank Ian McCann at SNP HQ for granting permission to reproduce the 2002 Draft Constitution in the appendices and Robbie Moffat for permission to reproduce the Scottish Provisional Constituent Assembly text.

Thanks are also due to Dr Craig McAngus for his advice throughout the project and for his comments on the text.

This project would never have come to fruition without the beneficial influence of Professor Chris Thornhill, Dr Thomas Lundberg, and Professor Michael Keating.

As always, I am thankful to my parents.

Above all, I must express immense gratitude to my wife, Eva Dominguez, for her willing and unstinting assistance in typing, editing and collating references. As far as I am concerned she is the world's best Research Assistant.

INTRODUCTION

Scotland's Unfinished Constitutional Revolution

On 18 September 2014 a referendum took place in Scotland to decide the question of whether Scotland should be an independent country. The independence referendum was the culmination of decades of campaigning for statehood by the Scottish National Party (SNP). Between its first major electoral breakthrough in the Hamilton by-election of 1967 and the achievement of an overall majority in the Scottish Parliament in 2011, the SNP had grown from a small fringe party with a (then rather far-fetched) commitment to Scottish independence, into a competent and professional party of government that was on the verge of achieving its founding aim.[1]

In the event of a 'Yes' vote in the 2014 independence referendum, Scotland would have recovered the independent statehood that was lost by the Treaty of Union more than three centuries ago. According to the plans of the Scottish government, the new Scottish state would have been based upon a new constitutional foundation: a written constitution. The SNP has long advocated a written Constitution for an independent Scotland and from the late 1960s to the present day, the party has had plenty of time to develop its 'constitutional prospectus' for an independent Scotland.[2] Moreover, it has supported a form of Constitution that, while still within the Westminster-derived 'family' of constitutions, differs in important matters of both substance and structure from the constitutional orthodoxies and traditional institutions of the United Kingdom.

This book tells the story of that constitution. It remains, of course, 'a constitution that never was', a constitution for a state which is not yet in existence. The Constitution of an independent Scotland, therefore, cannot be found in definitive form, but exists only in potentia, in various 'drafts', 'proposals' and 'interim' versions. Yet these constitutional proposals nevertheless reveal much about the Scottish national movement. They show that Scottish nationalism has long been concerned not only with a transfer of power from London to Edinburgh, but also committed to democratic constitutional change within Scotland. It has worked out a sustained – but not static – constitutional critique of the United Kingdom and mounted an ideological challenge, in the sphere of popular constitutional theory, to the institutions, practices and assumptions of the British State.

This book focuses on two of the most important of these constitutional texts. The first text is the so-called 'MacCormick draft', published by the SNP as '*A Constitution for a Free Scotland*' in 2002.[3] This, in overview, would provide for a unicameral parliament elected for fixed four-year terms by proportional representation. The monarchy would be retained, although certain Crown prerogatives would be curtailed. The conventional relationship between the head of state, government and parliament would be placed on an explicitly constitutional basis, with a prime minister formally elected by parliament. There would be an independent judiciary, chosen by the head of state on the advice of a non-partisan appointments committee. As a substitute for the delaying and revising power of a second chamber, a minority veto and referendum mechanism was proposed. The autonomy of local self-government would be guaranteed within the framework of a unitary but decentralised state.

The 2002 Constitution would also enshrine fundamental rights based on the European Convention, as well as social rights such as a right to fair working conditions, housing, education and healthcare. The right to vote in local and parliamentary elections would be granted to all citizens and residents of Scotland over the age of sixteen. All this would be embodied in a rigid Constitution, which could be amended only by a three-fifths majority vote of parliament, followed by a referendum.[4]

The second constitutional text to be considered is the 'draft interim Constitution' published by the Scottish government in 2014, which must be read in conjunction with the Scottish government's White Paper on independence, *Scotland's Future: Your Guide to an Independent Scotland*, published in November 2013. These promised a rather skeletal 'constitutional platform' for the transitional phase between independence and the adoption of a final constitution.

The restored Scottish state, according to the interim constitution, would have been born as a parliamentary democracy, based upon the sovereignty of the people, and founded upon a written Constitution that would – as a minimum – have enshrined the fundamental rights and freedoms of the European Convention on Human Rights in the nation's highest law. Provision was also made in the draft interim Constitution for the subsequent development of a permanent Constitution[5] through an inclusive Constitutional Convention to be created by the first post-independence parliament.

Although much of the referendum campaign in 2014 focused on practical issues of day-to-day policies, particularly in the fields of economic policy, currency, taxation, pensions and defence, the people of Scotland were asked not to vote for a new government, or for a new policy orientation, but, more fundamentally, for a new state embodied in the draft interim constitution. This new state was to be defined not only by its different flag, anthem and boundaries, but also by a new constitutional foundation. In a radical departure from British theory and practice, Scotland was to be built not upon the sovereignty of 'the Crown in Parliament' but upon 'the sovereignty of the people of Scotland', embodied in a written Constitution.

The 2002 and 2014 texts differ from one another in many ways. The 2002 text was proposed as a workable text for an enduring constitution, while that of 2014 was intended only to be an interim, transitional, text. The 2002 text was produced by a party in opposition, without civil service assistance, and in the absence of public scrutiny, whilst the 2014 was written by a party in government, with the assistance of civil servants, and under the intense scrutiny of a referendum campaign, in which the inclusion of certain policies in the text of the constitution (such as the prohibition of nuclear weapons) could be seen as electoral gambits.

Nevertheless, the two texts share certain similarities of status and form. They both represent the clearest and most explicit statements of the constitutional thinking of the SNP at their respective moments in time, and they both envisage Scotland as a democracy with a written constitution, and judicially enforced fundamental rights, with a unitary state structure, a unicameral parliament elected by proportional representation, and a responsible cabinet government topped by a ceremonial figurehead monarchy. They were both produced in reaction to the perceived shortcomings of the existing British system of government, which by the 1980s was seen by many (not only Scottish nationalists, but also more broadly across the British left and centre) as archaic, as lacking in democratic legitimacy, and as offering insufficient protection for human rights. Yet both texts were shaped, in different ways, by the enduring features and indelible example of the global 'Westminster model'.

As this short introductory survey already indicates, the Scottish independence movement is intrinsically associated with a process of both state-building and democratic re-constitutionalisation that could, at least in a British context, be described as a 'constitutional revolution'. The United Kingdom is unique in having evolved from a seventeenth-century monarchy to a parliamentary democracy without revolutionary upheaval and without adopting a written, fundamental constitution. The dominant British political tradition has embraced ad hoc solutions, has taken pride in piecemeal evolution, and has generally been suspicious of written constitutions, clear ground rules, abstract principles and judicially enforceable restrictions on parliament. By this measure, the proposals of the Scottish government and the SNP are quite radical.

Seen in the light of both domestic and international expectations, however, these constitutional commitments appear less radical, and more of a pragmatic response to the needs of a potential Scottish state in the early twenty-first century. Simply having a written constitution is not in itself a radical idea. Around the world, they are the norm. An old country such as the United Kingdom might long continue in the anomalous position of not having a written Constitution,[6] but a newly independent country such as Scotland would need a written Constitution and would be very likely to adopt one. The creation of a newly independent state is one of several contexts in which constitution-making is not only normal but necessary.[7]

To understand why a written constitution would be a necessity in a

Scottish context, even if perceived as something of an 'optional extra' in a British context, it is important to understand the roles and functions that a Constitution performs in relation to the state, the nation and society. At the risk of repeating some of what has been said in my earlier works,[8] it is worth briefly noting here that a Constitution is much more than a legal document that protects fundamental rights. It also defines and empowers the state, structures its political institutions and regulates interactions amongst these institutions. In other words, the Constitution does not merely limit state power, but also establishes, legitimates, regularises and depersonalises that power. It is, in every sense, foundational to the state-building project.

This regularisation and depersonalisation of power is important in all states which mean to enjoy democratic rule, but it is particularly so when the state is, like Scotland, rich in natural resources such as oil and gas. Although such natural resources can help enrich a country, they often also bring with them a so-called 'resource curse': a proneness to developmental lethargy, corruption and instability. The ability of the state to exploit a valuable income source with relatively little effort raises the stakes of political contestation for power, increasing incentives for foul play. A well-designed Constitution, by organising the powers of the state in ways that minimise corruption, can prevent authoritarian backsliding and defend the integrity of democratic processes against manipulation by incumbents, can provide real reassurance to citizens that the state belongs to the whole community of the realm and is not the private realm of the first minister, the SNP or any other person or party.

Furthermore, there is a growing body of literature on the political and sociological, as well as the narrowly legal, functions of Constitutions.[9] Constitutions are not addressed only to the judges and politicians who have to work with the fine print, but have a broader symbolic, declaratory and practical appeal to the general public. Constitutions can, for example, promote national cohesion and reinforce norms of democratic behaviour. In defining citizenship, recognising certain symbolic totems of nationhood, or by asserting particular policy directives as fundamental to the political system, Constitutions address matters of identity and values.[10] It is notable that even non-democratic countries often have written Constitutions that, although they do not uphold rights, do serve these important institution-organising, value-setting, nation-building, state-legitimating functions.[11] An independent Scotland would without doubt find a Constitution useful for all these purposes, as well as for the purpose of protecting fundamental rights and regulating democratic processes.

A new state would seek to establish its authority, its identity and its legitimacy in the eyes of foreign as well as domestic audiences. Thus, while being a mark of Scottish distinction vis-à-vis the United Kingdom, the idea of a modern, written, democratic constitution could also be a sign of Scotland's normality – of its desire to be, in the words of the SNP's 2002 policy paper on the constitution,[12] 'a normal European democracy'. Seen from the perspective of other comparable European nations – especially those in the 'Arc of Democracy' spanning from the Benelux countries through the Nordic countries to the Baltic – a written Constitution is not a radical innovation (as it might be seen in Britain), but a tried and tested, self-evidently sensible, necessity. In order to be seen as a serious and legitimate state in the eyes of our neighbours, Scotland would need one too.

Yet even in British terms, written Constitutions are hardly radical innovations. Written Constitutions are the normal foundations of modern democratic statehood in the Commonwealth; the vast majority of the many children of the prolific 'Mother of Parliaments' have written Constitutions. As such, the initial contrast between the emerging Scottish constitutional tradition embodied in the constitutional proposals of the SNP and what might be termed the British constitutional tradition becomes a lot less stark – and more interesting, from the point of view of comparative scholarship – if the British constitutional tradition is recognised as being broader than just that which pertains to this small island. Seen as a world-spanning concept, spread by the former British Empire and sustained even today by the Commonwealth, the global 'British tradition' appears much less hostile to written Constitutions.

So from the outset the arguments for and against having a written Constitution can be set aside. Not having a written Constitution would be quite absurd in the vast majority of democratic nations, in Europe, in the Commonwealth and around the world. An independent Scotland, if such a state were to exist and were to wish to be taken seriously by its peers, would almost certainly need, and most probably have, a written Constitution of some sort. It is from this perspective that this book sets out to chronicle, describe, analyse and assess the SNP's specific proposals for the Constitution of Scotland.

Scope and Structure of the Book

Since the rejection of independence in the 2014 referendum, academic attention in Scotland has shifted back from its brief interest in the design of a constitution for an independent Scotland to more familiar subjects, such as the working and enhancement of devolution, the piecemeal reform of British institutions, the study of nationalism as a phenomenon and the SNP as a party, and the territorial management of Scotland within the United Kingdom. The academic community in Scotland and elsewhere has produced a lively literature on all these themes since before devolution, and this book does not seek to add to that swelling body of work. It is not concerned, primarily, with the governance of Scotland within the United Kingdom. Instead it contributes to the previously very sparse academic literature on constitutional design in the context of an independent Scottish state.[13]

As such, this is the first detailed, book-length, treatment of the SNP's plans for the constitution of an independent Scotland. This is a subject of continued relevance, despite the result of the 2014 independence referendum. The success of the SNP in the 2015 general election and the 2016 Scottish Parliament election, while not in themselves a mandate for independence, show that the constitutional issue in Scotland is far from settled. At the time of writing, the result of the 2016 UK-wide referendum on membership of the European Union has just been announced, with England and Wales voting to leave the European Union, and Scotland and Northern Ireland voting to remain. It is far too early to tell what might be the outcome of this, but it does at least seem for the moment that independence for Scotland within the European Union is more likely now than it has ever been in the past. But even if an independent state is not (or not for now) to be, the SNP's constitutional historical proposals should be properly documented and analysed for their own sake. Regardless of the immediate future, the constitutional thought of the Scottish national movement is still of interest to scholars of Scottish politics for what its reveals about the SNP and its ideology, and to British politics because of the mirror they hold up to constitutional grievances and developments across the UK. This book draws attention to the existence of a Scottish nationalist constitutional tradition that has led to the articulation of constitutional values and to the creation of Scottish institutions that were expressly intended to be very different from those of Westminster, and yet have remained influenced by the Westminster model of which they are best seen as a derivative form.[14]

The SNP's proposed constitutional texts should also be of interest to scholars of comparative constitutional law, particularly in Westminster-derived democracies, because of what these documents reveal about the application of contemporary constitutional design to the context of a newly independent state that is both a modern European democracy and part of the great family of national political systems derived from Westminster's 'Mother of Parliaments'.

Accordingly, this book examines the historical trajectory of the constitutional question in Scotland, identifies an emerging Scottish nationalist tradition in constitutional thought, examines the SNP's proposals in their local, British and international contexts, and analyses the changing shape of these proposals over time. In particular, it presents the Scottish case as an example (albeit a stalled example) of contemporary constitution-building within the global family of 'Westminster model' Constitutions.

My analysis of Scottish constitutional proposals begins with two basic premises. The first is that a viable and acceptable Constitution must 'fit' the country for which it is intended.[15] It must reflect local standards that derive from the specific constitutional requirements of the country for which it is intended.[16] This means it should be 'rooted in a country's historical experience' and 'reflect values commonly held or respected by the people' and 'address current problems confronting the state'.[17] The second premise is that Scottish Constitutional proposals do not emerge in isolation, and that states in the contemporary world (if they do not wish to be seen as 'pariah states' and to be excluded from the club of international democratic respectability) must, as a minimum, conform to certain basic universal standards of democratic constitutionalism. These standards are embodied in a range of international instruments, from the European Convention on Human Rights to the Commonwealth Charter. It is against these criteria (domestic needs and international standards) that any constitutional proposal should be understood and evaluated.

The structure of the book follows from these two premises. Chapter 2 places Scottish constitutional proposals in their international context, particularly in the context of the global family of Westminster model constitutions. It traces the evolution of parliamentary and extra-parliamentary institutions through successive generations of the Westminster system, through the migration of constitutional ideas around the world, and through successive waves of democratisation.

Particular attention is paid to the codification of the conventions of parliamentary government and to the creation of independent 'fourth branch' institutions that provide an extra-parliamentary check against the misuse of power. It also discusses the rise of higher-law constitutionalism (that is, having a written constitution that provides for the judicial protection of human rights, and can be amended only by special procedures) and argues that a future Scottish Constitution would have to conform to European, Commonwealth, and increasingly global, norms in order to be legitimate in the eyes of both domestic and international audiences. These are not, therefore, design options that Scottish constitution-makers could consider at will, but unavoidable design requirements that would have to be reflected in any serious constitutional proposal.

Chapter 3 addresses the particular national context in which the SNP's constitutional proposals have been developed. It examines the sociological, political, religious, ideological and territorial needs that any Constitution for an independent Scotland would have to address.

Chapter 4 discusses the constitutional trajectory of Scotland since the beginning of the Scottish national movement; using a historical institutionalist framework, it considers how previous institutional choices, especially those surrounding the critical junction of devolution, influence and restrain the SNP's constitutional proposals.

The remaining chapters examine the SNP's constitutional proposals in light of these contextual parameters. Chapters 5, 6 and 7 are dedicated to the detailed exposition and analysis of the 2002 'MacCormick' text – dealing with, respectively, (1) the role, powers and composition of Parliament; (2) the head of state and the government; and (3) the judiciary, human rights, local government, and substantive provisions, including provisions on national identity, language and Church–State relations. The 2002 text is selected for analysis because, despite its advancing age, it remains the most comprehensive constitutional text yet to have been formally endorsed by the party. Unlike later texts, which set out constitutional aspirations only in general terms – as a manifesto commitment or White Paper – the 2002 text was a fully worked example of a constitutional text which could, in principle, have been adopted as Scotland's supreme law.

Chapter 8, finally, discusses more recent constitutional proposals, made after the SNP took office in 2007. Particular emphasis is placed on the draft interim Constitution published in 2014. The contrast between the 2002 and 2014 texts is discussed at some length to show the changing priorities of the SNP's constitutional policy, especially the apparent gap between the radicalism of the SNP's constitutional rhetoric and the rather uninspiring minimalism of its eventual proposals.

Before proceeding further, it is necessary to make a few personal disclaimers. For many years, I have supported Scottish independence in every public forum where I have had the opportunity to do so. In some of my previous writings, I have sought to persuade Scots that independence was both an attractive and a practical option. The case for independence is not, however, the subject of this work, and I seek in the pages that follow to make no partisan point.

Indeed, this book is not about Scottish independence as such. It does not include any analysis of the probable effects of independence on matters such

as the economy or public policy, discuss the politics of the independence campaign (except in passing, as it specifically relates to constitutional issues), or
speculate on the likelihood of independence in the future. Rather, the book's
aim is simply to review the SNP's constitutional proposals for an independent
Scotland from a detached perspective and in a dispassionate way. Although
it does cast judgment upon these proposals, it does not make any explicit
prescriptive recommendations for the form that a future Scottish Constitution
might take.[18] Likewise, this is not a book about Scottish nationalism, and
it does not discuss Scottish nationalism as a political or cultural movement,
except in so far as it relates specifically to the constitutional question.

Analysing Constitutional Proposals:
Some Preliminary Theoretical and Methodological Considerations

The word 'Constitution' has a variety of meanings. Finer's classic definition,
that 'Constitutions are codes of rules which aspire to regulate the allocation of
functions, powers and duties among the various agencies and officers of government, and define the relationships between these and the public',[19] requires
elaboration. Across most of Europe, in the United States, and in many former
British colonies, the word Constitution is chiefly used to refer to a supreme and
fundamental law, which is typically more difficult to change than other laws,
and which is upheld by a Supreme or Constitutional Court as the apex of a
hierarchy of legal norms – to what in Kelsenian terms is known as the fundamental norm, the *lex superior* from which other laws derive their authority.[20]

By this definition, a Constitution, as Finer says, prescribes the rights and
duties of the people, regulates the powers and functions of major public institutions, and defines the relationships between them.[21] Crucially, as Bergman et
al. emphasise, this code must be backed up by means of sanctions, which are
often enforced by the courts:

> [Constitutions are not] mere behavioural regularities that reflect habit, tradition, or
> self-interest. Such patterns may persist as long as the actors in question find them profit-
> able or convenient, but have no force or compulsion if that is no longer the case. [. . .][22]
>
> Therefore, for a rule to qualify as a mechanism of delegation or accountability, it
> must be enforceable. Voters, politicians, or civil servants must expect such rules to
> be backed up by direct or indirect sanctions from their principals, or from courts or
> other third parties that can enforce them.[23]

This concern for formal rules and sanctions reflects greater emphasis on
'calculus' than on 'culture' in determining the behaviour of actors, and is closer
to the 'rational choice' end of the institutionalist spectrum. It finds also expression in the 'principal-agent' model of constitutionalism, according to which the
Constitution is an instrument by which the people (as principal) regulate the
actions of the state (as agent):

> The rules of the constitution identify what the common objectives of the principal
> and the agent are, what activities the agent may never undertake, how policies are to

be enacted and implemented by the principal and the agent and how conflicts about the interpretation of the constitution are to be resolved. Human rights, separation of powers, checks and balances, judicial review – all these institutions – belong to the constitutional regulation of the principal-agent relationships in the State.[24]

Nevertheless, such a rule-based definition of Constitutions predates rational choice theory. It was popularised in the English-speaking world by Thomas Paine in his 1791 publication *The Rights of Man*, which defined a Constitution as:

> the body of elements to which you can refer, and quote article by article; and which contains the principles on which the government shall be established, the manner in which it shall be organised, the powers it shall have, the mode of elections, the duration of Parliaments [. . .] and, in fine, everything that relates to the complete organisation of a civil government.[25]

According to Paine, an unwritten Constitution, which cannot be produced on paper and quoted chapter and verse, is not really a Constitution at all. Likewise, a Constitution that is capable of being easily changed or overridden by the ordinary process of legislation is not worthy of the name. Thus, by Paine's definition, all talk of a 'British Constitution' is nonsense, for, as Paine continues, 'no such thing exists, or ever did exist'.[26]

Britain, uniquely amongst the nations of Europe, accepted mass democracy without pausing to adopt a fundamental, written Constitution (in Paine's sense of the word). This has affected the understanding, perhaps even the definition, of the word 'Constitution' as it is commonly used in British English, so that its meaning is not confined to one fundamental norm, nor to any specific long-term contract between the people as principal and the rulers as agents, but instead encompasses the plethora of rules and practices that describe (rather than prescribe) the form of government. For example, Richards defines the constitution in a typically British tradition: 'The constitution of a country is the body of rules and practices which regulate its government.'[27] A similar definition is provided by Anthony King:

> A constitution is the set of the most important rules that regulate the relations among the different parts of the government of a given country and also the relations between the different parts of the government and the people of the country.[28]

It is important to note that the definitions advanced by Richards and King do not require those rules or practices to have greater entrenchment than other rules and practices, nor to be specified in one or any number of documents. King goes on to draw a distinction between Constitutions (understood as formal, written documents) and 'most important rules' which apply in practice. These 'most important rules' are 'never written down'.[29] Moreover, such 'most important rules', according to King's argument, do not have to be enforceable, clear or binding – it suffices that they are descriptive rules, norms, traditions, customs, or 'behavioural regularities', which for the time being reflect behaviour.

This broader definition of constitutionalism calls for a historical institution-alist approach, which regards customs, norms, conventions and traditions as integral to the nature and working of institutions.[30] This is of particular rele-vance to the study of Westminster-derived constitutions, which, in many cases, place great reliance on such unwritten norms to regulate the most important relationships of parliamentary democracy.

As will be discussed in the following chapter, most countries derived from a Westminster root, outside of the UK itself, do possess a written, codified and entrenched law which is called the Constitution and which is superior to ordinary legislation (that is, they have a Constitution in the sense intended by Thomas Paine). However, following King's observation, these documents do not always contain 'the most important rules'.[31] The Canadian constitution is typical of this type of 'semi-written' constitution:

> ... the Canadian constitution is a conglomeration of British, Canadian and provincial statutes, the British common law, Canadian judicial decisions, and a number of real but invisible conventions, customs, values and assumptions, all clus-tering rather loosely and haphazardly around the central kernel of the BNA [British North America] Act and the more recent modifications in the Constitution Act, 1982.[32]

In other words, Van Loon and Whittington interpret the Canadian consti-tution ('most important rules') to include much more than the Constitution ('supreme and fundamental law'). Principles such as 'the conventions of Cabinet government' and the

> firm, though unwritten rule that the government must hold the support of a majority in the House of Commons or resign [are] not found in the British North America (BNA) Act, or in any constitutional document, yet they are as much a part of the Canadian constitution as the BNA Act itself.[33]

If this wider definition of constitutions is accepted, then we are faced with the problem of identifying the 'real' or 'complete' content of a given constitu-tion. It is clear that to rely solely on the careful textual study of the written law called the 'Constitution', where such a law exists, will not provide an adequate picture of the reality of the 'real' constitution – but where then do the bounda-ries of the constitution lie, and how are those practices which are properly regarded as 'constitutional' distinguished from those which are merely legisla-tive, administrative or incidental?

This problem of identifying what is, and what is not, part of the complete or 'real' constitution has been addressed by Palmer in a study of the New Zealand constitution.[34] Palmer identified two criteria for the recognition of a given practice as 'constitutional':

> Any practice, to be so designated [as definitely constitutional], must fulfil require-ments: (1) of existence (which includes highly probable continuance) and felt impor-tance; and (2) of constitutional function.[35]

Palmer settles the question of what has a 'constitutional function' by its influence on 'the generic exercise of public power – whether through structures, processes, principles, rules, convention or even culture'.[36] He uses the 'reality of affected actors' behaviour' to demonstrate that a practice meets the 'existence' requirement: 'If constitutional actors consistently act as if a rule exists, then in their perception it does.'[37] The constitution, therefore, comprises 'all those factors that significantly affect how public power is exercised'.[38]

Thus, for example, the rule (as it existed before the Fixed Term Parliaments Act 2011) that a government in the UK must resign, or else advise a dissolution, if it is defeated in the House of Commons on a matter of supply or confidence was regarded as a rule of the constitution because it met these two requirements. Firstly, the rule existed: all governments have acted accordingly, and have been universally expected and obliged by a sense of constitutional propriety to act accordingly. Secondly, the rule affected the generic exercise of public power. It was not a matter of mere administrative, particular or ephemeral significance, but of general significance to the process of how the UK was governed.[39]

A. V. Dicey divided the constitution into the 'law of the constitution' and the 'conventions of the constitution'.[40] The former includes 'legislation that influences the exercise of public power, to which can be added other formal instruments of the legislative, executive or judicial branches of government' – including such instruments as parliamentary Standing Orders, the Cabinet Manual and international treaties.[41] It also includes 'judgments in the common law that influence the exercise of public power' and the law of the royal prerogative.[42] The 'conventions of the constitution' include 'observed norms of political behaviour that are generally acknowledged to have attained a significance and status worthy of general acknowledgement'.[43] Palmer acknowledges this definition to be circular – the constitution is as the constitution does – but argues that this circularity '[captures] the iterative, endogenous nature of constitutional conventions'.[44]

These conventional rules can be 'consubstantial' with the text of the written (narrow) Constitution – present in, through, and under the written text, discernible only by 'reading between the lines'. For example, the 1901 Constitution of Australia makes only passing reference to the existence of ministers, who are to be appointed by the governor general, are to head administrative departments, and are to be members of the Federal Executive Council, by the advice of which the government of the country, under the legal style of 'Governor-General-in-Council' is conducted. Yet it is clear from the context that the (narrow, written) Constitution embodies and contains much more than a simple, literal, legalistic interpretation of its wording would indicate: it is, and was intended to be, the Constitution of a parliamentary democracy founded on the doctrine of ministerial responsibility.[45] Similarly, although the Australian Constitution contains no bill of rights, the High Court of Australia has, indeed, recognised this principle in developing the implied right of free speech on political matters – a right which, although unspecified in the text of the supreme law, is nevertheless inherent to the intent to the wider, normative, 'complete' constitution.[46]

To avoid the conceptual confusion surrounding the use of these terms, another approach is to adopt a lexicon that distinguishes between the 'Constitution' (the text, the 'supreme law') and the 'constitutional order' (the 'real', 'complete' constitution):

> The notion of the constitutional order here is a useful synonym for constitution-as-function, denoting the larger set of constitutional elements including, but not limited to, the written text.[47]

For the remainder of this book, this distinction will be maintained. The term 'Constitution', which will be capitalised when used in this sense, refers to the formal text of the supreme law. The term 'constitutional order', uncapitalised, will be used to refer to the 'real' or 'complete' constitution.

Given the importance of ideas, norms and culture one of the ways in which the supreme law ('Constitution') might influence the constitutional order is through the reflection, and thereby the continued shaping, of its founding values. The values embedded in the constitutional order can be stated explicitly in the formal text of the Constitution. The Constitution of the Fifth French Republic, for example, opens with a ringing endorsement and declaration of its core republican principles, upon which the rest of the text is really an institutional gloss:

> France is an indivisible, secular, democratic and social Republic.
> It ensures the equality before the law of all citizens, without distinction of origin, race or religion. It respects all beliefs. The national emblem is the tricolour flag, blue, white and red. The national anthem is the 'Marseillaise'. The motto of the Republic is 'Liberty, Equality, Fraternity'.
> Its principle is government of the people, by the people, for the people.[48]

The above provisions are not 'rules' in the sense usually meant by rational choice theorists. They have little to do with the 'thin', 'calculus' side of institutional analysis. In their absence, the rest of the Constitution – the operative rules concerning the election and the powers of the president and parliament, or the relationship between the government and parliament, or between lawmakers and the judiciary, for example, would not substantially be affected. Nevertheless, they have a declaratory effect. They speak to the cultural traditions of the French nation and its political history. They affirm that the Constitution stands on the side of the republic and not of reaction, and shows the nation to itself in its republican guise. In so doing, these words 'colour' the Constitution – giving it an explicit normative framework of aims, principles and values through which it can be interpreted.

Alternatively, the values of the constitutional order may be present in other documents, which are not themselves part of the Constitution. In the United States, for example, the Declaration of Independence has been argued to have normative status as part of the 'complete' constitution,[49] while in Ireland a similar status is sometimes attributed, especially by those on the left, to the Republic Proclamation of 1916.[50] These texts, although not part of the 'supreme law' or the written Constitution, are part of the underlying framework of normative values on which the written Constitution is based, and in reference to which politics takes place.

To measure the political effect of normative provisions such as these would be a substantial undertaking, and lies far outside the scope of this book. However, in the analysis of proposed Constitutions for a country such as Scotland, it is worth taking note of the 'fit' between the normative values expressed or implied in the Constitution and the prevailing political traditions of the country. A draft Constitution for Scotland, to be of any worth or relevance, must reflect aims, values and principles which are harmonious with those embodied in Scottish political traditions.

This brings us to the next consideration – the question of what would be, in the words of Neil MacCormick, one of the principal architects of the SNP's constitutional policy in the 1990s, 'a viable and acceptable constitutional order for a Scottish state'.[51] This question poses several methodological difficulties. The criteria of a 'viable' and 'acceptable' Constitution for Scotland must, from our present place in history, be a matter of judgment, and not of empirical fact. The only certain test of viability is whether something is found to 'work'; the only test for acceptability is whether it is broadly accepted by, and continues to be acceptable to, the people for whom it is intended. These tests can only be applied retrospectively, through the post hoc study of events. For the moment, we must be content with making our 'best judgment', based on extrapolation from the existing circumstances.

A historical institutionalist perspective does, however, provide some good guidance. It is not possible to pluck a Constitution out of 'thin air' and impose it on an unprepared country – at least, not without expecting a high probability of failure. Constitutions are, of course, capable of change. Specific constitutional 'technologies' can be pioneered in one country and then spread by the diffusion of constitutional ideas to another.[52] But the limits of 'viable' (that is, workable, practicable, sustainable) constitutional change in a given state will be determined, in part, by the historical experience of that state and its people. Institutional choices made early in a state's democratic history (for example, whether to abolish the monarchy or merely to strip it of its prerogatives, or whether to adopt a winner-takes-all or proportional electoral system) will structure future perceptions of what constitutional options are desirable or achievable. The relevant political elites and opinion-formers of a state which has opted for monarchy, for example, might tend to regard monarchy as a guarantee of stability and continuity, or as a venerated symbol of the nation's identity, such that abolishing it becomes unthinkable, whilst the citizens of a state which opted for a republic early in its democratic history might regard any hint of monarchy as foolish and absurd.

Choices about constitutional forms, then, are, like the political culture they produce and by which they are reinforced, 'sticky'. They can be changed, but not too far or too fast, and any change must be suited to the conditions of the country and people for which it is intended. Like a suit of clothes, the Constitution of a country must be tailored to fit.

Likewise, the limits of 'acceptability' (that is, legitimacy, tolerability in the eyes of public opinion) will be shaped by the values and expectations of the people. If a Constitution is to be acceptable it must embody the values, norms and principles of the people for whom it is intended – and these are derived, at least in part, from expectations arising out of historical experience.

These notions of viability and acceptability can be clarified by a hypothetical example. Imagine that a decision was taken in the United States of America to abolish the US Constitution and to replace it with something very closely modelled on the Basic Laws of Israel. While remaining within the liberal democratic fold, such a change would involve great and fundamental shifts in the form of government: from federalism to unitariasm, from presidentialism to parliamentarism, from highly personalised plurality elections to closed-list proportional representation, from a rigid constitution with strong judicial review to a flexible constitution with weak judicial review. We need hardly speculate on the (non-)viability of such a change. None of the established habits of patterns of US political behaviour would be unaffected: parties, pundits, politicians and people would flounder in confusion. The USA lacks the traditions, the assumptions, and even the political lexicon that have grown up around the Israeli Basic Laws: notions such as 'forming a government' or 'surviving a vote of no confidence' would be alien. A system that works well enough in a very divided but small society would be impractical on a continental scale. But most of all, it would be unacceptable – it would lack legitimacy because people would be deprived of rights and protections they have come to expect (such as being able to choose their presidents and governors, and to have their rights upheld in the Supreme Court against political majorities).

This is not to say that the Israeli constitutional system is necessarily better or worse than the current US system, merely that the constitution of a country, to be viable and acceptable, cannot ignore the circumstances, history and values of that country, and that these are, in turn, largely shaped by early choices made in a country's history. In a Scottish context, this means that constitutional proposals for an independent state would have to reflect certain values, norms and habits that have already become established in Scottish institutions and political life, and are congruent with Scotland's historical evolution and present circumstances.

It is important, however, to note that this notion, bounded by the concepts of 'viable' and 'acceptable', only sets outer limits or baselines. A viable and acceptable constitution is not necessarily an optimal one. When faced with various possible constitutional options, all of which can be regarded as 'viable' and 'acceptable', how is it possible to choose which is 'the best'? This is, of course, a normative question, to which historical institutionalism, as a way of understanding the nature, importance and development of institutions, can provide only partial guidance. Some key decision-makers might wish to retain (either out of self-interest or principle) as much as possible of the old, familiar form of government – 'warts and all'. Others might seek to react against the perceived failings of the former system, and, while not ignoring historical legacies, will seek to use them as a warning rather than as a model to be emulated.

The case of France is instructive here. After the Second World War, the previously dominant Radical party sought, if not to resurrect the Third Republic, at least to remake the Fourth Republic as closely in the image of the third as possible, while the Socialists and Communists sought to establish a unicameral system, with stronger socio-economic provisions and fewer restraints on the power of majorities.[53] The Gaullists, meanwhile, rejected the weakness and instability associated with parliamentarism and the 'régime d'assemblée', in favour of a rationalised semi-presidential system.[54] The boundaries of what was viable and acceptable in the French republican tradition set limits on all approaches: France was to be a secular republic based on universal suffrage. Even de Gaulle recognised that the government would have to be responsible to parliament and that parliament would have to have the final say in legislation.[55] Yet the limits of viability and acceptability could not prescribe which of these possible approaches would, in abstract, be 'the best'.

Likewise, studying the historical development of constitutional practice in Scotland, and surveying the current realities of Scottish politics, can determine the range of 'viable' and 'acceptable' constitutional possibilities. It can help to understand the constitutional proposals of the Scottish national movement and to assess whether they would provide a 'viable and acceptable constitutional order for a Scottish State'. There are, however, limitations to how far such an analysis can proceed. Even if the SNP's constitutional proposals are 'viable and acceptable', that does not mean either: (1) that they represent the only viable and acceptable option; or (2) that they represent the best available option.

I argue in the next three chapters that a 'viable' and 'acceptable' Constitution for an independent Scotland would be of the 'Westminster transformed'[56] type. It would be derived from the Westminster system, but would deviate from the standard Westminster model in important ways. This, I will argue, reflects the needs of Scottish society and profound trends and developments in Scottish constitutional thought and practice, as well as historical precedents that can be traced back to before the Union. Either a pure 'Westminster' model, or a complete rejection of the basic Westminster principles (parliamentarism, ministerial responsibility) would be unviable and unacceptable. To that extent, at least, the concept of a 'Westminster transformed' model ceases to be merely descriptive or analytical and becomes normative: it becomes a standard by which the 'goodness' of the SNP's draft Constitution can be judged.

Notes

1. G. Hassan (ed.), *The Modern SNP: From Protest to Power* (Edinburgh: Edinburgh University Press, 2009); J. Mitchell, L. Bennie and R. Johns, *The Scottish National Party: Transition to Power* (Oxford: Oxford University Press, 2012).
2. W. E. Bulmer, 'An analysis of the Scottish National Party's Draft Constitution for Scotland', *Parliamentary Affairs*, 64/4 (2011), 674–93; N. MacCormick, 'An idea for a Scottish Constitution', in W. Finnie, C. M. G. Himsworth and N. Walker (eds), *Edinburgh Essays in Public Law* (Edinburgh: Edinburgh University Press, 1991), pp. 159–81; SNP, *Citizens not Subjects* (Edinburgh: SNP, 1997); SNP, *A Constitution for a Free Scotland* (Edinburgh: SNP, 2002).
3. SNP, *A Free Scotland*.

4. SNP, *A Free Scotland*; W. E. Bulmer, 'An analysis of the Scottish National Party's Draft Constitution for Scotland', *Parliamentary Affairs*, 64/4 (2011), 674–93.

5. Of course, no Constitution is permanent. Although Constitutions are meant to last for decades and generations, only a handful have lasted for a century or more (see Elkins et al., *The Endurance of National Constitutions*, 2009). A 'permanent Constitution' is simply a Constitution that is intended to endure and is not self-consciously 'interim' or 'transitional' in nature.

6. Although it seems that the UK's unwritten system has now reached the limits of what can be achieved by ad hoc improvisation, as former certainties about what the UK is, and what it is for, have been eroded, and whatever internal coherence the UK's constitutional system might once have had has been undermined by layers upon layers of incongruous and short-sighted adaptation. The absurd solution of 'English Votes for English Laws' is just the latest instalment in a process of constitutional unravelling.

7. J. Elster, 'Constitutionmaking in Eastern Europe: rebuilding the boat in the open sea', *Public Administration*, 71/1–2 (1993), 169–217.

8. W. E. Bulmer, *A Model Constitution for Scotland: Making Democracy Work in an Independent State* (Edinburgh: Luath Press, 2011); W. E. Bulmer, *A Constitution for the Common Good: Strengthening Scottish Democracy After the Independence Referendum*, 2nd edn (Edinburgh: Luath Press, 2015).

9. C. Thornhill, *A Sociology of Constitutions: Constitutions and State Legitimacy in Socio-Historical Perspective* (Cambridge: Cambridge University Press, 2011); D. Lutz, *Principles of Constitutional Design* (Cambridge: Cambridge University Press, 2006).

10. W. E. Bulmer, *What is a Constitution? Principles and Concepts* (Stockholm: International Institute for Democracy and Electoral Assistance, 2014); W. E. Bulmer, *A Constitution for the Common Good*, pp. 80–4.

11. T. Ginsburg and A. Simpser (eds), *Constitutions in Authoritarian Regimes*, (Cambridge: Cambridge University Press, 2013).

12. SNP, *A Free Scotland*.

13. By way of analogical illustration, imagine a book written before the First World War concerned not with institutions of the Austro-Hungarian Empire, nor with the powers of the Bohemian Diet, but with the analysis of proposals for the Constitution of Czechoslovakia.

14. W. E. Bulmer, 'The emergent Scottish constitutional tradition: Scottish, Nordic and global influences', in K. P. Muller (ed.), *Scotland 2014 and Beyond – Coming of Age and Loss of Innocence* (Frankfurt am Main: Peter Lang, 2014), pp. 201–24.

15. Z. Elkins, T Ginzburg and J. Melton, *The Endurance of National Constitutions* (Cambridge: Cambridge University Press, 2009), pp. 34–5.

16. S. Levinson, 'Do Constitutions have a point?: reflections on "Parchment Barriers" and preambles', in E. F. Paul, F. D. Miller Jr and J. Paul, *What Should Constitutions Do?* (Cambridge: Cambridge University Press, 2011), pp. 166–8.

17. M. Böckenförde, N. Hedling and W. Wahiu, *A Practical Guide to Constitution Building* (Stockholm: International Institute for Democracy and Electoral Assistance, 2011), p. 47.

18. Those seeking a slightly more prescriptive, and much less dispassionate, discussion of such matters are directed to my earlier works, *A Model Constitution for*

Scotland: Making Democracy Work in an Independent State (Edinburgh: Luath Press, 2011) and *A Constitution for the Common Good: Strengthening Scotland's Democracy after the Independence Referendum* (Edinburgh: Luath Press, 2015).

19. S. E. Finer, *Five Constitutions: Contrasts and Comparisons* (Harmondsworth: Penguin Books, 1979), p. 15.
20. J.-E. Lane, *Constitutions and Political Theory* (Manchester: Manchester University Press, 1996), p. 171.
21. S. E. Finer, *Five Constitutions*.
22. T. Bergman, W. Müller, K. Strøm and M. Blombren, 'Democratic delegation and accountability: cross-national patterns', in K. Strøm., W. C. Müller and T. Bergman (eds), *Delegation and Accountability in Parliamentary Democracies*, Comparative Politics (Oxford: Oxford University Press, 2003), p. 112.
23. Ibid. p. 112.
24. J.-E. Lane, *Constitutions and Political Theory*, p. 180.
25. T. Paine [1791], 'The rights of man', in M. Foot and I. Kramnick (eds), *The Thomas Paine Reader* (London: Penguin Classics, 1987), p. 220.
26. Ibid. p. 221.
27. S. G. Richards, *Introduction to British Government* (London and Basingstoke: Macmillan Press, 1978), p. 11.
28. A. King, *Does the United Kingdom still have a Constitution?* Hamlyn Lecture Series 52 (London: Sweet and Maxwell, 2001), p. 1.
29. Ibid. p. 3.
30. P. A. Hall and R. C. R. Taylor, 'Political science and the three new institutionalisms', *Political Studies*, XLIV (1996), 938; D. Judge, *Political Institutions in the United Kingdom* (Oxford: Oxford University Press, 2005), p. 27.
31. A. King, *Does the United Kingdom still have a Constitution?*, p. 3.
32. R. J. Van Loon and M. S. Whittington, *The Canadian Political System: Environment, Structure and Process* (Toronto: McGraw-Hill Ryerson, 1987), p. 173.
33. Ibid. p. 172.
34. M. S. R. Palmer, 'Using constitutional realism to identify the *complete* constitution: lessons from an unwritten constitution', *American Journal of Comparative Law*, 54/3 (2006), 608.
35. Ibid. p. 594.
36. Ibid. p. 608.
37. Ibid. p. 594.
38. Ibid. p. 595.
39. The Fixed Term Parliaments Act 2011 limits the ability of the government to dissolve parliament at will. The House of Commons may now only be dissolved if a government enjoying the confidence of parliament cannot be formed within twenty-eight days following a vote of no confidence, or if a two-thirds majority of the members of the House of Commons vote for their own dissolution. These provisions replicate those introduced for the devolved Scottish Parliament in 1999. Interestingly, the Fixed Term Parliaments Act not only limits the prerogative of dissolution, but also gives the first formal statutory recognition – albeit in a somewhat implicit way – of the principle that the government must enjoy the confidence of the House of Commons, and so gives conventional restraints on the power of

the monarch to appoint and dismiss a prime minister some acknowledgement in statute.

40. A. V. Dicey [1914], *Introduction to the Study of the Law of the Constitution*, 8th edn (Indianapolis: Liberty Fund, 1982).
41. M. S. R. Palmer, 'Using constitutional realism to identify the *complete* constitution: lessons from an unwritten constitution', *American Journal of Comparative Law*, 54/3 (2006), 608.
42. Ibid. p. 608.
43. Ibid. p. 621.
44. Ibid. p. 621.
45. H. V. Emy, *The Politics of Australian Democracy: Fundamentals in Dispute*, 2nd edn (South Melbourne: Macmillan, 1978), pp. 3–16.
46. C. Saunders, *The Constitution of Australia: A Contextual Analysis*, Constitutional Systems of the World (Oxford: Hart Publishing, 2011), pp. 137–45.
47. Elkins et al., *The Endurance of National Constitutions*, p. 39.
48. Constitution of the Fifth French Republic, 1958, Article 2.
49. Elkins et al., *The Endurance of National Constitutions*, p. 44.
50. F. O'Toole, *Enough is Enough: How to Build a New Republic* (London: Faber and Faber, 2011), pp. 21–5.
51. N. MacCormick, 'An idea for a Scottish constitution', p. 160.
52. Elkins et al., *The Endurance of National Constitutions*, p. 28; S. Choudhry, 'Bridging comparative politics and comparative constitutional law', in S. Choudhry (ed.), *Constitutional Design for Divided Societies* (Oxford: Oxford University Press, 2008).
53. P. Williams, *Politics in Post-War France: Parties and the Constitution in the Fourth Republic* (London: Longmans, Green, 1958).
54. P. Avril, *Politics in France*, trans. J. Ross (London: Penguin Books, 1969), pp. 107–15; C. de Gaulle [1946], 'The Bayeux manifesto', in A. Lijphart (ed.), *Parliamentary versus Presidential Government*, Oxford Readings in Politics and Government (Oxford: Oxford University Press, 1992), pp. 139–41; D. Pickles, *France: the Fourth Republic* (London: Methuen, 1955); D. Pickles, *The Fifth French Republic: Institutions and Politics* (London: Methuen University Paperbacks, 1965).
55. C. de Gaulle [1946], 'The Bayeux manifesto'.
56. M. Glover and R. Hazell, 'Introduction: forecasting constitutional futures', in R. Hazell (ed.), *Constitutional Futures Revised: Britain's Constitution to 2020* (Basingstoke: Palgrave Macmillan, 2008).

THE GLOBAL DEVELOPMENT OF THE WESTMINSTER MODEL

It is perhaps no coincidence that the Commonwealth Games took place in Glasgow shortly before the independence vote. Had Scotland voted for independence in 2014, it would have joined the global family of countries – from Australia and Botswana to Vanuatu and Zambia – that have become independent from the United Kingdom. During the Games, Scotland's flag flew alongside those of many nations that had once been governed from London, but which now shouldered the burden (albeit with mixed degrees of democratic stability and socio-economic success) of independence.

At the opening ceremony of the Games, the Scottish anti-imperialist song 'Freedom Come All Ye' was sung by a South African performer – drawing a theatrical connection between Scotland's aspirations and those of a nation that had found the courage to democratically renew and reconstitute itself in recent times. Alex Salmond, then the First Minister of Scotland and leader of the SNP, cannot have failed to notice that symbolism. In the dining room of Bute House, the first minister's official residence in Edinburgh, Mr Salmond kept a decorative silver plate commemorating an inter-war meeting of the prime ministers of the Commonwealth nations. It is engraved with the signatures of the prime ministers of Australia, Canada, Newfoundland (which was then a dominion in its own right, having not yet joined Canada), South Africa and New Zealand. The significance of this highly polished sideboard *objet d'art* was self-evident. It represented the height of the SNP's constitutional ambition: for Scotland to be treated on a par with other independent Commonwealth realms – no more, no less.

As the British Empire slowly and erratically transformed itself into the Commonwealth of Nations, each of these countries faced the challenge of constituting itself as a democratic state. Every one of them, with the partial exception of New Zealand,[1] was given a written constitution at the time of independence, or adopted one soon afterwards, and in most cases these constitutions took the British Westminster model as their basis, and adapted British institutions to local needs. The institutions that were once unique to the unwritten 'British constitutional tradition' are now replicated, with an almost uncountable number of reformed variations, derived hybrids and local adaptations, in a global family of written Constitutions from Adelaide to Vancouver and from Port of Spain in Trinidad and Tobago to Port Moresby in Papua New Guinea.

This chapter discusses the idea of a Westminster model of constitutionalism. It presents the term 'Westminster model' as a useful typological category for the systematic classification of constitutions; it is not that they are all the same, but that they all share certain common features that make them distinguishable from other 'non-Westminster' Constitutions.

The first section attempts to identify those common features, and thereby to distill the 'essence' of the Westminster model from the many 'incidentals' of its appearance in different contexts. The following sections then examine three important developments in the family of Westminster constitutions: (1) the constitutionalisation of the conventional rules structuring the relationships between the head of state, prime minister, cabinet and parliament, particularly in terms of the powers of government formation and parliamentary dissolution powers; (2) the rise of extra-parliamentary, 'fourth branch' institutions that provide a check and balance on the governing majority, in order to protect the integrity of the state's 'non-political' administrative, judicial and election-management institutions from the power of the incumbent government; and (3) rigid constitutionalism, judicial review, and the constitutional recognition of fundamental rights.

What is the Westminster Model?

The term 'Westminster model' is widely used by comparative legal-political scholars, but it evades easy definition. According to Stanley de Smith, 'The Westminster model will never be a legal term of art, and the political scientist may also prefer to handle it circumspectly'.[2] Harshan Kumarasingham, whose work has done much to revive the study of Westminster models as a sub-field of comparative constitutional studies, notes that there is 'no rigid and idealised Westminster model', and that its 'malleable nature', 'ambiguous tenets', 'ever-present exceptions' and 'numerous mutations' make attempts to define it very difficult.[3]

If the term 'Westminster model' is to have typological or analytical value, sufficient to enable it to be used as a lens through which to examine constitutional proposals for an independent Scotland, its 'essential components' must be identified and set aside from the 'merely incidental details' of the British archetype.[4] Early attempts to define these 'essential components', such as the definition offered by de Smith, focused on the Westminster model's parliamentary characteristics:

> a constitutional system in which the head of state is not the effective head of government; in which the effective head of government is a Prime Minister presiding over a cabinet composed of Ministers over whose appointment and removal he has at least a substantial measure of control; in which the effective executive branch of government is parliamentary in as much as Ministers must be members of the legislature;

and in which Ministers are collectively and individually responsible to a freely elected and representative legislature.[5]

This definition, however, is far too broad. It would include many continental European parliamentary democracies, such as Italy, the Third and Fourth French Republics, and the Federal Republic of Germany, whose institutions have no kinship relation to the 'Westminster' family.

Arend Lijphart, in contrast, defines the Westminster model in terms of its majoritarian characteristics, using the terms 'Westminster' and 'majoritarian' interchangeably.[6] 'Westminster' democracies are defined by two-party politics, dominant single-party majority governments, weak or non-existent second chambers, flexible Constitutions, weak judicial review, centralised states, and a pluralistic interest group structure.[7] This approach produces difficulties of classification when applied to particular states. Canada, for instance, cannot be regarded as an example of the Westminster model according to these criteria, owing to its frequent minority governments, multi-party system, rigidly entrenched constitution, strong judicial review and federalism.[8] Yet a glance at a Canadian legislature, with its bewigged speaker, choir-stall layout and familiar terminology, will indicate that Canada's political system, despite these consensual structures, remains rooted in the Westminster tradition. In the words of the preamble to the British North America Act 1867, the Constitution is still 'similar in principle to that of the United Kingdom'.[9]

To avoid these difficulties of classification, it makes sense to consider the Westminster model, from a historical institutionalist perspective, not as a synonym for parliamentarism or majority rule, but as a set of culturo-institutional arrangements derived from British traditions[10] and sustained by informal 'norms, values and meanings'.[11] The Westminster model thus refers not only to the institutions of 'cabinet government, parliamentary sovereignty, majority party control [. . .], institutionalised opposition, ministerial responsibility, and a neutral civil service',[12] but also to a set of legitimating expectations and historical customs that embody political traditions and shape political behaviour.[13]

'Westminsterness' is above all a matter of common ancestry. At the risk of over-stretching a biological metaphor, the Westminster 'genus' can contain many species, which are adapted to the evolutionary pressures of different political and cultural environments, but which retain a certain familial resemblance. This resemblance can be seen in ineffable traditions, expressed in such details as the parliamentary seating arrangement,[14] and not – or at least, not necessarily – by institutional forms such as the electoral system, the absence of a written Constitution, or even a hereditary head of state. As Stanley de Smith noted in 1961, modern Commonwealth constitutions include such features as 'the limitation of parliamentary sovereignty, guarantees of fundamental human rights, [and] judicial review of the constitutionality of legislation', as well as the use of independent commissions to handle judicial appointments, manage the public service and ensure the impartial conduct of elections.[15] Thus, for example, Australia, with its constitutional rigidity, federalism and strong bicameralism,[16] and Ireland, with its proportional representation and elected president,[17] are still 'Westminster' systems, despite variation from the British archetype and from strict majoritarianism.

Harshan Kumarasingham makes a distinction between what he calls the 'New Westminsters' (the 'old' or 'white settler' dominions, where the populations were mostly of British cultural roots), and 'Eastminsters' (the countries of the Indian sub-continent, where British institutions were ingrafted, mainly through the influence of British and British-trained elites, onto populations with very different social structures, religious textures and cultural values).[18] In understanding the workings of the constitution in practice, in different sociological and cultural contexts, this is a useful distinction. In tracing the historical development of the Westminster model, however, the dictum that 'East is east, and West is west' only takes us so far. Despite the convenience of biological metaphors, constitutions do not evolve by random mutation and natural selection, but are consciously designed by the agency of human beings. Ideas can be adopted as well as inherited, and the transmission of constitutional characteristics can occur through learning as well as through inheritance.

In other words, the Westminster family can accommodate variations not only in response to local circumstances, but also in response to new constitutional ideas and technologies. The differences between the Constitutions of Ceylon (1946) and India (1950), on the one hand, and those of Canada (1867) and Australia (1901), on the other, might not, therefore, simply be a product of their socio-cultural contexts, but also be influenced by the ideas and technologies of their different historical epochs.

The remainder of this chapter discusses the emergence of new constitutional technologies, from the age of steamships and the electric telegraph to that of jet engines and space travel. These new constitutional technologies resulted in the development of a new form of Westminster Constitution in the second half of the twentieth century: one that was, on the one hand, more explicitly parliamentary than before, and yet, on the other hand, that placed greater extra-parliamentary constraints on the power of parliamentary majorities.

Varieties of the Westminster Model

Mark Glover and Robert Hazell have developed a framework for analysing variations of the Westminster system.[19] This was designed to categorise potential changes to British institutions, but it is also, with a few tweaks discussed below, well-suited to the analysis of constitutional proposals for an independent Scotland. It enables constitutional proposals to be viewed in terms of a series of reforms and modifications of the 'traditional' Westminster model as it operates (or rather, operated before 1997) in the UK.

This framework uses two dimensions of analysis that are similar, but not identical, to the 'executive-parties' and 'federal unitary' axis used by Arend Lijphart in the classification of 'majoritarian' and 'consensus' democracies.[20] The first dimension of Glover and Hazell's framework considers degree to which power is dispersed in the polity. It places 'concentration of power', characterised by centralism, uniformity, passive democracy and a two-party system, against 'dispersal of power', which is characterised by decentralisation, diversity, active and participatory democracy, and a multi-party system.[21] The second dimension marks the distinction between the 'political constitution' (reliance on parliamentary accountability and political control through the House of Commons) and the 'legal constitution' (reliance on legal, judicial, 'fourth branch' or other extra-parliamentary checks to prevent the abuse of executive power.[22]

These two dimensions can be put together to make four variants of the Westminster model.[23] The first, combining a concentration of power with reliance on parliamentary mechanisms of political constitutionalism, is the 'Old Constitution', or the unchanged Westminster model, as it stood prior to the reforms of 1997–2010. This is characterised by 'a highly centralised system of government', 'little or no devolution', 'very few checks and balances on the unfettered executive', 'parliamentary sovereignty', 'a strong two party system' with the governing party 'being able to do almost anything it wants, subject only to retaining the support of its parliamentary majority' and an absence of 'constitutional watchdogs apart from the Ombudsman and the Auditor-General'.[24]

The second variant represents 'Centralised Constitutionalism', or the 'Westminster Constitutionalised' system. In this variant, 'there is little decentralisation of power, but checks and balances are introduced to constrain the supremacy of Parliament and the discretion of the executive', including 'a bill of rights, a stronger judiciary and a range of constitutional watchdogs (Information Commissioner, Electoral Commission and so on)'.[25] This would involve the constitutional entrenchment of certain fundamental laws, which would be recognised as superior to ordinary Acts of Parliament. There would be 'a stronger human rights culture', as well as freedom of information and stricter regulation of political funding.[26]

The third variant is the 'Westminster Devolved' model. In a UK context, this would involve increased decentralisation to the so-called 'nations and regions', with Scotland, Wales and Northern Ireland gaining increased powers, more localism in England and more diverse approaches to public policy. However, in this variant there would be little change to the operation of the central government and little constitutionalisation of power, with 'only a weak bill of rights, a deferential judiciary and few constitutional watchdogs'.[27]

Finally, the fourth variant is the 'Westminster Transformed' model of 'Dispersed Constitutionalism'. In a UK context, further change in this direction would mean that 'power is dispersed geographically, with a lot of decentralisation', combined with 'a bill of rights, a strong and activist judiciary and a wide range of constitutional watchdogs'.[28] In this variant, 'Westminster itself undergoes fundamental reform, with an elected House of Lords, followed by PR for the House of Commons', resulting in a more diverse multi-party system and a higher likelihood of minority or coalition governments.[29] This Westminster transformed model is 'all the reformers' dreams come true', resulting in a radically different political system; although still clearly part of the 'Westminster' family, it would align much more closely to Lijphart's vision of a consensus democracy, in which 'the governing party is forced to build alliances with other parties to get all its legislation through' and 'faces further obstacles from a more powerful Supreme Court and more devolution'.[30]

Glover and Hazell's typology of variations on the Westminster model is clearly designed for the UK as a whole. It regards the territorial dimension, and the geographical devolution of power between Whitehall and the 'nations and regions' as one of the most important variables.[31] This is because constitutional reform and constitutional design in a UK context must deal, primarily, with the problem of territorial management: how to maintain sufficient autonomy for the nations and regions to placate any regionalist or nationalist movements, without giving away so much power that it inadvertently undermines the basis of the Union in the process. If we are analysing constitutional proposals for an independent Scotland, however, this question is resolved from the outset. The non-geographical elements of the 'dispersal of power' dimension are therefore a more relevant focus for analysing variations on the Westminster model in a Scottish context. These include proportional representation and multi-party politics, as well as mechanisms for the dispersal of power within and between institutions: between the prime minister and cabinet, the government and opposition, and the executive and legislature. It might also include a 'shift from representative to direct and deliberative democracy', with increased reliance on institutions such as initiative petitions, citizens' juries, and referendums.[32] With this slight shift of emphasis, this typology can be used for the classification, analysis and evaluation of proposed Constitutions for an independent Scotland. The fourth variant, in particular, is highly relevant, since the SNP's 2002 text can be seen, as will become clear in subsequent chapters, as a blueprint for a 'Westminster Transformed' Constitution for Scotland.

Explicit Parliamentarism:
The Constitutionalisation of Parliamentary Conventions

This section charts the evolution of parliamentary democracy in the written Constitutions of Westminster democracies. It traces how the 'implicit parliamentarism' of early Westminster-derived constitutions, based on unwritten and conventional relationships between the monarch (or governor general), prime minister, cabinet and parliament has largely been superseded, in later constitutions, by an 'explicit' form of parliamentarism, in which these key relationships are subject to written rules laid down in the Constitution.

The story of parliamentary constitutionalism begins in the late eighteenth century. The French and American revolutions brought about an initial spate of constitution-making, from which most patterns of modern democracy, be they presidential or parliamentary, ultimately derive.[33] Unlike in the Americas, where monarchs were deposed, the Revolutionary Constitutions of France (1791) and Spain (1812) sought to limit monarchs rather than abolish them. Strongly infused with the principle of national sovereignty, exercised through the legislative supremacy of a unicameral parliament, the Revolutionary Constitutions proclaimed the public nature of all authority and the legal equality of citizens in place of medieval, local and corporate privileges, yet still entrusted the executive authority to a crowned hereditary head of state.[34]

Despite their iconic status, these early constitutions were short-lived. After the rise and fall of Napoleon, the enduring achievements of the French Revolution were embodied in constitutions of a less radical, less ambitious nature. The first, and therefore arguably the most significant, of these post-Napoleonic Restoration era constitutions was the French *Charte Constitutionelle* of 1814. This short and elegant constitutional document was clearly based on British institutions of the time. It created a limited constitutional monarchy, in which the king exercised executive power through his ministers and shared legislative power with a bicameral parliament. Yet, although limited and constitutional, the monarchy of early Restoration era France, during the period from the Restoration until the Revolution of 1830, was at best only partially parliamentary.[35] The legal responsibility of ministers was constitutionally enshrined (Art. 13), but initially this responsibility extended only to cases of 'treason and peculation' (Art. 56). Scope for parliamentary control over the government was only 'general' and 'deeply ambiguous'.[36]

The French *Charte Constitutionelle*, which was reissued with minor textual amendments after 1830, provided a model for much nineteenth-century European constitution-making. Its influence can clearly be seen in the Constitutions of the Netherlands (1814, 1848), Belgium (1831), Spain (1837, 1845), Piedmont-Sardinia (1848), Denmark (1849) and Romania (1866).[37] Institutionally, all of these constitutions conformed to a common pattern, with a bicameral parliament, a limited suffrage, a brief catalogue of rights, an independent judiciary and a monarchical executive. Although in Piedmont-Sardinia (Italy after 1860), Belgium, the Netherlands, and some other countries, parliamentary conventions had developed by the middle of the nineteenth century, none of these Constitutions formally acknowledged the key principle of parliamentary government:[38] namely, that the government should be accountable to parliament, meaning that the government must maintain the confidence of parliament in order to attain and remain in office.[39] No mention was made, in any of the Constitutions listed above, of votes of investiture or of no confidence. The ministers were still formally chosen by the monarch, who was allowed to retain a moderately active, if practically limited, role in politics.

The end of the First World War marked a transition to democracy in many European countries, whether by the extension of the suffrage in those with a long history of representative government, or by the creation of parliamentary institutions in newly independent states. There was much ideological variation between the new Constitutions of the post-First World War era, seen in different levels of commitment to direct democracy, to judicial review and to decentralisation, different levels of presidential power and different degrees to which these Constitutions were strongly normative or simply procedural in their ambitions.[40] What they all had in common, however, was a commitment to democracy based on universal suffrage and, in most cases, proportional representation.

In many cases, the recognition of parliamentary democracy in these new Constitutions was explicit. The 1922 Constitution of Latvia, for example, provided that the president should bear no responsibility for his or her actions, except in two specific cases (that is, to propose a dissolution of parliament, and to nominate the prime minister).[41] The president's freedom of action in the appointment of the prime minister, meanwhile, was restricted by an explicit confidence requirement, which stated that the prime minister must have the confidence of parliament to hold office, and that a vote of no confidence in the prime minister by the parliament would result in the resignation of the government.[42]

Similarly, the Constitution of Poland (1921) codified many of the conventions of parliamentary democracy in key areas such as government responsibility, dissolution and assent to legislation. It stated that the president would exercise 'executive power through ministers responsible to the Sejm [lower House]' (Art. 43), that the Council of Ministers would bear 'joint constitutional and parliamentary responsibility for the general direction of the activities of the government' (Art. 56), and that this responsibility would be 'enforced by the Sejm by an ordinary majority' (Art. 58). It also defined powers of dissolution, allowing the Sejm to dissolve itself 'by its own vote, passed by a majority of two-thirds of those voting', and allowing the president to dissolve the Sejm 'with the consent of three-fifths of the statutory number of members of the Senate in the presence of at least one-half of the total membership' (Art. 26). The president was required to promulgate all statutes enacted by parliament (Art. 35) and was denied the right to refuse assent.[43]

After the collapse of liberal democracy across much of Europe in the inter-war years, the Constitutions of the post-Second World War era further intensified the trend towards the constitutional recognition of parliamentary democracy. The new Constitutions of France,[44] Germany[45] and Italy[46] sought to limit and define the powers of the head of state and to address some of the institutional causes of government instability that had been blamed, at least in part, for the collapse of democracy. In each of these post-Second World War Western European constitutions, negative parliamentarism, by which the head of state had a free choice of prime minister, subject only to the possibility of a vote of no confidence, was replaced by positive parliamentarism, whereby the head of state would only be able to appoint the prime minister following an authorising 'vote of investiture' or an election in parliament.[47]

Similar developments can be found in other, more recent, European Constitutions. For example, the Belgian Constitution of 1994, occasioned by the transformation of Belgium into a federalised state, took the opportunity to place the processes of government formation and removal on a clear constitutional foundation (Arts 96 and 101), although the king still has a co-ordinating role in the process.[48] Likewise, in Sweden, parliamentary government had been universally accepted by political convention since 1917,[49] but was not reflected in the Constitutional text until adoption of a new Constitution, providing for the investiture of the prime minister by a parliamentary vote, in 1974.[50]

This trend towards the constitutional recognition of parliamentary democracy in continental European constitutions, and the consequent limitation and codification of discretionary powers, was also paralleled in the Westminster-derived Constitutions. The 'first generation' dominion Constitutions – those of Canada (1867), Australia (1901) and South Africa (1910) – deviated from the British prototype by placing certain rights and privileges of parliament, such as the right to elect the speaker, which in Britain exist only by convention, on a constitutional basis.

Yet these early Westminster-export constitutions still maintained the polite fictions of the British system, relying only on custom and convention to regulate key practices of parliamentary democracy. According to de Smith, to 'bring strict law into accord with political reality', by explicitly stating parliamentary principles in the test of the Constitution, would have been 'unconventional, indecorous, unacceptable'.[51] Instead, parliamentarism was only 'coyly acknowledged' by such provisions as a requirement for ministers to be chosen from amongst the members of parliament.[52]

The first Constitution of Westminster extraction to reject these polite fictions, and to bring law and convention into closer proximity one with the other, was that of the Irish Free State. This severely restricted the powers and role of the governor general.[53] By seeking to 'remove every trace of ambiguity and mystery from the British constitutional model', these changes represented the assertion that the people of Ireland, and not the British Crown, were the fount of authority.[54]

The difference was not merely stylistic. Swift-MacNeill described the Constitution of the Irish Free State as the 'most momentous achievement in the history of the governing institutions based on the great prototype of the British Constitution'.[55] It sought not only to incorporate 'many of the principal conventions of the British Constitution into the positive law of the Irish Free State', but also to adopt 'variations of these conventions, indicative in themselves of the trend of opinion in the direction of reform of governing institutions'.[56]

The first independent Constitution of Ceylon (1946) was another pioneer in the transformation of Westminster conventions into positive constitutional law. It was less explicit than that of the Irish Free State in restricting the scope of conventional powers and allowed the governor general to exercise, on paper, broad prerogatives. For example, whereas the Constitution of the Irish Free State allowed the lower House of Parliament to elect the prime minister, the Constitution of Ceylon left this crucial appointment to the discretion of the governor general. However, these prerogatives were explicitly limited in Ceylon in three ways. Firstly, it was stated in the Constitution that there should be a prime minister and cabinet (rather than relying on the polite fictions of a 'Privy Council', as in the Constitution of Canada, for example). Secondly, the principle of the political responsibility of ministers to parliament, and of their dependence on the confidence of parliament, was constitutionally enshrined:

> There shall be a Cabinet of Ministers who shall be appointed by the Governor-General and who shall be charged with the general direction and control of the government of the Island and who shall be collectively responsible to Parliament. (Ceylon Constitution Order-in-Council 1946, as amended by the Ceylon (Independence) Order 1947: section 46)

Thirdly, Ceylon's Constitution explicitly stated that the prerogatives of the governor general were to be exercised only in accordance with British conventions:

> All powers, authorities and functions vested in ... the Governor-General shall ...
> be exercised as far as may be in accordance with the constitutional conventions,
> applicable to the exercise of similar powers, authorities and functions in the United
> Kingdom by His Majesty. (Ceylon Constitution Order-in-Council 1946, as amended
> by the Ceylon (Independence) Order 1947: Section 4(2))

This provision gave these unwritten and unspoken conventions the status of
positive constitutional law, although in the absence of a written codification of
the content of these conventions, the governor general remained as their sole
and self-adjudicating arbiter.[57]

The Constitution of India, adopted in 1950, likewise restricted the scope
of conventional powers, although in this case the symbolic element of a governor general was replaced with an indirectly elected president. The president
– according to the written text of the Constitution – was to be 'aided and
advised' by a Council of Ministers, which would be headed by a prime minister
and would be collectively responsible to the lower House.[58]

Although it was clearly intended during debates in the Constituent
Assembly that the President of India was to be bound by ministerial advice, and
that the government of India would be strictly parliamentary,[59] the wording
of the Indian Constitution as originally enacted, if read without reference to
the contexts and conventions of the Westminster system, could have given the
'impression that the functions of the ministers [were] merely advisory' and that
the president should exercise decision-making power.[60] This ambiguity was
largely resolved by the passage of the 42nd Amendment in 1976, which altered
Article 74 of the Constitution to specify that the president 'shall, in the exercise
of his functions, act in accordance with the advice tendered by the Council of
Ministers'. However, this amendment does not necessarily preclude the president from acting with discretion in 'a few well-known exceptional situations',
such as the choice of a prime minister who can command the confidence of the
majority in the House and the dismissal of a government that lost the confidence of the House but refuses to resign.[61]

The post-colonial Westminster Constitutions from the 1950s onwards
went even further in specifying prerogative powers and in transforming conventional rules into constitutional provisions. Most of the English-speaking
Caribbean Constitutions, for example, explicitly recognise the basic principles
of parliamentary democracy by requiring the head of state or governor general
to appoint as prime minister the person, being a member of the lower House,
who is 'best able' or 'most likely' to enjoy the confidence of a majority therein
and by requiring the prime minister to resign if the lower House passes a vote
of no confidence.[62] Some of the Commonwealth Constitutions go even beyond
this. In the Constitutions of the South Pacific, for example, it is not unknown
for the prime minister to be elected by parliament, removing even theoretical
discretion in government formation from the governor general (for example
Constitution of the Solomon Islands, 1978: Art. 33; Constitution of Tuvalu,
1978: Art. 63).

Furthermore, the range of 'exceptional situations' where the head of state
(typically, an indirectly elected figurehead president) or a governor general

may act without, or even contrary to, ministerial advice, is frequently 'set out in considerable detail' in these second-generation Westminster model constitutions.[63] The Constitution of St Lucia, to pick a typical example, explicitly authorises the governor general to dissolve parliament, 'acting in his own deliberate judgment': (1) if the office of prime minister is vacant, and no one can be found who enjoys the confidence of parliament; (2) following a vote of no confidence, if the prime minister does not advise dissolution or resign; conversely, the governor general may, at his discretion, refuse a dissolution requested by the prime minister if the governor general 'considers that the government [. . .] can be conducted without a dissolution and that a dissolution would not be in the interests of St Lucia'.[64] The Constitutions of Malta and Jamaica, amongst others, contain similar provisions. They not only enshrine the basic principles of ministerial responsibility to parliament, but also expressly define the exceptional circumstances in which the head of state or governor general may legitimately deviate from this principle of ministerial responsibiliy and act with personal discretion.

The theoretical right of governors general to exercise a neutral, discretionary power as an occasional constitutional arbiter is, in many cases, undermined by the fact that the governor general can (with a small number of exceptions, mostly in the South Pacific) be dismissed at will by the prime minister, and that any sustained difference of opinion between a governor general and the prime minister is likely to be resolved in the latter's favour. Indirectly elected presidents, even if they owe their election to the goodwill of the parliamentary majority, have a somewhat stronger position, by virtue of a fixed term office.[65]

One could argue that, symbolic value aside, too much is being made here of technical differences in the drafting of the Constitution (as text) which have little to do with the wider constitutional order (as working reality). In Canada, New Zealand and Australia, as well as in the UK, largely conventional arrangements have endured without catastrophic failure. Examples of continued reliance on wholly or mainly conventional arrangements can also be found in some of the older democracies of Europe, such as the Netherlands[66] and Norway[67,68]. However, the disadvantage of relying on conventions can be seen at moments of constitutional crisis. The head of state's reserve powers (those delicate, 'moderating' powers[69] that a head of state may sometimes be expected to exercise on his or her own personal discretion)[70] are shadowy and doubtful, and their limits difficult to discern. This can undermine the legitimacy of reserve powers, making their exercise a potential source of constitutional 'crisis'; at the moment when the Constitution is needed to provide clear guidance and to ensure certainty, it is silent and uncertain.

On this point, Australia's experience is instructive. Cheryl Saunders argues that there is 'consensus on the existence of a small central core of reserve powers', which include the right to appoint a new prime minister, after an election, if the incumbent prime minister is unable or unwilling to tender the pro forma advice necessary to appoint his or her successor, and to remove from office a prime minister who has lost the confidence of the House but refuses to resign.[71] '*Perhaps*' [my italics], Saunders continues, the governor general also has a discretionary power to 'refuse an early dissolution to a Prime

Minister who has lost the confidence of the House, if another Member is able to command a majority'.[72] There is 'much less agreement' over the question of whether a governor general can dismiss a government which has a majority in the House of Representatives, but is defeated on a vote of supply in the Senate and then refuses to resign or request a dissolution.[73]

For seventy-four years, this was a hypothetical question. Then, in 1975, the Senate rejected the budget proposed by Labour Prime Minister Gough Whitlam. The Senate, according to the text of the Constitution, had such a power. It is debatable, however, whether the exercise of that power to refuse supply was compatible with the conventions of the 'constitutional order'. Whitlam took the view that, as he still had the confidence of the House, he was not obliged either to resign or to request a dissolution. Sir John Kerr, the governor general, decided to exercise a reserve power to dismiss Whitlam, and called on the leader of the opposition, Malcolm Fraser, to form a government. When Fraser's government failed to win a vote of confidence in the House of Representatives, Fraser asked Kerr for a dissolution, which Kerr then granted.[74]

This chain of events sparked the most serious constitutional crisis in Australia's history. It was caused by doubt over whether the governor general had acted constitutionally – a doubt that arose because the limits of his discretionary authority were debatable, owing to the gulf between the wide powers given to both the Senate and the governor general in the written text of the Constitution and the unwritten conventional basis of the 'constitutional order'. That the Senate possessed the power to refuse a vote of supply was, by the text of the Constitution, quite clear; whether the Senate should exercise that power was subject to conventional rules of doubtful precision. Likewise, that the governor general had, by the text of the Constitution, a power to do what he did is undoubted; the question is whether by exercising that power Kerr violated the conventional rules of the wider constitutional order. Most of those who opposed Kerr's actions argued 'either that the Senate had violated a constitutional convention by blocking supply or that the Governor-General had violated a convention by refusing to accept the advice of his Prime Minister, or both'.[75]

If, for sake of argument, rules of the Saint Lucian Constitution had been written into the Constitution of Australia, a constitutional crisis could have been averted. There would be no question of the Senate's right to withhold supply, since the Constitution would explicitly deny the Senate's authority to block money bills for more than thirty days (Constitution of Saint Lucia, 1978: Art. 49). The question of whether an adverse vote in the Senate should be taken as a lack of confidence would not have arisen, as the Constitution would proclaim that the government is responsible solely to the lower House (Constitution of Saint Lucia, 1978: Art. 60). If there had nevertheless been some sort of impasse requiring the interjection of the governor general, there might still have been some concern over the wisdom or prudence of the governor general's exercise of authority, but the constitutional bounds of that authority – and therefore the propriety of its exercise – would have been much more clearly defined (Constitution of Saint Lucia, 1978: Art. 64).

This excursion into the Constitutions of St Lucia and Australia – both a very long way from Scotland – has two closer-to-home purposes. Firstly, it demonstrates the technical advances made in the design of Constitutions during the twentieth century. The attitude of reticence, shaped by deference to the Crown and belief in the mysterious, organic nature of constitutional conventions, was replaced by a desire for precision and clarity. At the same time, innovations were introduced – such as the election of the prime minister by parliament, as in the South Pacific examples noted above – that developed the Westminster system, rather than simply replicating it. Secondly, it shows the benefits of this transformation, and the superiority of a codified system over a convention-based arrangement. If a Constitution is intended to provide the basic rules of a polity, then these should be clear, explicit, and admit of as little room for ambiguity as possible.

Following the Kerr–Whitlam crisis of 1975, Australia sought to overcome the defects of an old Constitution that relied on unwritten – and therefore unclear and easily disputed or ignored – conventions to regulate the most important constitutional relationships between the governor general, prime minister and parliament. An amendment to the text of the constitution being politically untenable, this clarification of the rules was to be achieved by means of an experimental para-constitutional document: an 'authoritative but non-legally binding' declaration would 'recognise and declare' the conventional rules, thus placing them on a written foundation.[76] A list of 34 'Practices' covering matters from the appointment of a governor general to the independence of the judiciary, was adopted by a Constitutional Convention[77] of politicians in 1983, and a further 18 'Practices', specifically addressing the exercise of the governor general's powers, were added in 1985.[78] These 'recognised and declared' conventional rules are not justiciable and still depend on political actors to interpret, apply and enforce them, but the very act of declaring these rules in an authoritative public document does at least give them some definite content, as well as a more visible form. A similar process of recognising and declaring conventional rules has taken place in New Zealand, where another para-constitutional document, the Cabinet Manual, provides an official and authoritative – but not legally binding – statement of the major conventional rules.[79]

Reliance on conventional rules may in practice be acceptable in long-established democracies, and to 'recognise and declare' these conventional rules in a Cabinet Manual or other para-constitutional document may help to ensure that these rules are well understood – for reasons of civic education and democratic culture, as much as for reasons of procedural clarity – and are periodically adapted to current political needs and realities, so that they retain their clarity, legitimacy and vigour. Yet this approach is nevertheless a sub-optimal and rather outmoded form of constitutional design, which recent Westminster-derived constitutions, as well as most recent European constitutions, have rightly rejected. For even if para-constitutional documents can overcome some of the objections to reliance on conventional rules, in terms of visibility and certainty, they lack the democratic legitimacy that results from placing these rules in the text of a written Constitution. A written Constitution can in most cases be amended only by an inclusive democratic process that broadens the sphere of participation – through a requirement for a super-majority decision in parliament, two successive decisions separated by an intervening election, a referendum, or some combination of such hurdles. These amendment rules mean that the Constitution cannot be amended unilaterally by those in power to suit their own ends. These para-constitutional documents, in contrast, have no such protection. A Cabinet Manual, for example, is a statement of official practice, not of democratic rights. It is curated by the cabinet secretary, and the government can rescind it, amend it, and reissue it at will, without so much as a parliamentary vote on the matter.

A draft Constitution for Scotland, written in the twenty-first century, should not therefore be expected to replicate nineteenth-century modes of constitutional draftsmanship. It should be expected, at a minimum, to go as far as other recent Westminster model constitutions in codifying the main conventions of parliamentary democracy and in defining the reserve powers of the head of state in relation to government formation, the dissolution of parliament, and other sensitive prerogative powers. This would minimise the gap between the Constitution as text and the wider constitutional order, help to avoid constitutional crises caused by uncertainty over the extent and use of reserve powers, and give people a better understanding of the rules by which they are governed.

Constrained Parliamentarism:
Extra-parliamentary Scrutiny, Integrity and Non-maniulability Institutions

A second characteristic of recent Westminster model constitutions is the increasing reliance on 'integrity branch' institutions. This term can be applied to a variety of independent, depoliticised, extra-parliamentary institutions that are intended to 'deal more effectively with individual grievances, investigate claims of maladministration, enhance transparency, combat corruption, protect electoral democracy and regulate key services in the public interest'.[80] A non-exhaustive list of such institutions would include ombudsmen, auditors, electoral commissions, public service commissions and commissions for the appointment of judges. These are intended to protect the integrity of the state and to insulate democratic processes from the hazards of authoritarian backsliding, incumbent manipulation and corruption.[81]

Integrity branch institutions preserve the distinction between the government, which is composed of a particular party or coalition and (as the telling phrase 'government of the day' reveals) has only temporary status, and the enduring State that belongs to all citizens in common and transcends both partisan affiliations and any particular government. The flourishing of such institutions reflects the emergence of a new form of separation of the powers, which combines the effectiveness and clear accountability of the parliamentary system with countervailing institutions designed to control and constrain parliamentary majorities.[82] This 'constrained' form of parliamentarism recognises the advantages, in terms of efficiency and coherent policy development and implementation, of parliamentary government over systems designed around American-style separation between a Congress and separately elected president, but it also recognises that an executive supported by a disciplined majority in parliament needs additional checks and balances, from outside the parliamentary system, in order to limit the abuse of power, to uphold the non-manipulability of the law and political system, and to ensure accountability and transparency.[83]

This view is supported by Zifcak and Eckersley, who identify the role of integrity branch institutions as being to augment the periodic safeguard provided by elections with '*ongoing* safeguards to restrain a despotic government once it wins office'.[84] These ongoing safeguards are needed because in a modern parliamentary democracy, the executive is not effectively 'controlled' by parliament. When party loyalty and well-whipped majorities are the rule, parliament 'can no longer control the executive', and, therefore, 'the conventional doctrine that Parliament can and will hold the executive to account can no longer be regarded as an adequate foundation for democratic governance'.[85] To remedy these deficiencies, they propose the strengthening of integrity branch institutions as part of a package of measures, including the judicialisation of human rights and the codification of conventions.[86]

Some integrity branch institutions, such as Auditors General and Freedom of Information Commissions, are intended to support the party political institutions in promoting democratic contestation – for example, by rectifying the informational imbalance between the government and the opposition. They might therefore be regarded as part of a system of 'political', rather than 'legal' constitutionalism. Others, such as Electoral Commissions, are more clearly 'legal' in character, as they are intended to remove certain decisions from the clash of interests and egos found in day-to-day politics, and to place these decisions in a realm of dispassionate, impartial and rational-legal resolution.[87] As Philip Pettit notes, 'decisions in which elected politicians are likely to have self-seeking interests, inimical to the public interest' – such as decisions on public prosecutions and the redrawing of electoral boundaries – should, 'subject to the possibility of review in extreme cases', usually be 'put at arm's length on the grounds that no one should be judge in their own case'.[88]

The Swedish Instrument of Government of 1809 is credited with the creation of the modern office of Ombudsman. In essence, the ombudsman is simply a public prosecutor with special investigatory powers who is able to exert influence on the administration by offering advisory opinions, and by making official annual reports to parliament.[89] The ombudsman was for a long time unique to Sweden, and it may be Sweden's great contribution to the practice and ideas of liberal democracy; only in recent decades, starting with Denmark in 1953, has it become a 'well known article of legal export'.[90] Now, however, the office of Ombudsman, together with other integrity branch institutions, is widely diffused amongst the Constitutions of new, 'third-wave', democracies, including those adhering to the Westminster model. As noted by Elkins, Melton and Ginsburg, most Constitutions written in the last twenty years include not only provision for an ombudsman but also 'commissions for judicial appointments, electoral oversight, human rights and counter-corruption – bodies that were not considered by drafters in the nineteenth century'.[91]

Such institutions are prominent in the independence Constitutions of Commonwealth nations, where the list of bodies given constitutional recognition and protection from overt party-political interference may even include the commissions responsible for the police service and for the teaching profession.[92] The value of public accounts committees, ombudsmen, human rights commissions, auditors general, information commissioners, electoral commissions and similar oversight and regulatory institutions is officially recognised by the Commonwealth and has been commended to state-level constitutional designers and practitioners, on the grounds that these bodies may enhance 'public confidence in the integrity and acceptability of government's activities' and 'can play a key role in enhancing public awareness of good governance and rule of law issues'[93]

The Constitution of Malta provides a typical example of how these matters are handled in Westminster-derived Constitutions. The members of Malta's Electoral Commission (Art. 60), Public Service Commission (Art. 109), and the Broadcasting Authority (Art. 118) are appointed by the president, on the advice of the prime minister, 'given after the Prime Minister has consulted the Leader of the Opposition'. Although in practice 'consultation' is often little more than 'information', and although the prime minister can ultimately insist on the nominee of his or her choice, the spirit and intent of the Constitution is that these should be bipartisan appointments.[94] While the leader of the opposition only has a consultative role in those appointments, other integrity officials, such as the Auditor General (Art. 108) and the Ombudsman can be appointed only by a two-thirds majority vote of parliament, thus giving the opposition an effective veto. Members of integrity branch institutions also have a typical range of privileges and restrictions, intended to secure their autonomy: for example, ministers, parliamentary secretaries, public officers, anyone who is a 'member of, or a candidate for election to, the House of Representatives', and members of local councils, are excluded from appointment to the Public Service Commission (Art. 109). Similar rules apply to the Electoral Commission (Art. 60) and other integrity branch institutions (Arts 108; 118). These officers enjoy security of tenure for fixed terms, and may not be removed except for inability to discharge their duties, or for misbehaviour (Arts 60; 108; 109; 118).

The development and diffusion of integrity branch institutions is an important advance in constitutional technology. Their rise to prominence is neither coincidental nor surprising. Modern parliaments have become the seat of the government's power, in which the parliamentary majority routinely supports, rather than checks, the government. Parliamentary oppositions, committees and question time all still have their place, and competitive parliamentary elections remain the main means of democratic accountability, but these party political instruments must be augmented by extra-parliamentary checks and balances if a moderate, balanced and tempered system of government is to be maintained. As Bruce Ackerman points out, the combination of parliamentary government with such fourth branch institutions creates a 'new separation of the powers', which divides the governing, legislative and policy-making power of the cabinet-plus-parliamentary-majority from the scrutinising and rule-of-law-protecting powers of the minority, the people, the courts, and the integrity branch.[95]

A viable and acceptable Constitution for Scotland, conforming to the norms of contemporary Constitutions in Europe and the Commonwealth, and reflecting this major development in constitutional technology, would therefore incorporate such integrity branch institutions and ensure such bodies have the powers and independence necessary to perform their duties.

Human Rights, Judicial Review and Universal Constitutional Values

Proposals for the constitution of an independent Scotland have not been developed in isolation, but in the context of global norms for all democratic states. The central argument of this section is that Scotland's constitution-makers have remarkably little room for manoeuvre on the conceptual fundamentals of the constitutional system. Aside from any particular institutional or substantive bargains struck by the 'founders' of a Scottish state, a viable and acceptable Constitution would have to conform to a common model of legal constitutionalism, characterised by the establishment of a rigid, written Constitution, which entrenches human rights and basic democratic procedures beyond the reach of ordinary parliamentary majorities, and which enforces the distinction between the Constitution and ordinary law by means of judicial review. A Scottish Constitution that deviated too far from this common model would be grossly sub-optimal, and perhaps illegitimate, if not in the eyes of the Scottish people, then in the eyes of world opinion.

The latter half of the twentieth century saw the near-universal triumph of rights-based constitutionalism (rigid, judicially enforced constitutionalism with a commitment to the protection of guaranteed rights against majority decisions of elected assemblies) as the most widely used and accepted form of constitutionalism.[96] While stressing the limits to convergence, Goldsworthy claims that there now is a strongly judicialised 'common model' of democratic constitutionalism, which is 'increasingly regarded as desirable around the world' and is 'adopted in most countries that have achieved independence since the Second World War'.[97] The elements of the 'common model' identified by Goldsworthy include: (1) 'democratic elections for the legislature'; (2) 'guarantees of individual rights'; (3) 'an independent judiciary' with 'authority to enforce constitutional requirements' and 'exclusive authority to settle legal disputes'; and (4) 'a requirement that constitutional provisions can only be changed [. . .] by some special, democratic procedure', requiring 'broader consensus' and 'more careful deliberation' than ordinary legislation.[98]

The first of Goldsworthy's criteria is a defining characteristic of all democratic political systems. The other three mark a distinction between two alternative constitutional models: 'constitutional supremacy' and 'parliamentary sovereignty'.[99] Goldsworthy's criteria are all present in the 'constitutional supremacy' model, which enables the courts (or, in some jurisdictions, a specialist constitutional court, council or tribunal) to 'test or review parliamentary laws' against a rigid Constitution that guarantees certain rights and procedural processes against the whims of incumbent majorities.[100] The last three of Goldsworthy's criteria are not present in the traditional British model of 'parliamentary sovereignty', in which the legislature is sovereign in a 'formal, juridicial sense', statutes are 'supreme', and where the courts 'merely give effect to' laws enacted by Parliament, with 'no right to test or review' them.[101]

The chief characteristic of Goldsworthy's 'common model', or what Olivier calls 'constitutional supremacy' (they are treated synonymously) is the intimate connection between constitutional rigidity, judicial review, and guaranteed rights. According to the assumptions of this model, the three are inseparable. 'Judicial review', in this context, refers to the power of the courts to test the validity of statues against the Constitution.[102] Alex Stone Sweet draws a further distinction between 'judicial review', exercised by ordinary courts, and 'constitutional review', exercised by specialised constitutional courts occupying a guardianship position which is, strictly speaking, neither legislative nor judicial.[103] For these purposes, however, the two modes of review, which correspond to Cappelletti's distinction between decentralised and centralised judicial review,[104] are regarded as merely different mechanisms for achieving the same end – namely, to constrain legislatures under the higher norm of the Constitution. 'Constitutional rigidity' refers to the ease or difficulty with which the written text of a Constitution can be amended – as a rigid Constitution must be amendable only by a special procedure, which will usually include super-majoritarian rules, time delays, a referendum, or some combination of two or more of these mechanisms.[105] 'Guaranteed rights' are a set of substantive or procedural limits on the scope and use of public power, whether in the form of negative proscriptions or positive prescriptions, however narrow or wide-ranging, that the legislature and all other public authorities are bound to respect.

If the Constitution is of a rigid type, and proclaims that there are certain higher laws or norms that are binding even on the legislature, then, to ensure the protection of these laws and norms, there must be some judging institution, external to the legislature, with the authority to determine whether a violation has occurred. Otherwise, the legislature – which, in a modern parliamentary democracy usually means the government of the day with a well-whipped and loyal majority – would be judge of its own cause, and the Constitution would be only as strong as the morally restraining effect of its provisions on the consciences of legislators.[106]

Conversely, judicial review when applied to a non-rigid Constitution offers little protection against legislative absolutism. In the Irish Free State, for example, the parliament claimed for itself the right to amend the Constitution by ordinary legislation for an indefinite period; it simply tacked a rider on to bills saying that the legislation would amend the Constitution to the extent necessary to render the bill constitutional and thereby undermined all distinction between the Constitution and ordinary legislation.[107] A special amendment procedure is therefore necessary to protect the Constitution from the danger of such 'excessive flexibility', which might undermine its status, permanence and authority.[108]

This 'common model' was not always so common. Indeed, it was for a long time a rarity. Until the mid-twentieth century, distinct 'American',

'European' and 'Commonwealth' approaches to constitutionalism could be identified. Only the American tradition conformed exactly to what is now the 'common model'. From the earliest years of the republic, the USA relied on a rigid Constitution and judicial enforcement of a catalogue of specific rights.[109] In Europe and the Commonwealth, meanwhile, the development of constitutional rigidity was not accompanied by a similar rise in judicial review. Early Commonwealth Constitutions, such as those of Canada (1867–1982), South Africa (1910–61) and Australia (1901 – present), did not even possess a bill of rights or other charter of limitations on the scope of parliamentary power, except for those restrictions required by the federal or quasi-federal nature of these polities. Such Constitutions were limited to 'institutional arrangements', while the protection of rights was left in the hands of 'elective institutions and the common law'.[110] In Canada, for example, prior to the adoption of the Canadian Charter of Rights and Freedoms in 1982, judicial politics revolved mainly around the respective competences of federal and provincial legislatures.[111]

In Europe, there was a 'deep hostility toward[s] judges', and for most of the past two centuries 'delegation of power to judiciaries has been viewed as a necessary evil'.[112] The French Charters of 1814 and 1830, like many other European Constitutions of similar vintage, did proclaim a basic set of rights, but were silent on the subject of judicial review. By conserving the *Code Civil* and a system of administrative law with the Conseil d'État at its apex, the Charters tended in effect to confirm France's traditional distrust of 'le gouvernement des juges'.[113] The Belgian Constitution of 1831 and Dutch Constitution of 1848 expressly forbade judicial review of the constitutionality of statutes.[114] A similar reluctance to allow judicial control over the supremacy of statute continued well into the twentieth century. It can be found, for example, in the Polish Constitution of 1921.[115]

It is important to note that the rejection of judicial review of the constitutionality of laws was not, in Europe and the Commonwealth, a rejection of constitutionalism – the idea that there are superior rules that bind the legislator, and which need broader consensus before they can be changed – per se. Rather, it was a rejection of the judiciary's role as the chief interpreter and enforcer of the Constitution. Greater deference was shown to elected parliaments, rather than to unelected judges, as the proper guardians of constitutional guarantees.[116] An alert electorate, aided by the procedural regularities of either Napoleonic administrative law or English common law, was deemed the best guarantee of liberty. Legislatures, with constitutional principles (whether written or unwritten) behind them, and with the judgment of the electorate before them, were expected to act with moderation, deliberation and self-restraint when constitutional issues were at stake, and to refrain from passing what might be termed 'unconstitutional' laws.

In the latter half of the twentieth century, however, faith in the ability of electoral pressure and self-restraint to uphold democracy and to protect the rights of individuals and minorities was profoundly shaken by the 'unimaginable toxic brew of totalitarianism, Nazism, racism, genocide, and imperialism', which had 'inflicted incalculable human suffering until subdued by arduous and prolonged military intervention'.[117] From this horrific experience emerged a 'particular conception of constitutional ordering', which 'stands as the foundation of the postwar constitutional state' and which was intended to 'stabilize democracy and safeguard equal citizenship and respect for inherent human dignity as supreme or higher law'.[118]

In the post-war reconstruction of Western European democracy, the 'common model' of constitutionalism gradually emerged, albeit with important variations, as the norm in Europe and in most former British colonies, as well as in the United States:

> Successive waves of democratization in [the twentieth century] (for example, Germany and Italy after World War II, Southern Europe in the 1970s, the whole of Central and Eastern Europe after 1989) have transformed the juridical basis of the European state. New constitutions typically proclaim a long list of human rights; they establish a mechanism of defending the normative supremacy of the constitution; and they stipulate (non-legislative) procedures for how the constitutional law is to be amended).[119]

The German Basic Law of 1949 took this renewed commitment to constitutional entrenchment and judicial enforcement of fundamental rights furthest. It rests not simply on a procedural commitment to certain specified rights, but also makes a more teleological commitment to 'human dignity' as the foundation of the regime.[120] Human dignity is deemed so foundational to the German constitutional order that the rights protecting it are placed, in principle, beyond any subsequent amendment.[121]

The spread of judicial review in continental Europe was, however, slow. Well into the post-war period strong judicial review remained the exception rather than the norm. Most countries that had been invaded, rather than falling to home-grown authoritarian rule, chose to re-adopt their pre-war Constitutions: a list which includes Luxembourg, Belgium, the Netherlands, Norway and, initially, Denmark. Of these, only the Norwegian Constitution had, albeit in a limited fashion, developed a form of judicial review.[122] Besides Germany and Austria (the latter of which restored its 1929 Constitution, that, unusually for its time, provided for a special constitutional court with 'responsibility for determining the legality of all acts of state'),[123] only Italy – the other obvious case of inter-war democratic failure in Western Europe – made a clear commitment to judicial review in its post-war Constitution. Even in Italy, there was little consensus; the constitutional court was initially opposed by the left-wing parties[124] and did not become fully operational until 1956.[125]

France, the other major European democracy to reconstitute itself after the war, initially adopted a Constitution without justiciable rights.[126] The Constitutional Committee of the Fourth Republic, which was to determine whether laws were compatible with the Constitution before they were enacted, was a weak institution, to which appeal could be made only by a joint decision of the president and the second chamber (Constitution of the Fourth French Republic, Arts 91–3). Even after the establishment of the Fifth Republic in 1958, the newly formed Conseil Constitutionel was, at first, merely intended to protect the regulatory power of the executive from legislative encroachment;[127] it did not develop into a quasi-judicial check on the legislative power until 1971, when the Declaration of the Rights of Man and the Citizen, and the Preamble of 1946, which together provide a rudimentary bill of rights, were declared justiciable.[128]

Despite this slow start, judicial review has now become the norm in most continental European democracies.[129] In Spain, after the death of Franco, the Constituent Assembly 'never seriously considered *not* establishing a [constitutional] court'.[130] It also insisted on strongly enforced human rights and 'went out of its way to repudiate explicitly characteristic practices of the defunct dictatorship', for example by outlawing the death penalty and the trial of civilians in military courts.[131] Portugal had a more protracted transition, with constitutional review powers initially held by the military-backed Council of the Revolution, but by 1982 a new, civilian, constitutional court had likewise been established.[132] New democracies created in Central and Eastern Europe after 1989 also established constitutional courts with judicial review powers – a process which was notably strong in Poland, Hungary, Bulgaria and Latvia.[133]

This trend towards judicial review of the constitutionality of laws was not restricted to new democracies. The old democracies followed suit. In Belgium, successive waves of 'state reform', intended to transform a once unitary state into a federation, resulted in the creation of a Court of Arbitration, initially to protect the respective competences of the federal, community and regional authorities, but later having a role in the protection of fundamental rights.[134] In 1996, Luxembourg, not to be left out, likewise established a new Constitutional Court with responsibility for ensuring the 'conformity of the laws to the Constitution' (Art. 95ter).

Meanwhile, a similar pattern of development was taking place in the Commonwealth. As noted above, first generation 'Old Commonwealth' democracies – even federal ones – had Constitutions strongly influenced by British notions of parliamentary sovereignty. The Constitutions of the 'New Commonwealth' nations, in contrast, were based on 'constitutional supremacy', and in almost all cases included a justiciable bill of rights.

This tendency towards justiciable rights can be found both in 'home-grown' Westminster-influence Constitutions, such as those of Bangladesh and India, and in the vast number of Constitutions that were developed according to the 'Lancaster House template', mainly under the guidance of British Colonial Office officials.[135] Regardless of the misgivings of great post-colonial constitution-makers such as Sir Ivor Jennings,[136] Westminster-model Constitutions with judicially enforced human rights – substantively based, in most cases, upon the European Convention – proliferated around the world from the 1960s onwards. Today, of the sixteen Commonwealth realms (countries where the British monarch is head of state), which are unmistakably influenced by British traditions and unambiguously part of the global 'Westminster family', all but two (Australia and New Zealand) have justiciable fundamental rights provisions embedded in their Constitutions.

A brief survey of the world's constitutions illustrates the extent of this trend. Only 25 per cent of constitutions explicitly recognised judicial review in 1946, but that that proportion had increased to 82 per cent by 2006.[137] Amongst democracies, the percentage combining judicial review with constitutional rigidity is even higher: of the seventy-nine 'full democracies' and 'flawed democracies' identified in the 2010 Economist Democracy Index,[138] all but four adhere, in broad terms, to this 'common model' – the chief exceptions being the United Kingdom, the Netherlands, New Zealand and Israel.

Even these exceptional countries, which have not yet embraced the 'common model', display some tendency towards the constitutional rigidity and the judicialisation of politics. The Netherlands, which has long had a rigid Constitution but which lacks judicial review of the constitutionality of legislation, regards international human rights treaties as superior to domestic statutes and thus as a proper subject for judicial review in Dutch courts.[139] New Zealand has moved towards constitutional rigidity thanks to Section 268 of the Electoral Act 1993. This Act created several 'reserved provisions' concerning the duration of parliaments and the electoral system, which can only be amended by a three-fourths majority in parliament or by a referendum.[140] Israel, meanwhile, distinguishes between institutional 'Basic Laws' and other legislation, and in 1992 the Supreme Court claimed for itself the right to annul laws made by the Knesset that are incompatible with the human rights provisions of the Basic Laws.[141]

The constitutionalisation of rights also has an international dimension. States – at least, all states wishing to be seen as democracies and to be treated as decent members of international society – no longer have carte blanche in the treatment of their own citizens. Just as the collapse of democracy in the inter-war period and the rise of authoritarian populist regimes led to the subsequent constitutionalisation of rights and rise of judicial review in the post-war refoundation of Germany and Italy, so the brutal wrongs of the Holocaust renewed international commitment to universal human rights.[142] This was reflected in a profound desire to:

> collect together all the thinking of the past five centuries about rights and liberties, to organize it into a body of clear principles, and to affirm it as universally applicable to all human beings everywhere.[143]

The most symbolically important document to arise from this desire to codify rights was the Universal Declaration of Human Rights, adopted by the General Assembly of the United Nations in 1948.[144] In 1966, this Declaration was transformed into two Covenants that place binding obligations (though with no mechanism of enforcement except international monitoring) on states: the International Covenant on Civil and Political Rights (ICCPR) and the International Covenant on Economic, Social and Cultural Rights (ICESC), which have been ratified by the 'overwhelming majority of countries'.[145]

In Europe, the European Convention on Human Rights (1950) (a product of the intergovernmental Council of Europe, not of the European Union) has become a centrepiece of human rights law, with far reaching implications for the protection and definition of rights in the signatory states.[146] Backed by the European Court of Human Rights in Strasbourg, it was the first attempt to give 'specific legal content to human rights in an international agreement' to be combined with 'the establishment of machinery for supervision and enforcement'.[147]

The application of the European Convention has spawned a vast quantity of case law and academic literature which falls outside the scope of this book. The key consideration, from the point of view of Scottish constitution-making and of aiding our understanding and analysis of the SNP's constitutional proposals, is that these international covenants have a strongly normative influence of national constitution-makers, marking the boundaries of what an acceptable modern Constitution ought to contain.

Constitution-makers often seek to incorporate international human rights norms into national constitutional law.[148] Britain, in preparing new states for independence, has implicitly acknowledged the legitimacy of the European Convention as an acceptable baseline for human rights: as noted above, many of the bills of rights incorporated into the written Constitutions of the Commonwealth nations that gained independence from Britain after the 1950s were based directly on the European Convention on Human Rights. Its provisions were, in many cases, incorporated almost verbatim into the Constitution of each country, with only a bare minimum of local variation.

Aside from the Council of Europe and the European Convention on Human Rights, the main international organisation that might exert strong pressure in favour of the constitutionalisation of rights in a future Constitution of Scotland is the European Union. It is notable that the SNP's draft Constitution aimed to constitute Scotland as a 'normal, democratic, European country'.[149] This can be interpreted as more than a rhetorical device. It reflects the SNP's acceptance that 'the independence case depends on Scotland's being part of the EU'.[150] It also acknowledges the existence of European democratic norms and standards that Scotland would have to meet in order to be fully accepted into the European 'club'. Under the Copenhagen Criteria for European Union accession, these norms and standards include democracy, the rule of law and respect for human rights.[151]

The ability of the European Union to push states towards a convergent model of liberal democratic constitutionalism is demonstrated by Turkey's constitutional reforms of 2001, which were intended to facilitate membership,[152,153] and by the EU's partial shunning of Hungary over its controversial new Constitution which has been interpreted as a retreat from liberal democratic principles.[154] Even if the European Union were to pull apart under the strain of the debt crisis, or if Scotland were to choose to join the European Free Trade Area instead of the European Union, conformity to 'European' human rights standards, as embodied in the European Convention on Human Rights, remains vital to the legitimacy of the Scottish state.

The second international organisation which might push Scotland in the direction of a rigid, judicially enforced, rights-based Constitution is, of course, the Commonwealth. The Commonwealth Charter, adopted in 2013, commits states to democracy, human rights, separation of the powers, the rule of law and good governance, as well as to objectives such as gender equality, sustainable development, environmental protection and access to healthcare and education. The significance of this document lies in its quasi-constitutional character. Although it does not establish structures of government, it does proclaim principles and values that are constitutive in nature and provides a set of meta-constitutional norms against which any particular constitution can be assessed.[155]

Even before the Charter, the Commonwealth's Harare Declaration obligated its members to work for 'the protection and promotion of the fundamental political values of the Commonwealth', namely 'democracy', 'the rule of law and the independence of the judiciary', 'just and honest government' and 'fundamental human rights, including equal rights and opportunities for all citizens regardless of race, colour, creed or political belief'.[156] The institutional means of fulfilling these aspirations are set out in the *Latimer House Guidelines*[157] and further amplified by the *Principles on the Accountability of and the Relationship between the Three Branches of Government*.[158] While accommodation is made for countries such as the United Kingdom and New Zealand, which continue to rely on parliamentary sovereignty, the main thrust of these documents assumes that countries will adopt a 'common model' of constitutionalism.

The *Latimer House Guidelines* states, for example, that 'Courts should have the power to declare legislation to be unconstitutional and of no legal effect', and that 'judges should adopt a generous and purposive approach in interpreting a Bill of Rights',[159] while the *Principles on the Accountability of and the Relationship between the Three Branches of Government* recognises the role of the judiciary in upholding both domestic constitutional supremacy and international human rights law:

> The function of the judiciary is to interpret and apply national constitutions and legislation, consistent with international human rights conventions and international law, to the extent permitted by the domestic law of each Commonwealth country.[160]

The internationalisation of human rights, and the incorporation of standardised rights into national constitutions, has resulted in what Law and Versteeg have called a 'generic' set of rights.[161] These are the twenty-five most common rights, which appear in over 70 per cent of the world's constitutions:

> Accordingly, we can construct a hypothetical bill of rights that expresses the mainstream of global constitutionalism by selecting the twenty-five most prevalent provisions. This generic bill of rights contains both the average *number* of rights provisions and the most *common* rights provisions over the last six decades.[162]

The 'generic' rights of global constitutionalism identified by Law and Versteeg are: (1) right to life; (2) prohibition of torture; (3) prohibition of arbitrary arrest and detention; (4) right of access to court; (5) right to present defence; (6) prohibition of ex post facto laws; (7) right to counsel; (8) freedom of religion; (9) freedom of assembly; (10) right to vote; (11) right to private property; (12) equality guarantee; (13) right to privacy; (14) freedom of expression; (15) freedom of movement; (16) right not to be expelled from home territory; (17) presumption of innocence; (18) freedom of association; (19) judicial review; (20) right to work; (21) right to unionise and/or strike; (22) physical needs rights; (23) right to education; (24) women's rights; and (25) limits on property rights.

It is conventional to discuss rights in terms of 'generations'. First generation rights are those of the liberal revolutions of the eighteenth and mid-nineteenth centuries. They focus on civil and legal immunities, chiefly of a negative and individual nature. They place limits on the power, and especially the arbitrary power, of the state for the protection of the liberty of the individual. Second generation rights are those which emerged out of the Industrial Revolution, working class struggle and the attainment of universal suffrage. Often, these take the form of positive entitlements – to free education, public healthcare, decent working conditions and so forth – which demand a claim on public funds or active regulatory undertaking by the state. Third generation rights are those pertaining to the post-materialism of the 1960s 'sexual revolution', the US Civil Rights Movement, and the ecologist movement. These include, for example, protection from discrimination by the state or non-state actors (including private employers) on the grounds of race, gender, sexual orientation or matrimonial status.

Although, as Sunstein has argued, the usual distinction between so-called negative and positive rights is false – since even 'negative' rights demand action by the state and claims on public funds[163] – these generations nevertheless provide a useful shorthand tool for categorising the rights content of constitutions. According to Elkins et al.,[164] the trend over two centuries of Constitution-making has been towards the expansion of rights, with the continuation of first generation negative rights and the adoption of second and third generation rights. While agreeing with this general finding, Law and Versteeg see a divergence of constitutional rights provisions into two main paths: an 'Anglo-Saxon' or 'liberal' path, which is restricted chiefly to first generation rights, and a 'communitarian' path, which has embraced later generations of rights:

> constitutional evolution at a global level is also characterized by a degree of polarization between two competing paradigms or strains of rights constitutionalism – one libertarian in orientation, the other statist. Over time, constitutions are tending to gravitate toward one paradigm or the other. The result is the depopulation of the ideological middle ground and the formation of two competing clusters or families: within each family, constitutions are becoming more similar to one another, but the families themselves are increasingly distinct from each other.[165]

This divergence gets to the heart of the normative question of what a Constitution is and what it is for. The extent to which socio-economic and post-materialist rights can, and ought to be, constitutionalised is the subject of a vast literature. For some, the opposition to the constitutional definition of socio-economic rights may reflect a general distrust of rigid constitutionalism and judicial review, and a preference, as described above, for popular democratic control over decision-making over written, judicially enforced guarantees.[166] Others support the entrenchment and judicial enforcement of first generation rights, but oppose the inclusion of subsequent generations of rights. According to this classical liberal view: 'A constitution is supposed to limit the power of the state over the individual. Its aim is not to tell the government what it should do, but to clarify what it may not do.'[167] Implicit in this position is the notion of freedom as 'non-interference'; liberty, for a liberal, consists of an individual realm into which the state does not tread.[168] Rights, in this tradition, exist *against* the state, and we are free to the extent that we are not compelled or prohibited from certain actions by the state. In its liberal guise, therefore, the state is not an Aristotelian community united to pursue the good life together but simply a device for the protection of personal rights, prioritising individual choice without articulating a common vision of 'the good'.[169]

Support for the constitutionalisation of socio-economic rights may be inspired by various strands of left-liberal, civic-republican, social democratic, socialist or Christian-democratic thought: all these ideological traditions share a belief that the state exists not only to protect individuals in the maintenance of their private rights and in the pursuit of their own interests, but also to promote common goods and to ensure a socially just distribution of resources.[170] This does not mean, however, that the recognition of socio-economic rights necessarily implies that the Constitution commits itself to any one particular transcendental vision of desirable ends: there is scope for 'incompletely theorized agreement'[171] on the terms of a 'social contract' between those, for example, who see the mixed, welfare-capitalist economy as a welcome step towards socialism and those who see it as a necessary bulwark against socialism.

Whether the Constitution of Scotland should include references to second and third generation rights must ultimately be determined, therefore, by an appeal to the values and the policy preferences of Scottish political actors at the time of constitutional founding (and sustained, through time, by subsequent generations). As will be argued in Chapter 3, Scotland's strong Reformed and social democratic traditions, at least in the sense of elite opinion and self-identity, seem to support the case for a broader, more communitarian, concept of rights, even if these rights have a declaratory rather than justiciable status.

The essential point, however, is that a viable and acceptable constitutional order for Scotland would at least have to give recognition to a minimum set of first generation rights, with the European Convention being the baseline, and it is against that baseline that, in the first instance, the SNP's proposals should be judged. While this would require some deviation from British assumptions and practices, it need not exclude Scotland from the wider British-influenced family of Westminster model Constitutions. The Westminster model – if not in London, then in Valetta, Kingston, New Delhi, Ottawa and Gibraltar – recognises that majoritarian democracy alone cannot protect minorities, individuals and marginalised groups against gross abuses of power, and that there must therefore be constitutional limits on the arbitrary power of parliamentary majorities to erode those fundamental human rights that have, by hard experience and painful lapses, been found necessary for the maintenance of a civilised and free human society (freedom from torture, freedom from slavery, freedom of speech, assembly, association and religion, due process of law, and so forth). Viewed through a global lens, and freed from insular parochialisms, judicially enforced constitutional protections are the norm amongst Westminster-derived democracies.

Written constitutions and human rights provisions cannot therefore be seen as strange, 'foreign' innovations that are antithetical to the Westminster tradition. In a way, they are as 'British' as an Indian and a South African meeting in an Irish bar in Halifax, Nova Scotia, to watch the West Indies play Bangladesh at cricket – while eating haggis pakora.

Notes

1. New Zealand has a Constitution Act that establishes and regulates some of the principal institutions of government, but it has only the legal status of an ordinary Act of Parliament and can be amended by ordinary majorities. It therefore cannot be regarded as a 'written Constitution' with higher law status in the sense developed in Chapter 3 (see Palmer and Palmer, *Bridled Power*, 2004).

2. S. A. De Smith, 'Westminster's export models: the legal framework of responsible government', *Journal of Commonwealth Political Studies*, 1/1 (1961), 3.

3. H. Kumarasingham, *A Political Legacy of the British Empire: Power and the Parliamentary System in Post-Colonial India and Sri Lanka* (London: I. B. Tauris, 2013), pp. 2–3.

4. G. Wilson, 'The Westminster model in comparative perspective', in I. Budge and D. McKay, *Developing Democracy: Comparative Research in Honour of J. F. P. Blondel* (London: Sage, 1994), p. 190.

5. S. A. De Smith, 'Westminster's export models', p. 3.

6. A. Lijphart, *Patterns of Democracy: Government Forms and Performance in Thirty-Six Countries* (New Haven, CT: Yale University Press, 1999), p. 9.

7. Ibid. pp. 3–4.

8. R. J. Van Loon and M. S. Whittington, *The Canadian Political System: Environment, Structure and Process* (Toronto: McGraw-Hill Ryerson, 1987); A. Lijphart, *Patterns of Democracy*.

9. J. Webber, *The Constitution of Canada: A Contextual Analysis*, Constitutional Systems of the World (Oxford: Hart Publishing, 2015).

10. L. Wolf-Phillips, 'Post-independence constitutional change in the Commonwealth', *Political Studies*, 18/1 (1970), 18–42.

11. D. Judge, *Political Institutions in the United Kingdom* (Oxford: Oxford University Press, 2005), p. 27.

12. R. A. W. Rhodes, *Understanding Governance: Policy Networks, Governance, Reflexivity and Accountability* (Buckingham: Open University Press, 1997), pp. 198–9.

13. D. Judge, *Political Institutions in the United Kingdom*, p. 25.

14. P. Manow, *In the King's Shadow: The Political Anatomy of Democratic Representation* (Cambridge: Polity Press, 2010).

15. S. A. De Smith, 'Westminster's export models', p. 3.

16. C. Saunders, *The Constitution of Australia: A Contextual Analysis*, Constitutional Systems of the World (Oxford and Portland, Oregon: Hart Publishing, 2011); R. Zifcak and R. Eckersley, 'The Constitution and democracy in Victoria: Westminster on trial', *Australian Journal of Political Science*, 36/1 (2001), 61–80.

17. Bulsara, H. and B. Kissane, 'Arend Lijphart and the transformation of Irish democracy', *West European Politics*, 32/1 (2009), 172–95; A. J. Ward, 'Exporting the British constitution: responsible government in New Zealand, Canada, Australia and Ireland', *Journal of Commonwealth and Comparative Politics*, 25/1 (1987), 3–25.

18. H. Kumarasingham, *A Political Legacy of the British Empire*.

19. M. Glover and R. Hazell, 'Introduction: forecasting constitutional futures', in R. Hazell (ed.), *Constitutional Futures Revised: Britain's Constitution to 2020* (Basingstoke: Palgrave Macmillan, 2008).

20. A. Lijphart, *Patterns of Democracy*.

21. M. Glover and R. Hazell, 'Introduction: forecasting constitutional futures', p. 13.

22. Ibid. pp. 14–15.

23. R. Hazell, 'Conclusion: where will the Westminster model end up?', in R. Hazell (ed.), *Constitutional Futures Revised: Britain's Constitution to 2020* (Basingstoke: Palgrave Macmillan, 2008), p. 294.

24. M. Glover and R. Hazell, 'Introduction: forecasting constitutional futures', pp. 16–17.

25. Ibid. p. 17.

26. R. Hazell, 'Conclusion: where will the Westminster model end up?', p. 296.

27. M. Glover and R. Hazell, 'Introduction: forecasting constitutional futures', p. 17.

28. Ibid. p. 18.

29. R. Hazell, 'Conclusion: where will the Westminster model end up?', p. 297.

30. Ibid. p. 297.

31. Ibid. p. 295.

32. Ibid. p. 295.

33. J.-E. Lane, *Constitutions and Political Theory* (Manchester: Manchester University Press, 1996), pp. 63–5.

34. C. Thornhill, *A Sociology of Constitutions: Constitutions and State Legitimacy in Socio-Historical Perspective* (Cambridge: Cambridge University Press, 2011), pp. 211–19.

35. A. Cobban, *A History of Modern France (Vol. 2. 1799–1945)* (London: Pelican Books, 1961), pp. 71–92.

36. C. Thornhill, *A Sociology of Constitutions*, p. 228.

37. J.-E. Lane, *Constitutions and Political Theory*; C. Thornhill, *A Sociology of Constitutions*.

38. J. Macy and J. W. Gannaway, *Comparative Free Government* (New York: Macmillan, 1915); A. Stepan, J. J. Linz and J. F. Minoves, 'Democratic parliamentary monarchies', *Journal of Democracy*, 25/2 (2014), 35–51.

39. A. Siaroff, 'Varieties of parliamentarism in the advanced industrial democracies', *International Political Science Review/Revue internationale de science politique*, 24/4 (2003), 446.

40. A. Headlam-Morley, *The New Democratic Constitutions of Europe: A Comparative Study of Post-War European Constitutions with Special Reference*

to Germany, Czechoslovakia, Poland, Finland, the Kingdom of the Serbs, Croats and Slovenes and the Baltic States (London: Oxford University Press, 1928); C. R. Sunstein, *Designing Democracy: What Constitutions Do* (Oxford: Oxford University Press, 2002).

41. Constitution of Latvia, 1922, Article 53.
42. Constitution of Latvia, 1922, Article 59.
43. M. Brzezinski, *The Struggle for Constitutionalism in Poland* (Basingstoke: Macmillan Press, 2000), p. 50.
44. D. Pickles, *France: the Fourth Republic* (London: Methuen, 1955); P. Williams, *Politics in Post-War France: Parties and the Constitution in the Fourth Republic* (London: Longmans, Green, 1958).
45. E. Plischke, *Contemporary Government of Germany* (London: George Allen and Unwin, 1964); G. K. Roberts, *German Politics Today* (Manchester: Manchester University Press, 2000).
46. J. C. Adams and P. Barile, *The Government of Republican Italy*, 3rd edn (Boston: Houghton-Mifflin, 1972); F. Spotts and T. Weiser, *Italy: A Difficult Democracy* (Cambridge: Cambridge University Press, 1986).
47. T. Bergman, 'Formation rules and minority government', *European Journal of Political Research*, 23/1 (1993), 55–66; T. Bergman, W. Müller, K. Strøm and M. Blombren, 'Democratic delegation and accountability: cross-national patterns', in K. Strøm, W. C. Müller and T. Bergman (eds), *Delegation and Accountability in Parliamentary Democracies*, Comparative Politics (Oxford: Oxford University Press), pp. 109–220, pp. 148–52.
48. L. De Winter and P. Dumont, 'Belgium: delegation and accountability under partitocratic rule', in K. Strøm, W. C. Müller and T. Bergman (eds), *Delegation and Accountability in Parliamentary Democracies* (Oxford: Oxford University Press, 2003), pp. 253–280.
49. E. Holmberg and N. Stjernquist, *The Constitution of Sweden* (Stockholm: Swedish Riksdag, 1995), p. 14.
50. E. Lindström, *The Swedish Parliamentary System: How Responsibilities are Divided and Decisions are Made* (Stockholm: Swedish Institute, 1982), p. 91; O. Nyman, 'Some basic features of Swedish constitutional law', in S. Ströholm (ed.), *An Introduction to Swedish Law*, 2nd edn (Stockholm: Norstedts, 1988), pp. 68–9.
51. S. A. De Smith, 'Westminster's export models', p. 4.
52. Ibid. p. 4.
53. L. Kohn, *The Constitution of the Irish Free State* (London: Allen and Unwin, 1932), pp. 271–89.
54. A. J. Ward, 'Exporting the British constitution', p. 13.
55. J. G. Swift-MacNeill, 'Thoughts on the constitution of the Irish Free State', *Journal of Comparative Legislation and International Law*, 5/3 (1923), 52.
56. Ibid. pp. 52–53.
57. H. Kumarasingham, *A Political Legacy of the British Empire*, p. 138.
58. S. A. De Smith, 'Westminster's export models', pp. 4–5.
59. G. Austin, *The Indian Constitution: Cornerstone of a Nation* (Oxford: Oxford University Press, 1999).
60. Singh, M. P. V. N. *Shukla's Constitution of India*, 12th edn (Lucknow: Eastern Book Company, 2013), p. 418.

61. Ibid. p. 420.
62. D. O'Brien, *The Constitutional Systems of the Commonwealth Caribbean: A Contextual Analysis*, Constitutional Systems of the World (Oxford: Hart Publishing, 2014), p. 46.
63. S. A. De Smith, 'Westminster's export models', p. 6.
64. M. De Merieux, 'The codification of constitutional conventions in the Commonwealth Caribbean constitutions', *International and Comparative Law Quarterly*, 31/2 (1982), p. 266.
65. D. O'Brien, *The Constitutional Systems of the Commonwealth Caribbean*, pp. 50–3.
66. J. W. Sap, *The Queen, the Populists and the Others: New Dutch Politics Explained for Foreigners* (Amsterdam: VU University Press, 2010).
67. K. Strøm and H. M. Narud, 'Norway: virtual parliamentarism', in K. Strøm, W. C. Müller and T. Bergman (eds), *Delegation and Accountability in Parliamentary Democracies* (Oxford: Oxford University Press, 2013), pp. 523–52.
68. In Norway, the principle of ministerial responsibility to parliament and of the requirement of a government to tender its resignation after a vote of no confidence, long recognised in practice, was written into the Constitution only in 2007.
69. B. Constant, 'Principles of politics applicable to all representative governments', in B. Fontana (ed.), *Constant: Political Writings* (Cambridge: Cambridge University Press, 1988), pp. 171–305.
70. D. A. Low, 'Introduction: the Westminster model', in *Constitutional Heads and Political Crises: Commonwealth Episodes, 1945–85* (Basingstoke: Macmillan, 1988).
71. C. Saunders, *The Constitution of Australia: A Contextual Analysis*, p. 161.
72. Ibid. p. 161.
73. Ibid. p. 162.
74. H. V. Emy, *The Politics of Australian Democracy: Fundamentals in Dispute*, 2nd edn (South Melbourne: Macmillan, 1978).
75. A. J. Ward, 'Exporting the British constitution', p. 18.
76. C. J. G. Sampford, 'Recognise and declare: an Australian experiment in codifying constitutional conventions', *Oxford Journal of Legal Studies*, 7/3 (1987), 369.
77. Australian Constitutional Conventions were gatherings of politicians convened for the purpose of recommending amendments to the Constitution. 'Constitutional Convention' (capitalised) refers to these assemblies; 'constitutional convention' (uncapitalised) refers to the conventional rules.
78. C. J. G. Sampford, 'Recognise and declare', pp. 372–3.
79. M. S. R. Palmer, 'Using constitutional realism to identify the *complete* constitution: lessons from an unwritten constitution', *American Journal of Comparative Law*, 54/3 (2006), 587–636.
80. C. Saunders, *The Constitution of Australia: A Contextual Analysis*, p. 173.
81. B. Ackerman, 'The new separation of powers', *Harvard Law Review*, 113/3 (2000), 633–729; W. E. Bulmer, *A Constitution for the Common Good: Strengthening Scottish Democracy after the Independence Referendum*, 2nd edn (Edinburgh: Luath Press, 2015); P. Pettit, *Republicanism: A Theory of Freedom*

and Government (Oxford: Oxford University Press, 1997); P. Pettit, *A Theory of Freedom: From the Psychology to the Politics of Agency* (Cambridge and Oxford: Polity Press, 2001), p. 169.

82. B. Ackerman, 'The new separation of powers', pp. 633–729.
83. Ibid. pp. 633–729.
84. R. Zifcak and R. Eckersley, 'The constitution and democracy in Victoria: Westminster on trial', p. 63.
85. Ibid. p. 67.
86. Ibid. pp. 75–9.
87. T. Vallinder, 'When the courts go marching in', in C. N. Tate and T. Vallinder (eds), *The Global Expansion of Judicial Power* (New York: New York University Press, 1995), p. 14.
88. P. Pettit, *A Theory of Freedom: From the Psychology to the Politics of Agency* (Cambridge and Oxford: Polity Press, 2001), p. 169.
89. S. Jägerskiöld, S. 'Administrative law', in S. Strömholm (ed.), *An Introduction to Swedish Law*, 2nd edn (Stockholm: Norstedt, 1988), p. 83.
90. S. Strömholm (ed.), *An Introduction to Swedish Law*, 2nd edn (Stockholm: Norstedt, 1988), p. 41.
91. Z. Elkins, T. Ginsburg and J. Melton, *The Endurance of National Constitutions* (Cambridge: Cambridge University Press, 2009), p. 86.
92. De Merieux, 'The codification of constitutional conventions in the Commonwealth Caribbean constitutions', pp. 265–66.
93. Commonwealth Secretariat, *Latimer House Guidelines*, 1998, Art. IX.
94. W. E. Bulmer, 'Constrained majoritarianism: Westminster constitutionalism in Malta', *Commonwealth and Comparative Politics*, 51/1 (2014), 232–53.
95. B. Ackerman, 'The new separation of powers', pp. 633–729.
96. S. Choudhry, *The Migration of Constitutional Ideas* (Cambridge: Cambridge University Press, 2006); Elkins et al., *The Endurance of National Constitutions*; D. S. Law and M. Versteeg, 'The evolution and ideology of global constitutionalism', *California Law Review*, 99 (2011), 1163–254.; D. S. Law and M. Versteeg, 'The declining influence of the United States Constitution', *New York University Law Review*, 87 (2012); C. N. Tate and T. Vallinder (eds), *The Global Expansion of Judicial Power* (New York: New York University Press, 1995); C. Thornhill, *A Sociology of Constitutions*.
97. J. Goldsworthy, 'Questioning the migration of constitutional ideas: rights, constitutionalism and the limits of convergence', in S. Choudhry (ed), *The Migration of Constitutional Ideas* (Cambridge: Cambridge University Press, 2006), p. 116.
98. Ibid. p. 116.
99. P. Olivier, 'Parliamentary sovereignty and "judge-made" law; judicial review of legislation', in J. Hatchard and P. Slinn, *Parliamentary Supremacy and Judicial Independence: A Commonwealth Approach* (London: Cavendish Publishing, 1999), pp. 53–58.
100. Ibid. p. 54.
101. Ibid. p. 53.
102. A. Lijphart, *Patterns of Democracy*, p. 223.
103. A. Stone Sweet, 'Constitutional courts and parliamentary democracy', *West European Politics*, 25/1 (2002), 77–100.

104. M. Cappelletti, 'Judicial review in comparative perspective', *California Law Review*, 58/5 (1970), 1017–53.
105. A. Lijphart, *Patterns of Democracy*, pp. 228–30; M. Böckenförde, *Constitutional Amendment Procedures* (Stockholm: International Institute for Democracy and Electoral Assistance, 2014).
106. The Netherlands is an unusual – perhaps unique – case of a country with a written and rigid constitution, but a prohibition on the constitutional judicial review of statutes. The illogicality of this position is mitigated by the practice of pre-legislative 'political review' (as opposed to judicial review) of legislative bills, which is performed by the advisory Council of State and by the veto power of the indirectly elected Senate. Human rights are protected through the application of the European Convention, which has superior status to statutes and is justiciable. (See Andeweg and Irwin, 2009; Ten Kate and Van Koppen, 1995.)
107. M. Gallagher, 'The constitution and the judiciary', in J. Coakley and M. Gallagher (eds), *Politics in the Republic of Ireland*, 4th edn (Abingdon: Routledge, 2007), ch. 3, p. 74.
108. Elkins et al., *The Endurance of National Constitutions*, pp. 100–2.
109. P. Olivier, 'Parliamentary sovereignty and "judge-made" law', pp. 53–4.
110. C. Saunders, *The Constitution of Australia: A Contextual Analysis*, p. 259.
111. J. B. Kelly and C. P. Manfredi, 'Should we cheer? Contested constitutionalism and the Canadian Charter of Rights and Freedoms', in J. B. Kelly and C. P. Manfredi (eds), *Constested Constitutionalism: Reflections on the Canadian Charter of Rights and Freedoms* (Vancouver and Toronto: UBC Press, 2009), pp. 4–6.
112. A. Stone Sweet, 'Constitutional courts and parliamentary democracy', p. 78.
113. J. L. Lafon, 'France', in C. N. Tate and T. Vallinder (eds), *The Global Expansion of Judicial Power* (New York: New York University Press, 1995), pp. 289–91; C. Thornhill, *A Sociology of Constitutions: Constitutions and State Legitimacy in Socio-Historical Perspective*, pp. 210–11.
114. C. Thornhill, *A Sociology of Constitutions*, p. 244.; J. Ten Kate and P. J. Van Koppen, 'The Netherlands: toward a form of judicial review', in C. N. Tate and T. Vallinder (eds), *The Global Expansion of Judicial Power* (New York: New York University Press, 1995), p. 376.
115. M. Brezezinski, *The Struggle for Constitutionalism in Poland* (Basingstoke: Macmillan, 2000).
116. J. Ten Kate and P. J. Van Koppen, 'The Netherlands: toward a form of judicial review', pp. 376–7.
117. L. E. Weinrib, 'The postwar paradigm and American exceptionalism', in S. Choudhry, *Migration of Constitutional Ideas* (Cambridge: Cambridge University Press, 2006), p. 86.
118. Ibid. p. 86.
119. A. Stone Sweet, 'Constitutional courts and parliamentary democracy', p. 79.
120. C. Thornhill, *A Sociology of Constitutions*, p. 357.
121. C. Möllers, '"We are (afraid of) the people": constituent power in German constitutionalism', in M. Loughlin and N. Walker (eds), *The Paradox of Constitutionalism: Constituent Power and Constitutional Form* (Oxford: Oxford University Press, 2007), p. 97.

122. K. Strøm and H. M. Narud, 'Norway: virtual parlamentarism', p. 546.
123. C. Thornhill, *A Sociology of Constitutions*, p. 291.
124. M. Mandel, 'Legal politics Italian style', in C. N. Tate and T. Vallinder (eds), *The Global Expansion of Judicial Power* (New York: New York University Press, 1995), p. 265.
125. A. Lijphart, *Patterns of Democracy*, p. 227.
126. A. Stone Sweet, 'Constitutional courts and parliamentary democracy', p. 85.
127. Ibid. p. 85.
128. Ibid. p. 85.
129. C. N. Tate and T. Vallinder (eds), *The Global Expansion of Judicial Power* (New York: New York University Press, 1995).
130. A. Stone Sweet, 'Constitutional courts and parliamentary democracy', p. 85.
131. K. Medhurst, 'Spain's evolutionary pathway from dictatorship to democracy', *West European Politics*, 7/2 (1984), 40.
132. C. Thornhill, *A Sociology of Constitutions*, p. 347.
133. Ibid. pp. 358–60.
134. L. De Winter and P. Dumont, 'Belgium: delegation and accountability under partitocratic rule', pp. 274–5.
135. Lancaster House was the name of the building in London used by the Colonial Office for 'Constitutional Conferences' with the leaders of many colonies on the verge of independence.
136. W. I. Jennings, *The Approach to Self-Government* (Cambridge: Cambridge University Press, 1958).
137. D. S. Law and M. Versteeg, 'The declining influence of the United States Constitution', *New York University Law Review*, 87 (2012), 27.
138. L. Kekic, 'Democracy Index 2010: democracy in retreat' (London: Economist Intelligence Unit, 2010).
139. J. W. Sap, *The Queen, the Populists and the Others: New Dutch Politics Explained for Foreigners*; Ten Kate, J. and P. J. Van Koppen, 'The Netherlands: toward a form of judicial review', pp. 375–7.
140. G. Palmer and M. S. R. Palmer, *Bridled Power: New Zealand's Constitution and Government*, 4th edn (Melbourne: Oxford University Press, 2004).
141. R. Hirschl, *Towards Juristocracy: The Origins and Consequences of the New Constitutionalism* (Cambridge, MA: Harvard University Press, 2004).
142. A. C. Grayling, *Towards the Light: The Story of the Struggles for Liberty and Rights that made the Modern West* (London: Bloomsbury Publishing, 2007), p. 241.
143. Ibid. p. 242.
144. C. Sunstein, *The Second Bill of Rights: FDR's Unfinished Revolution* (New York: Basic Books, 2004), p. 100.
145. Ibid. pp. 100–2.
146. S. Greer, *The European Convention on Human Rights: Achievements, Problems and Prospects*, Cambridge Studies in European Law and Policy (Cambridge: Cambridge University Press, 2006).
147. I. Brownlie and G. S. Goodwill-Gill, *Basic Documents on Human Rights*, 4th edn (Oxford: Oxford University Press, 2002), p. 398.
148. M. Böckenförde, N. Hedling and W. Wahiu, *A Practical Guide to Constitution*

Building (Stockholm: International Institute for Democracy and Electoral Assistance, 2011), p. 105.

149. SNP, *A Free Scotland* (Edinburgh: SNP, 2002).

150. Michael Keating, cited by M. Steinbeis, 'Europeas letztes Aufgebot', *Die Welt Online*, 7 January 2012 <http://www.welt.de/print/die_welt/kultur/article 13802809/Europas-letztes-Aufgebot.html> (last accessed 20 January 2012); P. Lynch, *SNP: The History of the Scottish National Party* (Cardiff: Welsh Academic Press, 2002), pp. 185–7.

151. J. McCormick, *Understanding the European Union: A Concise Introduction*, 4th edn (Basingstoke: Palgrave Macmillan, 2008), p. 62.

152. S. Greer, *The European Convention on Human Rights: Achievements, Problems and Prospects*, Cambridge Studies in European Law and Policy (Cambridge: Cambridge University Press, 2006), p. 94.

153. Turkey's accession process to the EU has stalled, and its constitutional trajectory at the time of writing, under Recep Erdoğan, appears to indicate an increasing divergence between Turkey and European standards of democracy.

154. C. Boulanger, '"Is it a dictatorship and a police state yet?" Scheppele and Halmai on current Hungarian constitutional politics', *Verfassungsblog*, 11 July 2012) <http://verfassungsblog.de/dictatorship-police-state/> (last accessed 1 August 2012).

155. Much of the work done by a constitution is political, rather than legal in nature, and having a clear statement of values and principles to which the UK is formally committed – in the form of a Commonwealth Charter that is signed by the queen, no less – could provide a basis for people in the UK, without the benefit of a written Constitution, on which to claim rights and to hold the state to account. The Commonwealth Charter might also be used to inject a more democratic and tolerant spirit into the UK's rather narrowly authoritarian discourse on 'British values'.

156. Commonwealth Secretariat, *Harare Declaration*, 1991.

157. Commonwealth Secretariat, *Latimer House Guidelines*, 1998.

158. Commonwealth Secretariat, *Principles on the Accountability of and the Relationship between the Three Branches of Government*, 2003.

159. Commonwealth Secretariat, *Latimer House Guidelines*, 1998, Art. I.

160. Ibid. Art. IV.

161. D. S. Law and M. Versteeg, 'The declining influence of the United States Constitution', p. 14.

162. Ibid. pp. 14–15.

163. C. Sunstein, *The Second Bill of Rights: FDR's Unfinished Revolution*, pp. 198–202.

164. Elkins et al., *The Endurance of National Constitutions*, p. 28.

165. D. S. Law and M. Versteeg, 'The evolution and ideology of global constitutionalism', *California Law Review*, 99 (2011), 1243.

166. A. Tomkins, *Our Republican Constitution* (Oxford: Hart Publishing, 2005); R. P. Bellamy, *Political Constitutionalism: A Republican Defence of the Constitutionality of Democracy* (Cambridge: Cambridge University Press, 2007).

167. J. D. Tangelder, 'Reformed reflections: Canada's Social Charter', 1990 <http://www.reformedreflections.ca/cultural-political/can-soc-charter.html> (last accessed 2 February 2016).

168. J. W. Maynor, *Republicanism in the Modern World* (Cambridge and Oxford: Polity Press, 2003), pp. 43–8; P. Pettit, *Republicanism: A Theory of Freedom and Government*; Q. Skinner, *Liberty Before Liberalism* (Cambridge: Cambridge University Press, 1998); M. Viroli, *Republicanism*, trans. A. Shugaar (New York: Hill and Wang, 2002), pp. 45–51.

169. J. Gray, *Liberalism* (Milton Keynes: Open university Press, 1986), p. 81; I. Honohan, *Civic Republicanism* (London: Routledge, 2002), p. 19; J. W. Maynor, *Republicanism in the Modern World*, pp. 61–89; M. Ramsey, *What's Wrong With Liberalism: A Radical Critique of Liberal Political Philosophy* (Leicester: Leicester University Press, 1997), pp. 4–5.

170. C. Longley, 'Government and the common good', in N. Spencer and J. Chaplin (eds), *God and Government* (London: SPCK, 2009); D. Marquand, *The New Reckoning: Capitalism, States and Citizens* (Cambridge and Oxford: Polity Press, 1997); D. McIlroy, 'The role of government in classical Christian political thought', in N. Spencer and J. Chaplin (eds), *God and Government* (London: SPCK, 2009); P. Misner, 'Christian Democratic social policy: precedents for third-way thinking', in T. Kselman and J. A. Buttigieg (eds), *European Christian Democracy: Historical Legacies and Comparative Perspectives* (Notre Dame, IN: University of Notre Dame Press, 2003); M. Ramsey, *What's Wrong With Liberalism*; W. Storrar, *Scottish Identity: A Christian Vision* (Haddington: Handsel Press, 1990); C. Sunstein, *The Second Bill of Rights: FDR's Unfinished Revolution*.

171. C. R. Sunstein, *Designing Democracy: What Constitutions Do* (Oxford: Oxford University Press, 2002).

THE SCOTTISH CONTEXT

A viable and acceptable Constitution must 'fit' the country for which it is intended.[1] This means it must be 'rooted in a country's historical experience', 'reflect values commonly held or respected by the people' and 'address current problems confronting the state'.[2] In other words, in addition to conforming to universal standards of contemporary liberal democratic constitutionalism (discussed in the final section of the previous chapter), it must also reflect 'parochial' needs that derive from the specific constitutional requirements of the country for which it is intended.[3]

These particular needs can be embodied in the substantive provisions of a Constitution which recognise specific laws, policies or interests. For example, the Constitution of Sweden protects Sami reindeer herding rights,[4] while that of Nauru, in the South Pacific, has special provisions governing the distribution of royalties from the phosphate industry.[5] Parochial needs can also be considered more broadly in relation to the institutional form of the state. For example, the fact that the Constitution of Sweden provides for a large legislature elected by a party list system, while that of Nauru provides for a small legislature elected by a personal, plurality-based system, reflects the different needs of a medium sized industrialised European country, on the one hand, and a tiny Pacific micro-nation on the other.

This chapter, following an approach inspired by Walter Murphy,[6] considers how Scotland's 'commonly held or respected' values, as well as 'current problems confronting the state', such as sectarianism and different understandings of national identity, might shape the criteria of a viable and acceptable constitutional order. Recognising that 'Constitutions are rarely written in a vacuum, insulated from the political conflicts that swirl about them',[7] it is also necessary to survey the ethnic, religious, demographic and ideological cleavages of Scotland, and discusses how these cleavages might shape the boundaries of a viable and acceptable Constitution. Cleavages are here defined as 'a division in society along which conflict *may* arise [. . .] creating differences in interests, ideologies and identities that may translate into differing policy preferences'.[8]

The first section concerns national identity. Many in Scotland have 'nested' identities, considering themselves to be both Scottish and British. For this reason, a strong Scottish identity has not necessarily translated into rejection of the Union.[9] This could have serious repercussions for an independent Scotland: if the new Scottish state alienates those who emphasise their British identity, and fails to reconcile to itself those who voted against independence, then it might suffer from a debilitating crisis of legitimacy. The Constitution is substantively and symbolically crucial to this process of reconciliation. Substantively, the building of a stable, inclusive and effective democratic system, which provides adequately for material security and public goods, will count for much; it may over time foster a sense of civic, democratic, constitutional patriotism which takes pride in the stability of its institutions.[10] Symbolically, the Constitution has the potential, depending on its contents and presentation, either to be an agent of continuity and reassurance, cementing the Scottish state in an evolving 'social union' that modifies rather than negates British identity, or to be an instrument of radical rupture with the British past. It is argued that only the former course of action would, in the foreseeable future, be viable and acceptable.

The second section briefly examines the party system. It argues that, at present, Scotland has an evolving multi-party system, moving towards a dominant party system, in which the relationship between Scotland and the rest of the UK is one of the most important lines of disagreement between the parties, even overshadowing the left-right axis of politics. In the event of Scottish independence, this line of disagreement is likely to disappear, or at least to be greatly reduced in salience, continuing only as a vestigial marker of political identity. If Scotland were to become independent, a new party system might well emerge, and a Constitution for an independent state must be designed to work with various forms of party system – a dominant party, a two-bloc, or a multi-party system.

The third section considers the religio-ethnic cleavage structure of Scotland. While the existence of a sectarian division in Scottish society, does not call for a 'consociational' solution, it does require a Constitution that carefully manages and accommodates religious groups, perhaps by techniques such as 'recognition without empowerment'[11] augmented by constructive ambiguity and ambivalence.[12]

The fourth section considers the place of values and ideology. It argues that a Constitution for Scotland would have to at least pay lip service to communitarian and egalitarian values. This is inspired by the constitutive myth (if not the reality) of Scotland's commitment to social democracy, Labour radicalism, and the social justice teaching of the Kirk. There are two applications of this. Firstly, while a generic democratic Constitution, to be legitimate by universal standards, must as a minimum uphold first generation rights (as discussed in the previous chapter), a *Scottish* Constitution might also have to include certain second (if not third) generation rights that reflect and embody this social commitment. Secondly, the Constitution should permit and envision a fairly expansive role for the state in the realisation of common goods, and therefore should be designed to allow the effective and democratic exercise of public power, rather than merely limiting public power while protecting private power.

The fifth section discusses the implication of Scotland's geography on the Constitution. Scotland is a relatively small country. Its area is 78,772 square kilometers and its population is estimated at 5,254,800.[13] This equates to almost one-third of the landmass of the UK, and a little less than one-tenth of its people. In relative terms, Scotland is a similar size to Ireland and Denmark, somewhat smaller in both population and area than Sweden, and roughly equivalent to the three Baltic states, or the three Benelux countries, put together. Despite its relatively small size, however, Scotland is a diverse country, with multiple, cross-cutting and politically salient cleavages, which any Constitution would have to accommodate. There is scope for the emergence of politically salient centre–periphery cleavages in an independent state, such as between the central belt and outlying areas, or between the islands and the mainland, and that these cleavages have a potential bearing on viable and acceptable constitutional forms. While there is no basis for the creation of a federal system within Scotland, this regional diversity might be reflected in special constitutional provision for outlying areas (for example additional autonomy for island councils).

Running through this chapter are two recurring themes. The first is religion. It is almost impossible to speak of Scottish politics, even in a largely secular age, without some reference to religion, sectarian legacies, and church–state relations. Scotland is not unique in this respect. Many countries have strong religious interests (real or imagined, living or symbolic) that must be considered by constitutional designers. Nor should the influence of religion as a present force be overplayed: neither Calvin's *Institutes* nor Papal Encyclicals will determine the shape of Scotland's Constitution. Yet it remains the case that constitutional designers in Scotland must respond to the religious legacy, and still continuing religiously identified divisions, of the country. From the qualifications for succession to the throne to the content of the human rights provisions, one must tread carefully around religious or sectarian 'flash-points'.

The second recurring theme is a discussion between 'essentialist' and 'liberal procedural' paradigms of constitution-making.[14] These two paradigms give different weights to the 'institutional' and 'foundational' functions that the constitutional text is expected to perform.[15] From a liberal procedural perspective, the institutional function of the Constitution, which includes defining 'the legal and political structures of governmental institutions, and the procedures of future legislation', as well as specifying the 'legal limits of government power',[16] is most important. An essentialist or 'nation state' perspective gives greater emphasis to the 'foundational' function – the Constitution as a 'basic charter of the state's identity', which plays 'a key role in representing the ultimate goals and shared values that underpin the state'.[17]

These two paradigms differ in their ordering of state formation and nation building. An essentialist or 'nation state' Constitution assumes the prior existence of 'a presumably homogenous people',[18] whose values can be reflected in the Constitution that the people gives to itself. Following Carl Schmidt, '[the] people [*Volk*] must be present and presupposed as political unity if it is to be the subject of constitution-making'.[19] A liberal proceduralist Constitution, on the other hand, 'rests on an attempt to separate the *demos* (the citizens) from the *ethnos* (the people)'.[20] The Constitution is created not as the expression of the identity of a unified ethnos, but rather, following Jürgen Habermas, as a pragmatic agreement between individuals 'on the basis of a minimum consensus regarding procedures and institutions of conflict resolution within a democratic order'.[21] In practice, 'the distinction between these two paradigmatic constitutions is not intended as a strict categorisation', as almost all constitutions contain a mixture of both approaches in their origin, and are expected to perform, to varying degrees, both institutional and foundational functions.[22]

Combining Lerner's work with that of Elkins et al.,[23] this chapter explains the attraction for Scotland and the SNP of a Constitution of the liberal proceduralist type, especially in dealing with sensitive matters of national and religious identity. The reason for this decision is simply that a sophisticated constitutional consensus, capable of building a broad and lasting agreement on questions of identity, is unlikely to emerge, and that given the divisions of Scottish politics an essentialist document is unlikely to command the breadth of respect it would need in order to endure. The new Scottish state should have the constitutional latitude to develop its own civic identity, to overcome its remaining sectarian divisions and to renegotiate its church–state relations in the years and decades following independence, thereby allowing the wider constitutional order to develop organically within the permissive bounds of the written Constitution.

This does not necessarily mean that the Constitution should avoid important procedural technicalities or lack 'specificity' (defined as 'the level of detail in the Constitution and the scope of topics that the document covers').[24] Neither does it mean that the Constitution should restrict itself solely to procedural matters. Substantive issues on which a broad political consensus exists (for example, on the recognition of second and subsequent generations of rights) might safely be included, so long as those that concern divisive issues are left open, or framed in such a way as to be maximally inclusive, and thus amenable to future organic resolution.

Moreover, a liberal procedural Constitution is not to be confused with a Constitution that entrenches neo-liberal economic policies, or limits the state to the minimal 'night watchman' functions of classical liberalism. Rather, a liberal procedural Constitution provides a framework within which particular governments may espouse values and promote policies that go beyond liberalism. For example, Michael Manley, Prime Minister of Jamaica, was able to pursue a policy of 'democratic socialism', entailing a 'greatly enhanced role for the state in economic affairs', under Jamaica's liberal procedural Constitution.[25] In this way, the Constitution does not deny questions of identity or value, nor relegate the concept of 'the good' to the sphere of subjective private preferences. It merely prevents any one ideology from being identified with the constitutional order as a whole: under a liberal procedural Constitution, there can be governments of left, right, centre, or any other point of the political compass, but none of these parties or ideologies can be embedded in the constitutional order itself.

Finally, this is not to deny the foundational role of a liberal procedural Constitution as a state-building, or even nation-building, instrument over the longer term. By avoiding the constitutionalisation of divisive issues, while protecting the political processes and fundamental human rights necessary to maintain a democratic and pluralistic society, it is possible that a liberal procedural Constitution might, in time, give rise to a civic, constitutional patriotism, and become a source of beneficial stability[26] and (perhaps, eventually) a source of national unity and pride.[27]

National Identity

Scotland is divided in its sense of its own national identity. In response to a 'forced choice', asking respondents to come down on one side or other of a British/Scottish divide, 77 per cent gave their identity as Scottish, and 17 per cent as British – reflecting a 'long term shift' since the 1980s in favour of Scottish over British identity.[28] Scottish and British identities are not, however, mutually exclusive. Acknowledging this non-exclusivity, it has become standard to measure identities by means of the 'Moreno scale'.[29] This is a multi-option polling question, asking respondents to state whether they feel, for example, 'Scottish not British', 'More Scottish than British', 'Equally Scottish and British', 'More British than Scottish', 'British not Scottish', or 'None of these'.[30] In a survey conducted by the British Election Panel in 1999 – the year of the establishment of the Scottish Parliament – 22 per cent of respondents gave their identity as 'Scottish not British', 35 per cent as 'More Scottish than British', 33 per cent as 'Equally Scottish and British', and only 7 per cent as either 'More British than Scottish' or 'British not Scottish';[31] this means that while 57 per cent of the respondents privileged their Scottish identity over their British identity, at least 68 per cent acknowledged 'overlapping' Scottish and British identities.

While 'Scottishness' does correlate with support for independence and for the SNP there is no perfect alignment. Keating, citing the Scottish Social Attitudes Survey of 2005, notes that, 'Not surprisingly, SNP voters overwhelmingly prioritize their Scottish identity but two-thirds of Labour voters, a majority of Liberal Democrats and nearly half of Conservatives do so as well.'[32] Attitudes towards independence, rather than Scottish identity per se, is the salient political cleavage around which party competition is structured. This cuts both ways. In 1999, 11 per cent of those who self-identified (on a binary 'forced choice') as British, nevertheless favoured independence, compared with 31 per cent support for independence amongst those identifying as Scottish; conversely, 24 per cent of those identifying as British were opposed even to devolution, compared with 6 per cent of those who identified as Scottish.[33]

Over time, there has been a relative decline of British identity, and a corresponding rise of Scottish identity, but Scottish identity has not yet become universal and it is still, for the most part, nested within a British identity.[34] The continuation of these nested identities could present a problem to an independent state. It would have to reassure those who still claim some 'British' identity that they are nevertheless fully 'at home' in an independent state. It would, likewise, have to reassure those who vote 'No' in any future independence referendum that they can, despite any initial reservations about independence, still be fully included as citizens.

Maurizio Viroli draws a useful distinction between the *patria* and the *natio* which helps to understand how these overlapping, nested identities might be accommodated in the Scottish state.[35] *Patria* refers to the political, civic and legal entity – the *'res publica'*. This corresponds to the politically constituted *demos.*[36] The *natio,* on the other hand, corresponds to the *ethnos*, the cultural entity of which one is a part, regardless of its regime type.[37]

Neither a binary 'forced choice' nor the Moreno question captures the nuance of this distinction. Britishness has never been primarily an ethnocultural identity; it has always been a political, civic identity: the 1707 Union abolished Scottish and English statehood, but left much of civil society and cultural identity in the two countries intact.[38] 'British allegiance', writes Aughey, 'accommodates the identities of its different national parts'.[39] The British state was able to transcend, without having to assimilate, the previous identities of its constituent parts, allowing elites from all parts of the UK to participate in the 'high politics' of an imperial state while local subaltern elites were left to manage local affairs without excessive intervention.[40] To cite a banal example, Britain has a national anthem (characteristically, as a dynastic union state, an anthem which celebrates the unifying Crown rather than the diverse peoples), but there are only English, Scottish, Welsh or Irish folk songs.

Scottish nationalism is not, therefore, chiefly motivated by ethno-cultural considerations of identity; these were never seriously threatened by the Union – indeed, they were preserved and encouraged within it. The dominant mode of nationalism in Scotland is civic rather than ethnic in character.[41]

The prevailing aim of Scottish nationalism, then, has always been to rebuild the Scottish *patria*, based on a Scottish *demos*. What is at stake in Scottish nationalism is not a contest between Scottish *natio/ethnos* and British *natio/ethnos* identities, but a dispute about the political orientation of the Scottish *natio/ethnos* with respect to membership of, or withdrawal from, the British *patria*. The significance of this is that in asking people to choose between 'British' and 'Scottish' identities, or asking them to rank 'Scottish' and 'British' identities in order of salience using the Moreno question, one is really asking them to choose between their *natio/ethnos* (which is almost always Scottish, even amongst firm Unionists) and their real or aspirational *patria/demos* (which for those who favour independence is 'Scotland', and for those who do not is the 'United Kingdom').

In constitutional terms, this means that a strongly 'essentialist' Constitution,[42] that rests the legitimacy of the Scottish state on an appeal to the *natio/ethnos* – characterised, for example, by a nationalistic preamble that turns its back on the British past and seeks to promote a new all-embracing national identity[43] – would be out of place, as there is little need for such 'nation-building'. A more viable strategy would be to develop an inclusive, liberal procedural Constitution, which presents Scotland as *patria* – as a legal, civic, political entity, a *res publica*, or commonwealth, that 'goes beyond national, ethnic and religious identity' and 'provides a culturally neutral basis for political unity'.[44]

If national identity is malleable and created by states, as modernist theorists of nationalism assert,[45] then it is at least potentially possible for a liberal procedural Constitution to become a cornerstone of a renewed civic national identity. As Bruce Ackerman writes, the Constitution can become a 'central symbol' of a people's political achievement, promoting an 'enlightened kind of patriotism' that strengthens the Constitution's moral authority.[46] Thus, a Constitution that starts out as a practical, pragmatic basis for the Scottish *patria/demos*, might also – as in the case of the US Constitution – become 'a symbol of the people itself',[47] and so come to hold a central place in the self-identity of the Scottish *natio/ethnos*.

Short of a radical rupture which cannot in present circumstances be foreseen, such an identification of the Scottish *natio/ethnos* with the Constitution of the *patria* is not, however, likely to be immediate. As Sujit Choudhry noted (citing the failure, so far, of the Canadian Charter of Rights and Freedoms to consolidate Canadian national feeling), those who use Constitutions of a liberal procedural type as instruments of nation-building are facing a long and uphill struggle.[48] In the meantime, if the Constitution of Scotland is to take root, it must attempt to include and accommodate everyone in Scotland, including those whose attachment to the Scottish *natio/ethnos* is embedded within attachment to the British *patria/demos*.

Three areas in which a Scottish Constitution might strive to achieve this inclusivity can be identified. The first is to enshrine in the Constitution an inclusive definition of citizenship, with provision for dual English (or 'remainder of UK') and Scottish citizenship and reciprocal residency and voting rights. The second is to enable the Constitution to facilitate power-sharing and 'cross-border cooperation' in various fields. The SNP's public pronouncements indicated that an independent Scotland would seek to share certain powers with the rest of the former United Kingdom, perhaps using a structure similar to that of the current British–Irish Council, in order, inter alia, to administer a common currency and a common travel area. The third constitutional accommodation to 'British' identity is to maintain the monarchy. The monarchy would serve as an institutional link between the new Scottish state, the British state that precedes it, and the other realms of the Commonwealth. Scotland would, in effect, become the seventeenth 'realm', enjoying a constitutional status similar to that of countries such as Canada or Jamaica.[49] As further examined in Chapter 6, key aspects of traditional British usage, such as the oath of allegiance, could also be maintained, preserving a vestigial symbolic connection with a wider, historical, British imperial identity.

Taken together, these provisions might amount to the development of a so-called 'social union', in which it is recognised that the various parts of the former UK, although separate states having full recognition under international law, are not entirely 'foreign' to one another. A Constitution that recognises inclusive and reciprocal citizenship, facilitates power-sharing and cooperation across the border, allows for a common currency and maintains a shared monarch would necessarily keep the boundary between 'independence' and 'autonomy' porous. It would recognise that no state is ever fully 'independent', and that the sovereign states, dependent semi-states, and devolved quasi-states of these islands (not to mention the rest of Europe, and indeed the world) must find ways of addressing common problems. Such a 'porous' Constitution, allowing the Scottish state to enjoy the privileges of statehood while also continuing to be part of a wider 'British' sphere – just as Norway is, through the Nordic Council, part of a Scandinavian sphere – may be acceptable to those who primarily identify as British and those who vote 'No' to independence, in a way that a stridently 'nationalistic' Constitution, with separatist tones, would not.

The Scottish Party System

Prior to the 1970s, Scotland, in common with most of the UK, had a two-party system, with Conservative and Labour parties differing mainly on economic policies and competing chiefly on the basis of class identity.[50] Since the rise of 'territorial politics', this has changed: the SNP has risen from being a rather fringe party in the 1960s[51] to being the party of government.[52] As discussed in the previous section, attitudes to independence are now the most important line of division in the party system. This, rather than any great contest over social or economic principles, forms the dividing line between the SNP and Labour. Scotland has a two-dimensional party system with nationalist–unionist and left–right cleavages, resulting in a multi-party system that is reflected in[53] and reinforced by[54] the use of proportional representation for the Scottish Parliament. Devolved Scotland has therefore consistently had at least five parties being represented in parliament, of which at least four are 'significant' in terms of their ability to either hold office or to determine who holds office.[55]

At the time of writing, based on the 2015 general election result in which the SNP won 56 out of 59 Scottish seats in the House of Commons and on the SNP's victory in the 2016 Scottish Parliament election, Scotland seems to be heading towards a dominant party system, with the SNP as a catch-all popular party of the centre-left. There is no way of knowing how long this will last, and it is especially difficult to speculate on what would happen to the Scottish party system in the context of an independent state, if that were to come about in the future. With independence, the 'status question' of Scotland's place in or out of the UK would necessarily be settled, and the SNP's original *raison d'être* would then be fulfilled. It would be premature, however, to suggest that an independent Scotland would inevitably return to a left–right two-party system. In part, this is because party systems have a tendency to be 'frozen' at certain stages of their development[56] and the political enmity and personal distrust between those who supported independence and those who opposed it is unlikely to disappear overnight. It is also because of the existence of other potentially politically salient cleavages within Scotland, some of which have, until now, been 'buried' by the nationalist–unionist division. These other potential cleavages, whether sectarian, ideological or geographical, are considered in subsequent sections of this chapter.

Without being unduly speculative, it is possible to imagine three potential outcomes. Firstly, the SNP might continue as a dominant, even hegemonic, catch-all party of the broad centre, occupying a position which is almost identified with the political system as a whole, like that of the Christian Democrats in post-war Italy,[57] the Social Democrats in post-war Sweden,[58] the Congress party in post-independence India,[59] or Fianna Fáil during much of Ireland's history as an independent state.[60] In this dominant-party scenario, the SNP might occasionally share power with other minor parties, or even lose it on occasion to heterogeneous coalitions of opponents, but would be regarded as the new 'establishment' and the 'natural party of government'. Secondly, a two-party or two-bloc system might emerge, with SNP-led and Labour-led governments alternating in power, both occupying a similar 'slightly left' position on the ideological spectrum and competing for votes on grounds of patronage, personality, record and competence. Thirdly, a fragmented multi-party might emerge, in which newly opened divisions in Scottish society, long 'buried' by the politics of the Union, come to the fore. New parties might emerge (a Highlands and Islands party, a Christian Democratic party, or a populist party of the radical right, for example, are not beyond the realms of the imagination), meaning that coalitions have to be knitted together from diverse elements while the vote share of the established parties declines.

The crucial point, however, to bear in mind when assessing the SNP's constitutional proposals is that a workable Scottish Constitution would have to be robust enough to operate effectively with different types of party system. For example, to maintain democracy in a dominant party system, there would have to be extra-parliamentary checks and balances that can contain a long-dominant party without excessive complacency, corruption or abuse of power. To encourage stable coalition-building in a fragmented multi-party system, on the other hand, effective mechanisms to promote government formation and executive stability may be required.

Religious Influences and Sectarian Divisions

No survey of the Scottish context would be complete without mentioning the role of Christianity. Christianity in general, and the Reformed (that is, Calvinist, Presbyterian) tradition in particular, has had great historical influence on the formation of Scottish national identity, culture and thought.

Calvinism is a religion with profound political and constitutional implications.[61] With an emphasis on covenanted relationships, it readily embraces the idea of constitutional government formed upon the contractual consent of the community, most notably expressed in the 'National Covenant' of 1638. At the same time, its insistence on the sovereignty of God necessarily limits the authority of all human rulers: a sovereign parliament, unconstrained by higher laws or by transcendent principles of justice, would be unconscionable. Parliamentary sovereignty – whatever its status as a legal or political doctrine – was therefore alien to Scottish theo-constitutional principles. Canon Kenyon Wright, as one of the leading architects of the devolution settlement, for example, rejected the sovereignty of parliament by appealing to theological foundations:

From a Scottish constitutional (and theological) perspective this English tradition of state absolutism has always been unacceptable in principle. It is now intolerable in practice. The Scottish Parliament must be built upon philosophical foundations that are more coherent and credible than the notions which underpin the existing British constitution.[62]

Not only the ideas, but also the practice, of Presbyterianism have shaped Scottish democratic culture. The mixed constitution of 'aristocracy moderated by democracy' endorsed by Calvin[63] was replicated in the Presbyterian system of church government, in which collective bodies of elders ruled but congregations had an important role in selecting elders.[64]

The structure of the Kirk, culminating in the General Assembly, was formed on representative lines, but the principle of non-absolutism and constitutionalism prevailed even in respect of the General Assembly, whose powers were limited by the Barrier Act of 1697. This required the General Assembly to seek the approval of local presbyteries before making certain fundamental decisions – a procedure, incidentally, similar to that used for amending the Canadian Constitution,[65] the US Constitution,[66] and parts of the Indian Constitution.[67]

For the most part, the influence of such theo-political ideas on Scottish constitutional thought today is indirect, having been absorbed into the general civic and political culture, whence it has re-emerged in secularised and diluted form. Its effects are nevertheless profound. Secularised Calvinism blends naturally into a 'civic republican' ethos that favours a state that is constitutionally limited, but active and engaged rather than minimalist – a state wherein freedom is understood not simply as a matter of personal choice, but as active public-spirited engagement in the realisation of the common good through deliberative institutions.[68]

The Scottish Provisional Constituent Assembly's 1962 draft Scottish Constitution recognised the status of the Church of Scotland as a national church.[69] But, despite the historical cultural influence of Presbyterianism, it would be incorrect to see Scotland as a Presbyterian nation today. It is, like most Western countries, a nation characterised by religious pluralism and by divisions between an indifferently secular majority with only a nominal connection to religion, and various religiously active minorities.

Former divisions, arising in the nineteenth century, between the Church of Scotland and the Free Church of Scotland, are no longer as politically or socially salient as they once were. The most important religious divisions in Scotland today are: (1) that between those sections of the population – religiously practising or otherwise – that identify with, or have a cultural or historical connection to, Protestantism (mostly in Presbyterian form) and those which have a similar connection to Roman Catholicism; and (2) the division between the minority, mostly Christians, but also adherents of Islam and other faiths, who are actively practising and the majority who are not. The first of these divisions might for convenience be described, without any prejorative intent, as a 'sectarian' division; the second can be described as a 'secular–religious' division.

Constitution-makers around the world have to cope with the problem of how to recognise the religious identities and values of communities while preserving both the harmony of a pluralistic society and the rights of individuals within that society.[70] Politically articulated religious identities may even be responsible for the existence of states. For example, the Partition of the Indian subcontinent, which led to Pakistan and ultimately Bangladesh being separate from India, had much to do with the inability of the Congress Party and the Muslim League to come to terms on which they could construct a common polity.[71] In many other cases, deep disagreements over matters of religious identity remain at the centre of processes of constitutional change, from the concept of the 'civil state' (*dowla madaniyyah*) in Tunisia (2011–14) to the role of religious organisations in mobilising the 'No' vote in Kenya's 2010 constitutional referendum because of opposition to Kadhi courts and abortion rights.[72]

In this regard, Scotland is no exception. Although religious or ethnoreligious identity issues are not as marked or as divisive in Scotland as they are in some countries, the historically divided religious landscape of Scotland may still have consequences for constitutional design options. Matters such as the monarchy and the royal succession, abortion rights, same sex marriage and the status of denominational schools – all of which might reasonably fall under the purview of a written constitution – have the potential to arouse deep, if usually dormant, religious divisions. Mapping these divisions and understanding their nature is therefore essential to the project of re-constituting Scotland.[73]

Sectarianism can be defined as bigotry, antipathy and discrimination between 'Protestant' and 'Catholic' groups. However, the extent to which the sectarian division is truly 'religious' in nature is very debatable. These religious labels are often used as markers of communal identity rather than as indicators of active religious commitment. They mainly reflect a lingering ethnocultural division between 'indigenous' Protestant Scots and the descendants of nineteenth-century Irish, mainly Catholic, immigrants.[74]

These ethno-religious groups were, in the nineteenth century and in some cases long afterwards, correlated with socio-economic status. Protestants maintained control over skilled and higher-paying trades, while Catholics were 'used by employers to depress local wage levels' and often relegated to unskilled, low-paid work.[75] In consequence, the difference between Protestants and Catholics in working class Scottish communities was not a difference of personal religious opinion, but one of inherited, and therefore fixed, communal identity, having consequences for the whole of one's life chances. The continued existence of sectarian discrimination in education, employment and life chances is still widely perceived, although its continued extent has been disputed.[76]

Sectarianism is most vehement in West Central Scotland (in and around the Greater Glasgow conurbation), where it is often expressed through the proxy of football. Indeed, the term 'sectarianism' has become associated in the public mind with 'violence and hooliganism associated with the rivalry between Scotland's two biggest football clubs', Rangers and Celtic.[77] These clubs are historically associated with religio-ethnic identities; 87 per cent of

Rangers fans identified as Protestant and 93 per cent of Celtic fans identify as Roman Catholic.[78]

Although there is a 'clear indication that religion is of less significance in the east of the country than in other parts',[79] sectarian-related football violence is by no means limited to Glasgow. In 2002, a match between Celtic and Heart of Midlothian (a 'Protestant' team based in Edinburgh), resulted in the singing of paramilitary songs and street fighting.[80] Sectarianism is not only associated with football, however;[81] it is also 'influential in everyday life and in the corridors of power'. Attempting to eradicate sectarianism – and sectarian-motivated violence and disorder – has therefore been a policy priority of successive Scottish governments since devolution.[82]

The sectarian divide means that 'issues of an essentially religious nature can quickly become important political issues as well',[83] particularly when matters affecting the (real or imagined) interests of one group or the other is at stake – such as the public funding of denominational schools or the provisions of the Act of Settlement banning Catholics from the British Crown. Catholics were – traditionally at least – most likely to vote Labour[84] and to sympathise with Irish republican nationalism (but not Scottish nationalism).[85] Working class Protestants, on the other hand, have traditionally had close ties to the Conservatives (although this has greatly declined since its heyday in the 1950s–60s)[86] and to the Orange Order, a 'fundamentalist Protestant, unionist, loyalist and authoritarian' organisation which is alleged to have had connections with the far-right.[87]

The sectarian divide cuts across the distinct 'secular–religious' social cleavage, separating a religiously motivated minority of both Protestants and Catholics from the largely secular mainstream of Scottish society. According to the 2001 census, 42.4 per cent of the Scottish population claim some sort of adherence to the Church of Scotland, the largest Protestant group, while 15.9 per cent gave their religion as Roman Catholic.[88] While 66.9 per cent of the population claim some form of religious identification (with 27.55 per cent stating 'no religion'),[89] only around one in ten Scots regularly attend religious services.[90] It is interesting to note that this is approximately double the percentage of regular attendees in England, again indicating the relative strength and salience of religion in Scotland.[91]

In addition, about 2 per cent of the Scottish population (at least nominally) adhere to non-Christian religions, with Muslims, at 0.84 per cent of the total population, being the largest non-Christian religious community.[92] While there are some converts from amongst those with Scottish ancestry, most adherents of religions other than Christianity are, or are the descendants of, twentieth-century immigrants from the Commonwealth. 'Visible' ethnic minorities in Scotland, according to the 2001 census, account for around 2 per cent of the total population, with Asian Scots making up 70 per cent of this group (those from Pakistan being the largest ethnic minority, followed by Chinese, Indians and those of mixed ethnic backgrounds).[93]

The consequences of the religious composition of Scotland for the design of a Scottish Constitution and for the SNP's constitutional policy must now be considered. Much contemporary literature on comparative constitutional design focuses on the problems of democratic consolidation in 'deeply divided' societies.[94] A deeply divided society is one in which society is 'segmented' into distinct and (actually or potentially) antagonistic communities, defined by ethnic, linguistic, religious or ideological identity.[95] The most widespread response, which 'is to be found repeatedly in constitutions of "divided societies"' is a form of 'consociationalism' – meaning a system of government in which power-sharing at elite level is combined with autonomy for constituent groups.[96]

The extent to which consociationalism is necessary (or desirable) in a Constitution is related to the degree of heterogeneity in society. Donald Horowitz (who is critical of consociational institutions)[97] argues that the heterogeneity of a society can be seen on a 'spectrum'. At one end, there are 'severely divided societies', which are characterised by intense communal conflict; at the other, there are 'fluid societies' 'that have long contained groups whose descendants have blended into the general population' or 'whose interactions have been at relatively low levels of conflict'.[98] Between these two extremes, there is a 'middle category', where 'groups have strongly held political aspirations and interact as groups but where several favourable conditions have moderated the effects of ethnic conflict'.[99] In these countries intercommunal conflict is moderated by external forces that have fostered internal integration, by the presence of other cleavages (religion, class, often region) that 'compete for attention with ethnicity and are reflected in the party system', or by the fact that 'ethnic issues emerged late in relation to other cleavages and to the development of parties, so that party politics is not a perfect reflection of ethnic conflict'.[100]

Scotland probably fits into this middle category. Although sectarianism has a persistent, politically salient and occasionally violent presence in some corners of Scottish society, the ties of class, partisanship, region and British–Scottish identity cut across sectarian lines, blunting the importance of sectarianism as a primary determinant of both identity and voting behaviour. It is misleading to see Protestants and Catholics as monolithic, self-contained blocs, since 'individuals of all faiths and none now work together, drink together and, most significantly, marry each other'.[101]

This moderate degree of social fluidity is also reflected in voting behaviour. While traditionally there was, as noted above, a tendency for Catholics to support the Labour Party, and a historical connection between some parts of the working class Protestant population and an 'Orange', 'conservative' unionism, no party in Scotland today is based solely or even mainly on sectarian appeal: most Catholics might have voted Labour, but most Labour voters were not necessarily Catholic; some working class Protestants might vote Conservative on 'Orange' lines, but Orangemen do not make up the whole or even the majority of the Conservative vote.

Given this situation, consociational mechanisms, such as communal veto powers and '*proporz*' (proportional distribution of offices or resources between Protestants and Catholics), as found, for example, in the devolved institutions of Norther Ireland, are not required or desired in Scotland.[102] It is in the substantive, rather than the structural, parts of a Constitution that the influence of sectarian and secular–religious cleavages is most likely to be felt. Based on a study of democratic transition in South Africa, Murray and Simeon make a case for 'recognition without empowerment' as an alternative to consociationalism. This approach recognises and protects the diversity of society, without creating constitutionally entrenched lines of division: the Constitution is framed to protect and include diverse social, religious and linguistic groups, while downplaying the constituent or collective role of these groups in the political process.[103]

In other words, in a Scottish context, the substantive provisions of the Constitution, such as the monarchy, the national church, same sex marriage, the public funding of denominational (mainly Roman Catholic) schools, and the application of a constitutional 'right to life' to abortion and euthanasia, would be framed to take into account the range of religious views and sectarian identities in Scotland, while denying any political autonomy or veto power to religiously identified communities.

A similar difficulty attends constitutional rules on succession to the throne, the religious position of the monarchy, and issues such as same-sex marriage, abortion and euthanasia. It is impossible for a Constitution to come down on one side or the other of any of these issues (for example by providing explicit constitutional entrenchment of existing abortion rights, or an explicit rule that the 'right to life' extends to the unborn) without provoking disagreement. An illustrative example concerns the traditional oath taken by the monarch, promising to uphold the 'true Protestant religion and the Presbyterian form of church government'. As Norman Bonney writes:

> the oath can be seen as contributing to a national environment at the apex of the state for the sectarian expression of internal Protestant/Catholic religious differences [. . .]. But if the oath is abolished it could offend a substantial contrary body of opinion in Scotland evident in the Orange Order and its lodges and support for Glasgow Rangers and some other football clubs that are vocal supporters of the Protestant character of the United Kingdom state. The whole issue of the relationship of the monarchy to established religion in Scotland and whether existing arrangements should continue in an independent Scotland is thus likely to be a potentially very controversial one.[104]

In order to be viable and acceptable, a Constitution must tackle these 'foundational' issues – which reflect the nature, values and ethos of the society being constituted – in a way that allows as many relevant parties as possible to be comfortable with its provisions. There will almost certainly have to be room for negotiation between the various interested parties, so as to secure the broadest possible base of agreement. But, in these and similarly contentious cases, the best way to achieve the recognition required for broad agreement, and thus for stability, might be to agree to disagree. That is, to give the Constitution the breadth and latitude to accommodate various potential outcomes without privileging any, and then to undertake to resolve the remaining differences in an incremental way, outside of the 'constitutional realm', through the ordinary processes of parliamentary party politics.

'Ambiguity' (the use of deliberate omission or unclear language) and 'ambivalence' (the use of deliberately contradictory, but largely symbolic, provisions, giving each side something to hold on to) are two ways in which this might be achieved.[105] The Constitution of Italy provides good examples of the use of both techniques. Most Christian Democratic members of the Constituent Assembly wanted socio-economic rights to be included only in the preamble, as a moral guide to legislative action which would not be directly justiciable, while the parties of the left wanted to include these rights as directly justiciable guarantees.[106] The resulting Constitution was possible only because the text was ambiguously written. It satisfied the left by not specifying that socio-economic rights were merely 'directive principles', and satisfied the right by not stating them to be directly justiciable. By its ambiguous silence, the Constituent Assembly managed to postpone resolution of this question, to shift it from the exalted realm of constitution-making into the mundane realm of everyday legislative and judicial politics, and thereby to prevent this disagreement from halting the broader constitution-making project. Similarly, the Italian Constitution used ambivalence to patch over disagreement about the role of the Roman Catholic Church. The Constitution is secular, but it confirms the Lateran Pacts (a series of agreements between the Italian state and the Vatican, negotiated by Mussolini), which gives the Roman Catholic Church a range of legal privileges.[107] This ambivalence, by giving a symbolic 'victory' to both sides, made the Italian Constitution – if not perfect, by any means – viable and acceptable in its historical setting.

Ambivalence and ambiguity are messy. Where possible, they are to be avoided. Elkins et al. show empirically that there is a positive correlation between the level of detail in a Constitution and its longevity – because the ability to include such detail is evidence of broad agreement, and where Constitutions are based on broad agreement they are better placed to last.[108] If a consensus on church–state issues, sectarian interests and religiously sensitive legislation could be negotiated in detail, to the satisfaction of all interested parties, then so much the better. In the absence of such agreement, however, the second best option is to diffuse divisive questions. Techniques such as ambiguity and ambivalence can prevent the overall constitutional project (the entrenchment of human rights and democratic institutions and processes, on which a broad, if shallow, agreement *can* be reached) from being derailed by disputes over a few contentious issues.

The ultimate consequence of Scotland's religious cleavages might, then, be to push constitution-makers in the direction, at least as far as these sensitive questions are concerned, of a 'liberal procedural' document. Such a Constitution would avoid the lack of consensus on foundational values, identities or ultimate ends by restricting itself to a 'thin consensus' on democratic procedures and basic rights.[109] As will be discussed in the following section, the rights provisions might be quite extensive, and might reflect a broad 'social democratic' consensus on matters such as socio-economic rights, whilst nevertheless being framed in a way that strives to avoid religious or sectarian controversy.

A Social Democratic Scotland?

Not every constitutional choice is predetermined by factors such as a country's immediate historical trajectory, global trends in constitutional design, or the particular circumstances of its geography or demography. The constraints imposed by these limitations are real, but the role of ideology in framing constitutional choices must also be considered. In Scotland's case, the ideological consideration with the greatest bearing on constitutional design is Scotland's 'democratic', 'radical' or 'left' tradition, reflected in the preponderance of egalitarian and communitarian rather than hierarchical and individualist values and in a supposed preference for social democratic over neo-liberal policies. An early internal party submission on the SNP's constitutional policy claimed, for example, that any Constitution for Scotland, to work successfully, must reflect 'deep-seated democratic feeling' represented by 'the Declaration of Arbroath, the quite extraordinary democratic structure of the national church, and the political radicalism of the nineteenth and early twentieth centuries'.[110] This section explores this myth, examines its reality, and reflects on its consequences for the design of Scottish constitutional texts.

First the myth. Some of the stories that Scotland likes to tell itself boast of the country's democratic, egalitarian ethos and of its communal values. These are often, consciously or unconsciously, contrasted against the hierarchical, individualist, market-orientated values that supposedly prevail in England. Kenny MacAskill MSP, a former SNP justice minister in the Scottish government, exemplified this myth in the following terms:

> Scotland [. . .] is most certainly an egalitarian country. It has been forged on an anvil of historical events that have created a culture of equality and of public service. From the days of the Reformation and the creation of parish schools there has been a drive to educate all and for all to participate. Whether in the urbanised central belt or the rural crofting counties, communities grew up seeing the need for co-operation, whether against the excesses of the landlord or the industrialist.[111]

McCrone argues that the 'central motif' of this myth is 'the inherent egalitarianism of the Scots', according to which people are judged to be 'primordially equal'; inequality is therefore artificial and 'man-made'.[112] He goes on to note the ambivalence of this myth. On the one hand, it can lead to an 'activist interpretation', which 'takes the coexistence of man-made inequality and primordial equality, and argues for an active resolution of this apparent anomaly in favour of social equality'.[113] At its most radical, this may be reflected in the spirit of 'Red Clydeside' (a reference to the uprising in Glasgow after the First World War), of class struggle and trade unionism.[114] A more liberal interpretation, favouring equality of opportunity rather than outcome, is found in the meritocratic ideal of the 'lad o'pairts' – the poor boy made good.

On the other hand, it can provoke a more 'conservative response', whereby persistent inequalities, defined in terms of the 'distribution of resources, rewards and opportunities' are not only artificial, but also illusionary and irrelevant – they 'do not matter, so nothing needs to be done'.[115] Yet even this conservative interpretation of the myth can have important egalitarian properties. It might legitimate the wealth of the rich, but it deflates their pretentiousness and their claims to special, especially hereditary, privilege. If poverty is deemed unimportant because it makes a man no worse, then wealth is unimportant because it makes a man no better. Moreover, wealth does not imply a right to rule. As we are reminded by 'A man's a man for a' that', the Burns song chosen to be used at the first opening of the Scottish Parliament, the qualities of good sense and honesty may be found in the humble as well as the mighty.

The myth of Scottish egalitarianism, as a myth, cannot be falsified, because 'a myth cannot be disproved'[116]– although the limits and inconsistencies of this myth can be exposed by contrasting them against both persisting inequalities and the continued influence of neo-liberal thought and policies.[117] However, it is possible to test a 'common perception' arising from this myth, namely that 'Scotland's political values lie somewhere to the left of its neighbours and, in particular, England's'.[118] Rosie and Bond's analysis of citizens' policy preferences and political orientations, based on the British Social Attitudes Survey (2003), found little evidence to support this perception of left-leaning Scottish exceptionalism, as similar majorities in both Scotland and England thought that the gap between rich and poor was too large,[119] wanted to increase taxation and spending,[120] and supported free university tuition for at least some students.[121] Only on the question of welfare spending was there an appreciable and statistically significant difference, with 41 per cent in Scotland, as opposed to 34 per cent in England, believing that welfare benefits were too low.[122] Assessing respondents from different regions of the UK on a left–right scale of political values – including whether the government should redistribute income from rich to poor, whether big business benefits owners at the expense of workers, whether ordinary people get a fair share of wealth, and whether there is one law for the rich and another for the poor – Rosie and Bond found that 'Scotland falls more or less in the middle of a relatively narrow range of vales', with north-east England being most 'left wing', and south-east England being most 'right wing'.[123]

A 2011 study by John Curtice and Rachel Ormston found that people in Scotland were a little more in favour of 'tax and spend' policies than those in England, with 43 per cent of people in Scotland believing that the state should redistribute income compared with 34 per cent in England.[124] They also found, however, that the difference overall between England and Scotland on left–right economic and fiscal issues is modest, and that these differences had narrowed rather than widened since devolution.[125]

Nevertheless, Scotland still 'feels' more left-leaning than England – a phenomenon which Rosie and Bond, following Paterson,[126] attribute to the pattern of party competition, and to the fact that Scottish politics is dominated by 'a struggle between Labour and Nationalist parties, both advocating social democratic policies and adopting left-of-centre rhetoric', which pulls the 'centre of gravity' towards the left.[127] While 'simplistic views of Scotland as a naturally progressive country cannot be sustained', they argue that there is nevertheless a stronger basis for social democratic policies.[128]

The contrast between the legislative agenda, the political rhetoric, the governmental priorities, and the underlying values of the current (2015) Scottish government and those of the UK government, as well as the contrast between the reception given to Nicola Sturgeon in Scotland as leader of the SNP and that given to Jeremy Corbyn in England as leader of the UK Labour Party, would all appear to confirm that in the wake of the independence referendum there is still more of an appetite for left-of-centre politics in Scotland than at Westminster.

Scottishness is left-wing in another sense. Those who identify as solely or mostly Scottish on the Moreno scale tend towards the left, while those who feel equally Scottish and British, more British than Scottish, or only British, incline to the right; likewise, those who favour further steps towards independence tend towards the left, while those who favour a closer union tend towards the right.[129] Reasons for this association between Scottishness and left-leaning values can be found in the Scottish politics of the 1980s and 1990s, and in particular in the response of 'civic' or 'institutional' Scotland to Thatcherism. Whereas in England there was no clear basis, especially after the defeat of the trade unions and the collapse of Soviet Communism, on which a strongly rooted ideological opposition to Thatcherism could be mounted, in Scotland, anti-Thatcherism was to mobilise around a territorial and civic community:

> The difference in Scotland is that rejection of the neoliberal dispensation has a territorial expression and a territorial unit on which to base it. Defence of the welfare state in the 1980s and 1990s was linked to the campaign for self-government, giving it the extra momentum that previous home rule campaigns had lacked.[130]

It would be incorrect to say that Scottish nationalism was simply a product of Thatcherism. As noted in Chapter 2, dissatisfaction with the British constitutional order long pre-dated Thatcher's rise to power. Nevertheless, it is plausible to see institutional anti-Thatcherism as having an instrumental effect in driving demands for constitutional change, especially in inducing non-nationalists to support a fairly substantial measure of devolution:

> While demands for Scottish home rule go back to the nineteenth century, their intensification in the late twentieth century owed a great deal to the new conservatism that had dominated British politics since 1979. The Thatcher and Major governments, which never enjoyed even a plurality of support in Scotland, were widely seen as violating not just the welfare tradition of the post-war years but also deeper conceptions of community and solidarity embedded in Scottish self-understandings.[131]

In this – also mythologised – account, Mrs Thatcher's infamous address to the General Assembly of the Church of Scotland (her so-called 'Sermon on the Mound' speech) was central to the forging of this Scottish 'resistance' to Thatcherism. She was speaking to an assembly of ministers and elders of the Kirk – an audience that might be assumed to be 'traditionalist' and 'conservative' rather than 'progressive'. Yet this speech, and the reaction to it, reveals much about the nature of Scotland's ideological basis. With a telling choice of words, Kenny MacAskill MSP denounced Thatcherite individualism and lack of social conscience as a 'heresy'.[132]

MacAskill's choice of words hints at an important – even if mostly forgotten – religious dimension of the egalitarian myth. Variations on the Scottish egalitarian myth, whether expressed through a radical struggle for the economic condition of the working class, through a commitment to meritocratic education, or thorough a less material sense of moral equality despite differences in wealth, are commonly attributed to Calvinism, 'because the Kirk, and its secular arm, the parish, lay at the heart of each'.[133]

In Scotland, the opposition to Thatcherism was framed in moral terms, drawing on a deep (albeit never universal, and never uncontested) tradition of Calvinist social thought. As McCrone writes, 'The unalloyed pursuit of profit offends the moral economy of the community. [. . .] Money-making is judged to be too readily motivated by avarice and greed.'[134] Such concerns touch the left, but also offended the traditional, conservative, guardians of the 'moral economy'.[135]

Whilst, as noted in the previous section, the Reformed tradition promotes representative, constitutional government under the rule of law, it does not limit the state to a neo-liberal vision of 'minimal government'. On the contrary, the state according to Calvinism has a divine duty to promote the common good in active ways that go beyond the neutral defence of individual rights. As Storrar writes:

> The Calvinist stress on the responsibility of the local parish church for the welfare of the poor within the community, and the responsibility of the preacher to apply the word of God to the affairs of the community and nation, meant a theological tradition in Scotland which was concerned with questions of justice in society as much as with justification by faith.[136]

Instances of this tradition of socially concerned Presbyterians can still be found, for example, in bodies such as the Church of Scotland's 'Special Commission on the Purposes of Economic Activity', which brings together 'people from the financial services industry, poverty campaigners, academics, theologians and representatives from business and trades union organisations' in order to investigate how 'quality of life, well being and values, such as justice, cohesion and sustainability', rather than just 'growth' or 'shareholder value' can 'become the measures for economic activity'.[137,138]

According to this interpretation, Scotland is not a universally left-wing nation (as the mythologisers of 'Red Clydeside' assert). Rather, it is a country in which the rational egoist, utility maximising ethic of neo-liberal capitalism was rejected on grounds which are at least subconsciously theological. To a greater extent than in England, this rejection was shared by the traditional, moderately conservative, institutional elites as well as by the radical left. If this interpretation is correct, then Scotland's ideological orientation has much in common with that of continental European countries, where Social Democrats were traditionally faced not by a secular, market-liberal right, but by a centrist, welfare-orientated Christian Democratic party, and where the individualist amorality of market liberalism has never been elevated to the same position that it has held in 'Anglo-American' societies.[139] Whatever credence one gives to this 'Social Calvinist' interpretation of Scottish anti-Thatcherism, the fact remains that 'social democracy continues to be a key element in Scotland's political life'.[140]

Moreover, 'Scottish nationality has been rebuilt around themes of welfare and egalitarianism'.[141] Claiming a Scottish identity 'is to say that one has left-of-centre values', while 'to say that one is British is to assert distinctly more right-of-centre views'.[142] The SNP have attempted to capitalise on this by 'an emphasis on economic rather than cultural nationalism', with an independent Scotland portrayed as 'a haven from the depredations of Thatcherite economics and New Labour-style compromises'.[143]

The left-leaning orientation of Scottish politics is also found in a tendency to look to Scotland's Scandinavian neighbours for inspiration, as demonstrated, for example, in the frequent references of the architects of devolution to Scandinavian models of parliamentarism.[144] The idea that an independent Scotland would somehow emerge as a model 'Scandinavian-style' social democracy, effortlessly combining economic and industrial prowess with strong social welfare provision, environmentalism, progressive democratic politics and a peaceful foreign policy is central to the SNP's case for independence.[145]

Of course, this caricatured and optimistic portrayal ignores the cultural as well as institutional dissimilarities between Scotland and Scandinavia, as well as the fact that Scandinavian states (although still, on the whole, more social democratic than Anglo-American polities) have adopted certain neoliberal policies in an attempt to adapt to globalisation, deindustrialisation and the decline of the traditional social democratic voter base.[146] Nevertheless, this explicit Scandinavianism – what might be called 'keeping up with the Johansens' – reinforces the perception that an independent Scotland would be, for the most part, a social democratic Scotland, with its political centre of gravity on the left.

This ideological orientation has certain constitutional consequences. Firstly, it creates a strong case for the inclusion of socio-economic rights alongside 'first generation' civil and legal rights – although the manner of this inclusion, and the extent to which such rights can be rendered justiciable, remains moot. Secondly, it reinforces the need for the state to be able to act decisively and coherently in the delivery of democratically determined common goods. A US-style system, in which powers are deliberately divided and frustrated, must be rejected; instead, when there is a clear public support for a policy (which is not inconsistent with human rights or damaging to the basic institutions of the democratic state itself) then a government supported by a majority in parliament should have the authority to act without undue restriction. Thirdly, this further supports the case for proportional representation and an inclusive, power-sharing democracy. This is not, as usually argued, a response to diversity, but rather a normative choice that reflects the egalitarian self-conception of Scotland through its commitment to a 'high quality' democracy pursuing 'kinder, gentler' policies.[147]

The Territorial Dimension of Scottish Politics

'Territorial politics' has long been central to the study of Scotland and the Union,[148] but it has little place in the study of Scotland's internal politics, which has been dominated by issues of governance and identity.[149] This is because the main centre–periphery cleavage (using the terminology of Lipset and Rokkan)[150] in Scotland relates to the UK scale, with the SNP representing, in respect of Westminster, a 'peripheral' interest. In an independent Scotland this might well change. The 'centre' would no longer be London and the south-east of England, but Edinburgh and the Central Belt. This could lead to the emergence of a new 'territorial politics' within Scotland, reflecting differences of interest and outlook between different parts of a geographically diverse country.

The nature of this geographical diversity must be briefly described. Scotland's population is heavily concentrated in the industrial and post-industrial areas of the Central Belt, extending approximately along the M8 corridor. Beyond this lies a vast 'hinterland' of small towns, with rural settlements and small towns, stretching from the southern edge of the Central Belt to the border, and north from Stirling to the Highlands. The Highlands constitute a regional unit within Scotland, characterised by dispersed patterns of settlement, reliance on industries such as sheep farming, forestry and tourism, concentrated and largely absentee land ownership, and a distinctive Highland culture and way of life. It is in the Highlands and Islands, too, that Scotland's remaining Gaelic speaking population mostly resides. The number of native Gaelic speakers is small, but the continued vitality of the Gaelic language is of symbolic importance – for example, in the use of bilingual signage and the existence of BBC Alba, the Gaelic-language TV station.

Historically, there were marked urban–rural differences in voting behaviour, with the conurbations of the Central Belt being 'solid Labour', while rural and peripheral areas had a tradition of voting Liberal or Conservative, and, more recently, SNP. In part, this reflected different socio-economic realities. Much of the Central Belt was dominated by heavy industries, manned by unionised industrial workers, whereas the small towns and rural areas has a greater preponderance of farmers and independent small businesses. This legacy is still reflected in patterns of poverty and illness in Scotland: male life expectancy in the relatively prosperous area of East Dumbartonshire about seven years longer than in Glasgow.[151]

As a consequence of this variety, different parts of Scotland have different policy needs: in health, housing, transport, policing and a range of other policy areas, the challenges facing public services in Glasgow or Dundee are very different from those faced by service providers in, say, Fort Augustus or Lerwick. Thus, the territorial dimension of politics within Scotland, and its implications for constitutional design, cannot be ignored. In particular, the scope for sub-state devolution or decentralisation within an independent Scotland must be considered.

At present, Scotland is highly centralised. The present system of thirty-two unitary Councils can hardly be called 'local' at all. In comparative terms, they correspond more closely to the Spanish *provincia*, German *Kreis*, or French *département* than to the *ayuntamiento, Gemeinde* or *commune*:

> Scottish local authorities are very large and are in no really meaningful sense 'local', certainly not at community level. In them there is no way to ensure the democratic wishes of any individual community. Below them there is virtually no democratic structure whatsoever, and where there are (elected community councils still functioning) those structures have very little power and virtually no budget.[152]

These thirty-two authorities have little capacity to exercise policy initiative or even to adapt services to local needs. At least 70 per cent of local government functions are 'mandatory', meaning that the scope for innovative exercise of other, 'permissive' powers is only 'marginal'.[153] Policies of outsourcing and privatisation pursued since the 1980s have 'further reduced the power and the democratic accountability of local government in Scotland',[154] while close financial control is exercised by the Scottish government, through policies such as the 'ring-fencing' of funds, the merger of services into ever-larger units, and the adoption of a 'concordat' that freezes the Council Tax.[155] Moreover, owing to the absence of a written Constitution, local authorities have no constitutional basis, meaning that their boundaries, powers, and even their very existence, can be changed unilaterally by an Act of the Scottish parliament, or, indeed, the UK parliament.[156]

Some early supporters of Scottish independence were in favour of a federal or quasi-federal state. A submission to the SNP's constitutional committee made by P. J. Findlay in 1968 proposed the creation of sixteen provinces with constitutionally entrenched regional-level competencies, in addition to the then existing 197 burghs and 196 districts.[157] Such proposals must be treated with scepticism. No current demand for the federalisation of Scotland can be detected. Yet the principles of decentralisation and subsidiarity inherent in these proposals cannot so easily be dismissed. The importance of local self-government for the consolidation of democracy is a recurring theme of democratic thought, spanning civic republican, left liberal and Christian democratic traditions.[158] This importance is acknowledged in the European Charter of Local Self-Government, to which the UK became a signatory in 1997.[159] This Charter 'embodies the conviction that the degree of self-government enjoyed by local authorities may be regarded as a touchstone of genuine democracy',[160] and enjoins states, 'where practicable', to recognise the role of local government in their Constitution.[161]

To argue that a Constitution for Scotland would have to incorporate a new, highly decentralised system of local government, that it must grant substantial autonomy to the Highlands and Islands, or even that it should restore the burghs, would be to press the point too far. Nevertheless, there does seem to be a case, bearing in mind Scotland's geographical diversity, as well as the broader democratic case for subsidiarity and the dispersion of power, for giving local authorities some constitutional recognition. Such recognition would, on the one hand, protect local Councils from the further erosion of their existing powers and stop a future Scottish government from playing 'fast and loose' with local government election dates or electoral systems for partisan advantage. On the other hand, it would ideally leave scope, within the framework of a unitary system, for a more ambitious decentralisation of power in the future, should a demand for it ever arise.

Notes

1. Z. Elkins, T. Ginsburg and J. Melton, *The Endurance of National Constitutions* (Cambridge: Cambridge University Press, 2009), pp. 34–5.
2. M. Böckenförde, N. Hedling and W. Wahiu, *A Practical Guide to Constitution Building* (Stockholm: International Institute for Democracy and Electoral Assistance, 2011), p. 47.
3. S. Levinson, 'Do Constitutions have a point?: reflections on "Parchment Barriers" and preambles', in E. F. Paul, F. D. Miller Jr and J. Paul, *What Should Constitutions Do?* (Cambridge: Cambridge University Press, 2011), pp. 166–8.
4. Instrument of Government (Sweden) (as amended to 2011), Chapter 2, Article 17.
5. Constitution of Nauru, 1968, Art. 63.
6. W. F. Murphy, *Constitutional Democracy: Creating and Maintaining a Just Political Order* (Baltimore: Johns Hopkins University Press, 2007), pp. 24–5.
7. P. C. Ordeshook, 'Constitutions for new democracies: reflections of turmoil or agents of stability?', *Public Choice*, 90 (1997), 55.
8. M. Castle and R. Taras, *Democracy in Poland*, 2nd edn (Oxford: Westview Press, 2002), p. 152.
9. D. McCrone, *Understanding Scotland: the Sociology of a Nation*, 2nd edn (London: Routledge, 2001); L. Paterson, A. Brown, J. Curtice, K. Hinds, D. McCrone, A. Park, K. Sproston and P. Surridge, *New Scotland, New Politics?* (Edinburgh: Edinburgh University Press, 2001).
10. Elkins et al., *The Endurance of National Constitutions*, p. 35.
11. C. Murray and R. Simeon, 'Recognition without empowerment: minorities in a democratic South Africa', *International Journal of Constitutional Law*, 5/4 (2007), 699–729.
12. H. Lerner, *Making Constitutions in Deeply Divided Societies* (Cambridge: Cambridge University Press, 2011).
13. General Register Office for Scotland, 'Mid-2011 population estimate for Scotland', <http://www.nrscotland.gov.uk/files/statistics/population-estimates/mid-2011/mid-2011-population-estimates.pdf> (accessed 5 February 2016).
14. H. Lerner, *Making Constitutions in Deeply Divided Societies*.
15. Ibid. p. 16.
16. Ibid. p. 17.
17. Ibid. p. 18.
18. Ibid. p. 21.
19. Ibid. p. 20.
20. Ibid. p. 22.
21. Ibid. p. 22.
22. Ibid. p. 26; W. E. Bulmer, *A Constitution for the Common Good: Strengthening*

Scottish Democracy After the Independence Referendum, 2nd edn (Edinburgh: Luath Press, 2015).

23. Elkins et al., *The Endurance of National Constitutions*.
24. Ibid. p. 84.
25. J. R. Mandle, 'British Caribbean economic history: an interpretation', in F. W. Knight and C. A. Palmer (eds), *The Modern Caribbean* (Chapel Hill, NC: University of North Carolina Press, 1989), p. 250.
26. Elkins et al., *The Endurance of National Constitutions*, p. 35.
27. S. Choudhry, 'Bills of Rights as instruments of nation building in multinational states: the Canadian *Charter* and Quebec nationalism' in J. B. Kelly and C. P. Manfredi (eds), *Contested Constitutionalism: Reflections on the Canadian Charter of Rights and Freedoms* (Vancouver and Toronto: UBC Press, 2009), p. 246; P. H. Russell, 'The Charter and Canadian democracy', in J. B. Kelly and C. P. Manfredi (eds), *Constested Constitutionalism: Reflections on the Canadian Charter of Rights and Freedoms* (Vancouver and Toronto: UBC Press, 2009), pp. 300–1.
28. Paterson et al., *New Scotland, New Politics?*, p. 105.
29. Ibid. p. 102.
30. L. Moreno, 'Scotland, Catalonia, Europeanization and the "Moreno question"', *Scottish Affairs*, 54 (Winter 2006); F. Pallarés, J. Ramon Montero and F. José Llera, 'Non-state-wide parties in Spain: an attitudinal study of nationalism and regionalism', *Publius*, 27/4 (1997), 152; Paterson et al., *New Scotland, New Politics?*, p. 102.
31. Paterson et al., *New Scotland, new politics?*, p. 107.
32. M. Keating, 'The Strange death of unionist Scotland', *Government and Opposition*, 45/3 (2010), 378.
33. Paterson et al., *New Scotland, New Politics?*, p. 113.
34. M. Leith, 'Governance and identity in a devolved Scotland', *Parliamentary Affairs*, 63/2 (2010), 286–301.
35. M. Viroli, *Republicanism*, trans. A. Shugaar (New York: Hill and Wang, 2002).
36. H. Lerner, *Making Constitutions in Deeply Divided Societies*, p. 22; M. Viroli, *Republicanism*, p. 86.
37. M. Viroli, *Republicanism*, p. 86; H. Lerner, *Making Constitutions in Deeply Divided Societies*, p. 22.
38. A. Aughey, 'The wager of devolution and the challenge to Britishness', *Political Quarterly*, 78 (2009), 136–48.
39. Aughey, A. *The Wager of Devolution and the Challenge to Britishness*, pp. 144–5.
40. M. Keating, *The Strange Death of Unionist Scotland*.
41. M. Keating, 'Stateless nation-building: Quebec, Catalonia and Scotland in the changing state system', *Nations and Nationalism*, 3/4 (1997), 689–717.
42. H. Lerner, *Making Constitutions in Deeply Divided Societies*, pp. 19–21.
43. S. Levinson, 'Do Constitutions have a point?: reflections on "Parchment Barriers" and preambles'.
44. H. Lerner, *Making Constitutions in Deeply Divided Societies*, p. 27.
45. A. D. Smith, *Nationalism and Modernism* (London: Routledge, 1998).

46. B. Ackerman, *The Future of Liberal Revolution* (New Haven, CT: Yale University Press), p. 272.

47. H. Lerner, *Making Constitutions in Deeply Divided Societies*, p. 25; T. C. Grey, 'The Constitution as scripture', *Stanford Law Review*, 37/1 (1984), 1–24.

48. S. Choudhry, 'Bills of Rights as instruments of nation building in multinational states: the Canadian *Charter* and Quebec nationalism', p. 246.

49. N. Bonney, 'Scottish independence, state religion and the monarchy', *Political Quarterly*, 83/2 (April-June 2012), 360.

50. F. Conley, *General Elections Today*, 2nd edn (Manchester: Manchester University Press, 1994), pp. 204–5.

51. P. Lynch, *SNP: The History of the Scottish National Party* (Cardiff: Welsh Academic Press, 2002).

52. G. Hassan (ed.), *The Modern SNP: From Protest to Power* (Edinburgh: Edinburgh University Press, 2009).

53. J. Colomer, 'It's parties that choose electoral systems (or, Duverger's laws upside down)', *Political Studies*, 53/1 (2005), 1–21.

54. M. Duverger, *Political Parties: Their Organization and Activities in the Modern State*, 3rd edn (London: Methuen, 1964).

55. G. Sartori, *Parties and Party Systems: A Framework for Analysis* (Cambridge: Cambridge University Press, 1976), pp. 122–3.

56. S. M. Lipset and S. Rokkan, *Party Systems and Voter Alignments: Cross-National Perspectives* (New York: Free Press, 1967).

57. J. C. Adams and P. Barile, *The Government of Republican Italy*, 3rd edn (Boston: Houghton-Mifflin, 1972).

58. D. Arter, *Democracy in Scandinavia: Consensual, Majoritarian or Mixed?* (Manchester: Manchester University Press, 2006).

59. H. Kumarasingham, *A Political Legacy of the British Empire: Power and the Parliamentary System in Post-Colonial India and Sri Lanka* (London: I. B Tauris, 2013).

60. M. Gallagher, 'The constitution and the judiciary', in J. Coakley and M. Gallagher (eds), *Politics in the Republic of Ireland*, 4th edn (Abingdon: Routledge, 2007), ch. 3, pp. 72–102.

61. A. Kuyper [1898], *Lectures on Calvinism* (New York: Cosimo Classsics, 2007).

62. General Assembly of the Church of Scotland, 1989, cited in K. Wright, Submission to UK Constitutional and Political Reform Select Committee, 2012.

63. H. Höpfl (ed.), *Luther and Calvin on Secular Authority*, Cambridge Texts in the History of Political Thought (Cambridge: Cambridge University Press, 1991), p. 91.

64. G. D. Henderson, *Presbyterianism* (Aberdeen: Aberdeen University Press, 1954).

65. Constitution Act (Canada) 1982, Sect. 38.

66. Constitution of the United States of America, Art. V.

67. Constitution of India, Art. 368.

68. W. Storrar, *Scottish Identity: A Christian Vision* (Haddington: Handsel Press, 1990).

69. R. Moffat, 1993, Art. 4.

70. R. Hirschl, *Constitutional Theocracy* (Cambridge, MA: Harvard University Press, 2010); H. Lerner, *Making Constitutions in Deeply Divided Societies*.

71. G. Austin, *The Indian Constitution, Cornerstone of a Nation*, 2nd edn (Oxford: Oxford University Press, 1999).

72. J. Osur, *The Great Controversy: A Story of Abortion, the Church and Constitution-Making in Kenya* (Nairobi: Zeus Media, 2011); W. E. Bulmer and B. Mkangi, *Constitutional Change as a Response to Inter-Communal Violence: Kenya 2007–2010* (Stockholm: International Institute for Democracy and Electoral Assistance, forthcoming).

73. In my capacity as Research Director for the Constitutional Commission I was once summoned by the first minister's office to give a presentation on the need for a written Constitution before a group of Scottish government civil servants. Nothing caused so much consternation in the room as fear of the can of worms that might be opened by having to deal, in a constitutional text, with matters such as the status of the Church of Scotland or the privileges of denominational schools. I left with a sense that the handling of religious matters in the constitution was not only a delicate issue, but also one on which the future of the whole constitutional project could rest.

74. J. M. Bradley, 'Political, religious and cultural identities: the undercurrents of Scottish football', *Politics*, 17/1 (1997), 31.

75. D. McCrone, *Understanding Scotland*, p. 13.

76. S. Bruce, T. Glendinning, I. Paterson, M. Rosie, 'Religious discrimination in Scotland: fact or myth?', *Ethnic and Racial Studies*, 28/1 (2005), 151–68.

77. Ibid. p. 165.

78. J. M. Bradley, 'Political, religious and cultural identities', p. 27.

79. Ibid. p. 27.

80. E. Kelly, 'Challenging sectarianism in Scotland: the prism of racism', *Scottish Affairs*, 42 (Winter 2003), 32–56.

81. Ibid.

82. M. Steven, 'The place of religion in devolved Scottish politics: an interest group analysis of the Church of Scotland and Scottish Catholic Church', *Scottish Affairs*, 58 (2007), 97.

83. Ibid. pp. 97–98.

84. J. Mitchell, L. Bennie and R. Johns, *The Scottish National Party: Transition to Power* (Oxford: Oxford University Press, 2012), p. 51.

85. E. Kelly, 'Challenging sectarianism in Scotland'.

86. J. M. Bradley, 'Political, religious and cultural identities, p. 28; D. McCrone, *Understanding Scotland*, p. 19.

87. E. Kelly, 'Challenging sectarianism in Scotland'.

88. Scottish Government, *Analysis of Religion in the 2001 Census – Summary Report*, 2005 <http://scotland.gov.uk/Publications/2005/02/20757/53568> (last accessed 9 March 2012).

89. Ibid.

90. P. Brierley, *UK Church Statistics, 2005–2015* (Tonbridge: ADBC Publishers, 2011).

91. *The Scotsman*, 'Catholic Church moves into pole position', 24 May 2008, updated 25 May 2008 <http://www.scotsman.com/news/catholic_church_moves_into_pole_position_1_1433537> (last accessed 24 February 2012).

92. Scottish Government, *Analysis of Religion in the 2001 Census – Summary Report*.

93. Scottish Government, *Analysis of Ethnicity in the 2001 Census – Summary Report*, 2004 <http://www.scotland.gov.uk/Publications/2004/02/18876/32939> (last accessed 23 February 2012).

94. S. Choudhry, 'Bridging comparative politics and comparative constitutional law' in S. Choudhry (ed.), *Constitutional Design for Divided Societies* (Oxford: Oxford University Press, 2008); C. Sunstein, 'Designing democracy: what constitutions do' (Oxford: Oxford University Press, 2002); H. Lerner, *Making Constitutions in Deeply Divided Societies*.

95. J. G. Kellas, 'Nationalism and ethnic conflict: the contribution of political science to political accommodation', *Studies in East European Thought: Nationalism and Social Science*, 46/1/2 (June 1994), 108.

96. A. Lijphart, 'Constitutional design for divided societies', *Journal of Democracy*, 15/2 (2004), 97.

97. B. Reilly, 'Electoral systems for divided societies', *Journal of Democracy*, 13/2 (2002), 156–70.

98. D. Horowitz, 'Democracy in divided societies', *Journal of Democracy*, 4/4 (1993), 20.

99. Ibid. p. 20.

100. Ibid. p. 20.

101. D. McCrone, *Understanding Scotland*, p. 25.

102. G. Sartori, *Comparative Constitutional Engineering: An Inquiry into Structures, Incentives and Outcomes*, 2nd edn (Basingstoke: Macmillan Press, 1997); B. Reilly, 'Electoral systems for divided societies', p. 169.

103. C. Murray and R. Simeon, *Recognition without empowerment*.

104. N. Bonney, 'Scottish independence, state religion and the monarchy', p. 364.

105. H. Lerner, *Making Constitutions in Deeply Divided Societies*.

106. J. C. Adams and P. Barile, *The Government of Republican Italy*, 3rd edn (Boston: Houghton-Mifflin, 1972), pp. 55–6.

107. Ibid. pp. 224–31.

108. Elkins et al., *The Endurance of National Constitutions*.

109. H. Lerner, *Making Constitutions in Deeply Divided Societies*.

110. Findlay, P. J. *Contribution to the Constitutional Committee*, Second Draft, 1968 SNP Archives, National Library of Scotland, A/C No. 10090/98.

111. K. MacAskill, *Building a Nation: Post Devolution Nationalism in Scotland* (Edinburgh: Luath Press, 2004), p. 43.

112. D. McCrone, *Understanding Scotland*. p. 91.

113. Ibid. p. 91.

114. M. Rosie and R. Bond. 'Social democratic Scotland?', in M. Keating (ed.), *Scottish Social Democracy: Progressive Ideas for Public Policy* (Brussels: Peter Lang, 2007), p. 37.

115. D. McCrone, *Understanding Scotland*, p. 91.

116. Ibid. p. 91.

117. G. Hassan, *Caledonian Dreaming: The Quest for a Different Scotland* (Edinburgh: Luath Press, 2014).

118. M. Rosie and R. Bond, 'Social democratic Scotland?', p. 39.

119. Ibid. p. 42.

120. Ibid. p. 41.

121. Ibid. p. 45.

122. Ibid. p. 43

123. Ibid. p. 47.

124. J. Curtice and R. Ormston, 'Is Scotland more left-wing than England?', *ScotCen Special Edition*, no. 42 (2011).

125. Ibid.

126. Paterson et al., *New Scotland, New Politics?*

127. M. Rosie and R. Bond 'Social democratic Scotland?', p. 49.

128. Ibid. p. 56.

129. Ibid. p. 51.

130. M. Keating, 'The strange death of unionist Scotland, pp. 371–2.

131. M. Keating, 'Introduction', in M. Keating (ed.), *Scottish Social Democracy: Progressive Ideas for Public Policy* (Brussels: Peter Lang, 2007), p. 9.

132. K. MacAskill, *Building a Nation*, p. 43.

133. D. McCrone, *Understanding Scotland*, p. 98.

134. D. McCrone, *Understanding Scotland*, p. 99.

135. J. Hearn, *Claiming Scotland: National Identity and Liberal Culture* (Edinburgh: Edinburgh University Press, 2000).

136. W. Storrar, *Scottish Identity: A Christian Vision* (Haddington: Handsel Press, 1990), p. 33.

137. Church of Scotland Special Commission on the Purposes of Economic Activity, *A Right Relationship With Money* (Edinburgh: Church of Scotland, 2012).

138. It is interesting, if only as an anecdotal illustration, that Kevin McKenna, writing in response to the publication of the Scottish government's White Paper on independence in November 2013, attacked not only the 'intellectual paucity' but also the 'spiritual emptiness' of the Better Together (anti-independence) campaign (Kevin McKenna, 'The poverty of the Better Together campaign', *The Observer*, Saturday 30 November 2013).

139. G. Dierickx, 'Christian Democracy and its ideological rivals', in D. Hanley (ed.), *Christian Democracy in Europe: A Comparative Perspective* (London: Pinter, 1994); A. Geyer, *Ideology in America: Challenges to Faith* (Louisville, KY: Westminster John Knox Press, 1997); K. van Kersbergen, 'The distinctiveness of Christian Democracy', in D. Hanley (ed.), *Christian Democracy in Europe: A Comparative Perspective* (London: Pinter, 1994); P. Misner, 'Christian Democratic social policy: precedents for third-way thinking' in T. Kselman and J. A. Buttigieg (eds), *European Christian Democracy: Historical Legacies and Comparative Perspectives* (Notre Dame, IN: University of Notre Dame Press, 2003).

140. M. Rosie and R. Bond, 'Social Democratic Scotland?', p. 56.

141. M. Keating, 'The strange death of unionist Scotland', p. 372.

142. D. McCrone, *Understanding Scotland*, p. 27.

143. B. Jackson, 'The moderniser: Alex Salmond's journey', *Renewal: A Journal of Social Democracy*, 20/1 (2012), 5–8.

144. D. Arter, *The Scottish Parliament: A Scandinavian-Style Assembly?* (London: Frank Cass, 2004).

145. K. MacAskill, *Building a Nation*; D. MacLeod and M. Russell, *Grasping the Thistle* (Glendaruel: Argyll Publishing, 2006).

146. D. Arter, *Democracy in Scandinavia: Consensual, Majoritarian or Mixed?* (Manchester: Manchester University Press, 2006); M. Keating and M. Harvey, *Small Nations in a Big World: What Scotland can Learn* (Edinburgh: Luath Press, 2014).

147. A. Lijphart, *Patterns of Democracy: Government Forms and Performance in Thirty-Six Countries* (New Haven, CT: Yale University Press, 1999), pp. 258–300.

148. M. Keating, 'The strange death of unionist Scotland', p. 365.

149. M. Leith, 'Governance and identity in a devolved Scotland', *Parliamentary Affairs*, 63/2 (2010), 286–301.

150. S. M. Lipset and S. Rokkan *Party Systems and Voter Alignments*.

151. General Register Office for Scotland, 'Life expectancy for administrative areas within Scotland, 2005–2007', <http://www.nrscotland.gov.uk/files/statistics/life-expectancy-for-administrative-areas-within-scotland-2005-2007/j1009104.htm> (last accessed 5 February 2016).

152. E. Bort, R. McAlpine and G. Morgan, *The Silent Crisis: Failure and Revival in Local Democracy in Scotland* (Glasgow: Jimmy Reid Foundation, 2012), p. 5.

153. A. McConnell, *Scottish Local Government* (Edinburgh: Edinburgh University Press, 2004), pp. 15–16.

154. Bort et al., *The Silent Crisis: Failure and Revival in Local Democracy in Scotland*, p. 3.

155. Ibid. p. 3.

156. A. McConnell, *Scottish Local Government*, p. 7.

157. P. J. Findlay, *Contribution to the Constitutional Committee*, Second Draft, 1968, SNP Archives, National Library of Scotland, A/C No. 10090/98; A. McConnell, *Scottish Local Government*, p. 47.

158. M. Moos, 'Don Luigi Sturzo: Christian Democrat', *American Political Science Review*, 9/2 (1945), p. 278; A. De Tocqueville, *L'Ancien Regime*, trans. M. W. Patterson (Oxford: Basil Blackwell, 1962); J. S. Mill, 'Considerations on representative government', in H. B. Acton (ed.), *J. S. Mill: Utilitarianism, On Liberty and Considerations on Representative Government* (London: Dent, 1972); G. Hart, *Restoration of the Republic: The Jeffersonian Ideal in 21st Century America* (Oxford: Oxford University Press, 2002); R. Dagger, *Civic Virtues: Rights, Citizenship and Republican Liberalism* (Oxford: Oxford University Press, 1997); J. F. Pontuso, *Václav Havel: Civic Responsibility in the Postmodern Age* (Lanham, MD: Rowman and Littlefield, 2004), pp. 123–52.

159. A. McConnell, *Scottish Local Government*, p. 12.

160. Council of Europe, *Explanatory Report on the European Charter of Local Self Government ETS No. 122*, nd, <http://conventions.coe.int/treaty/en/Reports/Html/122.htm> (last accessed 18 May 2012).

161. Council of Europe, *European Charter of Local Self Government*, 1985, Art. 2, <http://conventions.coe.int/Treaty/EN/Treaties/Html/122.htm> (last accessed 18 May 2012).

4

THE EMERGENT SCOTTISH CONSTITUTIONAL TRADITION

Half a century ago, the idea that there might be a countervailing tradition of 'Scottish constitutional thought', less wedded to parliamentary sovereignty and less hostile to abstract constitutional principles, was preposterous to most constitutional scholars. In the orthodox view, north and south of the border, the United Kingdom was a centralised unitary state, divided only by class and never by nationality or geography.[1] Scotland's indigenous constitutional traditions barely warranted a mention in this account. However, a by-product of the rise of the Scottish national movement is the emergence of a 'distinctly Scottish' constitutionalism, expressed through a different constitutional lexicon and embodied in institutions that deviate from the 'Westminster norm'.

The term 'Scottish constitutional tradition' does not imply that such a tradition is universal, either in the academy or in popular usage. It makes no claim regarding the acceptance of such a tradition by the courts as a source of constitutional law. It simply refers to trends of constitutional thinking amongst those who have supported greater autonomy for Scotland and which have, to a greater or lesser extent, been absorbed into the lexicon and the assumptions of Scottish public life.

The Campaign for a Scottish Parliament, the Constitutional Convention, and the resulting Scotland Act and its associated provisions, marked a 'transformation' of the Westminster system in Scottish constitutional politics. Provisions such as proportional representation, the election of the executive by a formal vote of parliament, an independent commission for judicial appointments, and the entrenchment of the European Convention on Human Rights (ECHR), which were once labelled (with understatement) 'somewhat controversial', are now supported by an 'evident consensus' of Scottish opinion.[2] This section discusses why that change happened, and, more importantly, the consequences of that change for the future Constitution of Scotland.

The chapter begins with a description of Scotland's place in the 'Union Kingdom' (sic). It discusses how that place was threatened and how, in consequence and in reaction to that threat, a new constitutional space for institutional variation emerged. Much of this chapter is taken up with a detailed analysis of early home rule and independence constitutional pro-jects – showing how these proposals initially replicated, and then began to repudiate, the Westminster model. Other influences, both Commonwealth and Scandinavian, on these constitutional proposals are also considered. It is argued that the constitutional thought of the wider Scottish national move-ment has always been stuck, conceptually as well as geographically, between representing a thinly modified variation of the Westminster model, and other indigenous and external influences.

The immediate point of divergence was Scotland's popular reaction to Thatcherism. Scotland had its own 'big society' – in the shape of semi-autonomous indigenous legal, educational, cultural, religious and adminis-trative institutions – which gave it the civic resources, as well as a distinct mythology, through which a moral critique of Thatcherism could be turned into a constitutional critique of the British state. Thatcher's 'assault' on Scotland's institutional establishment and its embedded values gave popular impetus to the campaign for greater autonomy, leading to the creation of the devolved parliament. Crucially, the devolutionist movement also challenged the traditional majoritarian institutions of British democracy, in favour of more consensual (using the definition of Lijphart[3]) arrangements: it did not merely reject rule from Westminster, it also rejected the Westminster way of ruling.

This chapter argues that emerging Scottish constitutional norms include: (1) popular rather than parliamentary sovereignty, with a written Constitution as the highest act of the people; (2) proportional representation in place of plurality voting; (3) a more balanced relationship between the executive and legislature, and between the government and opposition, allowing non-executive MPs to have some policy influence; and (4) constitutional protection for human rights and civil liberties.

The Legacy of Independence

The first section of this chapter discusses the constitutional achievements of the pre-Union Kingdom of Scots, and examines how that legacy might determine the scope of constitution-building possibilities and might have influenced the constitutional proposals of the Scottish national movement.

During nearly four centuries of independence (1320–1707), Scotland developed its own institutions, including its own monarchy, government and administration, parliament, judiciary and legal system, church, universities and municipal burghs. Scotland also developed its own traditions of political thought used to justify or critique those institutions. Tracing the development of these institutions falls outwith the scope of this book. However, it is worth briefly considering these deep historical legacies, since a sense of continuity (real or imagined) between the pre-Union and the post-independence states and pre-Union institutions and principles has been invoked by some within the Scottish autonomy movement, at least on a symbolic level, to augment the legitimacy of new or projected Scottish institutions.

Kenny MacAskill MSP, for example, has sought to maintain this continuity, arguing that the current dissolved parliament is the same entity as that which Scotland had 'lost for nigh on 300 years'.[4] The same desire for continuity was voiced by Winnie Ewing MSP, who asserted, on opening the devolved parliament for the first time in 1999, that, 'The Scottish parliament, adjourned on the 25th day of March, 1707, is hereby reconvened'.[5]

The argument, in brief, is that the effect of pre-1707 constitutional legacies is more symbolic than substantive. Few wish, even if it were possible, to wind back the clock three centuries. A future Scottish constitutional order must be built on twenty-first-century constitutional principles, not seventeenth-century ones. Nevertheless, there is an important 'native' tradition of government, as distinct from the 'imported' Westminster tradition, on which constitution-makers can draw for ideas and inspiration, and as a source of historical legitimation.

The Kingdom of Scots (1320–1707), like most other European lands of its era,[6] was a constitutional monarchy of the *Ständestaat* type.[7] It was ruled by a hereditary monarch whose authority was both formally and informally constrained by the 'estates' of the realm,[8] under a feudal system that 'ensured that the ruler had limited power and was bound by mutual obligations and reciprocities'.[9]

The existence of a representative assembly, and of a government which acted with and through the major interests of the community, was therefore deeply entrenched in Scottish political life during the centuries of independence. MacKinnon argues that, 'parliamentary government is the salient fact of Scottish constitutional history',[10] and that:

> Legislation and government by the king and the Estates became actually, as well as in theory, the distinctive fact of the Constitution in its mediaeval form. The Parliament became a permanent institution; equally with the kingship an integral part of the national life.[11]

At its height, the Scottish parliament was a powerful institution. During the late fourteenth century, parliament assumed the authority to:

> control the expenditure of taxes which they granted; to regulate the coinage; to direct the administration of justice both by their legislative activity and the regular appointment of a parliamentary committee to deal with causes and complaints; to take measures to ensure the defence and the internal peace of the country.[12]

Moreover, parliament 'called to account royal officials', 'controlled the expenditure of the king himself' and made the king's councillors 'answerable and punishable by them for their actions'.[13] The parliament also 'took an active part in questions of peace and war',[14] and even on occasion issued special instructions to ambassadors.[15]

The pre-Union Scottish state not only developed its own political institutions, but also its own traditions of political thought used to justify or critique those institutions. These traditions can be found in the writings of Scottish political theorists such as George Buchanan[16] and Andrew Fletcher,[17] whose consistent theme was of limited, contractual, parliamentary monarchy. Most of all, however, this tradition is embodied in two iconic historical documents, the Declaration of Arbroath (1320) and the Claim of Right (1689), which neatly frame the epoch of independence.

The Declaration of Arbroath takes the form of a letter to the Pope from the Scots nobility, asking for his support in the wars of independence against the English.[18] It is significant, however, not only for its historical purpose, but also for its contemporary relevance in the mythology of Scottish constitutional nationalism. The Declaration speaks of the king being responsible to the 'whole community of the realm'. From this can be derived the principle, long integral to the SNP's constitutional policy,[19] that sovereignty in Scotland belongs to the 'whole community of the realm'. No one is above the community – not parliament, not even the king himself. As Kenyon Wright writes:

> [The Declaration of Arbroath's] stirring call to freedom is often quoted, but for me the most important part of it, which puts it so far ahead of its time, is the clear declaration that even the great Robert the Bruce is 'King, not only by right of succession according to our laws and customs, but also with the due consent of us all' and goes on to warn him that should he betray that trust 'we would instantly strive to expel him as our enemy and the betrayer of his own rights and ours, and we would choose another king to rule over us who would be equal to the task of our defence'. [. . .] A Commissioner at the Kirk's General Assembly in 1989 summed it up more succinctly – 'They said to Robert, you might be the King, but ye dae as ye're telt, or ye're on the burroo [that is, unemployed]'.[20]

Similar contractual principles are expressed in the Claim of Right Act of 1689[21] issued by the Estates of Scotland during the Revolution of 1688–9, which claimed that the king (James VII):

> by the advice of evil and wicked counsellors invaded the fundamental constitution of the kingdom and altered it from a legal limited monarchy to an arbitrary despotic power and hath exercised the same to the subversion of the protestant religion and the violation of the laws and liberties of the kingdom inverting all the ends of government whereby he has forfeited the right to the crown and the throne is become vacant.[22]

According to Kenyon Wright, the 1989 Claim of Right, like the 1689 Claim and the Declaration of Arbroath before it, proclaims 'the rejection of the absolute authority of the Crown, or the Crown in Parliament, to impose policy or governance on Scotland against her will'.[23]

To summarise, the last time an independent Scotland existed, it was constituted as a limited, constitutional, almost quasi-parliamentary, monarchy. It would be foolish to suggest that an independent Scotland in the twenty-first century should attempt to replicate medieval and early modern institutions. Yet it must be recognised that representative and responsible government, under the rule of law, is an autochthonous ('home-grown' and 'native to the soil')[24] concept in Scotland. This has two important implications. Firstly, whereas most states emerging from British rule in the twentieth century had little pre-colonial history of constitutional government to draw upon, and had to base their ideals and institutions solely upon British (that is, English) practices, Scotland has its own, pre-Union, constitutional history, which can be, and has been, used to criticise the British constitutional tradition. Secondly, as noted above, many institutions of the pre-Union Scottish state survived the Union – notably the judiciary and the legal system. Taken together, these mean that it is possible to think in terms not only of creating, but of restoring, a Scottish state, creating a thoroughly modern democratic constitution that can nevertheless derive legitimacy from a restored continuity with the country's own history.

Scotland in the 'Union-state'

The Union of 1707 'involved the abolition of both English and Scottish parliaments and their replacement by a new parliament of Great Britain'.[25] Yet this seemingly equal union affected the constitutional development of the two countries in different ways. England's constitutional history was not ruptured by the Union. The British parliament continued to operate as the English parliament before it had done, albeit with the addition of a few Scots members. Scotland's constitutional history, on the other hand, came to an abrupt end: its own parliament, which had existed since the late middle ages, was no more. As a consequence of the Union, 'Scotland was an unconstituted or, perhaps better, a de-constituted nation'.[26] Its own constitutional past was largely forgotten, and its future constitutional development, including expansion of the suffrage, the achievement of responsible government, and the creation of the post-war welfare state, would proceed only in the context of 'Westminster rule'.

The United Kingdom was traditionally classified as a unitary state[27] or even as a 'unitary and centralised' state.[28] This unitary concept of the UK led to the assumption that English constitutional practices and doctrines could be applied to the whole. In the year in which Winnie Ewing won the Hamilton by-election for the SNP, and shortly before the creation of the Kilbrandon Commission (see below), a textbook on British politics was able to assert that any minor Scottish peculiarities in the UK could be ignored 'for the sake of simplicity', and that 'for most practical purposes it is reasonable to treat the northern kingdom simply as part of a united political unit called Great Britain'.[29]

Yet, despite being a unitary state with a single, sovereign legislature, the UK never attempted to impose uniformity. Unlike most unitary and centralised states (which, in the Napoleonic tradition, have a uniform and standardised system of law and administration across the land), it allowed internal diversity, and 'in practice permitted varying degrees of autonomy and dispersal of power'.[30]

The Union that created the British parliament also insisted on the protection of existing Scottish rights and usages in several key areas of national life – the Presbyterian Church, the Scottish education system, the legal system and the municipal burghs. In this way, although the Union 'made two countries one' in terms of the institutions of high politics, it nevertheless 'ensured that

Scotland should preserve the definite nationality which she had won for herself and had preserved for so long'.[31] The existence of these civic and social institutions in Scotland meant that 'people in Scotland were educated, judged and worshipped God in a thoroughly Scottish way'; they 'carried on much as they had before, being self-governing in matters of the everyday, leaving matters of state, notably imperial ones, to the Westminster parliament'.[32]

In addition to this functional devolution of key aspects of Scotland's national life to semi-autonomous Scottish professional elites, Scotland in the Union also maintained many symbolic markers of its own identity, such as its own Royal Standard.[33] It is therefore more accurate to view the United Kingdom not as a 'unified kingdom', but as a 'union kingdom' – one in which certain 'pre-union rights and structures continue to exist'.[34]

From the late nineteenth century, the unique position of Scotland within the Union was recognised through the granting of administrative devolution. In 1885 the first Secretary for Scotland was appointed, although at first the office had limited powers and merely replaced the informal control of Scottish affairs previously exercised by the Lord Advocate.[35] In 1926, the post was given the status of a Principal Secretary of State, and thirteen years later the administrative departments under the control of the Scottish Office, responsible for health, local government, fisheries and agriculture, and Scottish home affairs, were relocated from London to Edinburgh.[36] By the middle of the twentieth century, the Scottish Office had emerged as a 'powerful intermediary between London government and Scottish civil society'.[37]

This administrative devolution was mirrored by the development of distinct Scottish mechanisms of influence in the UK parliament: the Scottish Grand Committee, consisting of all Scottish MPs, which held the second reading debate on bills applicable to Scotland only, and two Scottish standing committees, to which 'virtually all' Scottish legislation was referred at the committee stage.[38,39] In the absence of legislative devolution, these committees served as limited substitutes.[40] Participation in these committees enabled Scottish MPs at Westminster, despite the salient nature of party politics, to 'behave in a distinctive manner' and to 'seek distinctively Scottish policies'.[41]

These arrangements reflected acceptance by the British government of the distinctness of Scotland within the Union, and enabled the Scots to '[bargain] for as much autonomy as was available within the imperial order, while playing full parts in the politics of the United Kingdom as a whole'.[42] Kellas even argued that there was, before devolution, a distinct Scottish 'political system' consisting of its own civic, legal and educational institutions, its own judiciary and its own administrative departments based in Edinburgh, as well as some special recognition at Westminster.[43]

One must not, however, overstate the extent of autonomy Scotland enjoyed in the 'Union Kingdom'. Before 1999, Scotland had no parliament of its own: 'all Acts of Parliament affecting Scotland (even if they affected exclusively Scotland) were acts of the United Kingdom Parliament'.[44] Its executive branch was responsible only to the Westminster parliament through the British prime minister, and often the Secretary of State for Scotland belonged to the minority party in Scotland.[45] Although 'Scottish MPs did carve out their own niche at

Westminster', they could do so only 'within the boundaries of the British party system'.[46] This niche amounted to 'modifying the details of policy or lobbying for Scottish material interests rather than forging a distinct policy line'.[47] Besides, these accommodating arrangements between Scotland and the rest of the UK, depended, like much else in the British constitution, on convention, habit, custom, tradition and tacit agreements; there was no legal guarantee of Scottish rights or privileges.

The Road to Devolution

By the middle of the twentieth century, the reputation of British democracy was riding high. Through the gradual extension of the suffrage, coupled with the development of key conventions such as ministerial responsibility and the need for the government to enjoy the confidence of the House of Commons, Britain achieved a relatively peaceful transition from a liberal aristocratic constitutional monarchy to parliamentary democracy without a revolutionary rupture.[48] Moreover, this system of democracy had successfully exported these institutions across the empire, had withstood the Great Depression without falling to communism or fascism, and had gone on to win the Second World War and to create the National Health Service.

Scotland enjoyed all the benefits of sharing in this highly regarded, stable and effective democratic system. However, despite the 'success' of British democracy, not all Scots have been satisfied with the role allotted to Scotland within the Union. Discontent goes back well over a century. The Scottish Home Rule Association was formed in 1886, at the height of the British Empire. It was primarily a response to Irish home rule, and sought to rebalance the constitution into a quasi-federal system through 'Home Rule all round'.[49] It operated as a cross-party pressure group, being predominantly Liberal in its political orientation, but also including future Labour leaders such as Keir Hardie and Ramsey MacDonald.[50] The Scots National League, formed in 1920, was not content with home rule; it sought full independence for Scotland,[51] to be achieved through a 'decidedly political strategy which focused on establishing a separate party and contesting elections'.[52] A period of amalgamation followed: the Scots National League and the Scottish Home Rule Association, sharing a broadly centre-left outlook, united with the Glasgow University Student Nationalist Association in 1928 to form the National Party of Scotland; six years later, in 1934, the National Party of Scotland in turn united with the small, right-leaning Scottish Party to form the SNP.[53]

There was considerable popular support in Scotland for home rule during the post-war period. The Scottish Convention, which broke away from the fledgling SNP in 1942,[54] attempted to use the old Scots device of a 'Covenant' (a solemn undertaking by which the people bind themselves to one another, in imitation of the Solemn League and Covenant of 1638) to force home rule onto the agenda. Despite receiving around 2 million signatures, it failed to make any impact and was ignored by the UK government.[55] The Scottish National Party, meanwhile, remained a small, fringe presence in electoral politics. In the six general elections to the UK parliament held between 1945 and 1964, Labour won, on average, 47.3 per cent of the Scottish vote, the Conservatives 45.4 per cent, and the Liberals 4.65 per cent. The SNP polled a long way behind these three parties, with an average of just 0.9 per cent over this period.[56]

Only with the election of Winnie Ewing in the Hamilton by-election of 1967 did the electoral fortunes and public profile of the SNP begin to change. This surprising by-election victory was 'instrumental in providing the first devolutionary response' from the UK government.[57] In 1969 a Royal Commission (which became known as the Kilbrandon Commission) was established 'To examine the present functions of the central legislature and government in relation to the several countries, nations and regions of the United Kingdom'.[58] The Kilbrandon Commission reported in 1973: dismissing the alternatives, including federalism and independence, it advised 'legislative devolution' for Scotland.[59] The following year, the SNP won 30 per cent of the Scottish vote and 11 seats – a result that 'frightened Labour' into supporting home rule.[60]

The resulting Scotland Act, which received royal assent in 1978, would have given Scotland a devolved assembly twenty years earlier, had not it been thwarted by the 'Cunningham amendment', introduced by the Labour MP George Cunningham. This amendment required that the Act would not go into effect unless passed by 40 per cent of the Scottish electorate in a referendum – not just by a simple majority of those voting.[61] In the event, the referendum was defeated on this technicality, and devolution was indefinitely postponed following the Conservative victory of 1979. The SNP, meanwhile, collapsed into internal factionalism.[62]

Following the defeat of the devolution referendum, a Campaign for a Scottish Assembly (CSA) was formed, intending to 'keep the issue alive and mobilise support across the parties and within civil society'.[63] The CSA eventually evolved into the Scottish Constitutional Convention, which brought together a broad coalition of Scottish political, social, civic and economic interests, including the Labour Party and the Liberal Democrats, the local government association, the churches, the trade unions, the federation of small businesses, and a variety of social movements. Only the Conservative Party, big business – in the form of the Confederation of British Industry – and, once independence was ruled out of consideration, the SNP remained outside of the process.[64]

The first major public act of the Convention was to issue a Claim of Right for Scotland, asserting the sovereignty of the people of Scotland and their right to determine for themselves the form of government which best meets their needs.[65] Crucially, the Claim of Right did not merely criticise the territorial dimension of power: it objected not only to rule from Westminster, but also, more profoundly, to the Westminster way of ruling. It asserted that Scotland's problem was part of a wider British problem, and offered a radical and damning analysis of the flaws of the British constitution. As Paragraph 1.2 of *A Claim of Right for Scotland* states:

> Our direct concern is with Scotland only, but the failure to provide good government for Scotland is a product not merely of faulty British policy in relation to Scotland, but of fundamental flaws in the British constitution.[66]

Twentieth-century accounts of the British constitution typically attributed its success to three traits. Firstly, traditionalism – its reliance on well-established traditional rights and privileges, embedded in historical compromises and unspoken norms of parliamentary conduct, rather than on rational foundations expressed in written 'Declarations' or 'Constitutions'. Secondly, a plurality electoral system, coupled with adversarial politics, that generally favoured a straight two-way contest between government and opposition parties. Thirdly, a dominant executive, armed with the power of dissolution, and supported by an independent civil service with a strong public service ethos. Against this, most European models of democracy, characterised by abstract rights, written constitutions, proportional representation, and less dominant executives, were seen as inferior and inherently unstable.[67]

The Claim of Right inverted these three features, presenting them not as the secrets of Britain's strength and stability, but as problematic legacies, morally unsustainable and damaging the health of democracy. In the first place, the excessive power of the UK prime minister in relation to parliament and the rest of the political system was attacked:

The English Constitution provides for only one source of power: the Crown-in-Parliament. That one source is now embodied in the Prime Minister, who has appropriated almost all the royal prerogatives. She/he appoints Ministers who, with rare exceptions, can be dismissed at will, and has further formidable powers of patronage. Because of party discipline and the personal ambition of members, the consequence is that, so far from Parliament controlling the Executive (which is the constitutional theory), the Prime Minister is able to dominate Parliament.[68,69]

The excessive power of the prime minister coexisted, according to the Claim of Right, with a politically supine parliament under executive control:

Parliamentary procedures are subject to heavy pressure to conform with Government convenience and rest on the tacit assumption that the primary purpose of Parliament is to facilitate Government business. The power of dissolving Parliament has largely passed to the Prime Minister who, with rare exceptions, can manipulate it both to benefit and to control his/her party. In fact, if not in theory, the Prime Minister is Head of State, Chief Executive and Chief Legislator, and while in office is not circumscribed by any clear or binding constitutional limitation.[70]

The second purported flaw of the British system of government was that, owing to a disproportional voting system, it entrusted these powers to a prime minister whose party might have won only a minority of the votes:

This unique concentration of power is reinforced by a voting system which has always been commended as yielding strong government ... specifically, a large majority of the electorate may have voted against the Prime Minister yielding the enormous powers described above.[71]

Thirdly, the British system is marked by the absence of a written and codified Constitution, superior to ordinary law, which is enforceable in the courts and which can only be changed by extraordinary means. The core doctrine of the British constitution to which the Claim of Right objected was that of parliamentary sovereignty.

Parliamentary sovereignty is 'a combination of theory, history, political culture and institutional fact',[72] which has both a political sense and a legal sense.[73] In its political sense, the doctrine of parliamentary sovereignty is canonically expressed by Walter Bagehot's analysis of the British system of government as it operated in the mid-nineteenth century.[74] According to this account, political sovereignty is vested most especially in the House of Commons as the institution whose consent is necessary to sustain the cabinet (which is the effective decision-maker) in office and which must must give its ultimate approval to the cabinet's decisions. As sovereign, the House of Commons can make and break governments, turn the great machinery of state in this direction or that, and say to governments 'stop' and 'go'. Parliament is the ultimate decider.

Parliamentary sovereignty in its legal sense, as expressed by A. V. Dicey in his *Introduction to the Study of the Law of the Constitution*, is concerned not with the role of the Commons as the final repository of political power, but with the legal supremacy of an Act of Parliament over any other source of law.[75] There can be, in this scheme, no higher law, and nothing binding on the absolutism of parliament when Crown, Lords and Commons come together in this formal, solemn way to pass an Act.

> The principle of parliamentary sovereignty means neither more nor less than this, viz., that Parliament, thus defined, has, under the English constitution, the right to unmake any law whatever, and that no person or body is recognized by the law of England as having the right to set aside the legislation of Parliament.[76]

So, according to 'English' doctrine, the entrenchment of superior laws, which are binding on parliament itself, is impossible, meaning that neither the fundamental rights of citizens nor the basic principles and structures of democracy can be protected from unilateral change by parliamentary majorities:

> Every feature of the English Constitution, every right the citizen has, can be changed by a simple majority of this subordinated Parliament. That applies even to the requirement to hold Parliamentary elections every five years—or at all. It applies to the very existence of Parliament.[77]

As the Claim of Right states, it was the combination of these factors – an all-powerful prime minister, an unrepresentative electoral system, and the lack of a written Constitution – which rendered the British system of government particularly odious:

> It would be wrong to isolate any one of the above features. Any one of them might be tolerable without the others. Taken together, they represent an indulgence to party dogma and a hazard to human rights, in particular to the rights of minorities.[78]

Having outlined these objections to the British system, the Scottish Constitutional Convention went on to offer detailed plans for the design of a devolved Scottish parliament.[79] Labour and the Liberal Democrats 'became strongly committed to devolution',[80] and Labour's victory in the 1997 general election enabled these plans to be enacted into law.

The resulting Scotland Act of 1998 provided for a devolved parliament within the UK having legislative powers over all domestic matters with the exception of those – such as the constitution, defence, foreign affairs, macro-economic and fiscal policy, social security – which were reserved to Westminster. Moreover, the ultimate supremacy of the Westminster parliament – its ability to continue to legislate for Scotland, if it so chose, even in relation to devolved matters – was retained.

Devolution as a 'Critical Juncture': Westminster Rejected, Reformed or Replicated?

Devolution is normally considered in terms of the territorial politics of the UK. It can be understood as a partial restructuring of the British state, replacing the old union state with a 'quasi-federal structure' as part of a broader move towards multi-level governance.[81] It can even be presented as a 'conservative' – or at least defensive – policy, designed to protect the traditional, semi-autonomous institutional interests of Scotland from a UK government that 'relentlessly centralized power'.[82] From the point of view of British territorial politics, devolution was a splendid compromise – pragmatic accommodation between British and Scottish elites, who both recognised that a rise in pro-independence nationalism would be in the interests of neither party, and that protecting Scotland's autonomy within the Union was the best way of preventing it. As one critic put it, 'devolution was meant to be about legitimising the existing Labour state, its one party apparatus, nomenklatura class and extension into every aspect of Scottish public life'.[83]

For the purpose of this book, however, these questions of territorial politics or restructuring of the UK are less interesting than the institutional changes made to the internal government of Scotland. Devolution was never concerned only with the territorial locus of power; from the first days of the Constitutional Convention, there was a parallel concern for the nature of power, for the way in which it would be exercised, and for its distribution *within* the Scottish political system. The relevant critical juncture is not that Scotland got a *devolved* parliament, but that it got a *different type* of parliament, one that was intended and designed chiefly to avoid replicating the perceived flaws of Westminster.

Five key features of the Scotland Act mark a shift away from the traditional Westminster model. Firstly, the executive power in Scotland is vested not in the Crown, but in a statutory body, the Scottish executive/government.[84] The traditional notion of executive power being 'vested in' the Crown, but conventionally 'exercised' on the 'advice' of ministers is thereby rejected in favour of the notion (also found in the Swedish and Irish Constitutions) of government possessing executive powers, with the head of state in a strictly non-executive role.

Secondly, the Scotland Act provides for fixed-term parliaments, in the sense that parliament cannot be dissolved at will by the first minister.[85] Premature dissolution is possible, but only on the advice of the Presiding Officer, and only in certain circumstances, such as if a first minister cannot be appointed, or if parliament by a two-thirds majority votes for its own dissolution. This represents a major divergence from the Westminster model of executive dominance, since it means that a first minister who loses the confidence of the Scottish Parliament cannot appeal over the heads of parliament to the people, at least not without parliament first having the opportunity to form a new government.

Thirdly, the relationship between the government and parliament in Scotland is codified. The first minister is nominated by a formal investiture vote of parliament, and holds office, barring resignation or death, until there is a parliamentary election, or until removed by a vote of no confidence. This contrasts with the notions of tacit confidence on which the archetypical Westminster system is traditionally based. As a result of this rule, the Scottish government can suffer legislative setbacks in parliament without having its continuance in office called directly into question. This creates a balance of power between the government and parliament and, at least potentially, enables a give and take relationship between the government and parliament to arise. The effect of this was particularly evident during the period of SNP minority government (2007–11), during which the government even lost a vote on the budget, but was able to continue in office after making concessions to another party.

Fourthly, the Scotland Act adopted a system of proportional representation for elections to the Scottish Parliament.[86] Despite the SNP's current period of electoral dominance, proportional representation – especially when combined with fixed term parliaments and the formal election of the first minister – creates a situation in which coalitions and minority governments can be normalised, and in which the absence of a clear overall majority winner need not be treated as a matter of crisis.

The fifth reform reflects the nature of the Scottish Parliament's legal authority. Unlike the Westminster parliament, which (at least with the important exception of EU law) is sovereign, the Scottish Parliament is a 'creature of statute, open to challenge in the courts if it is seen as infringing the powers granted it in the Scotland Act'.[87] As a non-sovereign legislature, the Scottish Parliament is bound by both the ECHR and by a system of judicial review.[88] Bills passed by the Holyrood parliament become law on receiving royal assent, but bills are presented for assent by the Presiding Officer, not by the government, and there is a process of abstract judicial review by which the legality of the bill can be challenged by the Advocate General or Lord Advocate before the Presiding Officer makes the submission.[89] This process, quite unlike anything found at Westminster, is loosely akin to those of countries such as Ireland, France, Spain and Germany, which allow the constitutionality of legislation to be challenged before being enacted.

Shortly before devolution came into effect, a consultative steering group was established by the Scottish Office to examine the working practices of the new Scottish Parliament. From the outset, it was clear that Holyrood, in line with the expectations of the Scottish Constitutional Convention, was going to be a very different sort of parliament from that which sat at Westminster. It was to adopt 'modern methods of working', to be 'accessible, open and responsive to the needs of the public', and to encourage participation in decision-making by civil society organisations and individuals, a well as seeking 'views and advice from policy specialists' as appropriate.[90] It was also anticipated that committees would play an important role in the new parliament, able to initiate legislation as well as to 'scrutinise and amend the Scottish Executive's proposals' and to 'carry out wide-ranging investigative functions'.[91]

The consultative steering group adopted four key principles to guide their deliberations, based on the recommendations of the Scottish Constitutional Convention. These were: (1) 'power sharing', including 'the sharing of power between the people of Scotland, the legislators, and the Scottish Executive'; (2) 'accountability', including both the accountability of the executive to parliament and the accountability of the executive and parliament to the people; (3) 'access and participation', meaning that the parliament should be 'accessible, open, responsive' and that it should develop a 'participative approach' to policy making and law-making; and (4) 'equal opportunities', in the operation of parliament.[92]

These principles reflected the desire for a 'new politics' in Scotland that would redress the shortcomings of the Westminster system and would develop greater openness, power-sharing and accountability.[93] David Arter regards this desire for change, as embodied in the creation of the Scottish Parliament, as hope for 'a new type of democracy in which Parliament would not merely represent the people, but share power with them'.[94]

'New politics' was supposed to replace 'Westminster adversarial politics' with 'new institutions, new processes and a new political culture'.[95] There has been much scholarly discussion about the extent to which devolution has, or has not, lived up to these hopes and expectations. The initial assumption that proportional representation would end one party government in Scotland has clearly not been borne out by events.[96] Likewise, the anticipated moderate, consensual style of politics has failed to emerge, as parties, riven by tension between nationalists and unionists, remain 'competitive' rather than 'cooperative' in the electoral arena.[97]

Even accepting James Mitchell's statement that 'New politics is dead',[98] the Scottish electoral system still makes it more difficult for any one party to win an overall majority, while also enabling smaller parties with diffuse support to win a larger share of seats than they would under a single member plurality system. Since devolution, Scotland has been able to adapt to different governing arrangements: two minimal winning coalitions (1999–2003; 2003–7), a single party minority administration (2007–11 and 2016) and a single party majority (2011 – present). Early on, there were signs of more cooperative behaviour within parliament and its committees, although partisanship has once again become dominant.[99] Shephard and Cairney have argued that the new legislative processes initially strengthened the role of backbench MSPs in comparison to their Westminster counterparts, at least during the first session (1999–2003).[100]

However, for the purpose of this chapter, the focus is not on whether the attempt to create 'new politics' was successful in terms of behaviours, but on how the adoption of new institutions has shaped Scotland's constitutional trajectory, ushering in a new constitutional tradition that can help to explain and to evaluate constitutional proposals for a Scottish state. So, regardless of continuing debates about their lack of consensual effect, the fact remains that consensual institutions (such as proportional representation, stronger committees with provision for pre-legislative scrutiny, and fixed term parliaments) have *already* been established in Scotland. The critical juncture of the 1990s, from the point of view of identifying the criteria of a viable and acceptable Constitution, was not only the territorial *devolution* of power, but the new, more (institutionally if not behaviourally) consensual approach to the *distribution* of power. That is, a move away from the traditional Westminster system to a more 'Westminster transformed' variant. According to Neil MacCormick, these reformed institutions represent the 'common stock of democratic thought today'.[101] Therefore a traditionally majoritarian constitution for Scotland would no longer be a continuation of the status quo in Scotland; it would be a regressive return to the status quo ante, undermining the advance of the 1990s, of the Constitutional Convention, and of the devolution process.

Scotland and Reform of the 'British Constitution'

The development of the institutional changes in Scotland must be seen as a part of a UK-wide process, and as a response to a UK-wide complaint against the old ways of Westminster government. Scotland was merely fortunate in that these voices were able to combine with strong civic and religious traditions, an indigenous legal system and rhetorical appeals to democratic mythology to succeed in setting Scotland on a new constitutional trajectory.

The Constitutional Convention of the 1990s succeeded in making a political connection between the existing territorial tensions and the UK-wide desire for improved democracy. The Constitutional Convention used the popular mythology of a radical, Scottish democratic tradition to build a case against both rule from Westminster (deemed harmful to Scotland) and the Westminster way of ruling (deemed contrary to Scottish values and traditions). Scotland was not unique in sharing the reformers' concerns about the inadequacies of the Westminster system, and was not even unique in its institutional development (Wales, for example, was also given a proportionally elected assembly), but it was unique in its ability to articulate its critique of the Westminster system *through* its territorial politics, mobilising the mythology of its own indigenous, pre-Union constitutional tradition against the basic assumptions of the UK state.

The institutional developments in Scotland cannot simply be put down to the rise of territorial politics. It is important to note that the territorial question – Scotland's self-rule within the UK – preceded concern for the institutional transformation of Scotland's internal political structures by several decades. The first 'constitutions' for Scotland, in the form of the lapsed 1913 home rule bill and a subsequent bill introduced by Revd James Barr MP in 1927,[102] were remarkable for their adherence to the Westminster system and their lack of constitutional radicalism. The 1927 bill would have created a 148-member unicameral Scottish parliament elected by first past the post, with executive power vested in the Crown, acting on the 'advice' of the 'Scottish Privy Council'.[103] Likewise, the devolution bill of 1979 provided for an assembly elected by single member plurality, following the conventions of its Westminster parent.[104]

Something had happened between 1979 and 1999 to bring the way in which Scotland should be governed – not just the locus of government, or the extent of its powers, but its structures and practices – into question. While these institutional changes must be credited to the work of the Constitutional Convention, which was a vital catalyst for reform, the thinking behind them was not unique to Scotland. By the final decades of the twentieth century, many political voices in the centre and from the centre-left of British politics, notably the SDP–Liberal Alliance,[105] as well as groups such as Charter 88,[106] were dissatisfied with the increasingly centralised, majoritarian, executive-dominated nature of the UK's political system.

Such complaints had been voiced before Margaret Thatcher became prime minister. Indeed, it was a Conservative peer, Lord Hailsham, who introduced the phrase 'elective dictatorship' to describe the British system of government. Yet Thatcher's government (1979–90) brought the issue to a head. Thatcher waged war against the 'wets' (economically moderate 'One Nation' Tories who accepted the post-war welfare state and the social democratic settlement) in her own party, and enforced a hard neo-liberal ideological line that alienated many voters, especially in Scotland, Wales and the north of England. At the same time, the old, informal constraints on the power of the state were swept away: the aristocracy, the civil service, the church, the universities and all the other pillars of the old establishment – which, although far from democratic, had at least exerted a moderating influence on the government, and had made parliamentary absolutism mild and tolerable in practice – were side-stepped or eroded.

Old complacent claims in favour of the British Westminster system – namely, that it provided stability, responsible and effective government and clear choices between governing parties while also guaranteeing, in practice, human rights and respect for minorities – were increasingly replaced by criticisms of its exclusiveness and its unfairness to small parties. There was increasing disenchantment with its antagonistic and needlessly confrontational style of politics, and growing disquiet at its lack of moderation, balance, restraint and protection for civil liberties.[107]

Concern for the territorial dimension of politics, and a desire for some sort of devolved, regionalist or federal solution, was integral to many of these criticisms of the British system of government in the 1980s and 1990s.[108] Yet the interest of the reformers went beyond the territorial, to embrace subject such as electoral reform, reform of the House of Lords, protection of human rights, freedom of information, mechanisms of scrutiny and accountability, and parliamentary procedures.[109]

When the Labour government came to power in 1997, after eighteen years in opposition, it was committed to a programme of constitutional reforms that was intended to address many of the reformers' concerns. The Human Rights Act 1998, coupled with the creation of a new Supreme Court, introduced to the British political system the notion that Acts of Parliament can in principle be reviewed by the domestic courts against fundamental rights (although the full effect of this notion is diminished by the absence of any legislative entrenchment to prevent repeal of the Human Rights Act and by the inability of the Supreme Court to annul primary legislation it deems incompatible with the said Act).

As well as devolution to Scotland, Wales and Northern Ireland, the Labour government's package of reforms included the removal of most of the hereditary peers from the House of Lords,[110] freedom of information,[111] reform of local government in England,[112] measures to limit anonymous donations and to regulate the registration of parties and funding of campaigns,[113] the introduction of proportional representation for European parliamentary elections,[114] and the establishment of a Supreme Court for the UK.[115]

Yet according to Matthew Flinders, these reforms were not 'fundamental'[116] in that they did not result in power being 'dispersed in a manner which marks a stark departure from the previous constitutional arrangement'.[117] At the heart of Labour's reform project, Flinders argues, was a 'contradiction', with 'a principled commitment to a more consensual model of democracy' striving against 'practical awareness of benefits offered to a governing party of majoritarianism'.[118] Labour accepted 'a more consensus-orientated understanding of democracy' at the devolved or peripheral level, which was 'reflected in the voting system, party system, the nature of executive power and the cooperative relationship with interest groups, and a more balanced executive-legislature relationship', but was reluctant to carry through similar reforms at the UK-wide level.[119]

The result was a half-reformed political system that had lost what internal coherence it had formally possessed, without achieving a new coherence.[120] In 2005, after most of the Blair-era institutional reforms had been accomplished, the former Conservative MP Chris Patten wrote in dismay:

> We have an electoral system riddled with unfairness; a bicameral legislative structure that the government reorganises at regular intervals on the back of an envelope; courts whose judges are attacked by the executive because it does not care for the way they seek to protect our liberties; local government gutted by manic centralism; and an executive that displays under both Labour and Conservative leadership the attributes of what Lord Hailsham called 'an elective dictatorship'.[121]

Every major party went into the 2010 general election with at least one major institutional reform proposal in its manifesto. The winning coalition of Conservatives and Liberal Democrats began with a moderately ambitious package of proposed reforms – including reform of the House of Lords, fixed term parliaments, provisions for the recall of MPs, and a referendum on a new electoral system for the House of Commons. Very little of this programme was completed, however. Reform of the Lords collapsed in the now traditional and customary manner, over an inability to agree on the purposes of the House before tinkering with its form. A law permitting the recall of MPs was enacted, but its provisions were so restrictive as to be of little practical effect. The new electoral system offered for the House of Commons was alternative vote, a halfway house that pleased neither the supporters nor the opponents of proportional representation, and was consequently defeated by the people when put to a referendum. Only the commitment to fixed term parliaments, with restrictions on the prerogative of dissolution, made a successful journey from manifesto promise to statute; this reform was of immediate practical importance to the coalition government, since it prevented either party from pulling out of the coalition or from forcing a snap general election.

Even after these partial reforms to the UK at the centre, Scotland's institutional arrangements looked quite different from those of the UK as a whole. The electoral system is an obvious point of difference. By the time of the 2015 UK general election, proportional representation was the pipe dream of a rump of just eight Liberal Democrats at Westminster, but an established fact for both local and Holyrood elections in Scotland.

It must be acknowledged that the differences between Holyrood and Westminster have not always been to Scotland's advantage. One of the ironies of institutional politics in the UK in the opening half of the second decade of the twenty-first century was that Scotland, despite proportional representation, was ruled by a single-party majority government, while the UK as a whole, despite first past the post elections, was ruled by a coalition. Likewise, reforms to parliamentary procedures and committees under the leadership of Speaker John Bercow, coupled with the pressures of coalition government and a sense of independence on the government's back benches, meant that the House of Commons was arguably more robust as a legislative, deliberative and scrutinising assembly than the Scottish Parliament. The new-found strength of the House of Commons was evident, for example, in its refusal to allow the government to carry out bombing missions in Syria in 2013.

Although there is a desparate appetite in some quarters for further institutional reform at the UK level – as evidenced, for example, by the work of the Political and Constitutional Reform Committee under the leadership of Graham Allen MP during the 2010–15 parliament – the wholescale reconstitution of the UK remains a marginal issue; indeed, the leaning of the Conservative majority government elected in 2015 seems to be in the other direction, with repeal of the Human Rights Act being on its agenda.

In comparison with international trends and norms, the UK remains an outlier, having no codified Constitution, no formal distinction between constitutional and ordinary laws, and no system for the judicial review of the constitutionality of Acts of Parliament. The theoretical absolutism inherent in such a system was expressed by de Smith in these terms:

> The model of democracy so far adopted in the United Kingdom [. . .] equates democracy with majority rule, and therefore in theory allows Parliament, elected by the majority, to authorise anything from slavery to torture to detention without trial.[122]

Although the Human Rights Act of 1998 requires public authorities 'to act in conformity with the European Convention on Human Rights' and empowers the courts to strike down their decisions where they do not do so,[123] the Act itself has only ordinary statutory authority and is not entrenched. If there is an incompatibility between the rights protected by the Human Rights Act and another statute, the courts may only issue a 'declaration of incompatibility', which does 'not affect the validity, continuing operation or enforcement' of the incompatible statute, and which leaves parliament to remedy the incompatibility.[124] Lord Irvine, speaking as Lord Chancellor under Tony Blair, expressed this staunch commitment to parliamentary sovereignty, stating that although the government's constitutional reform agenda was 'ambitious and radical', it retained at its heart 'an unshakeable commitment to uphold parliamentary sovereignty.'[125]

Commitment to parliamentary sovereignty remains high amongst British elites. Given the majoritarian, executive-centred nature of the British political system, both major parties have been reluctant to accept judicial restrictions on parliament's ultimate decision-making power. The arguments proffered in favour of parliamentary sovereignty are many, and it would be wrong to see opposition to constitutional supremacy simply as a rejection of 'imported novelties' and 'continental theoretical ideas' by Burkean Tories. When filtered through the reality of a whipped partisan majority, parliamentary sovereignty accords with a 'trusteeship' view of democracy, in which ministerial discretion must not be limited or denied. Constitutional supremacy, according to this view, would bind the hands of statesmen, reducing their ability to respond to events as they see fit and potentially weakening the state – a view recently advanced, for example, by Alasdair Darling, the former Chancellor of the Exchequer.[126]

The defence of parliamentary sovereignty can also have a populist appeal, pitting 'elected politicians' against 'unelected judges'. The socialist left is disturbed by the class dynamics of the judiciary, which is seen as an elite body bent on the containment of democratic change. According to this view, the danger of strong judicial review is that it entrenches liberal, 'bourgeois', rights, and in particular the rights of property owners, against 'popular public power'.[127] The non-socialist, communitarian or civic-republican left is more concerned about the tendency of judicialisation to turn political questions on which society is divided, and which demand a discursive resolution, into 'technical legal matters, with the consequence that the bulk of the citizenry would cease to debate them and leave their resolution to lawyers and courts',[128] thereby undermining the view of politics as a 'conversation about the common good'.[129]

This concern is also articulated by Ran Hirschl, who argued that the rise of 'juristocracy' is motivated by self-interest; the desire of economic, legal and political elites to insulate decision-making from democratic politics, rather than by a sincere commitment to human rights.[130] Several academic proponents of reform to British institutions therefore remain sceptical of written Constitutions and judicial review, and would prefer to strengthen parliamentary controls over the executive – for example by reducing the power of whips, reforming parliament, or strengthening bicameralism.[131] Of course, a critique of dry legalism and of excessive reliance on courts and judiciaries, at the expense of public participation and democratic deliberation, need not be a critique of written constitutions or of justiciable rights as such; Blokker, for example, develops a notion of 'civic constitutionalism' that places more emphasis on the role of local democracy and referendums within legal-constitutionalist structures.[132]

Whatever the relative merits, in normative terms, of constitutional supremacy and parliamentary sovereignty, in a UK-wide context it might be politically impractical, under current circumstances, to reject parliamentary sovereignty and to adopt a supreme Constitution in accordance with the 'common model'. The Human Rights Act, devolution, the creation of the UK Supreme Court, and the attempt to develop a 'Cabinet Manual' to give great specificity and authority to constitutional conventions all point in the same direction: towards an ersatz Constitution that seeks to achieve many of the functional benefits of a written Constitution – stabilising and legitimating power – without challenging the sovereignty of parliament.

Maurice Sunkin, writing before the constitutional reforms of the Blair era, asked rhetorically, 'Who knows how long it will be before we have some form of written constitution, or at least a modern Bill of Rights?'[133] The answer, in the United Kingdom's case, might be never. The British state is old and would have to confront considerable institutional inertia. Writing a new, rigid, judicially enforced Constitution would have to overcome not only institutional conservatism but also many vested interests – from the conventional courtesy by which the Duke of Cornwall exercises a pre-legislative veto on matters affecting the Duchy, to the anomalous position of the City of London – whose privileges rely for their continuity on the secrecy of a system which is not only unwritten, but also 'unspoken', in the sense of being obscure to the ordinary citizen.[134]

A newly independent Scottish state, however, would be in a very different position. However strong support for parliamentary absolutism may be amongst those who fear the extension of judicial power, the recognition of parliamentary sovereignty is hard to imagine in an independent Scotland. For a contemporary democratic Scottish state to be created without a rigid, supreme, rights-based and judicially enforced Constitution would, both for domestic reasons and for international legitimacy, be almost unthinkable.

Scottish Nationalist Constitutional Thought

While constitutional change in the UK staggered between mild reforms and persistent inertia, some members of the pro-independence movement were thinking ahead, foreseeing the design of a future Scottish Constitution and making proposals for the Constitution of the new state they sought to create. This section narrates those proposals, from their first stirrings in the 1960s to the 2002 draft. It highlights certain common features of these proposals, most notably: (1) their concern to move away from the executive dominance and narrow majoritarianism of the pre-1997 British system of government;

and (2) the development of a doctrine of popular sovereignty in contrast to parliamentary sovereignty.

The first known draft Constitution for an independent Scotland was prepared by the Scottish Constituent Provisional Assembly (SCPA) (1957–62) under the direction of Roland E. Muirhead, a former SNP president and 'grand old man of the national movement'.[135] The SCPA was an offshoot of the Scottish Covenant movement, which had split from the SNP,[136] and no clear or direct link between the Muirhead text and the draft Constitutions later produced by the SNP can be traced. Nevertheless, this early predecessor of the SNP's draft Constitution reveals many of the same principles, and arrives at broadly similar institutional prescriptions.

This 'Muirhead' Constitution deviated from the traditional forms of the British political system in several ways.[137] It proposed: (1) a unicameral parliament elected by the single transferable vote system of proportional representation; (2) the abolition of the Crown prerogative of dissolution – Parliament was to sit for four-year terms, with early dissolution possible only with the agreement of a majority of its members; (3) a cabinet-style executive elected by the parliament from amongst its members; (4) a figurehead monarchy, stripped in many cases of even the outward forms of executive power; (5) an extensive list of guaranteed rights, including socio-economic rights as well as civil and legal rights, enforced by a Constitutional Court; (6) constitutional recognition of the role and status of local government; (7) the appointment by parliament of an Auditor General and of a 'Commissioner for Commonweal' (Ombudsman) several years before any such institution was established in the UK; (8) strong procedural rights for the opposition, including the right to a guaranteed minimum share of legislative time, the right to force a delay in the discussion of bills, and the right to remit bills to the Constitutional Court for advice on their constitutionality; (9) a rigid Constitution, amendable only by a two-thirds parliamentary majority followed by a referendum.[138]

The SNP began serious work on the drafting of a Scottish Constitution a few years later. This was in response to the Kilbrandon Commission, a Royal Commission set up to examine regional and national relations within the UK. The SNP's early attempts at writing a Scottish Constitution were sketchy and amateurish; there is a stark contrast between these efforts and the more polished and complete proposals of the SPCA, which contained several eminent lawyers.[139] Despite – or perhaps because of – this amateurism, the SNP's early proposals demonstrated an inventive approach that was open to constitutional innovation. A proposal submitted to the Constitutional Committee of the SNP in August 1968 by P. J. Findlay, for example, envisaged a unique 'Parliament of Three Estates' (clearly inspired by the pre-1707 Scottish parliament), in which directly elected members would sit alongside nominated members and indirectly elected 'Commissioners of the Provinces', to be chosen from sixteen provincial councils; another proposal provided for a 'hybrid Parliament', in which constituency members would serve for four years and list members would serve for two years in rotation.[140]

The SNP's constitutional proposals had begun to coalesce, by 1970, into a more recognisably modern and conventional form. At this stage, the party's draft Constitution was still sparse and vague on matters of detail, and could not have served as a working legal text. It focused on the composition and functioning of parliament and on basic rights, while the executive, judiciary, and other state authorities, received little or no attention. Nevertheless, the SNP's proposals by 1970 demonstrated a rather more systematic approach to constitutional design, informed by 'a study of the Constitutions in Europe and of the Commonwealth' and by 'an understanding of the problems arising from the existing constitutional structure of the United Kingdom'.[141]

While the European and Commonwealth nations were an explicit inspiration, the United Kingdom was seen primarily as an example of what to avoid. In evidence submitted to the Commission on the Constitution on 31 March 1970, D. Henderson noted that, 'We have tried to avoid in particular the dangerous situation in the UK, where heavy reliance on only two parties controlled by a system of party whips has led to the dominance of the legislature by the executive'.[142]

Further progress came in the late 1970s. The McIntyre Committee, consisting of Dr Robert McIntyre, Prof. Neil MacCormick, Dr Allan Macartney, Peter Chiene, Kenneth Fee, Isobel Lindsay and Barbara Park, produced the SNP's first truly complete draft Scottish Constitution.[143] In contrast with the rather patchy and vague drafting of earlier constitutional proposals, the 1977 text was the first to be presented in the form of a complete and workable constitutional document. It dealt with most of the principal institutions of state (head of state, executive, legislature and judiciary) and addressed the main constitutional issues (including sovereignty, territory, citizenship, fundamental rights and the process of amendment).

In outline, the 1977 text was similar to that of the SCPA published in 1964.[144] It would have constituted Scotland as a parliamentary democracy with a ceremonial monarchy; the written Constitution would contain justiciable fundamental rights, and would be amendable only by a super-majority in parliament followed by a referendum. The parliament would be unicameral and elected by proportional representation for fixed terms. An interesting and novel idea, designed to prevent excessive executive dominance, was incorporated into the 1977 text: a mechanism enabling a two-fifths minority of the members of parliament to suspend a bill, other than a money bill, for a year, thus effectively granting the parliamentary opposition the powers of an incongruent asymmetrical 'upper house'.

The main features of the SNP's 1977 draft Constitution were essentially unchanged in the 2002 version. The main differences between the 1977 and 2002 versions are: (1) archaic references to the 'Privy Council for Scotland' have been replaced, in the 2002 version, by a more modern and explicitly designated cabinet system; (2) local government, which was not mentioned at all in the 1977 text, was given its own article in the 2002 text; (3) socio-economic rights, such as rights to housing, social security and education, were incorporated into the 2002 text. Much of the similarity is due to a continuation of personnel: Neil MacCormick, vice covenor of the 1977 committee, was convenor of the 2002 committee.[145]

It is evident from this short survey of the development of Scottish nationalist constitutional proposals, that by the beginning of the twenty-first century a set of ideas were current, within SNP circles and the wider pro-independence movement, that rejected the traditional British notions of parliamentary sovereignty, executive dominance, majoritarian rule, in favour of popular sovereignty, constitutional supremacy, justiciable rights, proportional representation and a more equal balance of power between the government and parliament. These ideas represent a move – at least in thinking – towards a transformed variant of the Westminster model, which while still culturally and by descent part of the Westminster family, would operate in a less majoritarian (in Lijphart's terms) manner.[146]

Neither the 1962 nor the 2002 texts would allow the parliament of Scotland to enjoy the position of legislative sovereignty which that of the United Kingdom (at least under the orthodox understanding of the British system of government) enjoys. Instead, these constitutional texts sought to place certain constitutional limits on the power of parliamentary majorities, subordinating parliament to the people by means of a higher constitutional law that could be amended only with the consent of the people, acting in their original, sovereign, constituent capacity.

Popular sovereignty as articulated in these draft Constitutions and in other SNP constitutional policy documents,[147] has become a central – perhaps *the* central – doctrine of Scottish nationalist constitutional thought. The essence of this doctrine is that the powers of parliament, as the national representative and legislative body, have a derivative nature and limited extent, being subject to the ultimate power of the people to configure and reconfigure the state as they see fit. In the words of the 1989 Claim of Right, the 'sovereign right of the Scottish people' is, above all, 'to determine the form of Government best suited to their needs'.[148]

Popular sovereignty, like parliamentary sovereignty, has both legal and political aspects. Leading participants in the Scottish Constitutional Convention, notably its convenor, Kenyon Wright, had claimed that parliamentary sovereignty, in its legal as well as political manifestation, was alien to Scottish constitutional principles and traditions. These remonstrances against parliamentary sovereignty were couched in theological terms that recalled aspects of Reformed political thought. A resolution of the General Assembly of the Church of Scotland, adopted in 1989, is representative:

> From a Scottish constitutional (and theological) perspective this English tradition of state absolutism has always been unacceptable in principle. It is now intolerable in practice. The Scottish Parliament must be built upon philosophical foundations that are more coherent and credible than the notions which underpin the existing British constitution.[149]

It is possible to argue, in relation to Scotland, that while devolution has preserved the sovereignty of the UK parliament in its legal sense, its sovereignty in the political sense is no longer as secure as it was. The political sovereignty of parliament has been challenged both by the practical exercise of sovereignty by the people of Scotland through referendums and by the theoretical justification of Scottish popular sovereignty, as articulated in the Claim of Right of 1989.

It is worth reiterating here that while Claim of Right has a central position in nationalist constitutional thought (in the narrow, card-carrying SNP member sense), the principle of popular sovereignty that it expresses enjoys broader support. It was first adopted, as noted above, by an inclusive Constitutional Convention in which the Labour Party, the Liberal Democrats, the Scottish Trades Union Congress, Scotland's major churches and other political and civic organisations all played a prominent role. Its principles were not of their own invention but were derived from a long tradition of distinctly Scottish constitutionalism with roots that can be traced back through the theopolitical thought of the Scottish Reformation to the limited and contractual kingship of the Declaration of Arbroath.

When the Claim of Right was placed before the Scottish Parliament for endorsement in January 2012, it was approved overwhelmingly and was voted for by the Labour, Liberal Democrat and Green members, as well as by the SNP; only Conservative members abstained.[150] The Claim of Right's doctrine of popular sovereignty was even written into the report of the Smith Commission published on 27 November 2014, indicating its acceptance by Unionist opinion and by the British state, as well as by nationalist politicians.[151]

Yet the nature of the popular sovereignty so expressed in the Claim of Right is still contested, or perhaps insufficiently understood, even within the SNP's own leadership. In the 2002 draft Constitution, popular sovereignty is clearly asserted as a legal principle. The sovereignty of the people is manifest through the exercise of constituent power, in adopting and in amending – by referendum – the Constitution under which all other laws are made. According to this doctrine, the people do not abdicate their powers to parliament, nor even entrust their powers to parliament through an open-ended and implicit social contract; rather, the people merely delegate powers to parliament, under certain conditions, and subject to substantial and procedural limitations. This doctrine relies on Rousseau's distinction between the sovereign people as the constituent power and the institutions of government as subordinate authorities that must always be subject to the will of the sovereign people as expressed in the Constitution.[152,153]

In contrast, however, the 2014 text asserts the sovereignty of the people only in a political sense, while ceding effective legal sovereignty to parliament. That is to say, it formally recognises the people as the source and ultimate repository of legitimate authority, but allows constitutional changes to be brought about by the parliamentary majority, without any need for public approval. The sovereignty of the people, in this sense, is no different from that which operated in the Byzantine Empire:[154] a political doctrine (and rhetorical claim) which asserts that the state derives its moral authority from the people, but does not give the people a legally recognised means of exercising that authority through the constitutional amendment process. As argued above, such an arrangement, which would place no limits on the legal sovereignty of parliament, would be unable to offer the sort of constitutional guarantees that are demanded by both the circumstances of a newly independent Scottish state and by international standards.

Summary of Institutional and Contextual Constraints

Constitutional designs are not entirely a subject of free choice. The range of viable and acceptable constitutional options is circumscribed by the past development of a country's institutions, by the current state of constitutional thought and technologies, and by specific values and needs of the place and people for which it is intended.[155] The best analogy is perhaps that of piloting a raft down a river: skilful paddling gives Constitution-makers some control over direction and speed – and the ability to avoid the more obvious rocks – but they cannot go against the flow.

In Scotland, the historical 'flow' is determined by the institutional change that was begun in the 1980s and culminated in the Scotland Act 1998. The aim of the architects of devolution was not simply to create a 'Westminster-on-Forth', but to redress the excessive concentration of powers inherent in the traditional (that is, British, pre-1997) Westminster system, and to provide Scotland with more consensual institutions of parliamentary government, as defined by Lijphart, in which power would be more widely shared amongst a broader Scottish policy-making community, whilst also being more open and accountable to the people.

To that end, a number of institutional developments – including proportional representation, fixed term parliaments, the formal election of the first minister by parliament, stronger powers for committees – were introduced into the devolution settlement, either in the Scotland Act itself, or in subordinate instruments such as the parliament's Standing Orders. As discussed, the Scottish political system already has many elements of a consensus democracy, and (using Hazell's terminology) many of the features of a 'Westminster transformed' constitutional order.[156] What was once radical and innovative is now ordinary and accepted as the 'common stock of democratic thought in Scotland today' to which Neil MacCormick referred.

Consensus democracy is a 'kinder, gentler' form of democracy[157] that rests on a normative commitment to the diffusion rather than the hoarding of power.[158] While aspects of the 'consensus' model (such as strong bicameralism and federalism) are more suited to divided societies, other aspects (such as proportional representation, coalition government, balanced relationships between the executive and legislature, constitutional rigidity and judicial review) can be found in, and are suitable for, even small, highly integrated societies, such as those of Luxembourg[159] and Sweden.[160] The case for 'consensual' institutions, in a Scottish context, may rest less upon the need to overcome deep social divisions and more upon a normative commitment to a 'kinder, gentler' democracy which defines itself in opposition to the 'harsher, rougher' mores of Westminster.[161]

The extent to which these institutional changes have been reflected in Scottish political practice is debatable. Culture is stickier even than institutions, and for the most part Scottish political practice has remained largely adversarial, especially in plenary sessions. Nevertheless, as discussed in Chapter 2, these Scottish developments are set against a trend towards a new model of Westminster democracy that is characterised by rigid constitution-alism, justiciable human rights, increased reliance on extra-parliamentary 'integrity branch' institutions as mechanisms of scrutiny and control, and the codification of constitutional conventions. To revert to a system of first past the post elections, for example, or to give the Crown in Scotland a discretion-ary right to dissolve parliament at will, would no longer reflect the status quo, but a status quo ante that has been rejected.

Taken together, these considerations determine the background against which constitutional proposals for an independent Scotland have been made. As will be discussed further in the following chapters, the SNP's 2002 draft Constitution is a sensible, pragmatic, and not very radical response to these circumstances. To propose the continuation in Scotland of the British system of parliamentary sovereignty would deny the moral influence of the Claim of Right (which demands that sovereign power to 'determine the form of government' be exercised by the people directly, not handed over to their representatives). It would turn its back on the radically democratic (if admit-tedly ahistorical) reading of the Declaration of Arbroath, which stands at the heart of the constitutional nationalist's objections to the Union.[162] As such, it would go against the long-running constitutional policy of the SNP and the wider Scottish independence movement, which has long advocated a written Constitution enshrining popular sovereignty and constitutional supremacy.[163]

The institutions of devolved Scotland were created in an attempt to improve the quality of democracy – to reduce 'democratic deficits', to mod-ernise arcane procedures, to narrow the gap between people and their elected representatives and to make politics more accessible, open, accountable and mature. Even if these hopes have not been fully realised, and even if the cosy fog of consensual conviviality soon evaporated in the heat of bitterly polarised politics, the aspirational principles set out at devolution – power-sharing, accountability, access and participation, and equal opportunities – retain some normative value. Few in Scotland can actively desire a 'low quality' democracy that deliberately ignores these principles.

A viable and acceptable Constitution for Scotland, based on these criteria, would not only be one that fits within the broad institutional patterns of what is possible and achievable in Scotland's historical context, but also one which – given all the vagaries of politics, and the 'stickiness' of culture – does its best to promote and embody, through its institutional forms, these aspirational principles. This means a rigid Constitution, with judicial review of the consti-tutionality of legislation in order to uphold (as a minimum) the human rights standards set out in the European Convention on Human Rights. Recognising the positive role of the democratic state in the realisation of common goods, it would also, most likely, go beyond this minimum to include socio-economic rights. Such a constitution might retain the existing monarchy in a ceremonial role, but would place clear limits on the royal prerogative and specify the constitutional relationships between the queen, prime minister and parliament on an unambiguously parliamentary basis. Checks and balances would be provided partly by a strong parliamentary committee system and partly by a range of extra-parliamentary 'integrity branch' institutions.

Although there is still a lot of room for negotiation on the finer points of design and drafting, these elements would be likely to form what might be called the 'basic structure' (to borrow an Indian term) of a Constitution for an independent Scottish state. A Constitution with such a basic structure could be categorised in several ways: not only as a 'Westminster transformed' model[164] but also as an example of 'constrained parliamentarism',[165] as a 'mixture' of consensual and majoritarian elements,[166] or as a 'centripetal' Constitution that combines 'inclusivity', through proportional representation, with 'integration', through parliamentarism and a unitary state system.[167]

Turning from the structural to substantive provisions, a Scottish Constitution would have to account for the diversity of the population as discussed in Chapter 3. Although Scotland has no ethnic, cultural, linguistic, regional or religious cleavages that are sufficiently divisive as to require con-sociational politics system, a workable Constitution would probably have to be non-sectarian, while using constructive ambiguity or ambivalence to remove questions such as abortion and end-of-life rights (as far as possible) from constitutional controversy. While any well-written Constitution should be unambiguous on institutional procedures, reducing scope for conflict over the ground rules of democratic politics, it might be wise to avoid the deeply ideological, foundational or essentialist in favour of a more pragmatic, liberal procedural, approach.

These parameters, expectations and standards provide the basis on which the SNP's specific constitutional proposals – the 2002 and 2014 texts – can now be analysed and assessed in the following chapters.

Notes

1. A. Birch, *The British System of Government* (London: Allen and Unwin, 1967); A. King, *Does the United Kingdom still have a Constitution?*, Hamlyn Lecture Series, no. 52 (London: Sweet and Maxwell, 2001).
2. N. MacCormick, 'Is there a constitutional path to Scottish independence?', *Parliamentary Affairs*, 53/4 (2000), 723.
3. A. Lijphart, *Patterns of Democracy: Government Forms and Performance in Thirty-Six Countries* (New Haven, CT: Yale University Press, 1999).
4. K. MacAskill, *Building a Nation: Post Devolution Nationalism in Scotland* (Edinburgh: Luath Press, 2004), p. 15.
5. *The Scotsman*, 'The Scottish parliament, adjourned on 25th March 1707, is hereby reconvened', 13 May, 1999.
6. A. R. Myers, *Parliaments and estates in Europe to 1789* (London: Thames and Hudson, 1975).
7. J.-E. Lane, *Constitutions and Political Theory* (Manchester: Manchester University Press, 1996), p. 21.
8. A. Grant, *Independence and Nationhood: Scotland 1306–1469* (Edinburgh: Edinburgh University Press, 1984); J. MacKinnon, *The Constitutional History of Scotland: From Early Times to the Reformation* (Harlow: Longmans,

Green, 1924); J. Wormald, *Court, Kirk and Community: Scotland 1470–1625* (Edinburgh: Edinburgh University Press, 1981).

9. J.-E. Lane,*Constitutions and Political Theory*, p. 21.

10. J. MacKinnon, *The Constitutional History of Scotland*, pp. 269–70.

11. Ibid. p. 268.

12. Ibid. p. 281.

13. Ibid. p. 282.

14. Ibid. p. 283.

15. J. H. Burton, *The History of Scotland, From Agricola's Invasion to the Extinction of the Last Jacobite Insurrection* (Edinburgh and London: William Blackwood, 1901), p. 388.

16. C. F. Arrowood, *The Powers of the Crown in Scotland, Being a Translation, with notes and an Introductory Essay, of George Buchanan's 'De jure regni apud scotos'* (Austin: University of Texas Press, 1949).

17. J. Robertson (ed.), *Andrew Fletcher: Political Works* (Cambridge; Cambridge University Press, 1997).

18. E. J. Cowan, *For Freedom Alone: The Declaration of Arbroath* (Edinburgh: Birlinn, 2008).

19. N. MacCormick, 'An idea for a Scottish constitution', in W. Finnie, C. M. G. Himsworth and N. Walker (eds), *Edinburgh Essays in Public Law* (Edinburgh: Edinburgh University Press, 1991), p. 160; SNP, *Citizens not Subjects*, (Edinburgh: SNP, 1997), p. 3.

20. K. Wright, *'Expressing and Exercising Scottish Sovereignty'*, Open Democracy, 30 November 2009 <http://www.opendemocracy.net/ourkingdom/canon-kenyon-wright/expressing-and-exercising-scottish-sovereignty> (last accessed 3 January 2012).

21. The Claim of Right Act 1689 is not to be confused with the Claim of Right for Scotland 1989 – although neither the similarity of names nor the parallelism of dates is entirely incidental.

22. Claim of Right Act 1689 [modified spelling].

23. K. Wright, *'Expressing and Exercising Scottish Sovereignty'*.

24. L. Wolf-Phillips, 'Post-independence constitutional change in the Commonwealth', *Political Studies*, 18/1 (1970), 24.

25. M. Keating, 'Reforging the Union: devolution and constitutional change in the United Kingdom', *Publius*, 28/1, 'The State of American Federalism, 1997–1998' (Winter 1998), p. 219.

26. C. Craig, 'Constituting Scotland', *Irish Review*, no. 28 (Winter 2001), 2.

27. M. Keating, M., 'Reforging the Union', p. 218.

28. A. Lijphart, *Patterns of Democracy*, p. 17.

29. A. Birch, *The British System of Government* (London: Allen and Unwin, 1967), p. 15.

30. A. Gamble, 'The constitutional revolution in the United Kingdom', *Journal of Federalism*, 36/1 (2006), p. 21.

31. J. D. Mackie, *A History of Scotland*, 2nd edn (New York: Hippocrene Books, 1978), p. 263.

32. D. McCrone, *Explaining Scotland: Does the Exception Prove the Rule*, address given to Arts and Humanities Research Council Postgraduate Conference,

University of Strathclyde, 19 April 2008, transcript by Institute of Governance, Edinburgh, p. 5.

33. M. C. Meston, 'Scots law today', in M. C. Meston, W. D. H. Sellar and T. M. Cooper, *The Scottish Legal Tradition* (Edinburgh: Saltire Society, 1991), p. 1.
34. M. Keating, 'Reforging the Union: devolution and constitutional change in the United Kingdom', p. 219.
35. J. D. Mackie, *A History of Scotland*, p. 342.
36. Ibid. p. 367.
37. D. McCrone, *Explaining Scotland*, p. 6.
38. M. Keating, 'Parliamentary behaviour as a test of Scottish integration into the United Kingdom', *Legislative Studies Quarterly*, 3/3 (August 1978), p. 410.
39. At the time of writing, English Votes for English Laws has just been adopted by the House of Commons. Once again, Westminster has resorted to some sort of 'English Grand Committee' as a poor substitute for a devolved English parliament.
40. P. Lynch, *Scottish Government and Politics* (Edinburgh: Edinburgh University Press, 2001), p. 137.
41. M. Keating, 'Parliamentary behaviour as a test of Scottish integration into the United Kingdom', p. 411.
42. M. Keating, 'Reforging the Union: devolution and constitutional change in the United Kingdom', p. 219.
43. J. G. Kellas, *The Scottish Political System*, 4th edn (Cambridge: Cambridge University Press, 1989).
44. A. King, *Does the United Kingdom still have a Constitution?*, p. 26.
45. J. G. Kellas, *The Scottish Political System*, p. 28.
46. M. Keating, L. Stevenson, P. Cairney and K. Taylor, 'Does devolution make a difference? Legislative output and policy divergence in Scotland', *Journal of Legislative Studies*, 9/3 (Autumn 2003), 111.
47. Ibid. p. 111.
48. C. Thornhill, *A Sociology of Constitutions: Constitutions and State Legitimacy in Socio-Historical Perspective* (Cambridge: Cambridge University Press, 2011), pp. 237–40, 272–5.
49. P. Lynch, *SNP: The History of the Scottish National Party* (Cardiff: Welsh Academic Press, 2002), p. 28.
50. Ibid. p. 28.
51. Ibid. p. 33.
52. Ibid. p. 33.
53. Ibid. p. 35.
54. Ibid. p. 77.
55. Ibid. p. 28.
56. G. Hassan and P. Lynch, *The Almanac of Scottish Politics* (London: Politicos, 2001), pp. 349–52.
57. B. Jones and D. Kavanagh, *British Politics Today* (Manchester: Manchester University Press, 1979), p. 21.
58. Ibid. p. 21.
59. Ibid. p. 22.
60. M. Keating, 'Reforging the Union: devolution and constitutional change in the United Kingdom', p. 223.

61. P. Lynch, *SNP: The History of the Scottish National Party*, p. 149.

62. Ibid. p. 161.

63. M. Keating, 'Reforging the Union: devolution and constitutional change in the United Kingdom', p. 223.

64. Ibid. p. 223.

65. O. Dudley Edwards (ed.), *A Claim of Right for Scotland* (Edinburgh: Polygon, 1989).

66. Claim of Right, Para. 1.2.

67. A. Headlam-Morley, *The New Democratic Constitutions of Europe: A Comparative Study of Post-War European Constitutions With Special Reference to Germany, Czechoslovakia, Poland, Finland, the Kingdom of the Serbs, Croats and Slovenes and the Baltic States* (London: Oxford University Press, 1928).

68. Claim of Right, Para. 4.1.

69. Note the Claim of Right's use of the word 'English' when describing the UK. This is not, in this instance a result of careless nomenclature, but a deliberate attempt to attribute these flaws to the 'English' origins of the UK constitution.

70. Claim of Right, Para. 4.4.

71. Claim of Right, Para. 4.5.

72. G. Little, 'Scotland and parliamentary sovereignty', *Legal Studies*, 24/4 (2004), p. 543.

73. S. Gordon, *Controlling the State: Constitutionalism from Ancient Athens to Today* (Cambridge, MA: Harvard University Press, 2002), pp. 29–59.

74. W. Bagehot [1867], *The English Constitution* (London: Fontana, 1963).

75. A. V. Dicey [1914], *Introduction to the Study of the Law of the Constitution*, 8th edn (Indianapolis: Liberty Fund, 1982).

76. A. V. Dicey [1914], *Introduction to the Study of the Law of the Constitution*, 10th edn (Indianapolis: Liberty Fund, 1959), pp. 39–40.

77. Claim of Right, Para. 4.3.

78. Claim of Right, Para. 4.8.

79. P. Lynch, *Scottish Government and Politics*, pp. 11–13.

80. A. Gamble, 'The constitutional revolution in the United Kingdom', p. 27.

81. I. Bache and M. Flinders, 'Multi-level governance and the study of the British state', *Public Policy and Administration*, 19/1 (Spring 2004), p. 40.

82. A. Gamble, 'The constitutional revolution in the United Kingdom', p. 27.

83. G. Hassan, 'The forward march of Scottish nationalism and the end of Britain as we know it', *Renewal: A Journal of Social Democracy*, 19/2 (2011).

84. Scotland Act 1998, §44–54.

85. Scotland Act 1998, §2–3.

86. Scotland Act 1998, §5–8.

87. G. Leicester, 'Scotland', in R. Hazell (ed.), *The State and the Nations: The First Year of Devolution in the United Kingdom* (Exeter: Imprint Academic, 2000), p. 27.

88. C. M. G. Himsworth, 'Human rights at the interface of state and sub-state: the case of Scotland', in T. Campbell, K. D. Ewing and A. Tomkins (eds), *The Legal Protection of Human Rights: Sceptical Essays* (Oxford: Oxford University Press, 2011).

89. Scotland Act 1998, §32.

90. Scottish Office, *Report of the Consultative Steering Group on the Scottish Parliament*, 1998.

91. Scottish Office, *Report of the Consultative Steering Group on the Scottish Parliament*.

92. Scottish Office, *Report of the Consultative Steering Group on the Scottish Parliament*.

93. G. Reid, 'The fourth principle: sharing power with the people of Scotland', in B. Crick and A. Lockyer (eds), *Active Citizenship: What Could it Achieve and How?* (Edinburgh: Edinburgh University Press, 2010).

94. D. Arter, *The Scottish Parliament: A Scandinavian-Style Assembly?* (London: Frank Cass, 2004), p. 20.

95. M. Shephard and P. Cairney, 'The impact of the Scottish Parliament in amending executive legislation', *Political Studies*, 53/2 (2005), 303–4.

96. L. G. Bennie and A. Clark, 'Towards moderate pluralism: Scotland's post-devolution party system 1999–2002', *British Elections and Parties Review*, 13 (2003), 149.

97. Ibid. p. 152.

98. J. Mitchell, 'The narcissism of small differences: Scotland and Westminster', *Parliamentary Affairs*, 63 (2010), 98–116.

99. L. G. Bennie and A. Clark, 'Towards moderate pluralism', p. 152.

100. M. Shephard and P. Cairney 'The impact of the Scottish Parliament in amending executive legislation', pp. 314–16.

101. N. MacCormick, personal communication (interview), 2008.

102. P. Lynch, *SNP: The History of the Scottish National Party*, p. 31.

103. Hansard (House of Commons, 13 May 1927).

104. B. Jones and D. Kavanagh, *British Politics Today*.

105. I. Crewe and A. King, *SDP: The Birth, Life and Death of the Social Democratic Party* (Oxford: Oxford University Press, 1995).

106. R. Brazier, *Constitutional Reform* (Alderley: Clarendon Press, 1991), p. 11.

107. P. Ashdown, 'Beyond Westminster', Williamson Memorial Lecture, Stirling University, 15 April 1994.

108. B. Jones and D. Kavanagh, *British Politics Today*; R. Alexander, *The Voice of the People: A Constitution for Tomorrow* (London: Weidenfeld and Nicolson, 1997), pp. 107–23; A. King, *Does the United Kingdom still have a Constitution?*, pp. 63–5.

109. R. Alexander, *The Voice of the People*; R. Blackburn and R. Plant, 'Introduction', in R. Blackburn and R. Plant (eds), *Constitutional Reform: The Labour Government's Constitutional Reform Agenda* (Harlow: Addison Wesley Longman, 1999); R. Brazier, *Constitutional Reform*; M. Glover and R. Hazell, 'Introduction: forecasting constitutional futures', in R. Hazell (ed.), *Constitutional Futures Revised: Britain's Constitution to 2020* (Basingstoke: Palgrave Macmillan, 2008).

110. House of Lords Act 1999.

111. Freedom of Information Act 2000.

112. Greater London Authority Act 1998; Local Government Act 2000.

113. Political Parties, Elections and Referendums Act 2000.

114. European Parliament Elections Act 1999.

115. Constitutional Reform Act 2005.

116. M. Flinders, 'Majoritarian democracy in Britain: New Labour and the constitution', *West European Politics*, 28 (2005), 87.

117. Ibid. p. 62.

118. Ibid. p. 87.

119. Ibid. p. 88.

120. A. King, *Does the United Kingdom still have a Constitution?*

121. K. Wright, *'Expressing and Exercising Scottish Sovereignty'*, Open Democracy, 30 November 2009.

122. J. Hatchard and P. Slinn, *Parliamentary Supremacy and Judicial Independence: A Commonwealth Approach* (London: Cavendish Publishing, 1999), p. 193.

123. Ibid. p. 192.

124. Ibid. p. 193.

125. D. Irvine, 'Parliamentary sovereignty and judicial independence: keynote address', in J. Hatchard and P. Slinn, *Parliamentary Supremacy and Judicial Independence: A Commonwealth Approach* (London: Cavendish Publishing, 1999), p. 30.

126. A. Darling, speech given at *The Times Conference on the Future of the Union*, Royal Society of Edinburgh, Friday, 2 March 2012.

127. M. Mandel, 'Legal politics Italian style', in C. N. Tate and T. Vallinder (eds), *The Global Expansion of Judicial Power* (New York: New York University Press, 1995), p. 262.

128. P. H. Russell, 'The *Charter* and Canadian democracy', in J. B. Kelly and C. P. Manfredi (eds), *Constested Constitutionalism: Reflections on the Canadian Charter of Rights and Freedoms* (Vancouver and Toronto: UBC Press, 2009), p. 288.

129. A. Finlayson, 'Politics as an argument about the common good', in S. White and D. Leighton (eds), *Building a Citizen Society: The Emerging Politics of Republican Democracy* (London: Lawrence and Wishart, 2008).

130. R. Hirschl, *Towards Juristocracy: The Origins and Consequences of the New Constitutionalism* (Cambridge, MA: Harvard University Press, 2004).

131. T. Campbell, K. D. Ewing and A. Tomkins (eds), *The Legal Protection of Human Rights: Essays* (Oxford: Oxford University Press, 2011); A. Tomkins, *Our Republican Constitution* (Oxford: Hart Publishing, 2005); R. P. Bellamy, *Political Constitutionalism: A Republican Defence of the Constitutionality of Democracy* (Cambridge: Cambridge University Press, 2007).

132. P. Blokker, *New Democracies in Crisis? A Comparative Constitutional Study of the Czech Republic, Hungary, Poland, Romania and Slovakia* (London: Routledge, 2013).

133. M. Sunkin, 'The United Kingdom', in C. N. Tate and T. Vallinder (eds), *The Global Expansion of Judicial Power* (New York: New York University Press, 1995), p. 75.

134. S. Wilks-Heeg and S. Weir, *The Unspoken Constitution*, Democratic Audit, 2009 <http://www.opendemocracy.net/files/unspoken_constitution.pdf> (last accessed 5 January 2012).

135. P. Lynch, *SNP: The History of the Scottish National Party*, p. 84; R. Moffat, *Scotland's Constitution* (Glasgow: Moffat Press, 1993), p. 3.

136. P. Lynch, *SNP: The History of the Scottish National Party*.

137. A copy of the text of this Constitution is reproduced at Appendix A.

138. R. Moffat, *Scotland's Constitution*.

139. Ibid.

140. W. E. Bulmer, 'An analysis of the Scottish National Party's Draft Constitution for Scotland', *Parliamentary Affairs*, 64/4 (2011), 674–93.

141. D. Henderson, *Supplementary Evidence Submitted to the Commission on the Constitution*, 1970, SNP Archives, National Library of Scotland 10090/98.

142. Ibid.

143. SNP, *A Free Scotland* (Edinburgh: SNP, 2002).

144. There is some confusion about the dating of this draft. It appears to have been written in 1962, but not published until 1964.

145. N. MacCormick, personal communication (interview), 2008.

146. A. Lijphart, *Patterns of Democracy: Government Forms and Performance in Thirty-Six Countries* (New Haven, CT: Yale University Press, 1999).

147. SNP, *The Parliament and Constitution of an Independent Scotland* (Edinburgh: SNP, 1997).

148. O. Dudley Edwards (ed.), *A Claim of Right for Scotland*.

149. K. Wright, '*Expressing and Exercising Scottish Sovereignty*', Open Democracy, 30 November 2009.

150. W. E. Bulmer, *A Constitution for the Common Good: Strengthening Scottish Democracy After the Independence Referendum*.

151. Smith Commission, *Report of the Smith Commission for further devolution of powers to the Scottish Parliament*, 27 November 2014, <http://www. smith-commission.scot/wp-content/uploads/2014/11/The_Smith_Commission_ Report-1.pdf> (last accessed 12 November 2015).

152. K. Hutchins, 'Modelling democracy', *Global Society*, 12/2 (1998), p. 162.

153. Rousseau is often misunderstood (even by some respected constitutional scholars and political theorists) and presented as if he were an advocate of both direct democracy and unlimited governmental power. Neither is the case. For Rousseau, the sovereign power of the people is unlimited, but the people, through the constitutional laws that they enact, can establish a limited, constitutionally restrained, and elective, form of government. The exercise of sovereignty, through constitutional laws, is direct, but governing powers may be delegated.

154. A. Kaldelis, *The Byzantine Republic: People and Power in New Rome* (Cambridge, MA: Harvard University Press, 2015).

155. G. L. Negretto, *Making Constitutions: Presidents, Parties and Constitutional Choice in Latin America* (Cambridge: Cambridge University Press, 2013), p. 4–7.

156. R. Hazell, 'Conclusion: where will the Westminster model end up?'.

157. A. Lijphart, *Patterns of Democracy*, pp. 258–300.

158. Ibid. p. 2.

159. L. De Winter and P. Dumont, 'Belgium: delegation and accountability under partitocratic rule', in K. Strøm, W. C. Müller and T. Bergman (eds), *Delegation and Accountability in Parliamentary Democracies* (Oxford: Oxford University Press, 2003), pp. 253–80.

160. T. Larson and H. Bäck, *Governing and Governance in Sweden* (Stockholm: Swedish Institute, 2008); E. Holmberg and N. Stjernquist, *The Constitution of Sweden* (Stockholm: Swedish Riksdag, 1995).

161. A. Lijphart, *Patterns of Democracy*, pp. 258–300.

162. O. Dudley Edwards (ed.), *A Claim of Right for Scotland*; N. MacCormick, 'An idea for a Scottish constitution'.

163. W. E. Bulmer, 'An analysis of the Scottish National Party's Draft Constitution for Scotland', *Parliamentary Affairs*, 64/4 (2011), 674–93.

164. R. Hazell, 'Conclusion: where will the Westminster model end up?'.

165. B. Ackerman, 'The new separation of powers', *Harvard Law Review*, 113/3 (2000), pp. 633–729.

166. D. Arter, *Democracy in Scandinavia: Consensual, Majoritarian or Mixed?* (Manchester: Manchester University Press, 2006).

167. J. Gerring and S. A. Thacker, *Centripetal Theory of Democratic Governance* (Cambridge: Cambridge University Press, 2008).

2002 DRAFT I:
PARLIAMENT AND THE LEGISLATIVE POWER

This chapter and the two that follow it are devoted to the detailed analysis and evaluation of the 2002 draft Constitution. Although it has now been superseded and no longer represents the party's current policy, this text still has historical relevance, as a monument to the 'high point' in the SNP's constitution-making prior to the independence referendum.

It also has practical relevance, as by the detailed analysis of this text, including an examination of its flaws and weaknesses, the scholarly and public debate on a future Constitution for Scotland can be advanced; and, if ever there should be a second independence referendum and a future occasion to draft a Constitution for a Scottish state, a thorough combing of past attempts may glean some useful lessons.

This chapter addresses the legislative branch, including the composition of parliament and the electoral system, fixed term elections, the minority veto referendum procedure and parliamentary organisation.

Parliament and the Electoral System

The SNP's 2002 draft Constitution makes the following provisions with regard to the electoral system:

> elections to Parliament shall be conducted by a system of proportional representation so as to secure a fair reflection of the composition of Scottish society, both in general and with particular regard to party preference and to geographical diversity.[1]

The proposal to adopt proportional representation is an important variation on the Westminster model, which is integral to a move towards a 'Westminster transformed' system. Adopting proportional representation has far-reaching implications for the whole political system, increasing the likelihood of coalition or minority governments and in turn leading to a more balanced relationship between the legislature and executive[2] and promoting a more collegial decision-making style within cabinet.[3]

As Neil MacCormick wrote when the SNP's draft Constitution was first developed in the 1970s, proportional representation was regarded as a radical break from the Westminster tradition.[4] In a British context, it still is. In Scotland, however, as discussed in Chapter 4, proportional representation is an established fact, already integrated into the devolution settlement.

The significance of this provision in the draft Constitution, then, is not that it proposes the introduction of any novelty, but that it would entrench an existing achievement and prevent a majority government from taking any unilateral decision to revert to a majoritarian system.

The value of entrenching proportional representation can be seen in the experience of Ireland. In Ireland, the single transferable vote (STV) system has a long history, having been introduced for local elections by the British government in 1920. In 1921, STV was used for elections to the parliament of Southern Ireland (as then was); this decision was accepted in principle by both the British government and by a large bloc of Irish nationalist opinion, and the use of STV in the Irish Free State was confirmed two years later by the Electoral Act 1923.[5] STV, by then in regular use for sixteen years, was entrenched in the new Constitution of 1937.[6] Since then, it has withstood two attempts by the government to replace it for partisan ends. In 1959, a proposed constitutional amendment to replace STV with single member plurality (SMP) was narrowly rejected by the people, receiving 48.2 per cent of the vote; a second attempt in 1968 was more soundly defeated, this time winning only 39.3 per cent of the vote – a result that took further electoral reform off the agenda for a generation.[7]

Ireland's experience can be contrasted with that of France, where, since 1875, the electoral system has been regulated by ordinary or organic laws, amendable at will by parliamentary majorities.[8] During the Third and Fourth Republics this led to some egregious abuses, with incumbent majorities manipulating the electoral system for partisan advantage in 1885, 1889, 1919, 1927, 1946, 1951 and 1955.[9] This habit of electoral manipulation even continued into the Fifth Republic – in 1986, the Socialists replaced the double ballot majoritarian system with a list PR system, only for the Right, on regaining power, to reverse the decision.[10]

While such opportunistic manipulation is not necessarily inevitable, the contrast between France and Ireland shows, firstly, that incumbent majorities can easily be tempted to amend the electoral system for their own advantage – even when there is considerable weight of history behind the status quo – and, secondly, that constitutional specification makes it harder for them to do so.

The entrenchment of proportional representation in the SNP's draft Constitution is therefore good and prudent practice. However, although the principle of proportional representation is mandated, the draft Constitution does not specify any particular electoral system.

The requirement to reflect Scotland's 'geographical diversity' can be assumed to exclude nationwide list forms of proportional representation, such as that used in the Netherlands,[11] but a variety of other options – regional list PR, whether open or closed, STV, or a mixed member proportional (MMP) system – are available. The choice of system, and all other details of the electoral system, is left to parliament's discretion, to be dealt with by ordinary law:

> The Parliament of Scotland shall enact laws making detailed provisions for all matters concerned with the conduct of elections.[12]

Neil MacCormick was not overly concerned with variations between different forms of proportional representation. The priority, he said, was to 'end the winner-takes all system'; provided that the principle of proportionality be agreed, further details were not, he felt, of constitutional significance.[13] MacCormick's argument has some merit: technical differences between forms of proportional representation are arguably less important, in terms of effect on the operation of the polity as a whole, than the basic difference of principle between proportional and majoritarian systems.[14] Besides, no electoral system is objectively 'best',[15] and specifying the electoral system in the Constitution necessarily entrenches a set of imperfect and highly normative choices against easy subsequent revision.

The SNP's own position on the electoral system has varied. In 1997, the party officially favoured a unique hybrid of AV and MMP (a system similar to that currently used for the Scottish Parliament, but with the constituency members chosen by a preferential majority vote).[16] By 2002, in a footnote to the draft Constitution, they declared support for STV,[17] although this support has not been much voiced since. By 2012, however, it had become clear that the SNP intended to maintain the current MMP electoral system for an independent parliament – a stance confirmed by the first minister in parliament.[18]

From a historical institutionalist perspective, this acceptance of the current MMP system is predictable. The great advantage of MMP over STV – or indeed any other form of proportional representation – is that it is already in place, it exists, and it works. As discussed in Chapter 4, it emerged from public debate in the Constitutional Convention, was written into the Scotland Act, and has operated over four electoral cycles.

If the electoral system for an independent Scotland is now settled in favour of MMP, there is a stronger case for the detailed specification of the electoral system in the text of the Constitution. In the absence of such specification, a governing majority could manipulate the electoral system, by ordinary legislation, to serve its own immediate electoral interests. If it becomes acceptable – in a newly formed state, without the weight of long-established traditions behind it – for governments to tweak the electoral system for their own benefit, then the public perception of the fairness of the electoral process, even of democracy as a whole, could be jeopardised.[19]

It would not be necessary to change the highly visible (and therefore politically contentious) fundamentals of the electoral system in order to manipulate it. The draft Constitution does not specify the total size of parliament or the maximum or minimum number of members to be elected from each multi-member electoral district; nor, as discussed in Chapter 7, does it establish an electoral commission or boundary commission to ensure the impartial conduct of elections. Incumbent majorities would therefore be able to manipulate the electoral system in subtle ways – for example, by rigged districting or apportionment, by imposing high national thresholds for the allocation of list seats, or decreasing regional district magnitudes to reduce proportionality. These seemingly minor and technical matters can have a profound effect on the working of the electoral system.[20]

Under the 2002 text, any attempt to manipulate the electoral system could, of course, be judicially constrained, as all legislation, including the electoral law, would be subject to judicial review on the grounds of constitutionality. However, this could allow excessive room for judicial interpretation. What amounts to fairness, 'both in general and with particular regard to party preference and to geographical diversity',[21] is not self-evident. If it is usual, for example, for list-based proportional systems to apply an artificial threshold, then the difficulty lies in setting a 'fair' level. Would a 5 per cent national threshold (which would cause the Greens to lose representation, based on the 2011 election results) be acceptable? If so, what about setting it at 10 per cent (which based on the 2011 result would exclude the Liberal Democrats) or even 20 per cent (which would exclude the Conservatives)? This is not the place to answer these hypothetical questions, only to note that the 2002 text, by the ambiguity and imprecision of its provisions, would have left the way open to possible manipulation, and that it would be better, if the integrity and stability of the electoral system is to be safeguarded, to close any such loophole.

In summary, the 2002 draft Constitution's embrace of proportional representation is sound and reflects the established criteria of a viable and acceptable Constitution for Scotland. However, it is suboptimal in its refusal to specify the form of proportional representation to be used – that is, to reflect and entrench the consensus that has been formed around the existing MMP system – and in its lack of detailed provisions concerning matters such as national thresholds, formulas for the calculation of seats, dual candidacy, and other matters pertaining to the electoral system.

Fixed Term Parliaments

The SNP's 2002 draft Constitution recommended fixed term parliaments, with a four-year term. The relevant provision of the Constitution reads:

> The term of each Parliament shall be four years [. . .]. [T]he date for each General Election shall be appointed by proclamation of the Head of State to take place on a day not more than thirty days earlier nor more than thirty days later than the fourth anniversary of the preceding General Election.[22]

The decision to adopt fixed terms was intended to 'diminish the overweening power of the executive over Parliament',[23] which was perceived to exist under the traditional Westminster system. The argument, clearly advanced in the Claim of Right document discussed in Chapter 4, was that the power of the prime minister in the UK to dissolve the House of Commons at will – at least, prior to the Fixed Term Parliaments Act 2011 – strengthened the position of the executive and weakened that of the parliament:

The power of dissolving Parliament has largely passed to the Prime Minister who, with rare exceptions, can manipulate it both to benefit and to control his/her party.[24]

An effectively unrestricted power of dissolution in the hands of the prime minister benefits the incumbent party because it enables the prime minister to call an election at the most favourable time.[25] Perhaps more importantly, it also enables the prime minister to control his or her own party: the unpredictable threat of dissolution is a useful tool for maintaining party unity and keeping 'rebellious' backbenchers in check.[26]

This relationship between the prerogative of dissolution and the balance of power between the prime minister and parliament as a whole was noted by John Stuart Mill in the nineteenth century, who argued that, when armed with the power of dissolution, a prime minister could never be removed by an adverse vote in parliament, merely forced to choose between resignation and a general election which might see him returned to office.[27] Indeed, the presence of a strong power of dissolution in the UK, and its absence from the French parliamentary system of the Third and Fourth Republics, for example, was used by traditional 'old institutionalists' such as Williams[28] and Headlam-Morely[29] to explain why British parliamentarism 'worked' while its cousins in France and Central Europe 'failed'. In deciding to adopt fixed terms, therefore, the authors of the SNP's draft Constitution were deliberately choosing to modify the heritage of the Westminster system, opting for a novel (and 'continental') mechanism that would purposefully weaken the dominance of the executive and strengthen the position of parliament.

The desired effect of fixed terms – preventing the prime minister from dissolving at will, and thereby removing his or her ability both to benefit and control his or her party – could also have been achieved by interposing a neutral head of state between the prime minister and the decision to dissolve. This is the approach taken in the Constitutions of both Ireland and Malta, as well as in many Commonwealth realms.

The Irish Constitution, for example, allows the president, acting on his or her own absolute discretion, to refuse a dissolution requested by a prime minister who has lost the confidence of the Dáil.[30] This rule means a defeated government cannot automatically appeal from the Dáil to the people, especially if the president believes that an alternative government could be formed without a dissolution.

In practice, the Irish president's right to refuse a dissolution has never been exercised,[31] although situations have arisen in which this discretionary power might legitimately have been used, and its existence can still be politically important. In January 1982 the Fine Gael–Labour coalition government was defeated on the budget in the Dáil. President Hillery granted the prime minister's request for a dissolution, despite the fact that the opposition apparently requested him to refuse it.[32] If satisfied that an alternative government could have been formed, the president would have been within his rights to refuse a dissolution in this case.[33] Conversely, when Labour pulled out of a coalition with Fianna Fáil in 1994, President Robinson 'let it be known' that she would refuse a dissolution; in the event, however, the rump Fianna Fáil government resigned, rather than face defeat in a vote of no confidence, and a new government was formed without the need to ask for a dissolution.[34,35]

Malta, to cite another example from a Westminster-derived system, also relies on the interposition of the head of state to prevent a prime minister from dissolving parliament at will. As in Ireland, the President of Malta's agreement to a dissolution requested by the prime minister is usually, but not always, a foregone conclusion. Malta's Constitution potentially gives the president greater latitude to exercise discretion in this matter, since the power to refuse a dissolution is not dependent on the government having lost parliamentary support. Article 76(c) of the Constitution of Malta states:

> if the Prime Minister recommends a dissolution and the President considers that the Government of Malta can be carried on without a dissolution and that a dissolution would not be in the interests of Malta, the President may refuse to dissolve Parliament.

In other words, if the President of Malta judges that an alternative government could be formed without a dissolution (or even, arguably, that the government is merely seeking to maximise its electoral chances, and that a dissolution is therefore neither necessary nor desirable to secure a stable and continuing government), the president may stand in the way of the prime minister's intentions. In practice, owing to Malta's rigid two-party system, which makes any change of government between elections unlikely, the power to refuse a dissolution has never been used. Yet, even so, the specification of these provisions in the Constitution, rather than reliance on convention alone, means that the power to refuse a dissolution is real power and could be used in the future if the circumstances so demand.[36]

The potential interposition of the head of state in Westminster-influenced countries such as Ireland and Malta does not, however, deprive the prime minister of the right to advise a dissolution as and when he or she sees fit. Prime ministerial discretion is the norm, while the right of the head of state to refuse such advice is the occasional exception. Opting for constitutionally fixed terms reverses this situation, strengthening the hand of parliament, while also having the advantage of offering greater protection to the neutrality of a head of state who is hereditary rather than elected.

The phrase 'fixed term' does not, however, mean that election dates are necessarily set in stone. The 2002 draft Constitution contains several rules allowing electoral dates to be changed when the need arises. Firstly, the head of state (presumably acting on the binding advice of the prime minister – a subject which will be developed further in the next chapter) is allowed to set the date of a general election up to thirty days either side of the fourth anniversary of the preceding election. Without altering the substantial commitment to 'fixed terms', this rule allows for some minor flexibility, such as might be needed to avoid a clash with holidays, or to ensure elections fall, for convenience's sake, on the same day of the week.

The second exception provides for situations in which a government enjoying the confidence of parliament cannot be formed, where a deadlock between the parties can be broken only by recourse to a general election:

If at any time Parliament is unable to agree on a Government, in the sense that no person can be found who is able to command its confidence as Prime Minister, the Head of State may dissolve Parliament and by Proclamation appoint a date for the holding of a General Election to take place within one month of such a situation arising; and during the intervening period the Head of State may appoint an interim Prime Minister and Government.[37]

These proposed constitutional provisions are badly drafted, since the point at which the necessary condition of being 'unable to agree on a Government' arises is uncertain. This is because, as discussed in the following chapter, no timescale is specified for the election of a prime minister. It is easy to imagine a scenario in which the imprecision of these provisions could be highly problematic. Let us imagine, for example, that this Constitution were in effect, and that a governing minimal-winning coalition were to collapse because of an insurmountable disagreement between the coalition partners. This might lead to a vote of no confidence, with the former coalition partner joining with the opposition to vote against its erstwhile allies, resulting in the resignation of the government. In this case, it seems likely that the defeated prime minister would continue in office, albeit in a caretaker capacity, until a successor was elected, and would then resign in favour of that successor. This is the point at which confusion over the terms of the Constitution might arise. It could take time for a new prime minister to be chosen, following a realignment of the parties or the renegotiation of a coalition agreement. At what point, then, would the head of state be within his or her rights to demand a dissolution and to take the initiative in appointing a new prime minister?

It is also unclear whether this power of early dissolution would be exercised by the head of state acting solely on the advice of the incumbent prime minister (as a literal reading of the Constitution would suggest), or whether there is some scope for the head of state's personal discretion in this matter. Would refusal to act on such advice cause a crisis, even if the advice were tendered, or not tendered, for blatantly partisan motives?

The answers to these hypothetical, but not entirely improbable, questions cannot be found in the text of the draft Constitution: as argued more fully in the following chapter, they would have to be supplied by custom, convention and usage. The general tendency of convention is to favour the prime minister over independent decision-making by any other institutional actor. As a result, one of the advantages of having a fixed term parliament could be lost, or significantly diminished, simply through a lack of attention to detail in matters of constitutional design.

The draft Constitution is less satisfactory, in this respect, than the Scotland Act of 1998. The Scotland Act avoids the hypothetical difficulties identified above. Under its provisions, an early dissolution may be advised by the Presiding Officer only if a first minister has not been elected within a tightly defined period of twenty-eight days.[38] This time limit is arbitrary – although it is not unreasonable, being close to the average time taken for coalition formation in European democracies.[39]

It should be noted that the SNP's 2002 draft Constitution makes no provision for extraordinary dissolution in any circumstance other than that of being unable to form a government. This is highly restrictive. There might be times when, for pressing political reasons, a dissolution is required before the end of the fixed four-year term, even if a government is formed and is able to continue in office. Obviously, such flexibility cannot be taken too far in the direction of prime ministerial discretion, or the advantages of fixed terms would be lost, but a slightly more flexible approach to dissolution that that allowed by the SNP's draft Constitution could be advantageous. For example, it could be useful to enable members of parliament to seek a fresh mandate after a change of government, or to give the government a chance (at the risk of losing the election, of course) to bolster its political credibility in the face of a crisis or controversy. One possible solution, again based on the existing provisions of the Scotland Act, would be to allow parliament to dissolve itself by a two-thirds majority vote of its members.[40] This would allow the government and opposition to dissolve parliament by mutual consent, when both think it is necessary or expedient, but would not allow one side of the chamber to dissolve parliament without the agreement of the other.

If an extraordinary general election is held under the SNP's draft Constitution, then it does not reset the electoral calendar. In other words, the following 'ordinary' general election takes place on or around the fourth anniversary of the previous ordinary general election, regardless of the intervening 'extraordinary' election:

> The Parliament of Scotland elected at such a General Election shall serve for the remainder of the unexpired term of the Parliament so dissolved.[41]

This provision reflects a similar rule in the Scotland Act and in the Constitution of Sweden.[42] In Sweden the prime minister can dissolve parliament at will, without any interposition by the head of state, but a Swedish government has little to gain from calling an extraordinary election, since the next ordinary election is not thereby postponed. In consequence, since 1945, only one extraordinary election has been held in Sweden (in 1958), and no such election has been held since the adoption of the present Constitution in 1974.[43,44] The ability to dissolve the Riksdag is therefore 'at best a blunt instrument in the government's hand'.[45] The effect of a similar rule in Scotland is likely to be to dissuade the prime minister of Scotland from 'faking' a loss of no confidence in order to force an early election at a favourable time, since the prime minister could by this means only jeopardise, and not extend, his or her lease of power.

The third exception to the general principle of fixed terms applies in circumstances where Scotland is at war, and where the holding of a general election is therefore impractical:

> Parliament shall in time of war have power by resolution to extend its term for a period not exceeding one year.[46]

This provision is also less than ideal. Firstly, it can be invoked only in time of war, which is unduly restrictive. There might reasonably be other circumstances, such as a natural disaster or an epidemic disease, which demand a constitutionally legitimate means of delaying an election Indeed, this was a problem in Liberia in 2014, when the constitutionality of delaying elections to the Senate (due to the Ebola virus outbreak) was disputed.

Secondly, the invocation of this provision does not require a super-majority. This means, in essence, that the governing majority can, in time of war, delay elections and extend their incumbency, without having to have the agreement of the opposition. The potential for abuse of this power by the majority (although limited by the fact that it can only invoked in wartime) should not be neglected.

Thirdly, it is unclear whether this delay can be repeated. If so, potential exists for the perpetuation in office of a government at war, even if the opposition are convinced that elections could reasonably take place.

The decision to set the parliamentary term at four years, as opposed to any substantially longer or shorter period, must briefly be discussed. In principle, the shorter the period of time between elections, the greater the degree of citizen control over their representatives: as the Radical Whig maxim, recited by John Adams, put it, 'Where annual elections end, there slavery begins'.[47] Yet this must be balanced by the need for stability and continuity, by the desire to avoid constant rounds of electioneering, and by the principle of responsibility, which demands that a government be in office long enough for its record to be fairly judged by the electorate.

In practice, all EU-27 countries use either four-year or five-year terms. Of the ten EU states categorised by Lijphart as consensus democracies on the parties-executives dimension, all use four-year terms except for Italy and Luxembourg (which both have five-year terms).[48] Of the five EU states characterised as majoritarian, all use five-year terms except for Spain and Greece (which have four-year terms). The two EU countries with a clearly Westminster-influenced institutional heritage (Ireland and Malta) use five-year terms, as do all of the English-speaking Caribbean nations included in Lijphart's sample set (Jamaica, Bahamas, Barbados and Trinidad) – although two of the other Westminster-derived cases (Australia and New Zealand) have three-year terms.

It is also notable that the devolved Scottish Parliament is usually elected for four-year terms, although the duration of the current and previous parliaments has been extended to five years in order to avoid conflict with a UK general election under the Fixed Term Parliaments Act 2011. A four-year term, then, is well within comparative standards and can be regarded as a norm – albeit an as yet insecure one – in the Scottish context.

Overall, the basic principle of adopting fixed term parliaments, as outlined in the SNP's 2002 proposals, is a sound one: it would protect parliament from arbitrary dissolution, prevent the prime minister from using the threat of dissolution as a means of coercing backbenchers, and help achieve a balance of power between the executive and legislature, whilst at the same time allowing a means of breaking the deadlock by recourse to an extraordinary election if a workable government cannot be formed. However, the technical provisions on fixed term parliaments are poorly drafted, ambiguous, and even somewhat retrograde when compared against the existing provisions of the Scotland Act. The circumstances in which an early dissolution is legitimate are unspecified, as no time limit on government formation is laid down. Although unproblematic in most normal circumstances, the ambiguity of the draft Constitution's provisions could cause it to fail at moments of political crisis and heightened tension, when constitutional clarity is most sorely needed.

Unicameralism and Referendums

When the SNP's draft Constitution was first published in 1977, many of its provisions were indeed 'radical', at least by the Westminster standards of the time.[49] Today, as argued in Chapter 4, much of what then seemed bold and innovative (such as proportional representation, fixed term parliaments, the election of the executive by parliament, the acknowledgement of popular sovereignty and the judicial protection of human rights from parliamentary majorities) has now, for the most part, been accepted as an integral part of Scotland's constitutional heritage.

Yet, despite the advances that have occurred in the intervening years, there is one provision of the SNP's draft Constitution that is still as innovative today – at least in a British context – as it was when first proposed in the 1970s: the minority veto referendum procedure. This would enable a substantial minority of the members of parliament (two-fifths of the membership) to delay a bill, other than a money bill, for at least twelve months, subject to the right of the majority to override the delay by appealing to the people in a referendum.

The decision to adopt such a radical and unusual provision requires explanation. This lies in the SNP's longstanding antipathy to the House of Lords as traditionally constituted. This antipathy stems from the party's adherence to democratic and equalitarian principles – to which a partly hereditary chamber, representing political appointees and members of privileged noble and episcopal orders, was deemed incompatible. Indeed, the very idea of bicameralism was sometimes seen as an English invention. Giving England credit for the invention of bicameralism is, of course, ahistorical, as bicameral systems at least as venerable as that of England can be found elsewhere, such as in Hungary.[50] Even so, older histories of Scotland perpetuated the myth that unicameralism was Scottish, while bicameralism was distinctly English.[51] In the mythical 'crowned republic' of an idealised medieval Scotland, the nobles, clergy and burghers sat and voted together in one assembly, on equal terms, under a citizen-king who was first amongst equals, whilst in England the haughty Norman nobles separated themselves, so the story went, from the common folk.

Romantic history aside, unicameralism is the established norm in Scotland. The devolved parliament is unicameral. Early proposals for an independent Scottish parliament, such as that prepared by the SPCA and early SNP drafts, were also unicameral.[52] MacCormick even stated that he, personally, was not opposed to a second chamber in principle, but felt that the establishment of a second chamber would be unacceptable in Scotland.[53] Other tentative proposals for the establishment of a second chamber in Scotland – such as Lord Steel's plan for an 'external review panel' – have also failed to win approval.[54]

Unicameralism, then, was to a large extent required and inherited rather than 'chosen' by MacCormick. Yet unicameralism is associated with the majoritarian forms of government that MacCormick and the SNP were eager to avoid.[55] Lijphart identified strong bicameralism – where the second chamber has powers similar to those of the lower House and a differentiated composition which encourages the actual use of such powers – as one of the defining characteristics of a consensus democracy.[56] Hazell likewise identifies the reform of the House of Lords – that is, a move towards a wholly or mainly elective body, in which the government might not necessarily have a majority – as a step, in a UK-wide context, towards a 'Transformed' constitution.[57] Many others who have been concerned about checking the abuse of power have also favoured bicameral solutions.[58]

The proposed minority veto referendum procedure can therefore be understood as an attempt to 'compensate for the loss of an upper house's delaying power',[59] in circumstances where the majoritarian risks of unlimited unicameralism are fully acknowledged, but where the more usual option of bicameralism is, for contingent, historical and even irrational reasons, put out of reach:

> Having a single-chamber Parliament was regarded by some commentators as risky, but our response was that a robust committee system coupled with blocking rights for a substantial minority would be sufficient security against abuse of majority power.[60]

The minority veto referendum procedure is described in some detail in the 2002 draft Constitution. There is a period of ten days between the final reading of all bills, other than money bills, and their presentation for royal assent. During this period, any member of parliament would be able to sign a written motion calling for the bill to be suspended. If such a motion is supported by at least two-fifths of the total number of members of parliament, then the bill would be suspended. After the suspension of twelve months has elapsed (but no later than eighteen months from the date of suspension), Parliament may again vote on the bill. If the bill is confirmed by a majority of the members of parliament present and voting, then it is presented for royal assent. During its period of suspension, however, the bill may be submitted to the people by a majority vote of parliament; if the bill is then approved in the referendum, by a simple majority of the popular vote, it would be presented for royal assent without delay.[61]

Although relatively rare, such procedures are not unique. The Danish Constitution bears the closest resemblance to that proposed in the 2002 draft. In Denmark, a constitutional revision of 1953 abolished the second chamber and instead instituted a minority veto mechanism whereby one-third of the members of parliament would have the authority to refer bills to the people in a referendum.[62] This constitutional change was instigated by the Conservative and Radical parties in order to prevent excessive dominance by a Social Democrat majority.[63] It was therefore conceived as an unambiguously 'consensual' (majority restraining) device, the intention of which was 'not to transform

Denmark into a referendum democracy, but rather to introduce a mechanism which would force the Government to negotiate with the opposition'.[64]

Unlike in Denmark, the referendum mechanism in the SNP's 2002 draft would not, strictly speaking, finally decide the fate of a bill. The vote as envisaged in the text only confirms or overturns the suspensive veto. This means that if the bill were to be rejected in the referendum, it could still be enacted by parliament after the period of delay has elapsed – although, of course, blatant disregard for the voters' preferences might be 'politically imprudent'.[65]

Since the final decision rule is strictly majoritarian, the referendum should not be seen as a device intended to give special voice or protection to socio-cultural, political or regional minorities. Rather, it should be seen as a 'contes-tatory'[66] procedure, which protects popular majorities against parliamentary majorities.[67] It would help to diminish the 'agency loss' that occurs, in all representative systems, as a result of differences between elite and mass interests;[68] its deterrent effect would be most credible in situations where there is a notable difference between the policies pursued by the ruling majority in parliament and those favoured by the people.[69]

Unlike a second chamber (even a weak second chamber on the usual Westminster pattern), a minority veto referendum procedure does not provide an additional, reflective forum away from party politics, allow for the inclusion of experienced vocational representatives, nor enable the quality of bills to be improved through minor, technical amendments.[70] MacCormick's intention was that these other functions should be supplied by empowered parliamentary committees – which, as discussed in the following section, would be able to conduct hearings on proposed legislation.[71]

At present, there is no way of knowing whether this mechanism, if adopted in Scotland, would be used responsibly to promote constructive dialogue between the government and opposition on matters of major policy, or whether it would be used irresponsibly, in a manner that is obstructive, provokes brinkmanship and in the long run devalues its use.

It is clear, however, that including a minority veto referendum procedure in the draft Constitution represents an increasing openness to the referendum as an instrument of decision-making. Although once regarded as something alien to the Westminster tradition, referendums have now become an established part of Scottish political life, recognised as the way in which the sovereign people speaks. Provisions relating to the use of referendums are no longer uncommon in other Westminster-derived Constitutions. Ireland and Australia, for instance, require referendums to approve all constitutional amendments. Many of the English-speaking Caribbean countries require a referendum for major amendments to their constitutions, although in most cases minor amendments can be passed by a supermajority in parliament. The Australian state of New South Wales uses referendums as a mechanism for resolving disputes between the two Houses of its parliament.[72] The Cayman Islands even has a provision for citizen-initiated referendums.[73]

So, in proposing a minority veto referendum, the SNP's 2002 draft was being innovative in a British context. It was not, however, going beyond the norm of the provisions for direct democracy that exist in other contemporary democratic Constitutions, including some of those in the Westminster family.[74]

Parliamentary Organisation, Procedures and Committees

Much of the working arrangements of the UK parliament, in terms of its organisation, procedures and privileges, depend upon custom, convention and common law. Westminster-derived written constitutions, especially the more recent ones, do tend to make more explicit provision for matters of parliamentary organisation, elevating certain key principles from the realm of constitutional practice to that of constitutional law. Most post-colonial Westminster model constitutions provide in the constitutional text for the election of a Speaker, for the definition and protection of parliamentary privileges, for the mechanism of resolving disputes between the Houses in a bicameral system, for the process of dealing with public finances (such as the requirement for spending to be proposed by a responsible minister), for the determination of a quorum, and for similar purposes. Typical examples include the Constitution of Bangladesh, sections 72–76, and the Constitution of the Bahamas, sections 52–63.

The provisions of the SNP's draft Constitution with respect to the process of enacting legislation are quite elaborate. It states that, 'The Parliament of Scotland shall from time to time by resolution make provisions as to the procedures required for the passing Acts of Parliament',[75] and then goes on to describe, in some detail, what the 'normally required elements' of any procedure adopted by parliament ought to be.[76]

The standard legislative process, as mandated in the 2002 draft, consists of four stages: (1) publication of a bill (described as a 'proposed measure') and an initial debate in parliament on its general principles; (2) consideration of the bill in committee; (3) a report stage, during which amendments to the bill are debated and voted on in plenary session; and (4) a final plenary vote to pass or reject the bill as amended.[77]

MacCormick envisaged strong committees as a partial substitute for a second chamber, providing legislative expertise and detailed legislative scrutiny within a unicameral system.[78] The draft Constitution, which gives committees a central role in the legislative process, is clearly intended to give effect to that strength. To this end, committees may 'conduct hearings to which representations may be made by or on behalf of all persons or groups of persons interested in the subject matter of the proposed measure'.[79]

Upon closer inspection, however, the draft Constitution is less generous to committees than it initially appears. Under the prescribed legislative procedure, committees may only react to bills that have already been debated and approved in a plenary debate. This limits the role of the committee to one of scrutiny and peripheral amendment – the principle of a bill, having already been agreed upon, is hardly open to challenge. There is no mention, for example, of the right of committees to propose bills on their own initiative. This is not to say that the right of committees to introduce bills, which exists at present in the Scottish Parliament,[80] would necessarily be abolished by the draft Constitution, only that the continuation of such a right would depend solely on the Standing Orders of parliament, and not on any constitutional foundation.

Since the draft Constitution makes no provision for the involvement of committees in the pre-legislative stages, it must be assumed that civil servants and ministers are expected to provide the substance of bills, and present them ready-formed for parliamentary digestion. If this is the case, it is simply a continuation of existing practices and need not be problematic. Nevertheless, such practices may be regarded as a legacy of the old, unreformed Westminster way of thinking, which would do little to bring about a 'Westminster transformed' situation in which there is a more cooperative balance of power between parliament and the executive.

Scotland has adopted a form of 'cooptive' policy-making at the executive level, whereby relevant interest groups are coopted as 'insiders' and are given 'regularized access to the policy formulating bodies'.[81] Such consultative and cooptive forms of interest group activity are normally associated with a consensual style of democracy, in contrast to the majoritarian preference for competitive pluralism.[82] Yet the SNP's draft Constitution does not appear to entrench or protect such consultation. In other words, there is little in the draft Constitution to prevent a future government deciding that the extensive pre-legislative consultation hitherto practised is a frustrating, time-consuming and expensive distraction from the important business of getting things done, and reverting to a more majoritarian way of proceeding. Again, the claim is not that such authoritarian backsliding would necessarily occur, but simply that the 2002 draft Constitution, as such, contained no provisions that would clearly stop it.

Moreover, the committees may conduct hearings only 'during such period of time as is prescribed by resolution of the Parliament'.[83] That the activities of committees should be ultimately subject to the decisions of the parliament as a whole is a good, near-universal principle of parliamentary procedure, but, as phrased in the draft Constitution – with no standard minimum or maximum time limits, and no super-majoritarian requirements necessary to override these standard periods – it could enable a ruling majority to curtail the period of time in which committees can conduct hearings on an arbitrary or partisan basis.

The draft Constitution is silent about the size, appointment and composition of committees. There is no parallel to the rule found in the Scotland Act 1998 (Schedule 3) requiring committees to be reflective of the partisan balance of the chamber. It is reasonable to expect that the present practice of nomination by party business managers ('whips'), having due regard to the need for partisan balance, and taking into consideration the interests, expertise and experience of members,[84] would continue into the immediate future – but, if it were to continue, the rights of opposition members to fair representation on committees would depend solely on the Standing Orders, and not on any constitutional foundation.

In terms of the number of members, the devolved Scottish Parliament is small for the size of the country. The Norwegian parliament has 165 members, the Danish 179 and the Finnish 200 – despite all having a comparable population to that of Scotland.[85] The size of these legislatures is close to the 'norm', which is the cube root of population size.[86] In contrast, the Scottish Parliament, with 129 members, is 'undersized' (the cube root of a population of 5 million would be approximately 170). The decision to settle on 129 was not made for any reason of principle: it was chosen arbitrarily by Kenyon Wright, Convenor of the Constitutional Convention, in a hurried deal with the Liberal Democrats.[87] While sufficient for a devolved legislature, 129 members might be too few in an independent state that has to establish new committees for matters such as social security, broadcasting, defence and foreign affairs – especially as there is already a sense that the MSPs are overworked, and that committees are too small to be as effective as they should be.[88] An SNP constitutional policy document from 1997 envisages that the independent parliament of Scotland would consist of 200 members,[89] but the 2002 draft Constitution says nothing about this, and would leave the size of parliament to be determined by ordinary laws.

There is a provision in the 2002 draft limiting the number of ministers to one-fifth of the number of members of parliament. This is an innovative rule in a British context, although it exists in various other Westminster Constitutions, such as that of India. Such restrictions on the number of ministers are intended to re-balance power from the executive to parliament, by ensuring that there are always sufficient backbenchers on the government side to allow some scope for 'backbench revolts' and prevent domination by the 'payroll vote'.[90] A side-effect of this rule would be to place a de facto limit on the minimum size of parliament. Yet, even assuming a government of twenty ministers, parliament could be reduced to 100 members. Such a reduction would not only make it more difficult for smaller parties to secure representation, but could also 'render the committee system effectively unworkable'.[91]

Considering parliamentary organisation more broadly, the 2002 draft Constitution is remarkably sparse in detail, even compared with many of those in the Westminster tradition. Organisational devices introduced in the Scotland Act, such as the Parliamentary Corporate Body (which is responsible for parliament's services and facilities) and the Parliamentary Bureau (which arranges the order of business), find no place in the draft. There is no replication of the provision, included in the SPCA's 1962 draft, for one-third of legislative time to be reserved for opposition and private members' business.[92] There is no provision for a leader of the opposition, which is a norm in many post-war Westminster Constitutions. There are no provisions concerning the payment or allowances of members of parliament, and nothing concerning standards of parliamentary ethics.

The 2002 draft does specify that parliament would have the right to 'elect its own Presiding Officer',[93] but it has nothing to say about how the Presiding Officer is elected, whether the ballot is to be open or secret, or whether an absolute or simple majority is required. It is equally silent on how the Presiding Officer is to perform his or her duties. It might be presumed that they are to be an independent, non-partisan umpire in the British tradition – although it should be noted that the impartiality of the Speaker is not universally respected in Westminster-derived parliaments.

For the moment, impartiality is the convention in Scotland, and every Presiding Officer has set aside party membership on being elected to office.[94] However, there is nothing in the 2002 draft to reinforce this convention, nor to prevent the post becoming one of partisan legislative management in the future. This lack of constitutional specificity may be illustrated by a comparison with the provisions of the earlier SPCA draft:

> The National Assembly shall be presided over by a President who shall be elected from the Commissioners to the National Assembly at the first meeting of the first parliament after every General Election. The President shall be the constitutional representative of the National Assembly. He or she shall exercise their office with complete objectivity and impartiality and in accordance with the Rules of Procedure. He or she shall retain their office from the date of their election until the next General Election after which he or she shall be seated as a Commissioner in the National Assembly, without having submitted him or herself to the electorate. He or she shall be eligible for re-election to the office of President. The President shall be responsible for the effective functioning of the National Assembly and shall exercise domestic authority through a House Committee, and shall be controller of the administrative officials and employees of the Assembly. A Vice-President shall also be elected to assist the President and to act as his deputy as and when required.[95]

Under the 2002 draft, the parliament and its members would 'enjoy such privileges and immunities as are essential to the free, unimpeded and demo-cratic conduct of the affairs of the nation'.[96] Again, the exact nature of these privileges and immunities is undefined. Many Commonwealth Constitutions, for the sake of clarity and avoidance of doubt, try to distil the essential privileges of parliament, as developed in the laws, customs and traditions of the British House of Commons, into clear, enforceable constitutional rules. The Constitution of Malta, for instance, specifies not only that the House of Representatives may elect its own Speaker and may 'by law determine the privileges, immunities and powers' of the House and its members, but also that members have immunity from civil and criminal proceedings for 'words spoken before, or written in a report to, the House or a committee thereof or by reason of any matter or thing brought by him therein by petition, bill, resolution, motion or otherwise'.[97] The Scotland Act similarly gives members immunity from the laws of defamation.[98]

The 2002 draft says nothing of the frequency or duration of meetings of the parliament. In the absence of any legislative provisions to the contrary, the Crown – that is, the government – acting under residual prerogatives,[99] would have the power to summon and prorogue parliament at will. This would give the government a strong hand. For example, it could prorogue parliament to buy time if faced with a vote of no confidence, or refuse opposition requests to summon parliament during a recess to discuss urgent matters arising. In the devolved parliament, in contrast, the Presiding Officer may, in accordance with Standing Orders, summon parliament at his or her own initiative in emer-gencies, without having to depend on the government, so that the government cannot arbitrarily prevent parliament from forgathering.

In summary, the 2002 draft – except with regard to the stages for the passage of legislation – has little to say about the rules, procedures and privileges of parliament or its committees. Much would be left to be resolved by ordinary law, custom, and parliament's Standing Orders. The question is whether such reliance on extraconstitutional provisions is problematic. Certainly, it is not unusual for Constitutions to say relatively little about the rules and procedures of parliament. The consequences of such silence, though, can be unfavourable to active, power-sharing parliamentarism. In Ireland, for example, matters of parliamentary procedure have long been regulated by reference to British traditions and precedents.[100] 'Archaic' procedures have been retained,[101] while the provision of information and support to members is 'meagre'.[102] In consequence, the Dáil has 'failed to develop adequate procedures to make effective its scrutiny of the growing range of state activity'.[103] It is 'ill-equipped to hold the executive to account'[104] and remains a weak, reactive assembly, which 'has a comparatively modest role as a policy-maker' and 'does not perform it well'.[105] This comparison, however, only goes so far. The Scottish Parliament was created on a different trajectory, in a deliberate attempt to transform its working practices from the beginning. It might reasonably be assumed, then, that in the eyes of the drafters of the 2002 text, a hypothetical independent parliament would continue along that trajectory, and adopt a set of Standing Orders and working practices modelled on existing, 'transformed', provisions.

There is, nevertheless, a crucial distinction. Unlike the Constitution itself, which could only be amended by a three-fifths majority vote in parliament followed by a referendum, sub-constitutional instruments such as Standing Orders could be changed by a simple majority vote, with no special protection for the opposition or minorities. The rules regulating the balance of power between the government and parliament, majority and minority, plenary sessions and committees, and front and back benches would therefore be wide open to manipulation by governing majorities.

As Norton's study of the effects of procedural rules in the House of Commons concludes, ruling majorities with the theoretical power to amend rules for their own advantage do not often take advantage of their position: a sense of what is 'done' and 'not done', and a reluctance to use up political capital and parliamentary time in such sideshows, makes rules endure even in the face of strong governments.[106] Nevertheless, there is a risk that in a new state, a government that feels itself to be isolated and embattled against an opposition that resents independence and adopts an 'anti-system' stance (a circumstance which is not predicted, but also not impossible to envisage), could seek to govern in a closed, defensive way, excluding parliament and its committees as far as possible, and changing procedures to prevent what it sees as needless obstruction – thereby imperilling the deliberative and scrutinising power of parliament.

Obviously, it is neither possible nor desirable to embody all the rules and procedures of parliamentary organisation in the text of a written Constitution without the Constitution becoming unwieldy. Nevertheless, if the Scottish Constitution is to act as the foundation for a 'Westminster transformed' constitutional order, and is to prevent reversion to simple majoritarianism after independence, then there is a case for important procedural and organisational, particularly as these reflect the discursive and investigatory rights of the opposition and of minorities, to be specified in the Constitution.

Summary

This chapter has provided a detailed study of the provisions of the SNP's draft Constitution in so far as these relate to the election, composition, tenure, dissolution, internal organisation, committee structures, privileges and legislative processes of Parliament. The overall plan of the Parliament as presented in the draft Constitution – a unicameral Parliament, elected by proportional representation for fixed four-year terms, with the power to conduct committee hearings, to determine its own rules of procedure, and to elect its own Presiding Officer – clearly builds on the foundation of the Scottish Parliament and reflects existing practice in Scotland today.

In terms of its macro-level structures, it is a recognisably 'Transformed' derivative of the Westminster system, with power-sharing encouraged by proportional representation and fixed term Parliaments. The peak of this transformation is represented by the minority veto referendum procedure, which, although untried in a Scottish context, could shift the balance of power between the government and opposition in the latter's favour; it gives a two-fifths minority the ability to negotiate with the government from a position of strength, secure in the knowledge that they can force the government into making concessions in order to avoid a frustrating delay or a potentially embarrassing referendum defeat.

However, as a piece of constitutional architecture, the provisions of the SNP's 2002 draft Constitution with respect to Parliament are often vague and incomplete. In failing to specify the electoral system (and in the absence of a constitutionally-mandated independent Electoral Commission or Boundaries Commission), the draft Constitution would allow incumbent majorities to manipulate the electoral rules for their own advantage – for example by reducing district magnitudes or imposing high national thresholds to exclude minor parties. Whether incumbent majorities would actually attempt such a thing is not in question – the issue is simply that, were they to do so, the SNP's constitutional proposals would offer little protection. If one of the aims of the Constitution is to provide clarity and security for the fundamental rules of democracy, and thereby to protect the democratic constitutional order from manipulation by the government of the day, then the draft Constitution is insufficiently clear or robust.

Similarly, many of the rules that would intimately affect the daily operation of parliamentary democracy in an independent Scotland (in terms of the balance of power between the executive and legislature, the majority and minority parties, front and back benches, and the plenary assembly and committees), are left unstated in the draft Constitution. The draft Constitution has remarkably little to say about the orders, privileges and procedures of Parliament. Even its attempts to reinforce the powers of committees lack specificity, and could easily be set aside by a government fearful of criticism and backed by a well-whipped majority. Although the draft Constitution would not necessarily prevent the continuation of new practices adopted at the foundation of the Scottish Parliament (indeed, it must be assumed to allow their continuation, until determined otherwise), it would also do little to reinforce or protect these changes, and to prevent reversion, under a headstrong prime minister, to executive dominance.

If a future Scottish Constitution were to solidify (and even to reinforce) the 'Transformed' practices of the Scottish Parliament, it should perhaps take greater care to entrench major reforms in the text of the Constitution. This is not to suggest, of course, that the Constitution should replicate a full set of Standing Orders, only that it might perhaps lay down some basic principles governing the content of the Standing Orders for the protection of the rights of the opposition, of backbenchers, and of private members.

In summary, the 'constitutional policy' of the draft Constitution – in terms of principles and general structures – can be judged as viable and acceptable, but the 'constitutional draftsmanship' of the text is, in crucial aspects, deficient. These deficiencies are not, as such, catastrophic: they would not necessarily weaken democracy, nor even detract from the advances already made in Scotland since devolution. Much would depend on the use that is made of the text, in political circumstances that cannot, from the present perspective, be predicted. Yet they are nevertheless the sort of technical deficiencies that good constitutional draftsmanship, if serious about preserving a 'Westminster Transformed' form of democracy in Scotland, would seek to overcome.

These are also the kind of deficiencies that have in many cases already been overcome, either in the Scotland Act or in the Constitutions of other Westminster democracies. It would not be difficult to replace the open-ended text of the draft Constitution with respect to the electoral system with the clearer and more robust provisions of the Scotland Act, or to replace its vague provisions on the qualifications and privileges of members of Parliament, or the election and duties of the Presiding Officer, with a more specific and robust text. Even the SPCA's 1962 draft is a much more complete and better-written Constitution, in respect of these matters, than the SNP's 2002 text – and it would be a better foundation, in the event of independence, for future Scottish Constitution-makers to build upon.

Notes

1. SNP, *A Free Scotland* (Edinburgh: SNP, 2002), Article III, §3.
2. A. Lijphart, *Patterns of Democracy: Government Forms and Performance in Thirty-Six Countries* (New Haven, CT: Yale University Press, 1999), pp. 116–42.
3. B. Chubb, *The Government and Politics of Ireland*, 3rd edn (London: Longman, 1992), p. 188.
4. N. MacCormick, 'Is there a constitutional path to Scottish independence?', *Parliamentary Affairs*, 53/4 (2000), p. 723.
5. R. Sinnott, 'The rules of the electoral game', in J. Coakley and M. Gallagher (eds), *Politics in the Republic of Ireland*, 4th edn (Abingdon: Routledge, 2007), pp. 105–134, p. 107.

6. Constitution of Ireland, Art. 16.2.

7. M. Manning, 'Ireland', in D. Butler and A. Ranney (eds), *Referendums* (Washington, DC: American Enterprise Institute for Public Policy Research, 1978), pp. 204–6.

8. P. Campbell, *French Electoral Systems and Elections since 1789* (London: Faber and Faber, 1958).

9. Ibid.

10. J.-L. Thiébault, 'France: delegation and accountability in the Fifth Republic', in K. Strøm, W. C. Müller and T. Bergman (eds), *Delegation and Accountability in Parliamentary Democracies* (Oxford: Oxford University Press, 2003), p. 329.

11. A. Timmermans and R. B. Andeweg, 'The Netherlands: rules and mores in delegation and accountability relationships', in K. Strøm, W. C. Müller and T. Bergman (eds), *Delegation and Accountability in Parliamentary Democracies* (Oxford: Oxford University Press, 2003), pp. 498–522, p. 500.

12. SNP, *A Free Scotland*, Art. III, Sect. 4.

13. N. MacCormick, personal communication (interview), 2008.

14. A. Lijphart, *Patterns of Democracy: Government Forms and Performance in Thirty-Six Countries* (New Haven, CT: Yale University Press, 1999).

15. K. J. Arrow, 'A difficulty in the concept of social welfare', *Journal of Political Economy*, 58/4 (1950), pp. 328–46.

16. SNP, *The Parliament and Constitution of an Independent Scotland* (Edinburgh: SNP, 1997).

17. SNP, *A Free Scotland*.

18. Scottish Parliament Official Report, 31 May 2012.

19. It is interesting that the Smith Commission proposals, although falling outside the time frame for this book, state that certain substantial changes to the electoral system in Scotland should require approval by a two-thirds majority in the Scottish Parliament – a constitutional guarantee that would, for the first time, introduce a form of 'higher law' super-majoritarian rigidity into the system of government.

20. M. Böckenförde, N. Hedling and W. Wahiu, *A Practical Guide to Constitution Building* (Stockholm: International Institute for Democracy and Electoral Assistance, 2011), p. 191.

21. SNP, *A Free Scotland*, Art. III, Sect. 3.

22. SNP, *A Free Scotland*, Art. III, Sect. 5.

23. N. MacCormick, 'An idea for a Scottish constitution', in W. Finnie, C. M. G. Himsworth and N. Walker (eds), *Edinburgh Essays in Public Law* (Edinburgh: Edinburgh University Press, 1991), p. 166.

24. Claim of Right, Para. 4.4.

25. T. Saalfield, 'The United Kingdom: still a single chain of command? The hollowing out of the Westminster model', in K. Strøm, W. C. Müller and T. Bergman (eds), *'Delegation and Accountability in Parliamentary Democracies'*, Comparative Politics (Oxford: Oxford University Press, 2003), pp. 620–48, p. 627.

26. J. S. Mill [1861], 'Considerations on representative government', in H. B. Acton (ed.), *J. S. Mill: Utilitarianism, On Liberty and Considerations on Representative Government* (London: Dent, 1972), p. 367.

27. Ibid. p. 367.

28. P. Williams, *Politics in Post-War France: Parties and the Constitution in the Fourth Republic* (London: Longmans, Green, 1958), pp. 156–7, p. 231.
29. A. Headlam-Morley, *The New Democratic Constitutions of Europe: A Comparative Study of Post-War European Constitutions With Special Reference to Germany, Czechoslovakia, Poland, Finland, the Kingdom of the Serbs, Croats and Slovenes and the Baltic States* (London: Oxford University Press, 1928).
30. Constitution of Ireland, Art. 13.2.2.
31. R. Elgie and P. Fitzgerald, 'The president and the Taoiseach', in J. Coakley and M. Gallagher (eds), *Politics in the Republic of Ireland*, 4th edn (Abingdon: Routledge, 2007), ch. 11, pp. 305–27, p. 308.
32. J. Casey, *Constitutional Law in Ireland* (London: Sweet and Maxwell, 1992), p. 72.
33. Ibid. pp. 72–3.
34. M. Gallagher, 'Parliament', in J. Coakley and M. Gallagher (eds), *Politics in the Republic of Ireland*, 4th edn (Abingdon: Routledge, 2007), ch. 8, p. 217.
35. Ireland's provisions concerning presidential refusal of a requested dissolution are complicated by the fact that the Irish Constitution does not clearly specify the circumstances in which a government can be deemed to have lost the support of a majority in the Dáil. If the government is defeated on a specific motion of confidence, or on the budget, then the right of the president to exercise his or her discretion is quite evident. Other more ambivalent situations, however, are likely to draw the president into political controversy. It is notable that, to avoid such controversy, the 1997 Constitution Review Group recommended divesting the president of this discretionary power and adopting a 'constructive vote of no confidence' procedure instead (Constitutional Review Group, 1997, 26).
36. W. E. Bulmer, 'Constrained majoritarianism: Westminster constitutionalism in Malta', *Commonwealth and Comparative Politics*, 51/1 (2014), 232–53.
37. SNP, *A Free Scotland*, Art. III, Sect. 6.
38. Scotland Act 1998, Sect. 3.
39. R. Hazell, *The Political Rights of Constitutional Reform*, Stevenson Lecture at the University of Glasgow, 2 November 2010.
40. Scotland Act 1998, Sect. 3.
41. SNP, *A Free Scotland*, Art. III, Sect. 6.
42. N. C. M. Elder, *The Government in Sweden: The Executive at Work* (Oxford and New York: Pergamon Press, 1970), pp. 59–60; O. Nyman, 'Some basic features of Swedish constitutional law', in S. Strömholm (ed.), *An Introduction to Swedish Law*, 2nd edn (Stockholm: Norstedt, 1988), p. 65.
43. T. Bergman, T. (2003) 'Sweden: from separation of power to parliamentary supremacy – and back again?' in K. Strøm, W. C. Müller and T. Bergman (eds), *Delegation and Accountability in Parliamentary Democracies*, Comparative Politics (Oxford: Oxford University Press, 2003), p. 604.
44. An early election was nearly held in 2015, following the inability of the coalition of Social Democrats and Greens to pass the budget; in the event, the election was not held, because the government reached an agreement with the opposition parties to support the budget in return for specific policy concessions.
45. E. Holmberg and N. Stjernquist, *The Constitution of Sweden* (Stockholm: Swedish Riksdag, 1995), p. 29.

46. SNP, *A Free Scotland*, Art. III, Sect. 7.
47. J. Adams [1776], *Thoughts on Government* <http://press-pubs.uchicago.edu/founders/documents/v1ch4s5.html> (last accessed 10 March 2011).
48. T. Bergman, W. Müller, K. Strøm and M. Blombren, 'Democratic delegation and accountability: cross-national patterns', in K. Strøm, W. C. Müller and T. Bergman (eds), *Delegation and Accountability in Parliamentary Democracies*, Comparative Politics (Oxford: Oxford University Press, 2003), pp. 131–3.
49. N. MacCormick, 'Is there a constitutional path to Scottish independence?'.
50. A. R. Myers, *Parliaments and Estates in Europe to 1789* (London: Thames and Hudson, 1975).
51. J. H. Burton, *The History of Scotland, From Agricola's Invasion to the Extinction of the Last Jacobite Insurrection* (Edinburgh and London: William Blackwood, 1901).
52. R. Moffat (ed.), *Scotland's Constitution* (Glasgow: Moffat Press, 1993); W. E. Bulmer, 'An analysis of the Scottish National Party's Draft Constitution for Scotland', *Parliamentary Affairs*, 64/4 (2011), 674–93.
53. N. MacCormick, personal communication (interview), 2008.
54. C. M. G. Himsworth and C. M. O'Neill, *Scotland's Constitution: Law and Practice* (Haywards Heath: Bloomsbury Professional, 2009), pp. 86–7.
55. N. MacCormick, 'An idea for a Scottish constitution'; SNP, *The Parliament and Constitution of an Independent Scotland*; SNP, *A Free Scotland*.
56. A. Lijphart, *Patterns of Democracy*, pp. 203–11.
57. R. Hazell, 'Conclusion: where will the Westminster model end up?' in R. Hazell (ed.), *Constitutional Futures Revised: Britain's Constitution to 2020* (Basingstoke: Palgrave Macmillan, 2008), p. 297.
58. B. Ackerman, 'The new separation of powers', *Harvard Law Review*, 113/3 (2000), pp. 633–729; P. Pettit, *A Theory of Freedom: From the Psychology to the Politics of Agency* (Cambridge and Oxford: Polity Press, 2001); W. Riker, 'The justification of bicameralism', *International Political Science Review*, 12/1 (1992), pp. 101–16.
59. N. MacCormick, 'An idea for a Scottish constitution', p. 166.
60. SNP, *A Free Scotland*, p. 4.
61. SNP, *A Free Scotland*, Art. 10.
62. J. Fitzmaurice, *Politics in Denmark* (London: Hurst, 1981), p. 63.
63. M. Qvortrup, *A Comparative Study of Referendums: Government by the People* (Manchester: Manchester University Press, 2005), p. 131.
64. Ibid. p. 131.
65. W. E. Bulmer, 'Minority veto referendums: an alternative to bicameralism', *Politics*, 31/3 (2011), 107–20, 111.
66. P. Pettit, *Republicanism: A Theory of Freedom and Government* (Oxford: Oxford University Press, 1997).
67. W. E. Bulmer, 'Minority veto referendums'.
68. B. Manin, *The Principles of Representative Government* (Cambridge: Cambridge University Press, 1997).
69. W. E. Bulmer, 'Minority veto referendums', p. 118.
70. Ibid. pp. 118–19.
71. N. MacCormick, 'An idea for a Scottish constitution'.

72. New South Wales Constitution Act 1902, Section 5B.

73. Cayman Islands Constitution Order, Section 69.

74. For a fuller discussion on the potential for direct democracy in Scotland and a wider range of non-Westminster examples, see W. E. Bulmer, *A Constitution for the Common Good: Strengthening Scottish Democracy After the Independence Referendum*, 2nd edn (Edinburgh: Luath Press, 2015).

75. SNP, *A Free Scotland*, Art. III, Sect. 10.

76. Ibid. Art. III, Sect. 10.

77. Ibid. Art. III, Sect. 10.

78. N. MacCormick, 'An idea for a Scottish constitution'.

79. SNP, *A Free Scotland*, Art. III, Sect. 10.

80. D. Arter, *The Scottish Parliament: A Scandinavian-Style Assembly?* (London: Frank Cass, 2004), pp. 109–11.

81. Ibid. p. 11.

82. A. Lijphart, *Patterns of Democracy*, pp. 171–84.

83. SNP, *A Free Scotland*, Art. III, Sect. 10.

84. Standing Orders of the Scottish Parliament, 2011, Rule 6.3.

85. D. Arter, *The Scottish Parliament: A Scandinavian-Style Assembly?*, p. 12.

86. R. Taagepera, 'The size of national assemblies', *Social Science Research*, 1 (December 1972), 385–400.

87. K. Wright, personal communication, 2009.

88. D. Arter, *The Scottish Parliament: A Scandinavian-Style Assembly?*

89. SNP, *The Parliament and Constitution of an Independent Scotland*.

90. N. MacCormick, 'An idea for a Scottish constitution'.

91. D. Arter, *The Scottish Parliament: A Scandinavian-Style Assembly?*, p. 12.

92. R. Moffat, *Scotland's Constitution*.

93. D. Arter, *The Scottish Parliament: A Scandinavian-Style Assembly?*, p. 12.

94. Scottish Parliament, 'The Presiding Officer', 2012 <http://www.scottish.parlia ment.uk/abouttheparliament/22008.aspx> (last accessed 9 September 2012).

95. R. Moffat, *Scotland's Constitution*.

96. SNP, *A Free Scotland*, Art. III, Sect. 12.

97. Constitution of Malta, Art. 65.

98. Scotland Act 1998, Sect. 41.

99. SNP, *A Free Scotland*, Art. 2, Sect. 4.

100. M. Gallagher, 'The Oireachtas: president and parliament', in J. Coakley and M. Gallagher (eds), *Politics in the Republic of Ireland*, 5th edn (Abingdon: Routledge, 2010), ch. 7, p. 218.

101. B. Chubb, *Cabinet Government in Ireland* (Dublin: Institute of Public Administration, 1974), p. 65.

102. B. Chubb, *The Government and Politics of Ireland*, p. 199.

103. Ibid. p. 194.

104. N. Collins, 'Parliamentary democracy in Ireland', *Parliamentary Affairs*, 57/3 (2004), p. 611.

105. B. Chubb, *The Government and Politics of Ireland*, p. 65.

106. P. Norton, 'Playing by the rules: the constraining hand of parliamentary proce-dure', *Journal of Legislative Studies*, 7/3 (2001), pp. 13–33.

2002 DRAFT II:
HEAD OF STATE AND THE EXECUTIVE BRANCH

This chapter discusses the position of the head of state and the executive in the SNP's 2002 constitutional draft. The draft proposes a constitutional monarchy, in which the office of Head of State is vested in Elizabeth Windsor and descends to 'her successors as determined by the law of Scotland, acting in right of Scotland'.[1] At the same time, it provides an explicitly parliamentary form of government, in which many – although not all – of the conventional relationships characterising parliamentary democracy are constitutionally prescribed.

In analysing this combination of monarchy and parliamentarism, this chapter relies upon two key distinctions. The first is the distinction between the symbolic nature of monarchy (that is, the monarch as an iconic, ceremonial totem, who lends a romantic and quasi-sacred legitimacy to the state) and the constitutional function of the Head of State (as an office holder invested with specified powers under a democratic, parliamentary Constitution).

The second, related, distinction is that which exists between the powers of the Crown (the legal entity), which are largely exercised by the ministers, and the discretionary powers of the monarch (the person). Much confusion arises, in popular polemic debate between royalists and republicans, from a failure to appreciate these distinctions. One may, for example, support the symbolic monarchy as a Ciceronian moral rector, or as the embodiment of idealised Christian virtues,[2] whilst combining such ceremonial royalism with 'republican' principles that are opposed both to the Crown's prerogative powers[3] and to all forms of arbitrary power, both public and private.[4] This seemingly dichotomous position – simultaneously royalist and anti-monarchical – has a long history. It was, for example, the position taken by Henry Neville in his plans for the reform of the English system of government after the Restoration at the end of the civil wars,[5] by Andrew Fletcher of Saltoun in his proposals for a Scottish constitutional settlement before the Union,[6] and by Viscount Vilain in his decision, at the Belgian Constituent Assembly of 1830/1, to accept monarchy 'on the most liberal, the most republican, the most popular principles'.[7]

With these distinctions in mind, the first part of this chapter is dedicated to a discussion of the symbolic nature of the Scottish monarchy as envisaged by the draft Constitution. It argues that there is a deep ambivalence in the SNP's approach to the monarchy, combining an attempt to recast the institution in a democratic, national, ecumenical guise, while at the same time maintaining it as a symbol of legitimacy and continuity that binds Scotland to a wider British identity and maintains, albeit at a very subtle level, the 'Protestant' character of the state.

The second part of the chapter then charts the boundaries of the respective powers of the head of state and government as proposed in the draft. The argument advanced here is that the draft Constitution fails to define the extent of the head of state's personal prerogative in relation to three key areas: (2) nominating a prime minister in default of an election by parliament; (2) dissolving parliament if no prime minister able to enjoy the confidence of a majority can be appointed; and (3) refusing assent to legislation. It suggests that these uncertainties are problematic, and could lead to constitutional crises that a more robust constitutional design might easily avoid.

A Democratic and Non-sectarian Monarchy?

The SNP's decision to support the monarchy was written into the draft Constitution in 1977.[8] This decision was made after strong debate inside the SNP, as the party has long had a vociferous republican element within it, and has on occasion even had to expel republican dissent on its left wing.[9] That a party which has as its main aim Scottish independence should, despite the many republicans in its ranks, retain a formal loyalty to the British monarchy, has been portrayed by some – both for and against Scottish independence – as a sign of lukewarmness. It makes more sense, however, once one recalls that the party's original objective, at its founding in 1934, was to obtain for Scotland the same 'dominion status' within the British Empire that Australia, Canada, New Zealand, South Africa and the Irish Free State then enjoyed.[10] This basic constitutional position has remained remarkably constant ever since.[11] Moreover, the monarchy ties an independent Scotland not to the United Kingdom as currently constituted, but to a wider 'British' identity in which Scotland would have a continued share.[12] This identity has global dimensions, connecting Scotland to countries that have traditionally been lands of Scottish settlers, and which have been shaped by the Scottish diaspora.

The SNP's official commitment to the monarchy can be explained by two further considerations. The first is a pragmatic calculation, inspired by the desire to secure potential electoral support. As discussed in Chapter 3, there is a substantial block of opinion in Scotland, concentrated in (although not wholly confined to) the West Central Belt, and traditionally associated with the Rangers football club and the Orange lodges, that maintains a visceral loyalty to the Union, the Union flag, and the Protestant nature of the British state which is embodied by the monarchy.[13] By maintaining the monarchy after independence, the SNP hopes to mollify – or at least not to alienate – this block, reassuring them that a residually 'British' and culturally 'Protestant' identity may continue to be expressed through the personal Union of the Crowns, even after Scotland attains independence.

The second consideration may be termed 'romantic'. Its appeal is not to the 'British' monarchy, bound up with imperial traditions, but to the 'Scottish' monarchy that pre-dates the Union. According to this view, independence means the restoration of the 'Kingdom of Scots' that was lost by the Union and the re-formation of a Scottish State, at the hand of which will stand the Queen of Scots, 'restored' to her rightful inheritance:

> Those who find it surprising that the Scottish National Party ex-presses allegiance to the present royal house ought perhaps to remind themselves that it is a house which enjoys a much more ancient and uninterrupted title in right of Scotland than in right of any other part of the UK.[14]

Thus monarchism within the SNP has a profoundly ambiguous character. In appealing to the (probably ageing and dwindling number of) romantic nationalists within its old base, the monarchy is portrayed as an indigenous Scottish institution that an independent state will restore to its proper title and dignity – with the queen taking the traditional Scots title of 'Her Grace, Elizabeth I, Queen of Scots'. In reaching out beyond this base, to reassure those with a 'British', 'Unionist' or even 'Orange' identity, the monarchy is portrayed as a residually imperial institution, upholding both Protestant identity and the continuing social and cultural union with the wider 'British' and 'Commonwealth' spheres.

The text of the draft Constitution reveals these tensions concerning the 'British' and 'Scottish' characters of the monarchy. The personal union of the crowns is maintained, but it is a matter of historical accident, and not essential to the Constitution itself. Following the pattern of modern democratic monarchies such as Belgium,[15] the Constitution creates the office of head of state and vests hereditary rights in the monarch by an explicit constitutional delegation, while reserving to parliament the right to alter the law of succession.[16] Despite the conventional force of the Statute of Westminster, the personal union could be ended by a unilateral decision of Scotland's parliament.[17]

This means that a Scottish monarchy would not solely be an imperial remnant, as it was in the Ireland (1922–37) or Malta (1964–74), but could also have a 'national' and even 'democratic' character, because the monarch's legitimacy would be derived, under the Constitution, from the people. The Queen of Scots would not be 'the sovereign', as sovereignty (both in the political sense of being the ultimate source of legitimacy and the legal sense of having the authority to make constitutional law) resides solely in the people. The queen would be merely a constitutional public officer, deriving the chiefly ceremonial office of Head of State from the sovereign people in accordance with the Constitution and the law, and differing from other public officers only in the hereditary tenure and limited powers of the office.

In establishing a monarchy (the institution) that is both national and democratic, while retaining, for the time being, the British monarch (the person), the SNP's 2002 draft leaves a number of questions concerning the symbolic and ceremonial role of the monarch in the public life of Scotland open. In particular, the religious character of the monarchy is not defined. The succession is governed by the 'law of Scotland' – which, at the moment of independence, would presumably continue to include the provisions of the Act of Settlement barring Roman Catholics from the throne (the 1702 Act of Settlement was an Act of the English Parliament, but effectively incorporated into the law of Scotland by the Treaty of Union). However, the draft Constitution does not give the Act of Settlement any special status. If this is the case, then the parliament of Scotland could, in future, legislate to remove the ban on Roman Catholics inheriting the throne.

Similarly, the draft Constitution makes no mention of any accession declaration or coronation oath to be taken by future Kings and Queens of Scots. At present, these statements define the Protestant character of the monarchy, pledging the queen to 'maintain the Laws of God and the true profession of the Gospel' and to uphold 'the Protestant Reformed Religion established by law'.[18] Therefore, as Norman Bonney writes:

> There remains the possibility that the eventual proposals for an independent Scotland would insist, in line with the Scottish Parliament resolution of 1999, that the succession to the throne of Scotland should be non-discriminatory in religious terms, thus removing the exclusion from the succession to the throne of those in line who might have other denominations or faiths not in communion with the Church of England or no religion at all. This would mean that a Roman Catholic, a Muslim, a Mormon or an atheist might occupy the throne of Scotland and the line of succession to the thrones of Scotland and the remainder of the United Kingdom could eventually diverge.[19]

Yet it is notable that the draft Constitution, while not confirming the Protestant character of the Scottish state, does not deny it either. The Constitution does not, for example, explicitly repeal those parts of the Act of Settlement that are offensive to secular or Catholic sensibilities, nor does it prescribe a purely secular oath of office. In these respects, the draft Constitution enshrines ambiguity. It allows for a democratic, national and non-sectarian monarchy to be held by a British Protestant monarch. In this way, the draft Constitution avoids making fundamental or decisive statements about the nature of the State, leaving these questions open for on-going discussion and resolution.[20]

Written constitutions can be seen as both: (1) 'charters of government', that define the institutions of government, regulate political procedures, and protect the basic rights of citizens; and (2) 'national covenants', that seek to define the nation and to proclaim its purposes and values.[21] This means that constitutions can be very specific in some aspects, and vague or ambiguous in other aspects: for example, a constitution may leave questions of identity and ultimate ends open for wide-ranging public debate, while taking care to specify institutional or procedural matters with great clarity.[22] According to Hannah Lerner, there is sometimes an advantage to leaving questions of identity open, if leaving them open is the price to pay for getting agreement on the key structural and procedural aspects of the Constitution.[23] This relates to Cass Sunstein's notion of 'imperfectly theorized agreements': people from different ideological trends or subcultures may agree, on essentially pragmatic grounds, on institutional forms and constitutional rules, even while disagreeing on the reasons why those forms and rules are valuable.[24]

As argued in Chapter 3, Scotland's current political division into 'national-ist' and 'unionist' camps, overlaid with other sectarian, secular–religious and ideological cleavages, means that a Scottish Constitution would have to be – above all – a pragmatic liberal procedural document, in which democratic decision-making structures and basic rights are maintained despite disagree-ment over questions of religion, national identity or ultimate ends. This is not, of course, the same as saying that the Constitution should not have any pre-scriptive content, still less that it should proclaim liberalism in the ideological, economic or philosophical sense, but only that the constitution must accom-modate itself to the plurality of identities and ends in society, and provide forums through which these can be democratically reconciled.

In establishing a monarchy based on an ambiguous compromise between democratic, national and ecumenical principles, on the one hand, and British-imperial, Unionist and Protestant principles, on the other – while at the same time making parliamentary democracy the operative basis of the political system, the SNP's draft Constitution could well be an example of 'the form of government that divides us least' (to borrow Thiers' famous description of the French Third Republic).[25]

If so, the provisions of the draft Constitution with respect to the monarchy are not only viable and acceptable, but also an indication of the SNP's prag-matic and inclusive approach to the problem of gaining support and legitimacy for a Scottish state. The success of the monarchy as a unifying agent, which might help to smooth the transition to independence, would depend, however, on how the monarchy is portrayed in the public theatre of political symbolism. If such a constitution were ever to be adopted in an independent Scotland, it would be the responsibility of the Scottish government (through personal advice to the monarch tendered by the Prime Minister of Scotland, appointments to the royal household in Scotland, and ministerial control of royal protocol) to make constructive use of these constitutional ambiguities, and to decide how the two aspects of the monarchy (its democratic, national, non-sectarian aspect, and its British-imperial, Unionist, Protestant aspect) can be reconciled in practice.

A hint at how this could be developed can be seen in the difference between the State Opening of Parliament at Westminster, which is steeped in the tradi-tions of imperial monarchy, and the rather more low key public ceremonies surrounding the opening of the Scottish Parliament. If this is a reliable indica-tion, we might expect the Scottish monarchy to develop into a more 'national' and 'democratic' institution over time. It is even possible to imagine it develop-ing into a more 'ecumenical' institution, if a future parliament of Scotland (and this is all, of course, highly speculative) were to amend the coronation oath. Yet, so long as the personal union between the monarch of Scotland and that of the other Commonwealth realms remains, the fundamental ambiguity will not disappear: even if the Queen of Scots, in her constitutional position and in the ceremonial of her office, represents a national, democratic and ecumenical monarchy, she will continue, in her person, to represent a wider, British-imperial identity too. This would reflect the nested, multi-faceted nature of Scottish identity itself.

Head of State and Government

The remainder of this chapter discusses the powers and duties vested in the head of state and government under the SNP's draft Constitution. This discussion centres on two provisions of the text. The first of these is Article II, §4, by which all prerogative powers that were previously vested in the Crown in right of the United Kingdom are transferred to the Crown in right of Scotland:

> The residual powers of the Executive in Scotland at the date at which this Constitution comes into force shall be identical with the prerogatives of the Crown existing in the United Kingdom of Great Britain and Northern Ireland according to the law of Scotland immediately prior to that time, with the exception of any right, power or liberty or immunity belonging to the prerogative of the Crown which would be inconsistent with the provisions of this Constitution. Acts of the Parliament of Scotland shall override the residual powers of the Executive in any case of inconsistency.[26]

The second relevant provision is Article II, §3, which states:

> The Head of State shall be responsible for the exercise of all lawful governmental functions in Scotland, excepting functions expressly delegated to Ministers or other public authorities. The Head of State shall exercise such functions only upon the advice of his or her Ministers who shall be chosen from among the Members of, and who shall be directly answerable to, the Parliament of Scotland, and who shall be selected with a view to their ability to command and retain the confidence of Parliament, and whose appointment shall be confirmed by Parliament.[27]

Together, these provisions create a powerful 'Crown', the powers of which are exercised, in accordance with the Westminster tradition, on the advice of ministers responsible to Parliament.[28] It is by no means certain, however, that the head of state must always act upon, and be bound by, ministerial advice. The head of state in many parliamentary democracies is not only a symbolic totem, whose functions end with being the 'chief ribbon cutter'.[29] Rather, the head of state is a constitutional official, who possesses a neutral, 'moderating' power.[30] This may require the head of state, on 'highly charged' occasions, to take important 'public politico-constitutional decisions' according to his or her 'own deliberate judgment'.[31]

The degree of discretionary power allowed to constitutional monarchs in contemporary democracies varies. The monarch in the Netherlands is technically part of the government, and used to have extensive personal involvement in the complex process of government formation in a multi-party system.[32,33] In contrast, the King of Sweden is denied even theoretical executive power, and has no personal discretionary powers. He cannot dissolve the Riksdag, takes no part in the formation of a government and cannot grant — or withhold — assent to laws. His role is reduced, in law as well as in practice, to 'representational duties only',[34] such as declaring the opening of the Riksdag each year.[35]

As noted in Chapter 2, the approach of early Westminster-derived Constitutions such as those of Canada and Australia, was to leave the extent of the personal discretionary powers of the queen (or, rather, of the governor general) undefined in the text of the Constitution, and to allow the office, and its relationship with both the government and parliament, to develop in accordance with the unwritten conventions and traditions of the United Kingdom. Although this allowed for the rise of 'responsible government' – that is, government led by a prime minister and cabinet enjoying the confidence of the popular chamber – it has also had the consequence of greatly increasing the power of the prime minister in relation to the rest of the political system (since it is the prime minister, in many cases, who has inherited the prerogative powers of the Crown).[36]

The 'reserve' or 'discretionary' power of the head of state or the governor general in these early Constitutions is doubtful, disputed and undefined.[37] This weakens the procedural certainty of the Constitution, leading to crises of authority at the very moments when certainty is most needed (of which the 1977 Kerr–Whitlam crisis in Australia, is perhaps the most notorious example). Later Constitutions, such as those of Malta (1964) or St Lucia (1978), reduce this uncertainty, making a clearer distinction between the functions of the head of state and those of the government. Where certain reserve or discretionary powers are vested in the head of state, the extent of these powers and the circumstances of their legitimate use are precisely stated so as to avoid, as far as possible, constitutional crises.

The SNP's draft Constitution occupies an intermediate position between these constitutional types. It was intended to restrict the head of state to a 'ceremonial role rather than a position of power'.[38] Unlike in the Netherlands and Australia, where the parliamentary system rests solely on convention, the draft Constitution makes an explicit commitment to parliamentary government. The principle that the head of state acts only on the 'advice' (that is, binding direction) of ministers is unequivocally stated, and is coupled with the equally explicit principle that ministers are 'responsible' to parliament (that is, attain and remain in office only if they are supported by the confidence of parliament).[39] On the other hand, unlike the Maltese and Swedish Constitutions, where the head of state's discretionary powers are either explicitly abolished or narrowly defined, the SNP's draft leaves some questions of discretionary power unresolved.

There are three areas where this lack of precise resolution is most apparent, and where the consequences of a lack of constitutional precision are most serious: firstly, in the formation of government; secondly, in the dissolution of parliament if a government cannot be formed; and thirdly, in the refusal of assent to legislation. The first two of these are related, since the draft Constitution, as discussed in the previous chapter, limits premature dissolutions of parliament to situations in which a government cannot be formed;

these are covered in the remainder of this section. The third, refusal of assent, is covered in the next section.

The procedure for government formation (that is, for appointing the prime minister and ministers) proposed in the 2002 draft Constitution seems straightforward on first sight, since the head of state is effectively bound to appoint as prime minister the person who is elected to that office by a parliamentary vote:

> The Head of State shall appoint as Prime Minister whichever person being a Member of the Parliament of Scotland is elected by Parliament to serve in that office.[40]

As a variation on the Westminster system, this is remarkable. The formal election of the prime minister by parliament is a form of 'positive parliamentarism', since the government may take office only with the active support of the parliament.[41] This practice, which is also found in the devolved Scottish Parliament,[42] serves a number of symbolic purposes, besides limiting the personal discretion of the head of state in cases where a coalition must be formed. As Nyman notes, discussing similar provisions in the Constitution of Sweden, election provides democratic legitimation, demonstrating that the government derives its authority from parliament, and not from the king.[43] It also forces the parties to '[show] openly whether or not they tolerate a new cabinet before it forms'.[44]

The election of a prime minister by parliament can be described as a 'formal' election, because the chamber is rarely in a position to make a real choice; as Coakley remarks, in his study of Irish practice, in most cases the parliament 'simply registers the result of the proceeding general election by nominating the party leader who "won" that election'.[45] In some cases, however, Ireland's parliament does take a more active role in government formation: the selection of Garret FitzGerald to replace Charles Haughey in 1981 involved the Dáil members in 'hard post-election bargaining' and 'extensive negotiations'.[46] Yet even if the election has a 'formal' character most of the time, requiring an election is a good constitutional practice which ensures a legitimate and unambiguous process for the handover of power – a feature which, as Coakley argues, is 'particularly useful in countries where proportional electoral systems produce multi-party parliaments and where the identity of the premier-designate is not always apparent in advance'.[47]

Thus the principle of formal election by parliament stated in the SNP's draft is laudable. The procedure by which this election is to take place, however, is not specified. Nothing in the SNP's draft Constitution reveals whether the voting is to be open or by secret ballot, whether the election is to take place in one round or in several rounds, or whether an ordinary or absolute majority is required. In this respect the draft differs from some of the more recent Westminster-derived Constitutions, such as those of the Solomon Islands and of the Cayman Islands, where the rules and procedures for the election of a prime minister are specified in detail.

The SNP's draft therefore leaves scope for procedural uncertainty, which a good Constitution ought to minimise.[48] It is possible, for example, that a candidate for prime minister could win the support of a plurality of members of parliament, but not a majority; this, the supporters of that candidate might claim, is a valid election for the purposes of the Constitution; their opponents, meanwhile, might dispute the validity of such election, and demand a second round of voting to establish a clear majority. There is no way of knowing, from the text of the draft Constitution alone, who would be in the right in such a case.

The text of the Constitution would therefore have to be supplemented by law, parliamentary Standing Orders, or well-established conventions, in order to make the Constitution's provisions concerning the election of a prime minister by parliament sufficiently clear, robust, and workable. These provisions are part of the 'real constitution', as defined in the first chapter, even if not part of the 'Constitution as supreme law'. Provided that these instruments are in place, the lack of constitutional specification of the electoral process for the prime minister is not, in itself, necessarily problematic: the Scotland Act (§s 45–46), is equally imprecise for example, but its lack of precision is corrected by the Standing Orders, which prescribe a robust and unambiguous procedure for electing the first minister (§s 4.1 and 11.10). It might reasonably be assumed, working from historical institutional premises about the 'stickability' of institutions and of procedural rules in particular,[49] that current practices would be carried over into the new Constitution with minimal change; if so, that would most likely provide an adequate – if imperfect – solution to the problem.

Less satisfactory is the way in which the draft Constitution deals with situations in which a prime minister cannot be elected. It is here that the ambiguous power of the head of state becomes problematic. 'In default' of an election by parliament, the head of state is empowered to appoint as prime minister the member of parliament who 'in the opinion of the Head of State is best able to command the confidence of Parliament'.[50] This means that if parliament cannot agree on the election of a prime minister, or fails to elect a prime minister, the requirement for a formal election lapses, and the head of state has the discretion to appoint the prime minister.

The intention, clearly, is to ensure that 'the Queen's government is carried on', and that there is never a long vacancy in the office of prime minister. On closer inspection, however, this way of resolving an inconclusive prime ministerial election creates more problems than it solves. It is nowhere specified what conditions might be regarded as placing the election of a prime minister 'in default'. Is the election 'in default' if parliament fails to elect a prime minister within three months after a general election, or within three weeks, or three days, or three hours? After how long would the personal intervention of the head of state go from being an unconstitutional and unseemly interference in parliament's right of free election to being a necessary and legitimate exercise of the power of arbitration? These questions are unanswered by the text of the draft Constitution, which specifies no time limit.

Moreover, it is not clear, within a constitutional scheme in which the head of state acts on the advice of ministers, who has the power to act in this case. Could the head of state decide for herself or himself when the moment to intervene in the appointment a prime minister has come, or would this decision be dependent on the advice of the incumbent prime minister?

Neil MacCormick, being interviewed on the text of the draft, was unspecific on these points, insisting only that 'the usual conventions of parliamentary democracy would apply'.[51] Those conventions are doubtful, however, and there is no guarantee that a convention developed under the British constitution would apply under the written (but in this particular aspect, patchy) rules of the Scottish Constitution. That is to say, there exists a risk that the written rule of the Constitution, requiring the head of state to act always on ministerial advice, will come into contact with the conventional, vague, but sensible notion that such advice cannot be taken from a minister who has lost the confidence of parliament and is unable to form a government.

The difficulty is compounded by the fact that any action or inaction by the head of state, whether taken on the advice or without the advice of the incumbent prime minister, is open to question. It is easy to imagine a scenario in which a general election produces an inconclusive result, requiring the delicate negotiation of a coalition. Perhaps the negotiations stall, or take longer than usual. The people are anxious for a government. The bond markets are jittery. In this situation, the head of state might decide that the time has come to bring an end to the impasse, to declare the election to be 'in default'. Then the head of state may exercise the right either to appoint a prime minister under Article II, §5 of the Constitution, if the head of state thinks that such a prime minister can (for a while at least) hold together a governing majority, or else to appoint an interim prime minister and dissolve parliament under Article III, §6.

It appears from one reading of the Constitution (which would take the requirement to act only on ministerial advice, as stated in Article II, §3 in its broadest sense) that the head of state can only do this on the advice of the existing (potentially 'defeated') prime minister – in which case, the incumbent or 'outgoing' prime minister has a great advantage in coalition negotiations, since he or she has the ability to bring these negotiations to an end at any time.

Another reading would take Article II, §5 (on the head of state's right to appoint a prime minister in default of an election by parliament) and Article III, §6 (on the head of state's right to dissolve parliament if a government enjoying the confidence of parliament cannot be formed) as exceptions to the general rule of acting only on ministerial advice. By this latter reading, the head of state would be within her or his rights to refuse to act on the advice of the prime minister in such circumstances, allowing the coalition negotiations to work their course and denying the incumbent such advantage. On the other hand, if this latter reading is accepted, then the head of state would be able to intervene at will – either by appointing a prime minister, or by appointing an interim prime minister and then dissolving parliament – without waiting for the advice of the outgoing or incumbent prime minister; this would give the head of state a personal influence over coalition formation, since she or he would then be in a position to terminate the negotiations at any time.

Most of the time, of course, this is likely to be unproblematic. It may never be problematic, if additional rules are introduced, by legislation or by Standing Orders, regulating the process of elections and clarifying both the circumstances in which the election of a prime minister is deemed to be 'in default' (Article II, §5) and those in which a prime minister 'able to command the confidence of Parliament' cannot be found (Article III, §6). It seems ill-advised, however, for a new Constitution to leave such technical but critical aspects of procedure unresolved, and thus, potentially, to store up problems for the future. If these matters are unresolved (and it is the sort of issue which is likely to be low on any government's immediate list of priorities, until it is too late), then there is a risk that a constitutional crisis might occur, pitting the constitutional authority of the head of state against that of the prime minister at a time of division and confusion when the weakness of the Constitution would be most exposed. The draft Constitution must therefore be deemed somewhat deficient in this respect.

A further confusion is introduced by Article II, §3, which states that ministers other than the prime minister shall be 'selected with a view to their ability to command and retain the confidence of Parliament', and that their 'appointment shall be confirmed by Parliament'.[52] The best sense that can be made of the text is that the need for a confirmatory vote of parliament is absolute: it applies at all times, and no exception is made for those circumstances where the head of state, 'in default of an election', nominates the prime minister. Thus, the provisions described above, regarding the appointment of the prime minister, would be rather nugatory in effect: no workable government could be formed without its ministers having first received a formal vote of investiture.

These defects could easily be rectified. In Sweden, for example, the king plays no part in the government formation process, the initiative being transferred to the Speaker, who consults with the representatives of the parliamentary parties, and must then nominate a prime ministerial candidate for acceptance or rejection by the whole Riksdag.[53] If the candidate is rejected by an absolute majority of the Riksdag (that is, by 175 of the 349 available votes), the Speaker must nominate another candidate. This may continue for four nominations, after which, if all nominees are rejected, the Riksdag is automatically dissolved, without any intervention by the king; the government formation process recommences only after the general election. If not rejected, the candidate is deemed to have been appointed, and the Speaker – not the king – issues the prime minister's letter of appointment.[54] Malta, meanwhile takes an opposite course, making it explicit that the governor general (1964–74) or president (from 1974) has the undisputed right to appoint as prime minister the member of parliament who, according to his or her personal discretion, best enjoys the confidence of the majority.[55] Either of these two contrasting approaches would avoid the risk of confusion and dispute that is written into the SNP's draft. Of the two, the Swedish system is probably more suitable for Scotland, in so far as it insulates the monarch, who is supposed to be impartial, from all potential controversy.

Yet Scotland need not even look as far afield as Sweden for a solution to this problem. Scotland already has a tried, tested and robust process for the formation of a government. This creates a strict but realistic timetable for the election of a first minister by parliament within twenty-eight days after a general election or after the resignation or removal of the former first minister,[56] with a dissolution and general election held if parliament has not made the nomination during this time.[57] These provisions, together with those laid down in Sections 4.1 and 11.10 of the Standing Orders, exclude the head of state from the government formation process, limiting the queen's role to that of making a formal appointment based on parliament's elective nomination. The queen is thereby protected from the potential controversy of either having to act on her own initiative (which could be perceived as undemocratic and illegitimate in the absence of a clear constitutional mandate) or having to take the advice of an incumbent (or outgoing) first minister. Moreover, the rules currently in effect enable the appointment of minority governments, since they give a first minister supported by a plurality of MSPs an unequivocal parliamentary mandate.

Finally, the SNP's draft Constitution is unclear on the removal, tenure and resignation of the prime minister and other ministers. Article II indicates that ministers must enjoy the confidence of parliament, not only at the time of their appointment, but also during their continuance in office: ministers are to be 'selected with a view to their ability to command and retain the confidence of parliament' and are to be 'directly answerable to the Parliament'.[58] The implication of this is that those who lose confidence must resign, and that answerability involves the ability of parliament to remove ministers by a vote of no confidence. At no point does the draft Constitution explicitly state, however, that ministers must resign or be removed from office if a vote of no confidence is passed, nor is the process for holding votes of no confidence anywhere specified.

A consequence of this ambiguity is that it could, as in Ireland where a similar rule applies,[59] enable the government itself to treat every parliamentary defeat as a loss of confidence, and thereby force parliament into compliance. As Gruijters writes, commenting on similar provisions in the Netherlands, an unclear confidence rule can strengthen the hand of the government vis-à-vis parliament, since 'if the cabinet wants to have its way on a certain question, it states that it will regard a contrary decision by the [popular house] as a lack of confidence'.[60] In this respect, also, the draft Constitution is inferior to the provisions of the Scotland Act, which clearly prescribes that the first minister shall resign 'if the Parliament resolves that the Scottish Executive no longer enjoys the confidence of the Parliament'.[61]

Royal Assent

One of the deferential fictions of the traditional Westminster system, in which reality and appearance are so far removed one from the other, is that: (1) no law may be enacted without royal assent, but that (2) the power of the monarch to refuse royal assent to legislation, if it still exists at all, has fallen so far into disuse that its exercise would be almost inconceivable, and would invariably lead to a severe constitutional crisis.

The 2002 draft Constitution for Scotland would do little to resolve this muddle. It provides that royal assent must be given to a bill passed by the Parliament of Scotland in order for it to be enacted into law, but the text of the Constitution does not specify whether the head of state is obliged to grant assent, or whether, in certain extraordinary circumstances, a discretionary power to refuse assent might exist:

all such Acts as are passed in accordance with these procedures shall be submitted to
the Head of State for signification of Assent, and upon signification of such Assent
such Acts shall take effect as laws.[62]

There are two possible ways of reading these provisions. The first possibility is to consider Article III, §10, which refers to royal assent, in conjunction
with Article II, §4. The latter states that the powers of the Crown in Scotland
under the draft Constitution are, unless otherwise altered by Act of Parliament,
'identical with the prerogatives of the Crown existing in [the United Kingdom]
according to the law of Scotland immediately prior to [independence day]'.
This would imply that if the right of the monarch to refuse assent still exists
under the unwritten British Constitution, then an equivalent right would continue to exist under the written Constitution of Scotland. Such a reading shifts
the debate away from the text and into a discussion of the 'propriety' of a royal
veto under the conventional rules of the British system. As Low notes,

> Since 1707 no British monarch has refused assent to an Act of Parliament [. . .]
> though there is much conditional support for the view that this could still quite
> properly happen.[63]

The discussion of whether, when and under what circumstances, if any,
refusal to grant assent would be proper and legitimate is an arcane point of
constitutional rune-reading.[64] If such a discretionary power would exist under
the 2002 draft, then its existence would necessarily modify the general provision that the head of state must act solely and always in accordance with ministerial advice under Article II, §3, and, ultimately, the head of state would be
the judge of the propriety of its use. This would be akin to the situation under
the Constitution of Ceylon, in which the traditional British conventions surrounding the exercise of royal power were given constitutional authority by
reference, although never spelled out, and in which the governor general was
the sole judge of these conventions.[65] This would put the head of state in the
position of a 'guarantor' of the Constitution, of the wider constitutional order,
and of the public good, on the implied condition that assent is refused only in
the most rare and necessary circumstances.

A second possibility is that the provisions of the constitutional text would
overturn any implied conventional restrictions. Article III, §10 therefore maintains and affirms the right of the head of state to refuse assent, because no law
can be enacted without assent, and the text of the Constitution nowhere states
that the head of state is obliged to grant such assent. Adopting this 'strict con-
struction' position consistently, however, would also require Article III, §10
to be read in the context of Article II, §3, which requires the head of state to
act only on ministerial advice, without any implied, conventional exceptions
to that general rule. By this reading, the head of state would have the power
to refuse assent, but only when the refusal is authorised by ministers – a situation which will be highly unlikely in a parliamentary system where the prime
minister usually leads a parliamentary majority.

It should be clear, whichever of these readings is adopted, that the usual pattern should be for the head of state to grant assent to legislation without demur, hesitation or prevarication. In most circumstances, assent will be a symbolic act, which merely 'rubber stamps' the authoritative and final decision of parliament. However, the scope for constitutional crises arising from the existence of a disputed power cannot be entirely ignored.

To see why this constitutional obfuscation matters, the examples of Belgium and Luxembourg are instructive. These countries are both long-established constitutional monarchies, where the principle of ministerial responsibility is well-entrenched, and where the granting of royal assent was (until quite recently) believed to be a merely formal act, in which the king or grand duke had little or no discretionary power.[66] In both countries, however, the monarch has decided to withhold consent to legislation. Notably, they did not do so in defence of basic democratic principles, nor to prevent the passage of an egregiously unconstitutional bill, but to voice their displeasure at bills which offended their personal morality: an abortion bill in Belgium and a euthanasia bill in Luxembourg. In Belgium, the solution was for the king to be found 'incapable of performing his duties', and for the cabinet to grant assent on behalf of the king.[67] In Luxembourg, the solution was to amend the Constitution, ending the grand duke's hitherto undefined veto power,[68] and to stipulate in the Constitution that the grand duke must now grant assent to bills within three months; if he does not do so at the end of that period then the bill will become law, even without his assent, thus transforming a permanent veto into a mostly symbolic three-month suspensive veto.

These examples indicate that even in established democracies, where conventions limiting the monarch are widely respected, a monarch might still invoke the right to refuse assent to legislation. It is not difficult to imagine a future King of Scots threatening – however unwisely – to refuse assent to legislation that offends his personal views or interests, and this is a problem that constitution-drafters ought to anticipate and address.

In particular, the draft Constitution is markedly inferior to some of the more recent Westminster-derived Constitutions, which are constructed to avoid any room for confusion on this point. In the 1964 Constitution of Malta, for example, the governor general was constitutionally required to grant assent to all legislation passed by parliament 'without delay'.[69] Any possibility of discretionary authority is explicitly removed from the Constitution, such that the expression of assent is reduced to a mere formality; the only option open to a governor general (or, since 1974, a president) who could not in good conscience grant assent would be to resign.[70]

Ireland takes a different approach. Rather than abolishing the right of the head of state to refuse assent to legislation, the Irish Constitution recognises this right, while at the same time providing a procedure for its exercise that limits it to questions of unconstitutionality. The procedure is complicated: if the president believes that a bill passed by parliament may be contrary to the Constitution, then he or she may consult the Council of State for advice. The Council of State is an advisory body to the president, consisting of the incumbent prime minister, the deputy prime minister, the Chief Justice, the President of the High Court, the chairmen of the Dáil and the Senate, the Attorney

General, any former president, Taoiseach or Chief Justice who is willing and able to attend, and up to seven members appointed by the president at his or her discretion. Having heard the advice of the Council of State, the president may then, at his or her sole discretion, refer the bill to the Supreme Court, which decides on its constitutionality.[71] If the bill is deemed constitutional, the president must grant assent; if it is deemed 'repugnant to the Constitution', assent must be withheld.[72] Thus the president's discretionary power is not to grant or withhold assent to a bill, but to decide whether or not to refer it to the Supreme Court, which makes the final decision. Up to June 2009, this power to refer has been exercised on fifteen occasions, and on seven the court has found a bill wholly or party unconstitutional.[73]

The extent to which an Irish model of abstract review might be suitable for Scotland is discussed in Chapter 7; for now, the crucial point is that uncertainty concerning the validity or extent of the head of state's veto power is unacceptable for two reasons. Firstly, it leaves open an unacceptable risk that a future King of Scots may exercise the power, as the heads of state in Luxembourg and Belgium have done, to veto laws on grounds of personal scruple rather than for clearly constitutional reasons. Secondly, there is a danger that the ambiguous nature of the head of state's veto power under the draft Constitution could provide a false assurance. If the right to refuse assent is contested and ambiguous, and if in practice it can never be used without provoking a constitutional crisis, then it would be wise, in adopting a new Constitution for a new state, to provide instead a clear constitutional procedure for granting royal assent that avoids the capricious play of royal whims, while providing real protection against the enactment of unconstitutional laws.

Organisation and Powers of the Government

The previous sections of this chapter have largely been concerned with examining the extent of the personal, discretionary powers of the head of state. This section discusses those powers of the Crown that are vested in the ministers under the draft Constitution – including not only powers of internal administration, but also those of diplomacy and of war and peace.

The words 'cabinet' or 'Council of Ministers' are not to be found in the draft Constitution, although the text refers to ministers in the plural and collectively, and also speaks of 'the Government', clearly implying that a collegial, cabinet-style executive would be expected to exist. Likewise, the prime minister is not given any special status or powers in relation to the rest of the ministers by the text of the Constitution, although the clear implication is that the prime minister is head of the cabinet and leader of the government. The intention to replicate the basic Westminster-style pattern of a cabinet government, led by a prime minister and consisting of a number of ministers with departmental duties, is made explicit in MacCormick's commentary, which speaks of the 'continuation of a Cabinet system of executive government under an elected Prime Minister'.[74]

The powers of ministers under the draft Constitution are not clearly enumerated, but can easily be discerned from the text and from Scots law. Firstly, there are statutory powers, which may be conferred on a minister by law – for example by an Act of the UK parliament enacted before independence, by an Act of the devolved Scottish Parliament, by an Act of the Parliament of Scotland, or by European Community law. Secondly, ministers would exercise common law powers belonging to the Crown, such as the power to contract and the right, under the 'Ram doctrine', to do, in the exercise of the powers of the Crown, 'all those things which are not prohibited by law'.[75] Some prerogative powers derive from the common law, while others, which might be termed 'constitutional prerogatives', derive directly from the written text of the Constitution itself. In case of inconsistency between common law prerogative powers and statutory provisions, statutes take priority, meaning that statutes may abolish or restrict prerogative powers, but constitutional prerogatives would be superior to statutory provisions.[76]

In the absence of any specific constitutional or statutory rules to the contrary, ministers could therefore, under the cloak of prerogative power, do such things as award honours, summon and prorogue parliaments and grant pardons. The provision concerning the power of pardons, in particular, contrasts notably with the Constitutions of several other new Commonwealth democracies, where the procedure for the exercise of this prerogative is specified,[77] and where special advisory councils are often created to protect the pardons process from overt political manipulation.[78]

Likewise, Westminster-based Constitutions typically limit the prerogative of summoning and proroguing parliament. The Irish Free State Constitution (1922–34), for example, transferred the power to set the dates of parliamentary session from the Crown to the Dáil,[79] while the Constitution of Malta, in a formulation typical of constitutions of its type and era, mandates annual meetings of parliament and demands that the first meeting of parliament occurs within two months after an election.[80]

The SNP's draft Constitution for Scotland does not concern itself with such matters. It leaves them to be resolved by ordinary statues, or by parliamentary Standing Orders. The danger of this is that it increases the power of the government in comparison to that of the opposition. It would be perfectly constitutional (in the legal, if not in the moral, sense), in the absence of any statutory or parliamentary rules to the contrary, for the government to refuse to summon parliament for long periods, or to avoid potentially losing a vote of no confidence (and thus to prolong its tenure of power) by the peremptory use of the prerogative of prorogation. Although this might seem far-fetched, even alarmist – and, certainly, it would give rise to criticism, and perhaps be deemed contrary to the spirit, if not to the letter, of the Constitution – it should be remembered that the minority Conservative government of Stephen Harper in Canada did just that, and was thereby able, by use of the prerogative of prorogation, to cling to office.[81] In drafting a Constitution that is intended, at least, to reflect and protect the changes in parliamentary organisation and procedure wrought by the Constitutional Convention, the Scotland Act and the Consultative Steering Group, it would be better to be more specific, and to place stricter constitutional limits on the exercise of these powers.

The 2002 draft would, however, place two new restrictions on the prerogative power: the government may not declare war (Article III, §9) nor ratify treaties (Article III, §8) without the consent of parliament. In most circumstances, as long as the cabinet can rely on the support of a majority in parliament, this requirement is likely to be only a minor and formal restraint on the executive. Nevertheless, parliamentary resolutions have a deliberative and legitimating function. They at least ensure that the matter is directly put to, and fully debated by, parliament, and that the decision to ratify a controversial treaty, or to commit Scottish troops to a war, has a stamp of parliamentary legitimacy.[82]

The draft Constitution subordinates the treaty-making power to the supreme law. In other words, the Crown may not, even with the consent of parliament, enter into a treaty that is contrary to the Constitution, except by way of a constitutional amendment (that is, by a three-fifths majority in parliament followed by majority approval in a national referendum).[83] This means that parliament cannot, by treaty, conspire with other states to undermine popular sovereignty or encroach upon fundamental rights.[84] It is unlikely, however, that this restriction would lead to a situation similar to that which has existed in Ireland following the 'Crotty' case (1987), whereby the Irish Supreme Court ruled that treaties of European integration, being of a constitutional nature, would require approval by the people in a referendum.[85] This is because the draft Constitution explicitly states that Scotland's sovereignty may be limited by agreements 'freely entered into by it with other nations or states or international organisations for the purpose of furthering international co-operation, trade, and world peace',[86] and that Scotland shall be bound by 'all rights and obligations of European Union membership'.[87,88]

The restriction of war-making power under the draft Constitution is limited by the fact that it unambiguously applies only to formal (and thus, in practice, relatively rare) declarations of war. Whether this rule would also be applied to, say, the commitment of troops to a NATO interventions or to UN 'peace-keeping' operation must be resolved by custom and convention, or by judicial interpretation. It might reasonably be argued that any substantial military action undertaken by the government without a formal (if technical) parliamentary vote of approval is likely to be deemed illegitimate. Indeed, even in the Westminster parliament, where control of military and diplomatic affairs is very much a matter for the Crown alone, there is a developing conventional assumption in favour of holding a parliamentary vote before committing the armed forces.[89]

The draft Constitution contains no provision for the involvement of members of parliament in the decision-making processes of foreign affairs and defence prior to being presented in parliament with a ministerial statement, a fait accompli, and a request for approval. For example, there is no equivalent of Sweden's Foreign Affairs Advisory Committee, which the Swedish government must keep informed of foreign policy developments, and which has a constitutional right to be consulted on major questions of foreign policy.[90] Instead, parliamentary committees covering foreign affairs and defence would more likely provide reactive, post hoc oversight of military and diplomatic activities. The powers and effectiveness of such committees would ultimately depend on parliament's Standing Orders, which in turn would depend on the ruling majority's commitment not to alter Standing Orders to suit its own immediate ends.

More potentially problematic is the absence from the SNP's draft Constitution of any separation between government and administration. There is no equivalent to the 'Public Service Commissions' that feature so prominently in many new Commonwealth Constitutions. The principles of civil service impartiality, permanence and professionalism are not even mentioned in the draft Constitution. The recent proposals of UK Cabinet Office Minister, Francis Maude, to allow new governments to dismiss civil servants and to increase the number of political appointees,[91] show that these principles are no longer held as sacred as they once were, and that they cannot be safeguarded by conventional or statutory provision alone.

Without a constitutional commitment to the principle and practice of civil service professionalism and impartiality, there is a danger of severe regression. This could undermine the technical quality of administration (as institutional expertise and collective memory are lost), threaten the equal rights of citizens (as habits of impartiality die out, and are replaced by patronage and clientelism), corrode the civic 'public service ethos' (as the profit-maximising values of the boardroom replace those of public servants), and, in effect, put the whole state up for sale in a great auction of offices. Again, this is not a prediction of what would necessarily occur in an independent Scotland, only an observation that the absence of robust constitutional specification leaves many matters of importance to the good governance of the state to be resolved by ordinary law, which, in a parliamentary democracy, is largely a product of the government of the day. Therefore, if the draft Constitution does not lead to a corrupt spoils system, it will be because of the virtue and foresight of the government (in recognising that the short-term partisan advantages of corruption are vastly outweighed by the long-term decay of civic values and of the legitimacy of the state as an impartial public actor), rather than because of the virtue and foresight of the text of the Constitution itself.

Summary

This chapter has described the provisions of the draft Constitution with relation to the head of state and the executive branch. Even if there is a substantial minority – both within and outwith the pro-independence movement – in favour of a republic, there is no doubt that the structural decision to adopt a parliamentary executive under the symbolic mantle of a hereditary figurehead monarchy is viable and acceptable. This decision is congruent with developments in Westminster-derived constitutionalism discussed in Chapter 2, with the sociological and ideological landscape of today's Scotland discussed in Chapter 3, and with the institutional trajectory of Scotland covered in Chapter 4.

The problems with the 2002 text exist at the 'micro-level'[92] of detailed constitutional design. The basic weakness of the text as a constitutional proposal is a lack of precision and clarity in procedural matters, and especially in the demarcation of the limits of the head of state's personal discretionary powers. This is not to say that the Constitution, if it were ever – speaking purely hypothetically – to be adopted in an independent Scotland, would be incapable of serving as the foundation of a viable and acceptable constitutional order, simply to say that the role of the Constitution itself in the definition of that order is limited and not wholly satisfactory.

Much that is essential to the procedural functioning of the wider constitutional order is left to be defined by extraconstitutional and sub-constitutional sources, such as statute law, constitutional jurisprudence, parliamentary Standing Orders, and political conventions. An old state, with a settled party system and an entrenched ruling establishment, in which parliamentarism developed organically from limited monarchy, may well 'muddle through' with a set of unwritten conventional arrangements – although even there, the advantages of procedural clarity are evident, as shown by the attempt to transcribe existing customary practices into a Cabinet Manual during the premiership of Gordon Brown. In developing a new Constitution for a newly independent State, however, it is prudent to be clear, specific and precise about these procedural matters – to avoid, as far as possible, those uncertainties that may lead to potential constitutional crises by making the procedural parts of the text say in words what it is meant to mean in practice.[93] The SNP's 2002 draft Constitution fails to do this, and its provisions with regard to the head of state and the executive branch are therefore sub-optimal by the standards of other, more recently constituted, Westminster-influenced democracies.

Notes

1. SNP, *A Free Scotland* (Edinburgh: SNP, 2002), Art. 2, Sect.1.
2. G. H. Sabine and S. B. Smith (eds), *Cicero: On the Commonwealth*, Library of the Liberal Arts (New York: Macmillan, 1976).
3. A. Tomkins, 'Republican constitutionalism and constitutional reform', in S. White and D. Leighton (eds), *Building a Citizen Society: The Emerging Politics of Republican Democracy* (London: Lawrence and Wishart, 2008), ch. 3, pp. 33–43.
4. P. Pettit, *Republicanism: A Theory of Freedom and Government* (Oxford: Oxford University Press, 1997).
5. C. Robbins (ed.), *Two English Republican Tracts* (Cambridge: Cambridge University Press, 1969).
6. J. Robertson (ed.), *Andrew Fletcher: Political Works* (Cambridge: Cambridge University Press, 1997).
7. E. Lefebvre, *The Citizen Burgher: The Belgian Constitution of 1831*, discussion paper presented at Zentrum für Europäische Rechtspolitik, Bremen, 1997.
8. N. MacCormick, 'An idea for a Scottish constitution', in W. Finnie, C. M. G. Himsworth and N. Walker (eds), *Edinburgh Essays in Public Law* (Edinburgh: Edinburgh University Press, 1991), pp. 159–81.
9. P. Lynch, *SNP: The History of the Scottish National Party* (Cardiff: Welsh Academic Press, 2002), pp. 169–77.
10. SNP Manifesto 1935; SNP Archives, Acc. 10090/09.

11. W. E. Bulmer, 'An analysis of the Scottish National Party's Draft Constitution for Scotland', *Parliamentary Affairs*, 64/4 (2011), 674–93.
12. It may be noted in passing that the SNP's plans for independence set out in the White Paper included not only the retention of the shared monarchy but also a currency union and a 'social union', in which certain cultural ties would remain intact. In many ways, what was on offer was not so much a 'separate Scotland', as opponents had suggested, but a 'Scottish Free State' within a very different, more decentralised and more equal Union: not so much a 'United Kingdom', but '(Loosely) United Kingdoms'.
13. N. Bonney, 'Scottish independence, state religion and the monarchy', *Political Quarterly*, 83/2 (2012), 360–7.
14. N. MacCormick, 'An idea for a Scottish constitution', pp. 161–2.
15. C. F. Nothomb, *Principes de Démocratie : Le modèle de la Belgique fédérale* (Louvain-la-Neuve: Duculot SA, 1994), p. 15.
16. SNP, *A Free Scotland,* Art. 2, Sect. 1; N. MacCormick, 'An idea for a Scottish constitution', p. 165.
17. N. MacCormick, 'An idea for a Scottish constitution', p. 165; N. Bonney and B. Morris, 'Tuvalu and you: the monarch, the United Kingdom and the realms', *Political Quarterly*, 83/2 (2012), p. 368.
18. N. Bonney, 'Scottish independence, state religion and the monarchy', p. 365.
19. Ibid. p. 364.
20. Parenthetically, these provisions of the SNP's draft Constitution stand in contrast to those of the text prepared by the Scottish Provisional Constituent Assembly in 1964 (R. Moffat, 1993). That text maintained the British and Protestant character of the monarchy in unequiocal terms, rooting the monarchy of Scotland in the Act of Settlement (R. Moffat, 1993, Art. 27), while giving constitutional status to the establishment of the Church of Scotland (R. Moffat, 1993, Art. 4).
21. W. E. Bulmer, *A Constitution for the Common Good: Strengthening Scottish Democracy After the Independence Referendum*, 2nd edn (Edinburgh: Luath Press, 2015).
22. S. Levinson, 'Do constitutions have a point?: reflections on "Parchment Barriers" and preambles', in E. F. Paul, F. D. Miller Jr and J. Paul, *What Should Constitutions Do?* (Cambridge: Cambridge University Press, 2011), p. 155.
23. H. Lerner, *Making Constitutions in Deeply Divided Societies.*
24. C. Sunstein, 'Designing democracy: what constitutions do' (Oxford: Oxford University Press, 2002).
25. A. Knapp and V. Wright, *The Government and Politics of France*, 5th edn (Abdingdon, Routledge, 2006), p. 4.
26. SNP, *A Free Scotland,* Art. II, Sect. 4.
27. SNP, *A Free Scotland,* Art. II, Sect. 3.
28. N. MacCormick, 'An idea for a Scottish constitution', p. 161.
29. D. A. Low, 'Introduction: the Westminster model', in *Constitutional Heads and Political Crises: Commonwealth Episodes, 1945–85* (Basingstoke: Macmillan, 1988), p. 4.
30. B. Constant, 'Principles of politics applicable to all representative governments', in B. Fontana (ed.), *Constant: Political Writings* (Cambridge: Cambridge University Press, 1988), pp. 183–93.

31. D. A. Low, 'Introduction: the Westminster model', p. 4.
32. J. W. Sap, *The Queen, the Populists and the Others: New Dutch Politics Explained for Foreigners* (Amsterdam: VU University Press, 2010).
33. This power has since been curtailed in the Netherlands by a change to parliamentary Standing Orders, and since 2011 the government formation process has been controlled by the House of Representatives.
34. E. Holmberg and N. Stjernquist, *The Constitution of Sweden* (Stockholm: Swedish Riksdag, 1995), p. 16.
35. Riksdag Act (Sweden): Chapter 1, Article 6.
36. A. Tomkins, 'Republican constitutionalism and constitutional reform', p. 37.
37. D. A. Low, 'Introduction: the Westminster model', p. 5.
38. SNP, *A Free Scotland*, p. 6.
39. Ibid. Art. 2. Sect. 3.
40. Ibid. Art. II, Sect. 5.
41. T. Bergman, 'Formation rules and minority government', *European Journal of Political Research*, 23/1 (1993), pp. 55–66.
42. W. E. Bulmer, 'An analysis of the Scottish National Party's Draft Constitution for Scotland', *Parliamentary Affairs*, 64/4 (2011), 674–93.
43. O. Nyman, 'Some basic features of Swedish constitutional law', in S. Ströholm (ed.), *An Introduction to Swedish Law*, 2nd edn (Stockholm: Norstedt, 1988), p. 68.
44. T. Bergman, 'Sweden: from separation of power to parliamentary supremacy—and back again?' in K. Strøm, W. C. Müller and T. Bergman (eds), *Delegation and Accountability in Parliamentary Democracies*, Comparative Politics (Oxford: Oxford University Press, 2003), p. 602.
45. J. Coakley, 'Selecting a prime minister: the Irish experience', *Parliamentary Affairs*, 37/1 (1984), p. 411.
46. Ibid. p. 411.
47. Ibid. p. 415.
48. Z. Elkins, T. Ginsburg and J. Melton, *The Endurance of National Constitutions* (Cambridge: Cambridge University Press, 2009).
49. P. Norton, 'Playing by the rules: the constraining hand of parliamentary procedure', *Journal of Legislative Studies*, 7/3 (2001), pp. 13–33.
50. SNP, *A Free Scotland*, Art. 2, Sect. 5.
51. N. MacCormick, personal communication (interview), 2008.
52. SNP, *A Free Scotland*, Art. 2, Sect, 3.
53. O. Nyman, 'Some basic features of Swedish constitutional law', p. 67.
54. E. Lindström, *The Swedish Parliamentary System: How Responsibilities are Divided and Decisions are Made* (Stockholm: Swedish Institute, 1982), p. 91.
55. Constitution of Malta, Arts 80 and 85.
56. Scotland Act 1998, Sects 45–6.
57. Scotland Act 1998, Sect. 3.
58. SNP, *A Free Scotland*, Art. 2, Sect. 3.
59. P. Mitchell, 'Ireland: O What a Tangled Web – delegation, accountability and executive power', in K. Strøm, W. C. Müller and T. Bergman (eds), *Delegation and Accountability in Parliamentary Democracies*, Comparative Politics, (Oxford: Oxford University Press, 2003), p. 430.

60. J. P. A. Gruijters, 'The case for a directly elected prime minister in the Netherlands', in A. Lijphart (ed.), *Parliamentary versus Presidential Government* (Oxford: Oxford University Press, 1992), p. 191.
61. Scotland Act 1998, Sect. 45.
62. SNP, *A Free Scotland,* Art. 3, Sect. 10.
63. D. A. Low, 'Introduction: the Westminster model', p. 5.
64. D. A. Low, 'Introduction: the Westminster model'; V. Bogdanor, *The Monarchy and the Constitution* (Oxford: Oxford University Press, 1997); T. Saalfield, 'The United Kingdom: still a single chain of command? The hollowing out of the Westminster model', in K. Strøm, W. C. Müller and T. Bergman (eds), *Delegation and Accountability in Parliamentary Democracies* (Oxford: Oxford University Press, 2003), p. 640; G. Taylor, 'Two refusals of royal assent in Victoria', *Sydney Law Review,* 29 (2007), 85–130.
65. W. I. Jennings, *The Constitution of Ceylon* (Bombay: Oxford University Press, 1949).
66. J. Fitzmaurice, *The Politics of Belgium: Crisis and Compromise in a Plural Society,* 2nd edn (London: Hurst, 1988); L. De Winter and P. Dumont, 'Belgium: delegation and accountability under partitocratic rule', in K. Strøm, W. C. Müller and T. Bergman (eds), *Delegation and Accountability in Parliamentary Democracies* (Oxford: Oxford University Press, 2003), p. 253–80.
67. P. Montgomery, 'Belgian king, unable to sign abortion law, takes day off', *New York Times,* 5 April 1990.
68. D. Charter, 'Grand Duke Henri of Luxembourg opposes euthanasia and loses power', *The Times,* 4 December 2008.
69. Constitution of Malta, Art. 72.
70. W. E. Bulmer, 'Constrained majoritarianism: Westminster constitutionalism in Malta', *Commonwealth and Comparative Politics,* 51/1 (2014), 232–53.
71. Constitution of Ireland, Art. 26.
72. M. Gallagher, 'The changing constitution', in J. Coakley and M. Gallagher (eds), *Politics in the Republic of Ireland,* 5th edn (Abingdon: Routledge, 2010), ch. 3, p. 85; Constitution of Ireland, Art. 26.
73. M. Gallagher, 'The changing constitution', p. 85.
74. N. MacCormick, 'An idea for a Scottish constitution', p. 162.
75. C. M. G. Himsworth and C. M. O'Neill, *Scotland's Constitution: Law and Practice* (Haywards Heath: Bloomsbury Professional, 2009), pp. 177–9.
76. SNP, *A Free Scotland,* Art. II, Sect. 4.
77. Constitution of Malta, Art. 93.
78. Constitution of St Vincent and the Grenadines, Sect. 66.
79. Constitution of the Irish Free State, Art. 24.
80. Constitution of Malta, Art. 75.
81. 'Harper goes prorogue', *The Economist,* 7 January 2010.
82. F. R. Tesón, 'The liberal constitution and foreign affairs', in E. F. Paul, F. D. Miller Jr and J. Paul (eds), *What Should Constitutions Do?* (Cambridge: Cambridge University Press, 2011).
83. SNP, *A Free Scotland,* Art. III, Sect. 8.
84. F. R. Tesón, 'The liberal constitution and foreign affairs', p. 135.
85. M. Gallagher, 'The changing constitution', p. 83.

86. SNP, *A Free Scotland*, Art.1, Sect. 1.

87. Ibid. Art. 1, Sect. 2.

88. In the same way, the 2002 draft Constitution would enable Scotland to share certain powers and functions, by treaties, with the rest of the former UK. It would even be possible, for example, for an independent Scotland to negotiate something like a British version of the Benelux Union or the Nordic Council, perhaps based on the existing British–Irish Council, through which to co-operate in various policy areas.

89. United Kingdom Cabinet Manual, 2011, 5.36–5.38.

90. E. Lindström, *The Swedish Parliamentary System: How Responsibilities are Divided and Decisions are Made*, p. 44.

91. O. Wright, 'Ministers plot end to Civil Service neutrality', *The Independent*, London, 1 August 2012.

92. A. Ágh, *The Politics of Central Europe* (London: Sage, 1998), p. 87-8.

93. S. A. De Smith, 'Westminster's export models: the legal framework of responsible government', *Journal of Commonwealth Political Studies*, 1/1 (1961), pp. 2–16; Elkins et al., *The Endurance of National Constitutions*); S. Levinson, 'Do constitutions have a point?: reflections on "Parchment Barriers" and preambles'.

2002 DRAFT III:
JUDICIARY, RIGHTS AND SUBSTANTIVE
PROVISIONS

The previous two chapters have discussed what might loosely be termed the 'political' aspects of the SNP's draft Constitution: the parliament and the government, or legislative and executive branches. This chapter goes on to discuss the legal and substantive aspects of the draft Constitution.

A recurring theme of this chapter is that the 2002 draft Constitution is a 'procedural'[1] document. It is thin on rhetoric and is based upon no specific foundational or teleological ideology, beyond a commitment to the procedures of democracy and to a relatively generic set of human rights. The chapter argues that this is a prudent course of action, in so far as it concerns the substantive content of the Constitution.

Nationalism, Statehood, Citizenship, Religion and Identity

As well as establishing the institutions of government and defining the rights of citizens, modern Constitutions often have nation-building and regime-defining functions. As such, a typical modern constitution proclaims what the country stands for, and what it will not stand for. It reflects the values, aspirations and identity of the nation; it says who 'we the people' are, what we hold in common and where we are going.[2]

In many cases, these symbolic and formative functions are performed by a preamble. Preambles (or preamble-like opening provisions) are the point at which the 'presumptive ends' of a Constitution meet 'the particular means' that the Constitution establishes; there the authors of a Constitution 'proclaim their intentions' and 'communicate their deepest aspirations for the newly created polity'.[3]

For a Constitution which is supposedly the product of a 'nationalist' party, the SNP's 2002 draft Constitution is curiously devoid of what might be called nation-defining features. There is no preamble. It gets straight down to the prosaic text of institutional regulation, without either rhetorical flourishes or theoretical posturing. Moreover, except for a declaration of the sovereignty of the people, the text contains no explicit theory of government on which the state is based, nor any mention of the ultimate ends of the polity. There are no provisions regulating such symbolic matters as the national flag, state emblem or anthem.

Although by no means unique amongst Westminster-derived constitutions, the prosaic nature of the SNP's draft stands in contrast with, say, the Irish Constitution (which devotes its first three articles to defining the *nation*, even before it defines the *state*), to the Constitution of Malta (which devotes several articles to defining the national flag, anthem, language and religion), and to the Constitution of India (which is preceded by a highly symbolic preamble).

This is not to say that the draft is 'value-neutral'. No Constitution, even the most open-ended, ever can be. Rather, the SNP's 2002 draft is one which leaves, as Himsworth and O'Neill put it, 'underlying principles or values to be deduced from the rules of the constitution' and 'implied from the text, rather than laid down'.[4] Reading between the lines in this way, the 2002 draft clearly shows a commitment to certain underlying values, such as democracy, human rights and social justice, which are implicit in the text. These values might be rather thin and generic, and would of course be in need of continual re-definition and re-affirmation through the noisy daily life of democratic politics under a living constitution. It is nevertheless fair to say that these would be legitimate as foundational values, as they would be likely to command a broadly shared, deeply permeating, and long-lasting consensus of support in Scotland.

Although shying away from the more rhetorical and ideological aspects of constitutional nation-building, the SNP's 2002 draft does address two of the most important foundations of state-building: (1) determining who is, and who is not, a citizen of the state, and (2) defining the territory of the state.

With regard to matters of citizenship, the draft makes quite extensive provisions. It prescribes that from the outset: 'Every person whose principal place of residence is in Scotland at the date at which this Constitution comes into force', as well as 'every person whose place of birth was in Scotland or either of whose parents was born in Scotland' would have the right of citizenship by default.[5] The draft would also give the parliament of Scotland the authority to legislate for the acquisition and loss of Scottish citizenship by birth, marriage and naturalisation. This authority is subject to certain caveats, preventing the involuntary deprivation of citizenship and preventing discrimination on the acquisition of citizenship on 'any ground such as sex, race, colour, religion, personal beliefs, abilities, status or sexual orientation'. The text would also guarantee the continued permanent residency rights of those who choose to renounce Scottish citizenship on independence.

Thus the draft Constitution offers broad, inclusive access to the rights of citizenship. It would enable many people who might be regarded as 'English' by origin to be citizens of Scotland. On one level, this can be seen as a tactical concession. It provides reassurance to people born outwith Scotland, and perhaps to those Scots who identify primarily as British and are opposed to independence, that independence would not deprive them of the right to live and work in Scotland, even if they choose not to be citizens of the new state. It therefore makes independence seem less threatening and less disruptive. On another level, it also makes a statement about the relationship between nation-hood and citizenship. An open and residence-based approach to citizenship reflects the SNP's commitment to a civic and inclusive, form of nationalism: to be a Scottish citizen is not to be a child of the 'Scottish nation', but simply to 'belong' as a member of the political community.[6]

As well as citizens, a state needs territory. The 2002 draft devotes consider-able attention to stating Scotland's territorial claims. The opening lines of the Constitution assert the sovereign right of the people of Scotland over 'the terri-tory and natural resources of Scotland'.[7] The territory of Scotland is defined as:

> all those areas over which the Court of Session and High Court of Justiciary have exercised jurisdiction since the time of, and in virtue of, the ratification of the Articles of Union of 1707, and all the territorial waters appertaining thereto under interna-tional law . . .[8]

This curious provision, defining Scotland by reference to the Treaty of Union, was intended, according to MacCormick, to maintain a 'continuing legal definition of Scotland as a country which existed before, and has persisted throughout, the period of incorporation in Great Britain'.[9] It reveals a desire, however vestigial, to constitute the Scottish state not as a new creation, but as the restored continuation of the Kingdom of Scots that was, on the one hand, absorbed into the Union three centuries ago, but which, on the other hand, has maintained its own legal identity and had never been completely assimilated.

The 2002 draft Constitution states that 'the extent of Scotland's rights to territorial waters and natural resources beyond territorial waters shall be determined according to international law' (Art. 1, §2), and that the 'sover-eignty of the Scottish state extends over all such rights in relation to exploita-tion of the resources of the sea, the sea bed and the sub-soil thereof beyond the territorial waters as are enjoyed and exercised by states under international law' (Art. 1, §3). Of course, if Scotland were to become an independent state, then it would possess all the rights to territorial waters and exclusive economic zones that pertain to states under international law, without having to specify these claims in the Constitution. Indeed, to specify these claims, not just once, but three times, in the first three sections of the text (Art. 1, §1–3), reveals the sort of ardency that often stems from a profound sense of insecurity. The inclu-sion of these words, so earnestly and repetitively, in the text of a Constitution which does not even take the care to define with any precision the electoral system or the privileges of parliament, can be interpreted as an indication of the extent to which the control of resources – especially maritime and off-shore resources – remains integral to the SNP's independence project. That there is no constitutional provision for an independent, ring-fenced, 'oil and gas fund', into which the revenues from fossil fuel resources can be poured, is also a telling and perhaps worrying sign. For all the SNP's talk of wishing to ensure the better, wiser and more sustainable use of these resources, there is nothing in the Constitution to prevent a government from yielding to the temptation to burn revenues now, in order to spend lavishly without raising taxes or debt level, and to forget about the consequences faced by future generations.

The relationship between Church and State is another subject on which the 2002 draft Constitution is conspicuously silent. Following Article 9 of the ECHR, it guarantees the right to 'the free confession and the free practice of religion', subject only to such lawful restrictions as are 'necessary for the protection of public order or public health or for the protection of the rights and freedoms of others'.[10] It also guarantees freedom from religious discrimination in the exercise of other constitutional rights (Art. VI, §1). It would clearly be unconstitutional, for example, to place religious qualifications on property rights (Art. VI, §14), employment rights (Art. VI, §15), voting rights (Art. VI, §17) or the right to an education (Art. VI, §22).

What the draft Constitution does not do, however, is to declare the ideological stance of the state vis-à-vis religion. It could be said to be 'secular by omission', especially in contrast to states which refer explicitly to deities or divine sanction in their fundamental laws – such as Canada's claim that its Charter of Rights and Freedoms rests on 'the supremacy of God', or Greece's theologically dense invocation of the 'Holy and Consubstantial and Indivisible Trinity'.[11] It does not, for example, give constitutional recognition to the status of the Church of Scotland. It does not entrench the provisions of the Church of Scotland Act 1921, which gave effect to the Articles Declaratory of the Constitution of the Church of Scotland in Matters Spiritual and so cemented the position of a church that was at once 'established' and 'free'.[12]

As noted in Chapter 6, the draft Constitution says nothing about the coronation oath and is ambiguous about the Protestant succession and about the monarch's formal allegiance, if any, to religious principles. Perhaps more importantly, in terms of sectarian politics, the Constitution neither abolishes the existing provision for the public funding of religious schools, nor does it explicitly affirm the constitutionality of such provision. In leaving all these questions open, to be settled by legislative policy and judicial interpretation, the Constitution refuses to commit itself to one model of Church–State relations. Using the definitions of Ran Hirschl, it does not embrace 'secularism as neutrality' or '*laïcité*', but neither does it constitutionally entrench the currently prevailing de facto balance of 'weak establishment' and 'multiculturalism'.[13]

With regard to language, the 2002 draft does recognise the place of Scots and Gaelic, and makes them co-official with English. However, little emphasis is placed on language as a marker of the state's identity. This contrasts, for example, with both the Irish Constitution, which gives Irish preeminent status,[14] and with the draft Constitution for an independent Quebec prepared by Daniel Turp, which cites 'ensuring the quality and influence of the French language' as an 'objective' of the state.[15] Again, this can be seen as a reflection of social and linguistic realities in Scotland, as well as underlining the inclusive civic nationalist nature of the movement.

Some Constitutions contain a number of provisions that extend well beyond what has traditionally been regarded as the 'constitutional' sphere and far into the realm of what might be regarded as the proper sphere for ordinary legislation. This is traditionally regarded as poor drafting practice, since the inclusion of elements with little or no relevance to the 'constitutional order' in the text of the Constitution blurs the distinction between what is, and what is not, truly 'fundamental to the governance of the state'.[16] The SNP's 2002 draft Constitution cannot be accused of this. Other than the few foundational provisions relating to territory and citizenship, as discussed above, which are necessary for defining the extent of the state's authority and the bounds of its membership, the draft has a minimal substantive content.

This scope for pluralism might be the draft Constitution's greatest strength. Without disputing the centrality of Neil MacCormick's personal contribution, the draft Constitution was produced by committee, wrangled over through the SNP's internal policy-making structures, and amended over the years.[17] It reflects the tensions and bargains within the SNP – between urban and rural, left and right, secular and religious, Protestant and Catholic – that reflect, albeit imperfectly, the cleavages within wider Scottish society.[18] The text of the Constitution reflects the scale of agreement and disagreement within the party, tempered by the party's expectations of what those outside it may be willing to accept. The party was able to agree on the principles of parliamentary democracy, on the protection of basic human rights, and on the inclusion of socio-economic rights that are supported by the broad mainstream of Scottish political opinion. Yet it left the nature, identity and aspirational *telos* of the state unspecified, to be continuously re-defined by ordinary democratic politics.

Moreover, the 2002 draft was shaped by its intended process of adoption. Successful Constitutions are almost always a product of wide negotiation, including elites, experts and everyone else. However, the 2002 draft was originally intended (according to Neil MacCormick and to the SNP's policy documents of the time), to be submitted to the people as part of the independence package. By voting for independence the people would be voting to become independent under this Constitution. As envisaged, there would be no Constituent Assembly, no round-table agreement and no public consultation. This lack of wider negotiation or consultation with interests outside of the SNP, balanced by the awareness of its authors that their draft would have to win approval in the court of public opinion, no doubt made them cautious, eager to reassure and unwilling to include anything that could be seen as divisive.

Socio-economic Rights

A similarly non-prescriptive, procedural approach is evident with respect to the inclusion of socio-economic rights. The draft includes a right to work and to 'conditions of work which are fair and which respect the dignity of the person' (Art. VI, §15), the right to social insurance and benefits in event of unemployment, and the right to old age pensions (Art. VI, §15). It also includes a right to housing (Art. VI, §20), a right to public healthcare (Art. VI, §21) and a right to education (Art. VI, §21). These rights are not included in the ECHR – although many of them are found in other instruments, such as the Social Charter and the Charter of Fundamental Social Rights of Workers.[19]

By including these rights, the Constitution thereby clearly envisages an active role for the state in promoting the well-being of citizens through the regulation of markets and through the provision of public services and redistributive transfer payments. Yet it leaves the roles and boundaries of state, society and market open to political debate, and allows a broad degree of political latitude in how to achieve and fund the common goods which are constitutionally mandated. The provisions of the text in relation to public healthcare may be taken as a representative example of this approach to socio-economic rights:

> Everyone has the right to the provision of reasonable health care to secure wellbeing and human dignity within an acceptable level of overall cost and subject to prevailing conditions of medical practice. Parliament shall be responsible for securing by legislation that health services are properly maintained and are available on fair terms to all persons.[20]

This provision clearly establishes a right to healthcare accessible to all, at a reasonable standard to secure human dignity and well-being, and creates a corresponding duty upon parliament to provide by legislation for the effective realisation of this right. But no direction is given as to how that right is to be realised. It might be realised, as in Scotland at present, through a publicly funded, state run National Health Service. It might also be realised, through a regulated and subsidised system of universal and compulsory medical insurance, in which both the insurers and the providers are largely private entities, as in the Netherlands. The general ends are prescribed by the Constitution; the ways and means, the extent and the priorities are left to be decided through sub-constitutional politics.

The provisions in relation to other forms of state activity in social and economic activity are similarly expressed in terms of open-ended directions to parliament. Nevertheless, these socio-economic rights are not separated from the rest of the human rights provisions in a non-justiciable set of 'Directive Principles'. In this regard, the draft differs from the Irish, Maltese, Indian and several other Westminster-derived Constitutions. It is possible that an activist court could find in these socio-economic rights a real constraint on legislative action. To stay with the example of public healthcare, for example, it is not inconceivable that a legislative attempt to retreat from the principle of universal coverage, available to all and free at the point of delivery, could be regarded as unconstitutional and struck down by the courts; a decision of such magnitude, which would alter the very basis of the social contract, would not be within the competence of a mere parliament, but would have to go back to the sovereign people – who, no doubt, would reject any encroachment on such a sacred principle. In this way, the constitutional provisions, although allowing broad latitude to elected politicians, do provide some fundamental guarantees to the people.

Here it is worth noting that the framers of the draft Constitution were in favour of a range of additional rights and entitlements beyond those listed in the constitutional text. These would include, amongst others: rights intended to promote greater gender equality, such as 'stronger equal pay legislation, child care and nursery provision';[21] rights for disabled people 'in the areas of employment, education and training, access to public places, housing, transport, communications and the provision of goods, services and facilities';[22] sexuality rights 'specifically to prohibit discrimination on the grounds of sexuality in eligibility for employment, housing or services';[23] children's rights, including implementation of the UN Convention on the Rights of the Child;[24] and workers' rights, including 'a practical and enforceable right to a statutory minimum wage', 'equal rights to join, participate in and be represented by a trade union without discrimination', and 'employment contracts which place acceptable limits on flexible contracts and ban the use of zero hour contracts'.[25] These additional rights and entitlements would exist only on a statutory, rather than a constitutional, basis – although some of them may well attain the status of 'super-statutes' and so become 'politically entrenched'.[26]

The drafters of the text thereby drew a clear distinction between the progressive set of rights and entitlements that they would like to see in place (their political agenda) and the more restricted set of rights they believed should be entrenched in the Constitution (as the common basis of a democratic society). In so doing, the framers wrote a draft Constitution that was intended to enable progressive policies, while not making the legitimacy of the Constitution contingent on the acceptance of those progressive values. In this way, the SNP's 2002 draft reveals an implied commitment to a broad and pragmatic pluralism; it represents in general terms the commonly held values of Scottish society, including provision for the poor and protection for the weak, without being a utopian manifesto.

Popular Sovereignty, Constitutional Supremacy, the Judicial Review

Chapter 2 argued that there is a 'common model' of contemporary liberal democratic constitutionalism. This entails the supremacy of a rigid Constitution over ordinary law and the judicial enforcement of rights. Not only is this common model widespread, but it is increasingly the only form of constitution that would be perceived as internationally legitimate in a new state. Chapter 4 discussed how Scotland, since devolution, has already moved in the direction of this common model: the Scottish Parliament is not a sovereign legislature, since the Scotland Act and Human Rights Act are akin, for the purposes of the Scottish Parliament, to a fundamental law.[27]

Therefore, even if all criticisms levied against rigid constitutions and the judicial protection of rights are true, and even if there might be good reasons why a long-existing state (such as the UK) does not rush to adopt a new written constitution (at least not without careful consideration of the alternatives), it would be almost inconceivable for a Scottish state to adopt a system based on the legal sovereignty of parliament, without any higher law constitutional protections. European and world opinion, and an appeal to what are perceived to be the universal standards of modern liberal democracy, would require the Constitution of a new state to adhere, at least to a minimal degree, to a common model of constitutional rigidity and judicial review.

This section will consider the conformity of the SNP's 2002 draft Constitution to this common model of legal constitutionalism. It examines the place that the 2002 draft Constitution would envisage for itself in the constitutional order of a Scottish state: the status of the Constitution as a supreme law, the process of constitutional amendment, and the apparent tension between its commitment to popular sovereignty, on the one hand, and the prominent role of the judiciary in upholding the Constitution and fundamental rights, on the other.

The first point to be made is that, in its overall form, the draft Constitution does adhere closely to this pattern, entirely rejecting the doctrine of parliamentary sovereignty. The draft Constitution states that it 'shall be the supreme law of the land'.[28] It cannot be amended by legislative acts, but only by a special procedure involving a three-fifths majority decision of parliament followed by a referendum.[29] As a consequence of this legal supremacy and rigidity, the courts would be expected to defend the Constitution against the legislature, and empowered to 'review legislative and executive acts to secure their conformity with the Constitution and the guaranteed rights it entrenches'.[30]

The draft Constitution contains a 'Bill of Rights'[31] that is closely based on the European Convention on Human Rights (ECHR) and its protocols. It is intended to 'give full effect to fundamental rights as recognised throughout Europe'.[32] The listed rights include: the right to life (Art. VI, §2); freedom from torture (Art. VI, §3); freedom from slavery (Art. VI, §4); personal liberty, including due process of law and 'habeas corpus' rights (Art. VI, §5); right to a fair public trial (Art. VI, §6); prohibition of retrospective laws and punishments (Art. VI, §7); privacy in personal affairs, family life and correspondence (Art. VI, §8); freedom of thought and conscience, and free confession and practice of religion (Art. VI, §9); freedom of opinion and expression (Art. VI, §11), freedom of peaceful assembly and association (Art. VI, §12); the right to marry and found a family (Art. VI, §13); the right to private property (Art. VI, §14); and the right to vote (Art. VI, §17).[33] There are also some Scotland-specific rights, such as right of access to open land (Art. VI, §16). All these rights are preceded by a right of remedy through the courts for any violation of these or other protected constitutional rights, and by a general principle of non-discrimination in the application of rights (Art. VI, §1).

The draft Constitution enables its fundamental rights provisions to be suspended by law 'during times of war or other periods of grave emergency'.[34] The government may declare a state of emergency, but any such declaration must be approved within two weeks by a resolution of parliament, passed by a three-fifths majority vote. A state of emergency may be renewed, at three-month intervals, by a further resolution. These rules are intended to prevent the abuse of states of emergency by requiring a supermajority for their continuance beyond a specified time period. Even during a state of emergency, certain rights are absolute: the right to life, freedom from torture, freedom from slavery and freedom from retrospective laws cannot be suspended.

The set of rights explicitly provided in the draft Constitution maps very closely on to the expected contents of a 'generic' Bill of Rights according to Law and Versteeg.[35] In this respect, the SNP's draft steers a middle course between a narrowly liberal-individualist approach that would limit rights to negative prohibitions on state power and exclude socio-economic rights in their entirety, and, at the other extreme, a highly communitarian and progressive set of rights.

It is notable that the draft Constitution does not simply incorporate the European Convention by reference (as the Scotland Act does), but rather specifies each right directly in the text of the Constitution. This may have symbolic importance. For the courts to overturn an Act because it violates (as a right-wing tabloid might put it) 'dictates of Strasbourg Eurocrats', is politically more difficult than for the courts to overturn an Act because it violates the fundamental rights of the people as enshrined in Scotland's supreme law. The first creates potential tension between human rights and national pride; the second makes the defence of human rights itself a matter of national pride, building a sense of 'constitutional patriotism' and contributing in some small way, as the Charter of Rights and Freedoms has done in Canada, to the 'emergence of a more rights-conscious and democratic constitutionalism'.[36]

This embrace of constitutional supremacy backed by judicial review can be portrayed as a liberal principle. It purports to 'protect the rights of every Scottish citizen' and 'to place restrictions on what politicians can and cannot do'.[37] Without repeating the arguments made earlier, some scholars have strong reservations against this liberal presupposition of rights, on the grounds that the entrenchment of rights diminishes the reach of democracy.[38] As MacCormick himself notes, 'Our opponents considered entrenched bills of rights to be anti-democratic, because of the discretion they remove from elected politicians'.[39]

Critiques of constitutional supremacy also expose the perceived bias of liberal rights against progressive policies: so-called 'juristocracy', rather than entrenching democracy, human rights and egalitarian socio-economic policies, can actually protect elite interests by insulating policy-making from the clash of democratic politics.[40] Its effect, according to this argument, is to constrain the scope of politics: to 'de-legitimate popular public power and thus to give free rein to private economic power'.[41]

Neil MacCormick accepted the argument that constitutional supremacy and judicial review tend to shield individuals against public power, yet treated this as a positive case for the rejection of parliamentary sovereignty. As he put it: 'democracy, with all its other virtues, contains no guarantee of justice to unpopular individuals or minorities, who can always be outvoted'.[42]

However, it would be wrong to see constitutional supremacy simply as a device for protecting individuals, private rights or minorities at the expense of democratic decision-making. The draft Constitution devotes only about half of its total word-count to the specification of rights. As mentioned in the previous section, this includes not only civil and legal rights that protect individuals from the abuse of public power, but also socio-economic rights that put a positive burden on the public to assist and support members of society. The other half of the Constitution is devoted not to liberal rights, but to democratic processes. It establishes a parliamentary government based on universal suffrage, proportional representation and regular elections. It sets out the powers of the various institutions of the state, provides mechanisms for the transfer of orderly power and ensures the accountability of officers of state to parliament and ultimately to the people. It therefore gives at least as much prominence to active democratic control over public affairs as it does to the protection of private rights.

Moreover, the legal supremacy of the Constitution flows from, and is intended to embody, the 'sovereignty of the people'.[43] The sovereignty of the people is not a liberal principle of minimal government, but a democratic principle appealing to the legitimacy of collective public political action. Where the Constitution is adopted and changeable by means of referendums, the higher law of the constitution can be seen as a democratic mechanism to ensure that the mere representatives of the people in parliament (whose office, even if elective, is restricted to the few) cannot usurp sovereignty for themselves.[44]

Liberal theorists, defining liberty in terms of 'non-interference', are often opposed to the sovereignty of the people, since it confers upon the people a power which is arbitrary and unlimited over each individual person.[45] The legal sovereignty of the people is made manifest when the whole people, by referendum, have a theoretically unlimited power to change their fundamental law, and even the power to overrule rights.[46] The SNP's draft Constitution gives a simple majority of the people, on the proposal of a three-fifths majority in parliament, just such a power:

> This Constitution, including this Article of this Constitution, may be amended only by the following procedure: The passing of a proposed measure at its third stage by a majority of three-fifths of the whole membership of the Parliament of Scotland followed, within a period of between two and six months, reference to the proposed measure to a National Referendum in which a majority of those voting shall have voted for the proposed measure.[47]

It is notable that there are no clauses that are stated to be beyond this power of amendment. This characteristic is shared with most Westminster-influenced Constitutions, but it can be contrasted with those (such as that of Bangladesh) which expressly prohibit the amendment of certain foundational articles, as well as those such as India where the 'Basic Structure' of the Constitution has been deemed unamendable.[48]

Thus it can be said that the draft Constitution, were it to come into effect as an act of the whole people endorsed by a referendum, would bind the hands of the parliament, but would not attempt to bind the hands of the people themselves, in whom sovereignty resides. Rights are protected not from the sovereign people, but only from their elected representatives. This being the case, rights in Scotland under the draft Constitution would not be 'pre-commitments', in the sense of rules that are normatively prior to the sovereign people and beyond the domain of their sovereign power. Rather, rights would be instituted and upheld by the sovereign people on a basis that can be renegotiated over time – albeit at a deeper and more deliberate level than that applied to ordinary, sub-constitutional policy or legislative decisions. To this degree, at least, it could be argued that the Constitution, while proceduralist rather than prescriptive in terms of its substantive content, is 'civic-republican' rather than 'liberal-individualist' in nature, and that its constitutionalism has a 'civic' and not merely 'legal' character.[49]

At the same time, however, the draft Constitution institutes some protection against brute majoritarianism. The requirement for changes to the constitution to be approved by a majority of the sovereign people is a democratic device;[50] unlike indirect methods of constitutional amendment, such as the need for an intervening election, it gives the people a clear and more decisive voice in approving or rejecting amendments.[51] However, the referendum alone offers little protection to minorities.[52] The 2002 draft remedies this by requiring a three-fifths majority in parliament in order to put an amendment to the people. In this way, a healthy and pragmatic balance is struck between the protection of minorities in the proposition of amendments and the sovereignty of the people in their approval.

These restraints on the amending power might also increase the scope for the 'real', 'living' constitution to evolve around the text, without a formal amendment or reference to the people:

> If the methods of securing formal amendment are difficult (as in the United States, where ratification by three-fourths of the state legislatures presents a high hurdle), there will be pressure to adapt the Constitution through judicial or other interpretation.[53]

The use of the words 'judicial *or other interpretation*' (my italics) is revealing. As is now evident, the SNP's 2002 draft is a rather skeletal Constitution. It leaves a broad space not only for judicial interpretation, but also for 'fleshing out' through ordinary legislation and parliamentary Standing Orders, and even by conventional practices which might be inherited by the new state or which might develop over time and acquire the status of normatively binding (if unwritten and unenforceable) rules. If the Constitution thereby opens up 'an invitation to conversation' about its meaning,[54] participation in the conversation is not limited to judges; it is also open to elected, party political actors and to members of the public, using arguments that are inherently political as well as legal in nature.

The judiciary's role, then, is not to limit the people's sovereign and original power of making fundamental law, nor to take conversations about rights out of the political and into the legal realm, as critics of judicial review allege,[55] but simply to maintain the hierarchy of laws and to limit the delegated and entrusted power of parliaments and governments under the fundamental law. As Cappelletti puts it:

> When two such laws are in conflict, it is the judge who must determine which law prevails and then apply it. When the conflict is between enactments of different normative force, the obvious criterion to be applied is that the higher law prevails: *lex superior derogat legi inferiori*. A constitutional norm, if the constitution is rigid, prevails over an ordinary legislative norm in conflict with it, just as ordinary legislation prevails over subordinate legislation [. . .].[56]

Besides, the draft Constitution would, in principle at least, entail only a small increase in the power of judicial review. As discussed in Chapter 4,

EHCR rights are already embedded within the Scotland Act (§32). While at the UK level the Human Rights Act does not allow judges to annul incompatible legislation, Acts of the Scottish Parliament are already subject to review on the grounds of compatibility with convention rights.[57] The draft Constitution would not change this arrangement. The Scottish Parliament would remain, as it is at present, a legally subordinate and not a supreme legislature. Only, instead of being subordinate to the Crown-in-Parliament at Westminster, it would be subordinate to the Scottish people voting in constitutional referendums.

Turning now to the structure of the judicial review process, the first point to note is the decision to avoid the creation of a 'Constitutional Court' on the 'Kelsenian' model, having exclusive and centralised jurisdiction over constitutional interpretation; instead, judicial review is decentralised, and is exercised by ordinary courts in the course of ordinary legal processes.[58]

At the apex of the system would be the Court of Session, sitting as a court of not fewer than seven judges, as the court of final appeal for all cases concerning the interpretation or application of the Constitution.[59] MacCormick attributed this decision to 'Scots legal conservatism' rather than to the 'intrinsic superiority' of this design.[60] Nevertheless, there are good reasons why this model of decentralised judicial review might be highly appropriate in a Scottish context. A decentralised system is common in countries with a history of British rule: decentralised judicial review is found, for example, in Australia, Canada, Ireland, India and most English-speaking Caribbean states. European democracies, influenced by civil law (that is, Roman or Napoleonic law), are inclined towards centralised models. In part, this reflects the superior status of common law judges over their civil law counterparts. Common law judges are typically recruited from lawyers in private practice, and have considerable professional privilege that sets them apart from the civil service. Civil law judges, in contrast, have traditionally held a more subordinate position vis-à-vis the executive, being recruited to judicial office early in life and often alternating between judicial and prosecuting duties.[61] Thus, in a civil law country the establishment of a centralised and specialised body for constitutional review, distinct from the ordinary judiciary, augments the strength and independence of review mechanisms, but in a common law country the ordinary courts are better placed to fulfil this role.

Scots law 'occupies a position somewhere midway between' the civil law and common law traditions,[62] but in terms of the status, recruitment methods and professional characteristics of the judiciary, and their distinctiveness from the civil service, it is closer to the common law model. Moreover, the Court of Session has a continuous history of almost 500 years; it existed before, and has been maintained within, the Union; and defence of the privileges of the Court of Session, as the highest court of Scotland, is a point of national pride amongst certain Scots lawyers.[63]

The professional, historical and 'national' legitimacy of the Court of Session gives the institution a strong starting point – a reserve of political capital – from which to exercise its powers of judicial review. This bodes well for the preservation of constitutionalism in an independent state. Unlike other newly independent or democratising states, which often have to establish a new institution of judicial review without firm historical foundations,[64] Scotland has the benefit of an existing institution that can swiftly consolidate its judicial review functions, and which – unlike the Supreme Court of the United Kingdom – can exercise these functions in a way that does not offend 'national' sentiment.

According to Ginsburg, judiciaries newly equipped with the power of constitutional review take time to establish their institutional authority.[65] Initially there will be a period of low judicial intervention, as the habits ingrained by unlimited parliamentary sovereignty still shape the judiciary's concept of its own role. This is then followed by a period of expansion of judicial power, as the judiciary begins to explore and test the limits of its place in the constitutional order. This growth period ends in the establishment of a new plateau, where the power of judicial review is accepted as an ordinary part of the political process.[66] This expected pattern is broadly borne out by the experience of countries such as Ireland, Malta and India, where judicial power took time to establish itself.[67]

The draft Constitution makes no provision for 'abstract' review – that is, review of the constitutionality of a bill before it receives assent, based on a theoretical analysis of its provisions.[68] The courts can only settle questions that emerge from the ordinary judicial process and are based on an actual, concrete, case. Abstract review can be regarded as an additional protection for human rights, since it allows the constitutionality of a law to be tested without waiting for an unfortunate (or brave) person to hazard their all in order to vindicate their rights, and it prevents 'patently unconstitutional' laws from reaching the statute book.[69]

Various models of abstract review exist. As discussed in Chapter 6, Ireland combines abstract review of legislation with a modified form of veto power in the presidency, such that the President of Ireland may refer bills of doubtful constitutionality to the Supreme Court, and must refuse assent to bills that are found by the court to be unconstitutional. Sweden, in contrast, balances a relatively weak system of concrete judicial review, with effective pre-legislative scrutiny.[70] This is exercised by a 'Law Council', consisting of members of the Supreme Court and the Supreme Administrative Court.[71] The Law Council has a wider remit than a court, since it considers not only the constitutionality of proposed legislation, but also its coherence, its compatibility with other laws, its relationship to the legal system in general, and its practical applicability. The Constitution of Sweden requires that the Law Council be consulted before taking a decision on a wide range of matters, including the Fundamental Laws, broadcasting, the availability of public documents, civil rights, local government taxation, and administrative law.[72] The advice of the Law Council may be overridden by the government and the Riksdag: it is, ultimately, 'a consultative and not a decision making body'.[73] Failure to obtain the opinion of the Law Council before enacting legislation does not invalidate a resulting law. Nevertheless, because of the moral authority of the Law Council and the public nature of its proceedings, attempting to needlessly bypass it, or flagrantly ignoring its advice, would be seen as a breach of convention and could have 'important political repercussions'.[74]

Neither the Irish system of presidential intervention, nor Sweden's powerful Law Council would necessarily be entirely suitable for Scotland. The operation of the Irish system puts a personal and discretionary power in the hands of the elected president[75] that would almost certainly be inappropriate in the hands of an unelected, non-partisan and legally irresponsible monarch, while Sweden's Law Council is embedded in a system of highly legalistic and technocratic governance[76] that would be difficult to replicate in Scotland.

However, it would be possible to imagine an equivalent mechanism of pre-legislative scrutiny, in which the constitutionality of bills could be tested before being enacted. Such a process already exists in the Scottish Parliament. Firstly, the Presiding Officer and the minister in charge of a government bill must certify that the bill is 'constitutional' (that is, within the competence of the Scottish Parliament) before it is introduced.[77] Secondly, the Lord Advocate, Advocate General and Attorney General have the right to stay the submission of a bill for royal assent, pending review of its constitutionality by the UK Supreme Court.[78]

Such arrangements, suitably modified for an independent state, would provide a double check against unconstitutional legislation: firstly a political check, which forces ministers and parliamentarians to consider the constitutionality of bills at an early stage of the legislative process; secondly a legal check, giving the Court of Session the chance to conduct abstract review, and, if a bill is found to be unconstitutional, to prevent it from receiving royal assent.

The Judiciary: Appointments and Tenure

In a British context, the perceived conservative bias of judges, their mixed record on the defence of civil liberties and their deference to the executive is a common complaint, both amongst those hostile to the judicial enforcement of rights[79] and those who favour stronger judicial review.[80] If judicial review of the constitutionality of legislation is to play a significant part in the political system, the constitution must take steps to ensure that the judiciary is professionally competent, independent and trusted by the general public to perform its duties in an impartial way.

For Commonwealth nations, the 'Latimer House Principles', which are intended to promote 'good governance, the rule of law and human rights', provide some guidance as to what might be regarded as 'viable and acceptable' in this respect.[81] These Principles recognise the role of judges in interpreting and applying national Constitutions, human rights conventions and international law, and so emphasise the need for an 'independent, impartial, honest and competent judiciary' if the task of 'upholding the rule of law, engendering public confidence and dispensing justice' is to be fulfilled.[82]

Judicial appointments 'should be made on the basis of clearly defined criteria and by a publicly declared process', including 'equality of opportunity for all who are eligible for judicial office' and 'appointment on merit', while also recognising 'the need for the progressive attainment of gender equity and the removal of other historic factors of discrimination'.[83]

Once appointed, judges should have 'appropriate security of tenure and protection of levels of remuneration'; they should enjoy 'adequate resources' so that the judiciary may 'operate effectively without any undue constraints'; they should not be 'subject to suspension or removal' except 'for reasons of incapacity or misbehaviour that clearly renders them unfit to discharge their duties'; and, 'interaction, if any, between the executive and the judiciary should not compromise judicial independence'.[84]

There is nothing particularly radical or novel in these provisions. They are endorsed by the law ministers of Commonwealth countries and are based on recommendations from the Commonwealth Parliamentary Association, the Commonwealth Legal Education Association, the Commonwealth Magistrates' and Judges' Association and the Commonwealth Lawyers' Association.[85] They reflect not only 'best practice' in the Commonwealth, but also the minimum standards of most liberal democracies – to the extent that a substantial deviation from these standards would call into question a state's liberal democratic credentials.

The provisions of the SNP's draft Constitution can now be examined in light of these Principles, beginning with rules on judicial appointments. Ginsburg identifies three main methods of appointment applicable to supreme courts: professional, cooperative or representative.[86] Professional appointments are conducted internally: for example, on the nomination of the executive, with existing judges acting as gatekeepers to ensure competent selection. Cooperative appointment systems require the joint approval of two or more appointing authorities, such as presidential nomination subject to legislative approval. Representative mechanisms make use of two or more appointing authorities, who, in distinction to the cooperative model, act separately and not jointly: for example, in Italy, one third of the Constitutional Court is nominated by the president, one third by parliament and the remaining third by the judiciary. To these three may also be added a fourth mechanism: 'single-body appointments', where one body, usually the president or prime minister, appoints judges without a formal need for professional screening, 'advice and consent' or any wider participation in the appointment process.[87]

MacCormick argued that the pre-devolution mechanism of judicial appointment – essentially a 'single-body' mechanism, in which judges were chosen by government patronage, after a process of informal and secretive 'soundings' – was unsatisfactory.[88] Instead, the draft Constitution envisaged the creation of a 'Commission on Judicial Appointments', which would have the right to advise the head of state on judicial appointments.[89] When first proposed, in 1977, this was a novel proposal, at least in a British or Scottish context (similar institutions existed in new Commonwealth Constitutions from the Caribbean to the South Pacific, as well as in the Constitutions of several European democracies). Indeed, to seek to limit the traditional patronage powers of the Lord Advocate and prime minister in this regard was considered almost 'insulting'.[90]

Today, however, the idea of a judicial appointments commission is no longer novel. The Judicial Appointments Board (Scotland), placed on a statutory basis by the Judiciary and Courts Act 2008, now already fulfils the intended functions of the Commission on Judicial Appointments. This is a further indicator of Scotland's rejection of traditional Westminster institutions and its, albeit cautious and partial, embrace of a 'Westminster transformed' model in which extra-parliamentary institutions of 'legal' constitutionalism help to constrain the arbitrary power of governments.

The Commission on Judicial Appointments, as envisaged by the 2002 draft, would consist of just five members: the Lord Advocate, the Presiding Officer of the parliament, a senator of the College of Justice elected by his or her fellow senators, and two 'eminent and impartial persons' elected to serve for a term of ten years by the parliament.[91]

This balanced composition, with a mixture of *ex officio*, legal and lay members, is common for comparable institutions in other Westminster-derived countries. Ireland's Judicial Appointments Advisory Board (JAAB), for example, consists of four *ex officio* senior judges, the Attorney General, a barrister and a solicitor, and up to three other members appointed by the government.[92] Similarly, the Judicial Service Commission of Jamaica consists of three *ex officio* judicial members and three members nominated by the prime minister 'after consultation with the Leader of the Opposition' – of which one must be a former appellate judge and two must be chosen from a list of nominees submitted by the General Legal Council.[93] Although the body proposed by the draft Constitution is smaller, it is also broadly similar, in terms of this mixture of legal and lay members, to the existing Judicial Appointments Board (Scotland), which consists of three judicial members appointed by the Lord President, two legal members appointed by ministers (one solicitor, one advocate), and five lay members also appointed by ministers.[94]

The wording of the Constitution states that the head of state 'shall make appointments [to various senior judicial offices] upon the advice' of the Commission (Art. 5, §3). This clearly means that no such appointment may be made without, or contrary, to the advice of the Commission. It also seems to imply that a nomination advised by the Commission cannot be refused. If this is so, then the Commission under the draft Constitution would be the real appointing power, not a pre-screening body for appointments that effectively lie in the gift of the executive. It is therefore a more formidable institution than similar bodies in other countries. The Irish Judicial Appointments Advisory Board, for example, is restricted to nominating seven candidates per vacancy, with no order of preference, from amongst which the government may (but is not obliged to) make the appointment.[95] Malta's Commission for the Administration of Justice is likewise limited by the fact that it can only advise the prime minister on judicial appointments when the prime minister asks for such advice, something that the prime minister is under no legal obligation to do.[96]

The purpose of similar judicial appointment commissions in most countries with a history of British rule is to insulate the judiciary from political patronage, and to ensure an independent, neutral and competent judiciary. They serve to put the traditional system of 'soundings' on a more formal, systematic and (sometimes) transparent and meritocratic basis. It is expected that they should be free from partisan pressure and political patronage, and should appoint judges according to 'neutral competence' rather than for overt ideological reasons. This neutralism is congruent with a model of judicial review that is formal and technical – where the task is to discover and apply the one true meaning of the Constitution.[97] This, of course, can be contested on the grounds that 'neutrality' is a myth that hides hegemony, perpetuates the socio-economic status quo and seeks to exclude crucial decisions from democratic control.

The 2002 draft responds to such criticism by introducing an element of democratic contestation into the judicial appointments process, since two of the five members of the proposed Commission would be elected by parliament. It is not inconceivable to imagine a scenario in which issues such as the reconciliation of privacy and freedom of speech with respect to journalism or the balance between religious freedom and equal access to public schools are expressed in parliamentary votes on the election of Commissioners, and then reflected in the Commission's judicial selections. In practice, the fact that the elected law Commissioners could be outvoted by the Lord Advocate and the members chosen from the judicial and legal professions would probably moderate the overt politicisation of the body.

The draft Constitution does not mention the qualifications required of judges. This stands in contrast to many Commonwealth Constitutions, which restrict judicial appointments to those with suitable qualifications and experience. Malta's Constitution, for example, limits appointments to the superior courts to those who have served for at least twelve years as a magistrate or advocate;[98] the Constitution of Queensland (Australia), on similar principles, requires judges to be chosen only from amongst those who are barristers or solicitors of at least five years' standing.[99]

Although it would be quite improper, the text of the Constitution does not expressly forbid judges from combining their judicial office with active membership of a political party, or even with another, perhaps elective, public office. Similarly, although judges would enjoy security of tenure once appointed, and may only be removed from office on grounds of misconduct by a two-thirds majority vote of parliament,[100] there is no protection for judicial salaries and nothing to prevent judges being assigned to other duties against their will.

These important matters are unaddressed in the draft Constitution, and are instead left to ordinary law, custom, or subsequent interpretation. It might be reasonable to assume that existing statutory and customary rules would continue to apply in the event of independence, and that there is no pressing need to make plain what everyone within the judicial system already understands. However, one of the functions of a written Constitution is to set out rules that are binding, authoritative and easily understood by the citizens; to be a yardstick of good practice, and a means of preventing that decay and corruption that inevitably sets in when things are based only on unspoken understandings of propriety. A written Constitution for Scotland should at least issue authoritative guidance on matters such as the qualifications and qualities required of judges and the standards of behavior, integrity and impartiality to be upheld by them.

In regard to the appointment, organisation, tenure and independence of the judiciary, therefore, the SNP's draft shows itself to be sound in principle, but somewhat lacking in matters of detail. These details are, however, quite simple, and might easily be rectified, based on international standards such as the Latimer House Principles and the practice of other Westminster-derived Constitutions.

Integrity Branch Institutions and Standards in Public Life

As discussed in Chapter 2, the term 'integrity branch' can be applied to a range of institutions, including Electoral Commissions, Public Service Commissions, ombudsmen and auditors.[101] The term is therefore used in a somewhat more general sense than that originally intended by Ackerman.[102] These varied institutions have at their root the common function of ensuring the non-manipulability of the democratic order by separating the permanent institutions of the state from the arbitrary power of the ruling majority – whether by protecting electoral procedures from partisan pressure, by ensuring scrutiny and oversight of financial and administrative acts, or by insulating the civil service from political influence.[103] The increasing prominence of integrity branch institutions can be seen in the 'democratic re-foundations' of Western Europe after 1945, of Southern Europe in the 1970s, and of Central Eastern Europe in the 1990s, as well as in the post-colonial Constitutions of the new Commonwealth.[104] Strong integrity branch institutions, which take contestation out of the party political arena of parliament and into special-ised non-partisan forums, are a form of 'legal constitutionalism', and, in the Westminster-derived tradition, are a defining characteristic of a 'Westminster transformed' political system.[105]

The 2002 draft Constitution is therefore quite unusual, amongst contempo-rary European and Commonwealth Constitutions, in making no provision for integrity branch institutions (except, of course, for the Commission on Judicial Appointments discussed in the previous section). It makes no mention of an ombudsman to protect citizens from maladministration. It says nothing about the institution of an Auditor General to safeguard the public purse. There is no institution to uphold the integrity of the civil service – as noted in the previous chapter, even the principle of a non-partisan, permanent and professional civil service is absent from the text. The draft Constitution also lacks provision for an Electoral Commission to oversee the administration of elections, and has no place for a Boundaries Commission to oversee the re-districting and re-apportionment of seats.

This does not mean that a hypothetical Scottish state operating under the draft Constitution would necessarily lack integrity branch institutions. Existing statutory institutions, such as the Scottish Public Services Ombudsman and Auditor General for Scotland, could presumably continue in being. Other institutions not currently in existence in Scotland, which would be needed in an independent state, such as an Electoral Commission and a Public Service Commission, could easily be created on a statutory basis.

Yet the advantage of constitutional entrenchment, over-reliance on statu-tory institutions, is that the Constitution can protect integrity branch insti-tutions from manipulation by the government. It enables non-partisan or

cross-partisan appointment to be prescribed and the powers of integrity institutions to be specified; it can place security of tenure rules, incompatibility
rules, and rules on the impartial conduct of integrity branch officers, beyond
the 'meddling' reach of ruling majorities.

The absence of such constitutional protection for the independent authority of integrity branch institutions in the SNP's draft Constitution places all
such rules and safeguards at the mercy of the ruling majority, subject only to
the flexible and imprecise limits of political acceptability. Rather than being
'constraints' on the arbitrary power of the government,[106] integrity branch
institutions could, at least *in potentia*, become highly manipulative tools of
government power.[107] They could even become sources of lucrative political
patronage – part of a corrupt, opaque, unaccountable 'quangocracy'.

Combined with the majority's unfettered control of parliament's electoral
rules, timetable, procedures, privileges and committees (as discussed in Chapter
5), this could easily lead, without any violation of the written Constitution, to
a great concentration of unaccountable power in the executive. For example,
there would be nothing to prevent the first government to win office under
the draft Constitution from establishing an Electoral Commission (with broad
powers over electoral processes, voter registration, districting and apportionment, and the registration of political parties) that is wholly appointed on a partisan basis by the incumbent ministers, whose members hold office for relatively
short terms, and which in consequence enjoys little 'integrity' in its actions.

This bleak outlook is not a prediction of what is likely to happen in an
independent state; it is merely an analysis of what the 2002 draft Constitution
could potentially allow to happen. The absence of guarantees for integrity
institutions is not a fatal flaw of the Constitution – it would only be damaging
if combined with a government policy of anti-constitutionalist power hoarding, which is intolerant of transparency and democratic contestation, and
which tries to undermine institutions outwith its control (such as that pursued,
some argue, by Orbán in Hungary today).[108]

Yet, since preventing such concentration and corruption of power is one of
the essential requirements of a Constitution for Scotland – being integral not
only to the 'Westminster transformed' model, as argued in Chapter 2, but also
more broadly to contemporary standards of good governance – its inability to
guarantee the autonomy of integrity branch institutions can only be regarded
as a serious omission and as something that falls short of the usual standards
of Westminster model constitutions.

An issue allied to that of 'integrity' is that of standards in public life. Some
Constitutions include a normative, if non-enforceable, statement of good
conduct, which is morally binding on those in positions of public trust or
leadership. The 1978 Constitution of the Solomon Islands, for example, lists a
number of responsibilities that apply to public officers, including civil servants,
local councillors, parliamentarians, ministers, members of integrity branch
institutions and even the governor general (Art. 93). These responsibilities
– which extend also to spouses, households, agents and trustees – include a
general obligation of good conduct in both private and public life, an undertaking to avoid conflicts of interest and all situations which could demean their

office, or allow their integrity to be called into question, as well as a specific prohibition on using public office for any personal gain (Art. 94). These moral requirements may be backed up by legislative force, and parliament is enjoined to make provision for the disclosure of the financial affairs of public servants (Art. 95). Similar provisions are found, for example, in the 2010 Constitution of Kenya.

These matters are not peripheral to the governance of the state. Even if not included in the Constitution (as text), they are crucial to the satisfactory operation of the 'real' constitutional order. A good Constitution can be undermined by a lack of civic virtue in the wider constitutional order.[109] The need for 'virtuous' leadership in a polity is a recurring theme, in particular, of the civic-republican constitutional tradition; the problem of how to inculcate civic virtue has recently, following the 'rediscovery' of that tradition, received more scholarly attention.[110] Classical republican concerns for virtuous leadership in the polity can be seen, for example, in Cicero's requirement in his constitutional model for the restoration of the Roman Republic, that senators must maintain 'unblemished behaviour', must 'set an example to the rest' and must 'have a grasp of public affairs'.[111]

These provisions, like those found in the Constitutions of Solomon Islands and Kenya noted above, can best be understood not as procedural or substantive rules, but as normative directions to the political leadership on how they ought to behave. The inclusion of a 'Leadership Code' or 'Code of Ethics' gets to the heart of what a Constitution is for: does the Constitution provide, in an Aristotelian sense, for a common notion of the good life, or does it simply provide procedures and ground rules so that people with few common standards and values can commodiously cohabit a geographical space? Is democracy just a set of decision-making procedures, in which differences are settled by the counting of votes expressing the individual interests and opinions of each person, or is it a commitment to a certain type of society, in which public deliberation and good governance have some intrinsic value?

Although found in several new Commonwealth Constitutions,[112] such 'Leadership Codes' or 'Codes of Ethics' do not at present form part of the standard *acquis* of constitutional law. It would be somewhat churlish to criticise the draft Constitution for its failure to include them. However, one does not have to subscribe to civic-republicanism, or look longingly back to republican Rome, to appreciate the importance of honest, capable and public-spirited leaders in a democracy. A Constitution can make a commitment to honest government and transparent processes without necessarily being committed to any one teleological vision of the good life. Besides, the question is not whether honest leadership is preferable to corrupt demagoguery, but whether the Constitution should commit itself to such leadership, claiming and lauding these principles as 'normative directives' endogenous to the Constitution, or whether the Constitution should remain 'neutral' on these matters, and let the impulse for good government and virtuous leadership come from beyond the Constitution (for example, from the expectations of a political culture and public opinion that is formed exogenously). Even if the Constitution makes no normative appeal to the qualities of politicians as civically virtuous 'servant-leaders', it might still be necessary to provide, on a pragmatic, procedural basis, an authoritative statement of what is, and what is not, acceptable behaviour. In the wake of the parliamentary expenses scandal of 2009, which highlighted the weakness of informal exogenous constraints, the case for the inclusion of a Code of Ethics, even in a liberal procedural Constitution, is perhaps stronger than ever before.

The aim of these provisions is not to normatively inculcate virtuous traits of character, but simply to prevent specific acts that would undermine procedures of democratic contestation by the power of money or patronage. The inclusion of such provisions in the text of a written Constitution, making fair procedures more resilient against corruption, could be seen as enhancing, rather than negating, its liberal procedural character. The absence from the SNP's Constitution of any institutions designed to ensure the fair, neutral, processes for the exercise of public power – and, in particular, the absence of an Electoral Commission, combined with the lack of any commitment to an impartial civil service – while not necessarily crippling to the Scottish polity as a whole, could be considered as a serious weakness of the SNP's 2002 draft Constitution.

Local Government

Article IV of the 2002 draft Constitution concerns local government. It requires that there should be local authorities elected by the people by proportional representation, 'in a manner similar to the election of members of Parliament'.[113] The structure and competences of these local authorities, including their 'composition, areas of authority, and financial and taxing powers', would be determined by ordinary legislation (Art. IV, §2). This is subject only to two constraints: firstly, any power vested in a local authority by law must be exercised autonomously, without direction or interference from the central government (Art. IV, §1–2); and secondly, any existing power vested in the three Island Councils cannot be limited, nor the territorial jurisdiction of the Island Councils altered, without the consent of the islanders to be affected, by way of a referendum (Art. IV, §3).

These provisions are similar to those of several Westminster model Constitutions in unitary states. Ireland, Malta and Bangladesh, for example, each take a similar line in enshrining the principle and some very skeletal ground rules for local government, while leaving their powers, duties, funding and operation to the discretion of parliament.[114]

Yet these similar constitutional provisions could accommodate very different forms of local government. Under the SNP's draft Constitution, the Parliament of Scotland could decide to establish a 'quasi-federal' system of internal devolution, with powerful regional assemblies enjoying broad fiscal, administrative and regulatory autonomy – even the power of secondary legislation – over policy areas such as infrastructure, transport, rural development, policing, public health, education and so forth. It could establish hundreds of local municipalities, forming a lower tier of administration, bringing parish-pump participation – backed by fiscal autonomy, and led by highly visible directly elected provosts – to small towns and city neighbourhoods across the country. Alternatively, as local authorities would have no powers or fiscal resources, except those conferred by parliament, parliament could decide to pursue a centralising policy, choosing standardisation over local responsibility. Parliament could, without in any way violating the text of the Constitution, erode the existing powers of local councils, forcibly merge authorities into ever larger units, and impose ever tighter fiscal controls to further reduce the scope for discretionary spending. Which of these outcomes would be more likely is a matter of conjecture; but the 2002 draft would allow for either.

Since 1975 there has been a trend towards centralisation in Scotland.[115] This shows no signs of abating, as the current Scottish government has transferred police and fire services from regional bodies to national authorities. The dominant discourse on local government in Scotland has been about service provision and cost saving, not about the role of local autonomy in cultivating an active, engaged, responsible civic culture[116] or distributing power more widely across society.[117] It is not inconceivable that independence might rupture this trend. It might bring new political dimensions, hitherto hidden from view – such as urban–rural and centre–periphery cleavages – more clearly into the frame of Scottish politics. It is not beyond the realm of imagination, for example, to envisage a Highlands and Islands Party arising, which puts pressure on the Scottish government to devolve powers north of the Great Glen.

This is speculation, of course, but the key point is that in refusing to be drawn on these particulars, and in refusing to commit itself to either centralised or decentralised patterns of governance, the SNP's draft Constitution once again shows its skeletal, minimal, liberal procedural nature. It does not depend, for its validity or acceptability, on embracing either a centralising or decentralising, once and for all, vision of Scotland. It simply provides a mechanism by which these issues can be argued over, decided, criticised and reformed, through the ordinary daily interactions of competing and cooperating political parties in parliament. If there is demand, in a newly independent state, for decentralisation, this draft Constitution would allow for it; if not, it will not put any great hurdles in the way of a centralised state.

Summary

The draft Constitution's basic form, as a supreme and rigid Constitution, enforced by judicial review, adheres to the 'common model'[118] of modern liberal democratic constitutionalism. Although this model may be radical and contentious in a UK context, it is a tried and tested, normal, standard thing around the world, including in most other 'Westminster' democracies.

In a Scottish context, it is a continuation of the move, impelled by the devolution settlement, towards a 'Westminster transformed' system; it would maintain the status of the Parliament of Scotland as a subordinate body, exercising delegated powers – only, they would be delegated from the sovereign people of Scotland, on terms that the people can change by referendum, rather than being devolved by the Crown-in-Parliament at Westminster. To this extent the draft Constitution's provisions on popular sovereignty, constitutional supremacy and rigidity, and judicial review can be judged not only as 'viable and acceptable', but virtually essential.

The specific human rights provisions of the draft Constitution are also sound. Being based on the European Convention, the Constitution's Article VI mainly entrenches rights that are already incorporated into Scots law by the Human Rights Act and the Scotland Act. The socio-economic rights included in the draft Constitution are hardly radical: they reflect the broad ideological centre ground of Scottish politics, as discussed in Chapter 3, and are framed in a way that maximises parliamentary, rather than judicial, discretion in their realisation. These provisions are, in comparison with many other modern constitutional rights instruments, rather skeletal.[119]

This, together with the lack of a preamble and silence on a range of substantial and foundational matters, indicates a commitment to a liberal procedural Constitution. In refusing to be drawn on questions of identity, teleological purpose, religious affiliation, ideological orientation or even sub-state governance structures, the draft Constitution eschews for the most part nation-defining or ideological functions. It simply provides a minimal and rather pragmatic framework for self-governance, allowing these questions to be settled, over time, through ordinary, parliamentary, sub-constitutional, democratic politics. Given the cleavages of Scottish society discussed in Chapter 3, and especially divergence on questions of national identity and sectarian belonging, this approach must – in the absence of a revolutionary nation-forging 'moment', that cannot at this time be foreseen – be accepted as the best, perhaps the only, way ahead.

The same reluctance to be pinned down to specifics, however, is less desirable when extended to the procedural, institutional, parts of the draft Constitution. The absence of provisions regulating the existence, powers and composition of integrity branch institutions is a serious, although not fatal, omission: this, together with a lack of procedural clarity concerning the rights of the opposition in parliament, parliamentary committees and other scrutinising and controlling mechanisms, could lead to a situation in which unaccountable power is concentrated in the executive. This would be contrary to the constitution's own declared intentions.[120] It could also, potentially, reverse Scotland's institutional development since the 1990s, undermining the attempt of the Constitutional Convention, the Scotland Act and the Consultative Steering Group to create in Scotland a more open, accountable and consensual democracy.

Notes

1. H. Lerner, *Making Constitutions in Deeply Divided Societies* (Cambridge: Cambridge University Press, 2011); W. E. Bulmer, *A Constitution for the Common Good: Strengthening Scottish Democracy After the Independence Referendum*, 2nd edn (Edinburgh: Luath Press, 2015).

2. Y. P. Ghai and J. Cottrell Ghai, *Kenya's Constitution: An Instrument for Change* (Nairobi: Katiba Institute, 2003); W. E. Bulmer, *A Constitution for the Common Good*.

3. S. Levinson, 'Do constitutions have a point?: reflections on "Parchment Barriers" and preambles', in E. F. Paul, F. D. Miller Jr and J. Paul, *What Should Constitutions Do?* (Cambridge: Cambridge University Press, 2011), pp. 155–62.
4. C. M. G. Himsworth and C. M. O'Neill, *Scotland's Constitution: Law and Practice* (Haywards Heath: Bloomsbury Professional, 2009), p. 22.
5. SNP, *A Free Scotland* (Edinburgh: SNP, 2002), Art. 1, Sect. 4.
6. C. M. G. Himsworth and C. M. O'Neill, *Scotland's Constitution: Law and Practice*, p. 4–5.
7. SNP, *A Free Scotland*, Art. 1, Sect. 1.
8. Ibid. Art. 1, Sect. 3.
9. N. MacCormick, 'An idea for a Scottish constitution', in W. Finnie, C. M. G. Himsworth and N. Walker (eds), *Edinburgh Essays in Public Law* (Edinburgh: Edinburgh University Press, 1991), pp. 159–81.
10. SNP, *A Free Scotland*, Art. VI, Sect. 9.
11. S. Levinson, 'Do constitutions have a point?: reflections on "Parchment Barriers" and preambles', p. 169.
12. G. D. Henderson, *The Church of Scotland: A Short History* (Edinburgh: Church of Scotland Youth Committee, 1958).
13. R. Hirschl, *Constitutional Theocracy* (Cambridge, MA: Harvard University Press, 2010).
14. Constitution of Ireland, Art. 8.
15. D. Turp, 'L'avant-projet de loi sur la souveraineté : texte annoté,' *L'Action nationale*, LXXXV/8 (October 1995), pp. 52–77.
16. A. King, *Does the United Kingdom still have a constitution?* Hamlyn Lecture Series, no. 52 (London: Sweet and Maxwell, 2001).
17. N. MacCormick, 'An idea for a Scottish constitution', p. 160; SNP, *A Free Scotland*.
18. P. Lynch, *SNP: The History of the Scottish National Party* (Cardiff: Welsh Academic Press, 2002); J. Mitchell, L. Bennie and R. Johns, 'Who are the SNP members?', in G. Hassan (ed.), *The Modern SNP: From Protest to Power*, (Edinburgh: Edinburgh University Press, 2009).
19. J. McCormick, *Understanding the European Union: A Concise Introduction*, 4th edn (Basingstoke: Palgrave Macmillan, 2008), p. 180.
20. SNP, *A Free Scotland*, Art. VI, Sect. 21.
21. Ibid. Annex A, 2A.
22. Ibid. Annex A, 2C.
23. Ibid. Annex A, 2D.
24. Ibid. Annex A, 2E.
25. Ibid. Annex A, 2F.
26. W. N. Eskridge Jr and J. Ferejohn, *A Republic of Statutes: The New American Constitution* (New Haven, CT: Yale University Press, 2010).
27. C. M. G. Himsworth, 'Human rights at the interface of state and sub-state: the case of Scotland', in T. Campbell, K. D. Ewing and A. Tomkins (eds), *The Legal Protection of Human Rights: Sceptical Essays* (Oxford: Oxford University Press, 2011).
28. SNP, *A Free Scotland*, Art. 1, Sect. 2.
29. SNP, *A Free Scotland*, Art. VII.

Constituting Scotland

30. N. MacCormick, 'An idea for a Scottish constitution', p. 161.
31. The term 'Bill of Rights' is a misnomer. The draft Constitution does not use the term, neither does it establish a separate Bill of Rights distinct from the 'frame of government', as some earlier Constitutions did (for example Constitution of Pennsylvania, 1776). Nevertheless, it is common in British English to refer to all constitutional catalogues of rights, and not just the first ten amendments to the US Constitution, as a Bill of Rights. The term, while technically incorrect, is used for convenience.
32. SNP, *A Free Scotland*, p. 5.
33. The draft Constitution would reduce the age qualification for voting from eighteen to sixteen. The consequences of this change – which must be regarded as marginal in the wider context of the Constitution as a whole – are not considered in this book.
34. SNP, *A Free Scotland*, Art. 6, Sect. 24.
35. D. S. Law and M. Versteeg, 'The declining influence of the United States Constitution', *New York University Law Review*, 87 (2012).
36. P. H. Russell, 'The *Charter* and Canadian democracy', in J. B. Kelly and C. P. Manfredi (eds), *Constested Constitutionalism: Reflections on the Canadian Charter of Rights and Freedoms* (Vancouver and Toronto: UBC Press, 2009), p. 300–1.
37. SNP, *A Free Scotland*, p. 4.
38. R. P. Bellamy, *Political Constitutionalism: A Republican Defence of the Constitutionality of Democracy* (Cambridge: Cambridge University Press, 2007); R. Hirschl, *Towards Juristocracy: The Origins and Consequences of the New Constitutionalism* (Cambridge, MA: Harvard University Press, 2004); A. Tomkins, *Our Republican Constitution* (Oxford: Hart Publishing, 2005).
39. SNP, *A Free Scotland*, p. 5.
40. R. Hirschl, *Towards Juristocracy: The Origins and Consequences of the New Constitutionalism*.
41. M. Mandel, 'Legal politics Italian style', in C. N. Tate and T. Vallinder (eds), *The Global Expansion of Judicial Power* (New York: New York University Press, 1995), p. 262.
42. N. MacCormick, 'An idea for a Scottish constitution', p. 162.
43. SNP, *A Free Scotland*, p. 6.
44. J. Kane and H. Patapan, *The Democratic Leader: How Democracy Defines, Empowers and Limits its Leaders* (Oxford: Oxford University Press, 2012), pp. 92–3.
45. P. Pettit, *Republicanism: A Theory of Freedom and Government* (Oxford: Oxford University Press, 1997; P. Pettit, *A Theory of Freedom: From the Psychology to the Politics of Agency* (Cambridge and Oxford: Polity Press, 2001); J. W. Maynor, *Republicanism in the Modern World* (Cambridge and Oxford: Polity Press, 2003); R. Gargarella, *The Legal Foundations of Inequality: Constitutionalism in the Americas 1776–1860* (Cambridge: Cambridge University Press, 2010).
46. K. Hutchins, 'Modelling democracy', *Global Society*, 12/2 (1998), 162; J. Kane and H. Patapan, *The Democratic Leader: How Democracy Defines, Empowers and Limits its Leaders*, p. 92.
47. SNP, *A Free Scotland*, Art. VII.

48. M. Khosla, *The Indian Constitutions* (New Delhi: Oxford University Press India, 2012).
49. P. Blokker, *New Democracies in Crisis? A Comparative Constitutional Study of the Czech Republic, Hungary, Poland, Romania and Slovakia* (London: Routledge, 2013).
50. B. Ackerman, 'The new separation of powers', *Harvard Law Review*, 113/3 (2000), 666–8.
51. R. B. Andeweg and G. A. Irwin, *Governance and Politics of the Netherlands*, 3rd edn (Basingstoke: Palgrave Macmillan, 2009), p. 153; M. Böckenförde, *Constitutional Amendment Procedures* (Stockholm: International Institute for Democracy and Electoral Assistance, 2014).
52. A. Lijphart, *Patterns of Democracy: Government Forms and Performance in Thirty-Six Countries* (New Haven, CT: Yale University Press, 1999), pp. 218–23.
53. Elkins et al., *The Endurance of National Constitutions* (Cambridge: Cambridge University Press, 2009), p. 66.
54. S. Levinson, 'Do constitutions have a point?: reflections on "Parchment Barriers" and preambles', p. 155.
55. A. Tomkins, *Our Republican Constitution*.
56. M. Cappelletti, 'Judicial review in comparative perspective', *California Law Review*, 58/5 (1970), 1034.
57. C. M. G. Himsworth,'Human rights at the interface of state and sub-state: the case of Scotland', p. 82.
58. M. Cappelletti, 'Judicial review in comparative perspective'; K. Rosen, 'Judicial review: old and new', *Yale Law Journal*, 81/7 (1972), 1411–20.; A. Sajó, *Limiting Government: An Introduction to Constitutionalism* (Budapest: Central European University Press, 1999), pp. 232–8.; C. Thornhill, *A Sociology of Constitutions: Constitutions and State Legitimacy in Socio-Historical Perspective* (Cambridge: Cambridge University Press, 2011).
59. SNP, *A Free Scotland*, Art. 5, Sect. 2.
60. N. MacCormick, personal communication (interview), 2008.
61. T. Ginsburg, *Judicial Review in New Democracies: Constitutional Courts in Asian Cases* (Cambridge: Cambridge University Press, 2003), p. 166; J. C. Adams and P. Barile, *The Government of Republican Italy*, 3rd edn (Boston: Houghton-Mifflin, 1972), p. 144.
62. M. C. Meston,W. D. H. Sellar and T. M. Cooper, *The Scottish Legal Tradition* (Edinburgh: Saltire Society, 1991), p. 66.
63. N. MacCormick, personal communication (interview), 2008.
64. T. Ginsburg, *Judicial Review in New Democracies: Constitutional Courts in Asian Cases*, p. 36.
65. Ibid. p. 36.
66. Ibid. pp. 65–77.
67. C. N. Tate and T. Vallinder (eds), *The Global Expansion of Judicial Power* (New York: New York University Press, 1995); M. Khosla, *The Indian Constitutions*.
68. T. Ginsburg, *Judicial Review in New Democracies: Constitutional Courts in Asian Cases*, p. 38.
69. Ibid. p. 39.
70. B. Holmstrom, 'The judicialization of politics in Sweden', *International Political*

Science Review/Revue internationale de science politique, 15/2 (1994), 155–7; M. Cappelletti, 'Judicial review in comparative perspective', pp. 1036–44; O. Nyman, 'Some basic features of Swedish constitutional law', in S. Ströholm (ed.), *An Introduction to Swedish Law*, 2nd edn (Stockholm: Norstedt, 1988), p. 62; N. Stjernquist, 'Judicial review and the rule of law: comparing the United States and Sweden', *Policy Studies Journal*, 19/1 (1990), 113.

71. E. Holmberg and N. Stjernquist, *The Constitution of Sweden* (Stockholm: Swedish Riksdag, 1995), p. 36.

72. Instrument of Government (Sweden) 1974 (as amended to 2011), Ch. 8, Art. 18.

73. E. Holmberg and N. Stjernquist, *The Constitution of Sweden* (Stockholm: Swedish Riksdag, 1995), p. 36.

74. B. Holmstrom, 'The judicialization of politics in Sweden', p. 159.

75. M. McDunphy, *The President of Ireland: His Powers, Functions and Duties* (Dublin: Browne and Nolan, 1945).

76. J. Ziller, 'European models of government: towards a patchwork of missing pieces', *Parliamentary Affairs*, 54/1 (2001), 102; T. Larsson and H. Bäck, *Governing and Governance in Sweden* (Stockholm: Swedish Institute, 2008).

77. Scotland Act 1998, Sect. 31.

78. Scotland Act 1998, Sect. 33.

79. J. A. G. Griffith, 'The political constitution', *Modern Law Review*, 42/1 (1979), pp. 1–21; A. Tomkins, *Our Republican Constitution* (Oxford: Hart Publishing, 2005).

80. H. Kennedy, *Just Law: The Changing Face of Justice – And Why It Matters To Us All* (London: Chatto and Windus, 2004).

81. Commonwealth Secretariat, *Principles on the Accountability of and the Relationship between the Three Branches of Government*, 2003, p. 10.

82. Ibid. p. 10.

83. Ibid. pp. 10–11.

84. Ibid. p. 11.

85. Ibid.

86. T. Ginsburg, *Judicial Review in New Democracies: Constitutional Courts in Asian Cases*, pp. 42–5.

87. Ibid. p. 44.

88. N. MacCormick, 'An idea for a Scottish constitution', pp. 162–3.

89. SNP, *A Free Scotland* (Edinburgh: SNP, 2002), Art. 5, §3.

90. N. MacCormick, 'Is there a constitutional path to Scottish independence?', *Parliamentary Affairs*, 53/4 (2000), 723.

91. SNP, *A Free Scotland*, Art. 5, Sect. 3.

92. Ireland: Courts and Court Officers Act 1995, Sect. 13.

93. Constitution of Jamaica, Art. 111.

94. Judiciary and Courts (Scotland) Act 2008.

95. D. G. Morgan, 'Selection of superior judges In Ireland', a paper from the conference on Judicial Reform: Function, Appointment and Structure, held by the Centre for Public Law, University of Cambridge on 4 October 2003.

96. Constitution of Malta, Art. 101A; W. E. Bulmer, 'Constrained majoritarianism: Westminster constitutionalism in Malta', *Commonwealth and Comparative Politics*, 51/1 (2014), 232–53.

97. T. Ginsburg, *Judicial Review in New Democracies: Constitutional Courts in Asian Cases*, p. 70.
98. Constitution of Malta, Art. 96.
99. Constitution of Queensland, Sect. 59.
100. SNP, *A Free Scotland*, Art. V, Sect. 3.
101. C. Saunders, *The Constitution of Australia: A Contextual Analysis*, Constitutional Systems of the World (Oxford: Hart Publishing, 2011), p. 173.
102. B. Ackerman, 'The new separation of powers', pp. 633–729.
103. Ibid. pp. 633–729 ; P. Pettit, *A Theory of Freedom: From the Psychology to the Politics of Agency* (Cambridge and Oxford: Polity Press, 2001), p. 169.
104. S. A. De Smith, 'Westminster's export models: the legal framework of responsible government', *Journal of Commonwealth Political Studies*, 1/1 (1961), pp. 2–16; Elkins et al., *The Endurance of National Constitutions*, p. 86; C. Thornhill, *A Sociology of Constitutions*.
105. R. Hazell, 'Conclusion: where will the Westminster model end up?' in R. Hazell (ed.), *Constitutional Futures Revised: Britain's Constitution to 2020* (Basingstoke: Palgrave Macmillan, 2008).
106. P. Pettit, *Republicanism: A Theory of Freedom and Government*; B. Ackerman, 'The new separation of powers', pp. 633–729.
107. W. E. Bulmer, 'Exclusionary constitutionalism: developments in Chile and Hungary', in S. Bisarya (ed.), *Annual Review of Constitution Building Processes, 2014* (Stockholm: International Institute for Democracy and Electoral Assistance, 2015), pp. 47–56.
108. *The Economist*, 'Orbán and the wind from the east', 14 November 2011; C. Boulanger, '"Is it a dictatorship and a police state yet?" Scheppele and Halmai on current Hungarian constitutional politics', *Verfassungsblog*, 11 July 2012, <http://verfassungsblog.de/dictatorship-police-state/> (last accessed 1 August 2012); W. E. Bulmer, *A Constitution for the Common Good*.
109. N. Bobbio and M. Viroli, *The Idea of the Republic* (Cambridge and Oxford: Polity Press, 2003), pp. 94–5.
110. R. Dagger, *Civic Virtues: Rights, Citizenship and Republican Liberalism* (Oxford: Oxford University Press, 1997); I. Honohan, *Civic Republicanism* (London: Routledge, 2002); J. W. Maynor, *Republicanism in the Modern World*; P. Pettit, *Republicanism: A Theory of Freedom and Government*; J. A. G. Pocock, *The Machiavellian Moment: Florentine Political Thought and the Atlantic Republican Tradition* (Princeton, NJ: Princeton University Press, 1975); M. Viroli, *Republicanism*.
111. N. Rudd, *Cicero: The Republic and The Laws* (Oxford: Oxford World's Classics, 1998), p. 153.
112. These provisions seem to crop up wherever Professor Yash-Pal Ghai has had a hand in the development of a constitutional text. The practical restoration of the ancient idea that a Constitution can not only establish institutions and protect rights, but also define the ethical standards expected of public officials, appears to be one of his original (and, as yet, not fully explored or appreciated) contributions to contemporary constitutional design.
113. SNP, *A Free Scotland*, Art. IV, Sect. 4.

114. Constitution of Ireland, Art. 28A; Constitution of Malta, Art. 115A; Constitution of Bangladesh, Arts 59 and 60.
115. E. Bort, R. McAlpine and G. Morgan, *The Silent Crisis: Failure and Revival in Local Democracy in Scotland* (Glasgow: Jimmy Reid Foundation, 2012).
116. Ibid.
117. A. McConnell, *Scottish Local Government* (Edinburgh: Edinburgh University Press, 2004), pp. 5–23.
118. J. Goldsworthy, 'Questioning the migration of constitutional ideas: rights, constitutionalism and the limits of convergence', in S. Choudhry (ed.), *The Migration of Constitutional Ideas* (Cambridge: Cambridge University Press, 2006), pp. 115–41.
119. Elkins et al., *The Endurance of National Constitutions*; D. S. Law and M. Versteeg, 'The declining influence of the United States Constitution', *New York University Law Review*, 87 (2012).
120. N. MacCormick, 'An idea for a Scottish Constitution'.

THE SNP'S CONSTITUTIONAL POLICY 2002–14: FROM LIBERAL PROCEDURAL CONSTITUTIONALISM TO DEMOCRATIC POPULISM?

Much had changed in the twelve years between the publication of the SNP's draft Constitution in 2002 and the holding of the referendum on independence in 2014. The SNP had moved from opposition, through a period of minority government, to majority government status. The party had recast itself as a party of government and begun to accustom itself to power.[1]

These developments had implications for the development of the party's constitutional policy, such that by the time of the referendum, the SNP's 2002 draft Constitution was little more than a historical document. Although the traces and influences of the 2002 text can clearly be seen in the later proposals of the Scottish government, it was superseded by the 2013 White Paper and the 2014 draft interim constitution. This chapter, accordingly, examines the constitutional policy of the SNP and the wider pro-independence movement during the years leading up to the independence referendum. It focuses on a comparison between the 2002 text and the text of the draft interim Constitution published by the Scottish government in June 2014.

The SNP's Constitutional Policy in Government

From the publication of *A Constitution for a Free Scotland* in 2002 until the SNP's coming to power in a minority government after the 2007 Scottish Parliament elections, constitutional policy remained far in the background. The party was more preoccupied with the internal structural reforms that would enable it to present itself as a credible, electioneering machine.[2]

Constitutional policy stagnated and even appeared to regress. The constitutional debate in Scotland focused almost exclusively on the 'status question' (the relationship between Scotland and the rest of the United Kingdom) to the exclusion of the wider 'constitutional question' (the constitutional arrangements for a Scottish state). The so-called 'National Conversation', a rather half-hearted consultation exercise undertaken by the Scottish government during the period when the SNP governed with a minority in the Scottish Parliament, framed the debate solely in terms of a sliding scale of Scottish autonomy, ranging from the devolved status quo, through implementation of the Calman Commission proposals and some sort of 'devolution max', to independence. Little thought was given to the constitutional form that the future Scottish state might take in the event of achieving such independence. Indeed, in the SNP's electoral rhetoric, the 'i-word' (independence) was downplayed, in favour of focus on competence in government and a more general sense of 'standing up for Scotland'.

The Scottish government's White Paper, *Your Scotland, Your Voice* (2009), put forward a strongly convincing case for independence, but had little to say about the Constitution of a Scottish state:

> According to the White Paper, Scotland could gain independence with only a few incidental changes to our current political institutions. All that would be required is the repeal or amendment, by the Westminster Parliament, of the offending parts of the Scotland Act and the Act of Union: abolishing the concept of 'reserved matters', prohibiting appeals to the British courts, and, in short, giving the Scottish Parliament sovereignty over all aspects of policy (subject, as applicable, to EU law and to European Convention on Human Rights). There would, of course, be many incidental matters to be settled as part of the transfer of sovereignty, from the apportionment of national debts, through the status and pensions of UK civil servants in Scotland, to the division of military assets, but none of these would affect Scotland's form of government.[3]

While retreating from explicit constitutional proposals, and although expressed in the cautious, civil service terms of a government rather than a party document, *Your Scotland, Your Voice* did continue to hint that a written Constitution for Scotland might be on the agenda:

> An independent Scotland could consider further progress, for example . . . formulating and agreeing a fully codified and written constitution. These issues would be decided within Scotland, either by the Scottish Parliament, or, as at the moment for major constitutional change, through a referendum.[4]

The SNP's policy document which accompanied the 2002 draft Constitution had suggested that the Constitution would be 'presented to the people of Scotland in advance of the [independence] referendum', and would 'come into force following the country's transition to independence'.[5] In other words, the 2002 draft Constitution was presented as a finished and final constitutional proposal; it would be put to the people as part of the independence package, and would come into effect – without much further ado – in the event of a Yes vote. The referendum would be, in effect, a referendum on the proposed Constitution, and not on the general idea of independence. There were sound post-colonial precedents for this plan. In several cases, former British colonies attained independence by means of a referendum in which they voted not for independence in the abstract, but for an 'Independence Constitution' that had been drafted in advance (usually by agreement between the Colonial Office and the parliamentary leaders of the country about to become independent).

The referendum in Malta held in 1964 was one example of this process. In other cases, such as Celyon, there was no referendum, but a Constitution was bestowed upon the country about to become independent by UK Orders-in-Council, transforming the constitutional basis of the country from that of a Crown Colony to that of a self-governing dominion.[6]

To apply this to a Scottish context, it would be quite easy to imagine an SNP government having come to power in Holyrood with a manifesto commitment to hold a referendum on a new constitutional dispensation (based, for example, on the 2002 text). If the 'pro-Constitution' side won that referendum, they would then expect and require the UK parliament to pass a Scotland (Independence) Act, which would provide for the granting of the new Constitution to Scotland by Order-in-Council. The new Constitution would be 'made in Scotland', and would have been approved in the independence referendum, but it would be authorised, to avoid legal rupture, by the UK parliament and by the Queen-in-Council. This process would be supported by many strong precedents from post-colonial transitions.

However, *Your Scotland, Your Voice* signalled a major change in the SNP's approach to the constitutional transition. Instead of the previously outlined process, in which constitutional development would precede a vote on independence, the approach shifted to one in which constitutional development would take place only after independence.

This change in approach makes tactical sense from the point of view of the SNP leadership. Firm constitutional proposals could be a hostage to electoral fortune in the referendum. Several highly placed members of the Scottish government feared that to release a proposed text, and to campaign on the basis of that text, could cause some people who might otherwise have supported independence to vote against it on the grounds of some constitutional disagreement.[7] Kicking the constitution into the long grass would enable consensus to be built around the general idea of independence, while leaving the resolution of disputes about what that might actually mean, in constitutional terms, until after the referendum. Moreover, being in government made the SNP more reliant on the civil service for policy advice, and the civil service, in its risk averse way, would be inclined to shy away from constitutional development.[8]

The change in approach also represents a more general trend in constitutional design – away from closed, elite-driven, template-orientated processes, towards processes in which public engagement figures more strongly. In the era of post-war decolonisation, the Constitutions of newly independent countries could be drafted by small groups of civil servants, working with the government and main opposition parties of the country concerned, through a brief and closed Constitutional Conference. They would in most cases minimally adapt a standard 'Lancaster House' template to meet the needs of the country. The resulting constitution would represent a mixture of standard 'Westminster-export' institutional features with some specific constitutional bargains or guarantees designed to appease, reassure, include or disarm, particular political pressures. Thus Kenya in 1963 got regionalism and bicameralism,[9] and Malta in 1964 got unicameralism, the constitutional establishment of Roman Catholicism and the single transferable vote.[10] Yet the overall shape, structure and content of the two Constitutions was remarkably similar, despite the obvious differences between the two countries, in terms of their histories, cultures and levels of economic development.

Even those Westminster-derived Constitutions that were not directly produced by Colonial Office civil servants were constructed through elitist channels, with only a minimum of public engagement. The Constitution of India was produced by a Constituent Assembly that was indirectly elected, on a limited franchise, representing only a minority of the Indian people.[11] The Constitution of Ireland was produced largely through the personal action of the prime minister, de Valera, assisted by Irish civil servants and trusted private advisors; although it was approved by a vote of parliament and then confirmed by a referendum, there was little public discussion of, or influence upon, the text during its gestatory stages.[12]

In such circumstances, constitution-making was a process engaged in by elites: *for* the people, and sometimes *with* the people (whose assent to the constitution may be necessary, as in the Irish example), but never *by* the people. Such an elite-led approach, however, was increasingly seen as illegitimate in contemporary Scottish circumstances. After the financial crisis and the parliamentary expenses scandal, trust in politicians was low.[13] A new form of constitutionalism began to emerge: what might be termed a 'populist ethical constitutionalism', in which the Constitution would serve as a rule of proper conduct and as a statement of values and principles, by which the people would be able to hold elites to account.[14] If constitutions express the values and principles of the people, and if they are intended to be a statement of what the people demand of their representatives, then an elitist, technocratic formulaic approach to constitutionalism will not do. A democratic constitution, in this sense, is not only one that creates democratic institutions and processes, and so enables the people to govern themselves by democratic means, but one that emerges from the people, and serves as a democratic 'covenant' for the transformation of society.

The more the constitution is expected to do, in terms of articulating values, bringing about social change and prescribing policies, the greater the need for public participation in its formulation. A 'liberal procedural' constitution is an empty bottle, into which substance is poured by the daily life of ordinary democratic politics. A 'covenantal', 'prescriptive', or 'essentialist' constitution (the three words, if not quite synonymous, have broadly overlapping meanings) is a full bottle, and it is necessary for the people, who must drink it, to choose its contents.

So the emergence of this concern for values, principles and standards to be constitutionally mandated necessarily implied a shift towards a more open, democratic and participatory constitution-making process. Such a process could not occur before the independence referendum, since it was impossible for the half of the country that opposed independence to be drawn, even on the grounds of 'contingency planning', into a discussion of the constitutional arrangements for a Scottish state. For them to have done so would have been to admit that a Scottish state would be possible, viable and maybe even helpful to the achievement of their declared aims.

A further impetus to the idea of participatory constitution-making was given by the experience of Iceland, which adopted several innovative techniques to 'crowd-source' a new constitution.[15] Delaying constitution-making until after independence could therefore be seen as a democratic measure, intended to allow scope for a longer, more open, more inclusive and more participatory constitutional process. This would allow the voices of 'ordinary citizens' to be heard, and not just those of the institutional 'grey suits' who crowd around Holyrood.

The 2013 White Paper and the 2014 Draft Interim Constitution

A consequence of the decision to delay constitution-making until after independence, however, was that a newly independent state would exist, from independence day until the adoption of the new constitution, in a constitutional limbo. To prevent this, and to avoid the uncertainty that would result, an interim constitutional arrangement would have to be put into place. This was exactly what the SNP government planned to do.

On 26 November 2013, the Scottish government issued a White Paper, *Scotland's Future*, outlining its vision of an independent Scotland. The White Paper, by setting forth the Scottish government's long-term policy programme on such issues as healthcare, university funding, childcare provision, taxes and pensions, provides the most comprehensive statement to date of the SNP's ideological vision. It will no doubt provide scholars with raw material for years to come, as they seek to analyse the strange political phenomenon of the SNP.

However the SNP is labelled, *Scotland's Future* rejected the hegemonic 'deep ideology' of the UK state, its agenda of privatisation, deregulation, post-industrial crony capitalism, permanent austerity, official British nationalism, quixotic great power pretentions, Europhobia, perpetual military engagement, and the shifting of social burdens from the rich to the poor which has become the 'London orthodoxy'.[16] Behind all of these specific policy proposals lay the central claim of the SNP's case for independence: namely, that compared to the lacklustre performance of the UK, a Scottish state would be better able, and more inclined, to serve the people of Scotland in practical, tangible ways; or, more precisely, that the people of Scotland, having attained democratic control over their own institutions, laws, policies and spending decisions, would be better able than the UK government to protect and advance their own interests.[17] In other words, although *Scotland's Future* might look like a glorified SNP manifesto, it differed from an election manifesto in that its promises are not predicated on a change of government but on a change of state.

Chapter 10 of *Scotland's Future*, in which the constitutional basis of the proposed Scottish state was described, was therefore the foundation on which the whole depended. It contained proposals for a 'permanent' Scottish Constitution that were broadly in accordance with the SNP's previous policy announcements: popular rather than parliamentary sovereignty; binding protections for human rights; the supremacy of the Constitution over ordinary legislation; and provision for socio-economic rights, including rights to universal education and healthcare, as well as European Convention rights.[18]

The 2013 White Paper also promised the development of an 'interim constitutional platform'. This would be a rather minimal framework of institutional
rules, based on the existing Scotland Act. It would make only such adjustments
to existing, devolved institutions as would be required to see the state through
the first months and perhaps years of independence, until such time as a new
constitution could be adopted by the people. The promises made in relation to
the interim constitutional platform were thin and vague. The whole approach
was cautious and minimalist; any radical constitutional change would have to
wait until after independence.

The draft interim Constitution, published in June 2014, was the Scottish
government's attempt to make good this promise of an interim constitutional
platform. Even in comparison to such meagre expectations, the draft interim
constitution was a disappointment. Expressed in the form of an Act of the
Scottish Parliament containing just thirty-seven short sections, the draft interim
Constitution deviated in many ways from the SNP's earlier constitutional proposals. Whereas the 2002 text set out to contain, as most constitutions do,
the principal rules by which the institutions of the state would be established
and regulated, the 2014 draft interim text was laconic in the extreme. The
legislative and executive branches of the state were briefly mentioned in two
sections amounting to a total of no more than forty-six words. These stated
that legislative power would be vested in the Scottish parliament and executive
power in the Scottish government, without bothering to address such matters
as the size of parliament, the methods of its election, the qualifications and dis-
qualifications of members, the election of the Presiding Officer, the adoption
of Standing Orders, the pay and allowances of members, the organisation of
committees, the grounds for dissolving parliament, the composition of the government, the manner in which the government was to be chosen and removed,
or, indeed, any other institutional detail that one would normally expect in a
Constitution.[19]

Other institutional aspects were equally neglected. Section 9 retained the
monarchy, and while prerogative powers were rendered subject to both the
constitution and to acts of the Scottish parliament, the extent of these powers
was nowhere defined, nor were conventions of ministerial responsibility anywhere specified. Likewise, although the constitution sought to recognise the
independence of the judiciary and the role of the High Court and the Court of
Session as Scotland's supreme courts in criminal and civil matters respectively,
no provision was made for judicial appointments, for the security of tenure of
judges, the power of pardon, or the role of law officers.

In short, the 2014 interim draft Constitution would have failed to perform
the core tasks of a constitution, such as defining the institutional structures of
the state and regulating the basic procedures by which the state would be governed. Bizarrely, these were deemed to be of merely sub-constitutional importance. These institutional provisions were to continue to be embedded not in
the Constitution, but in the Scotland Act, which was to be minimally amended
to meet the needs of an independent state.

The draft interim constitution contained no explicit process for its
own amendment and, although it was implied by provisions stating that

parliament's power would be 'subject to the constitution',[20] there was no supremacy clause that would have rendered Acts of Parliament null and void if incompatible with the constitution. In other words, the status of the constitution as a higher law was, at best, unclear. Even if the constitution were deemed by the courts to be superior to ordinary Acts of Parliament, the absence of a specific amendment procedure, combined with the grant of plenary power to parliament under Section 10, would appear to give parliament the authority to amend the constitution at will by ordinary statutes. The difference between the constitution and other laws would therefore be mainly a symbolic one which would be of little avail in restraining the wayward power of parliamentary majorities.

In comparison to the 2002 text, therefore, the 2014 draft interim constitution was both more conservative and more radical. It was very conservative both in its maintenance of existing institutions and in its continued reliance on a British, piecemeal and incremental approach to constitutionalism in which the constitution per se would be little more than a super-statute and would play only a minimal role in defining the institutions of the state. Instead of defining the institutions of the state, the role of the draft interim constitution would simply have been to define the state itself; that is, the draft interim constitution was intended to fulfil more of a declaratory than a regulatory function.

To return to the terminology of Hannah Lerner, as discussed in Chapter 2, the 2014 text was less 'liberal procedural', and more 'essentialist', than the 2002 text. The purpose of the 2014 text was not to define the powers of state institutions and protect the rights of citizens, but to proclaim the identity of the Scottish state, and to assert in very general terms the principles on which the new Scottish state was to set out its prospectus. It is in these principles, however sparse and generic they may be, that the radical elements of the draft interim constitution were made manifest. In comparison to the sparseness of its institutional provisions, the draft interim constitution contained some substantive innovations, such as committing the state to a peaceful and multilateral foreign policy (Section 19), to nuclear disarmament (Section 23), to children's rights (Section 29), and to the protection of the environment and natural resources (Section 31). It also contained a greater degree of constitutional nationalism, taking care to name the state, to define its flag and to provide for the adoption of an anthem (Section 8). The problem with this approach, however, is that whereas the 2002 text made an attempt to be a constitution for the whole country – a common procedural basis and framework of rights around which disparate parties, ideologies, interests and identities could pragmatically unite to engage in political action – the 2014 text sought rather to model Scotland in the SNP's own image, and to embed the party's programmatic stances in the constitutional text.

To judge the SNP's constitutional thought too harshly on the basis of the draft interim constitution would be unfair. Whereas the 2002 text purported to be a full, final and enduring constitution, the 2014 draft was explicitly intended to have no more than an interim status. It was not presented as a final constitutional destination, but simply as a bridge to statehood. Given the existence of broadly accepted and relatively well functioning parliamentary institutions under the Scotland Act (which, as discussed above, had already incorporated many of the SNP's earlier and more novel constitutional ideas), the extreme brevity of the 2014 draft may be partially excused; it avoided either reinventing the wheel on the one hand or opening up a potentially distracting and very technocratic debate about institutional reform on the other. There was an obvious political incentive to leave such details until after the referendum.

Nevertheless, the absence of constitutional specificity in relation to institutional forms and entrenched higher law status would have resulted in a situation in which a bare majority in the first post-independence parliament would have had total and unrestrained control of the state. As a guarantee against fears that an independent Scotland would degenerate into a one party state, the draft interim constitution was a failure, offering no reassurance – especially to those who did not support the SNP – that rights would be respected and democratic processes upheld after independence.

Similarly, although the draft interim constitution made provision for the appointment of a Constitutional Convention, which was to have been responsible for the development of a final, post-independence, constitution, it left the composition, terms of reference, timetable and organisation of the Constitutional Convention to be determined by the Scottish Parliament. In other words, there would have been nothing, constitutionally speaking, to prevent the SNP majority from imposing its own final constitution on its own terms and in its own time without reference to the other parties, to civic society, or to the people at large. None of this is to say, of course, that the SNP would have acted in bad faith, only that if (like the incumbent rulers of many newly independent and resource rich states) they had been so tempted, there would have been no constitutional barriers to effectively restrain them.

Finally, implicit in the 2014 text is an understanding of popular sovereignty that differs substantially from that articulated in the 2002 draft and in the Claim of Right. In the 2002 text, popular sovereignty and constitutional supremacy combined to restrain parliamentary absolutism. There was a clear distinction in mandate and authority between the limited, conditional and constitutionally bound power of the elected representatives of the people in parliament assembled, on the one hand, and the plenary, constituent power of the people themselves, on the other. For the representatives of the people to claim sovereign power would, in such terms, be a usurpation of popular sovereignty. The 2014 text blurs this distinction between popular and parliamentary sovereignty. Although it made bold assertions that 'In Scotland, the people are sovereign' and that 'the people have the sovereign right to self-determination and to choose freely the form in which their state is to be constituted and how they are to be governed', the vesting of constituent power in parliament, and not in the people, marked a failure – whether deliberate or otherwise – to embed the sovereignty of the people in resilient constitutional forms. In other words, the effective legal sovereignty of the people was denied, even as the rhetoric of political popular sovereignty was boldly affirmed.

Explaining the Change: Insights from Latin America?

Roberto Gargarella,[21] based on a study of Latin American constitutions from the early 1800s to the present day, identifies three constitutional models that can be very useful to us in the analysis of different proposals for a Scottish Constitution: the conservative, the liberal and the radical. Conservative constitutions are orientated around a commitment to the preservation of order and authority; they seek to protect existing hierarchies of power and to maintain traditional social values and practices.[22] Liberal constitutions are concerned, primarily, with the protection of individual rights and the restriction of state power, whether this power is used for conservative (tradition defending) or radical (inequality removing) ends.[23] Radical constitutions are based, above all, on a principle of democratic populism; they seek to elicit and to apply the will of the people with a minimal degree of filtering or restraint.[24]

Gargarella's typology focuses on the purpose, ideology and ethos of the constitutions being classified, rather than their structural features. This typology therefore cuts across other forms of classification, such as whether a state is unitary or federal, or has a presidential or parliamentary form of government, or a majoritarian or proportional electoral system. However, Gargarella argues that certain constitutional provisions, both in terms of structure and substance, generally follow from each of these models. Conservative constitutions typically concentrate power in the executive branch, while weakening legislatures, courts, sub-national authorities and other potentially competing centers of power. They minimise opportunities for direct, public participation, while adopting a minimalist approach to rights, which allows political authorities wide discretion in restricting rights on grounds of state security or to prevent assaults on the traditional moral order. Liberal constitutions are similarly skeptical about the role of the people in decision-making, but in seeking to limit power, typically provide for extensive checks and balances and a separation of powers between different branches of government as well as a division of competences between central and local authorities. Radical constitutions typically concentrate powers in elected legislatures and are skeptical of judicial constraints, although they may provide opportunities for direct public participation, through mechanisms such as recall votes and referendums.

The SNP's 2002 draft Constitution can be seen as a hybrid of the liberal and radical types. Although radical in its commitment to popular sovereignty, proportional representation, the use of referendums and extensive social rights, its liberalism was evident in the role assigned to courts in the protection of fundamental rights and in various mechanisms designed to weaken the executive and to strengthen checks and balances. Liberalism could also be seen in the relative lack of nation-defining provisions.

The 2014 draft interim constitution, in contrast, is perhaps best understood as a mixture of radical and conservative elements: somewhat radical in its substantive commitments to environmental protection, the stewardship of natural resources, children's rights and nuclear disarmament, but conservative in its treatment of institutional provisions and, in particular, in its concentration of power in the governing majority.

Another Latin American scholar, Gabriel Negretto, provides some insight into why this change might have occurred. Negretto's study of the constitution-making processes of Latin American democracies shows that while the range of viable and acceptable institutional options is shaped by historical background and other circumstances that are exogenous to the constitution-making process, the selection of particular institutional forms is largely a product of inter-party and intra-party bargaining.[25] Parties that are engaged in the constitution-making process have a common interest in reaching an agreed and workable solution (because, with the possible exception of a few 'spoilers', no one wants to live in a failed state), but they also each have separate interests in maximising their own share of power.[26]

One of the several determinants of institutional choice, according to Negretto, is the degree of electoral uncertainty. Parties that expect to win elections will generally seek institutions that concentrate power in the hands of majority winners, because they envisage themselves as holding office and being able to exercise those powers. Meanwhile, parties that expect to lose elections, or who because of electoral uncertainty have no clear expectation of winning, might favour institutions that disperse power more broadly, in order to protect their interests if they lose elections.

This at least partially accounts for the differences between the 2002 and 2014 texts. In 2002, the SNP was an opposition party with no experience of government. Constitutional provisions intended to restrain the governing majority – such as a rigid constitution with a super-majority amendment mechanism, or the minority veto referendum system – would appear beneficial to the party's interests. In 2014, the SNP was a party of government, with both a parliamentary and a popular majority behind it. In these circumstances, institutions that would leave the majority party unfettered, and that would give the SNP sole control over the transition from an interim to a permanent constitution, would be more appealing.

Conclusion: Towards 'Northminster' Constitutionalism?

The campaign for Scottish autonomy, as discussed in Chapter 4, has long been a thoroughly constitutionalist and democratic movement, which has articulated a radical constitutionalist critique of the British system of government that goes beyond a mere dispute between the London centre and the Scottish periphery. It has sought not only to redistribute power from London to Edinburgh, but to constitute a Scottish state that would be more democratic, more inclusive and more humane than that which it replaces.

These objectives were clearly visible in the 2002 draft text, which represented a marked shift towards a 'Westminster transformed' system. The 2002 text sought to correct the over-concentration of unassailable and unaccountable power in the hands of a prime minister leading a solid parliamentary majority; so many of its provisions – including the minority veto referendum mechanism, fixed term parliaments, proportional representation, the restriction of crown powers in relation to war and treaty-making, the limitation of the 'payroll vote', the rigid super-majority rules for the amendment of the constitution and the judicial enforcement of fundamental rights – are aimed at dispersing power more broadly, at increasing the strength of parliament and the judiciary against the executive, and at protecting the people from the abuse of power by majoritarian winners. The counter-majoritarian protections of the 2002 text were not replicated in the 2014 version. The 2014 text was not greatly concerned with the distribution power, but merely sought to ensure that power would in principle originate from, and in practice operate on behalf of, the people of Scotland.

Although far from perfect, the 2002 text was at least a satisfactory starting point, which, as this book has argued, met the contextual criteria of viability and acceptability. A few relatively small and uncontroversial improvements (for example, the inclusion of provisions for an ombudsman and auditor general, for an Electoral Commission and a guarantee of civil service impartiality, for the regulation of pardons, honours and other powers, and for strengthening of parliamentary processes) would have rendered it a good Constitution – at least by the lights and standards of our times.

In contrast, the 2014 draft interim constitution fell far short even of the basic standards that might be expected of an interim document. The text was proposed on behalf of a government as a means of legitimating a transition process to independence – and this, one supposes, it would have done, in so far as it would have proclaimed and defined Scottish statehood. What it would have failed to do, however, is to have constituted the state that was thereby established, in the sense of regulating the institutions of power and placing limits upon the arbitrariness of incumbent majorities. Indeed, the whole purpose of this patchy and unsatisfactory document, despite its shiny veneer of constitutionalism, seemed to be to place as few restraints as possible on the government's freedom of action. Even as a temporary, transitional expedient, it would not have provided the necessary constitutional guarantees for the safety of Scottish democracy.

The 2002 and 2014 constitutional draft texts represent two different variations on the Westminster model, addressing different perceived shortcomings of the British archetype: one, a democratic constitutionalist variation, framed in liberal proceduralist terms, that would transform the Westminster system through a combination of more diffused powers and better protection for human rights; the other, a democratic populist variation, framed in a more ideological and prescriptive form, that would hail democracy and pay homage to popular sovereignty, while in fact placing unbounded power in the hands of the parliamentary majority.

It is revealing, for example, that the constitutional rhetoric of the official Yes campaign and of SNP leaders in the lead-up to the referendum presented the Constitution mainly in terms of the more communitarian policy positions it could entrench – universal education and healthcare, for example – and not in terms of maintaining a basic distinction between the government of the day and the State as such.

Somewhat ironically, this focus on policy was quite indicative of the residual 'Britishness' of Scottish popular constitutional culture on the eve of the referendum. Having a national independence movement in which the Constitution, although vital to the state-building process, is not central to the electoral debate, is a remarkably 'British' thing (in the insular rather than global sense of the term). This lack of attention to the institutional aspects of constitutional design and state-building was a grave miscalculation. It perpetuated the notion – even if people did not necessarily voice it in these terms – that an independent Scotland would be an 'SNP state', and that voting Yes was, in effect, voting for Alex Salmond to remain as 'First Minister for Life'. This idea was an obviously false one, as Alex Salmond has never been anything other than a sincere democrat, but there was nothing in the SNP's constitutional proposals, in the period immediately before the referendum, to convincingly dispel it.

Thus the interim constitution failed not only to build on an anti-establishment desire for a more democratic form of government (which would have endeared it to the Left), but also failed to reassure the more conservative sections of the population that all would be well in an independent state – that their rights would be secured, and that the new state would be one in which they would have a place. Ultimately, the people were asked to vote, on trust, for a constitutional 'blank cheque'.

Yet, despite these differences between the 2002 and the 2014 texts, and despite the shortcomings of the latter, both represented a challenge to the orthodoxies of the British constitutional system from within the family of Westminster-derived Constitutions. Although the 2014 draft interim Constitution did not provide for entrenchment by any super-majoritarian procedure or requirement for a referendum, and although the text was sparse and minimal, it nevertheless labelled itself as a 'Constitution', with a political status above ordinary laws. Had it been adopted, it might have occupied a position not unlike that of the Basic Laws in Israel or the Constitution Act in New Zealand – not quite a 'proper Constitution', but more than just another statute. Moreover, it should be remembered, the 2014 text was intended only as an interim measure. It provided quite explicitly for its replacement by a final constitution; as such, whatever its shortcomings, it could have opened the door to a further process of constitutional change that might have resulted in a very different (and more robust) Constitution.

Other 'innovations' introduced at the time of devolution, including proportional representation, unicameralism, fixed term parliaments and the election of the executive by a formal vote of parliament, were common to both texts (albeit constitutionally protected in the 2002 draft and merely implicitly carried over from the Scotland Act in the 2014 draft). Popular sovereignty, although articulated legally and constitutionally in the 2002 text, and only politically in the 2014 text, was at least proclaimed by both as a principle on which the legitimate exercise of power should be based. Thus both texts inverted the traditional British system in which power flows downwards from the Crown.

Harshan Kumarasingham drew a distinction between 'Westminster' and 'Eastminster' constitutions, with the latter as an adaptation of the former suited for a particular set of national contexts.[27] Perhaps the constitutional proposals of the Scottish national movement point to what might be called an emerging 'Northminster' model: a constitutional order for the northern kingdom, in which the inherited and generic features of the Westminster system are infused with some distinctly Scottish ideas and institutions. If there were to be an independent Scottish state in future, and if it were to be based on a Constitution not unlike, say, the SNP's 2002 draft, then it could be a state that preserves the best aspects of the Westminster model, while reforming or removing the less appealing aspects of that model.

One result of the defeat of independence in the 2014 referendum may be the indefinite postponement of holistic, 'big bang' approaches to constitution-making in Scotland – that is, a root-and-branch redrawing of the constitutional system that results in a new written Constitution. The countries of the 'New Commonwealth', which became independent in the 1960s, 70s and 80s, had a clean break between colonial and independent status. One moment the flag went down in a self-governing Crown Colony, and the next moment the flag went up in a sovereign, independent country. At that symbolic moment the constitutional order fundamentally changed, from one in which the legal sovereignty of Westminster was acknowledged, to one in which the supremacy of the new independent Constitution would prevail. There was never any doubt about when the day of independence had arrived, or about which constitutional order was in place. In contrast, the countries of the 'Old Commonwealth', such as Australia, Canada and New Zealand, had a longer and less obvious route to full independence. Although Australia and Canada adopted written, legally supreme and procedurally entrenched Constitutions during that process, the adoption of the Constitution bore no clear temporal connection to the achievement of independence. Indeed, de facto independence was achieved in these Old Commonwealth countries long before this independent status was formally and legally recognized, and there was a period of theoretical ambivalence, during which their independence was recognized in the law of those countries, but not fully accepted by the adherents of Dicey's orthodoxies in the United Kingdom.[28]

The 'New Commonwealth' pattern would have been replicated if the independence referendum had gone the other way in September 2014. On independence day, Scotland would have achieved a new constitutional order – based, for the time being, on the Interim Constitution, and then replaced in due course by the Constitution that the Constitutional Convention, to be established under Section 33 of that Interim Constitution, would have adopted. A transition to independence following the Brexit vote may provide another opportunity for such a clean break and a root-and-branch approach to constitution building.

However, it is also possible – and I say this as nothing more than a speculative possibility, not as a prescription or a prediction – that Scotland's constitutional development will take a more circuitous path. A piecemeal accretion of more powers, a quiet but persistent assertion of claims by Scotland, and a gradual acquiescence to those claims by the UK government, may result in Scotland becoming imperceptibly independent, in fact, long before the constitutional and legal doctrines of the United Kingdom reluctantly catch up with, and adjust themselves to, that reality.

If that were to happen, then it is possible that some sort of constitutional framework will emerge that makes a distinction between constitutional laws and other laws, and that gives constitutional laws entrenched status, while falling short of a fully codified, rigid Constitution. The provisions contained in the Scotland Act 2016, which would require certain changes to electoral law in Scotland to be approved by a two-thirds majority of the Scottish Parliament, are indicative of the kind of 'manner and form' restrictions that might be used to protect the basic institutional structure and human rights against the absolute power of incumbent parliamentary majorities. Such a half-written, partially codified, semi-entrenched constitutional system could at least offer some institutional stability and protection to minorities, although the broader social, declarative and transformative purposes of a constitution would not be well served by this approach.

We have no way of knowing what the future might bring. From 19 September 2014 until 24 June 2016, it seemed that Scotland would remain in the United Kingdom – although it might be a very different, and less united, kingdom. At the time of writing, however, the independence movement appears to have been revitalised by the decision of England and Wales to leave the European Union. Should the opportunity to establish an independent Scottish state arise again in the future, it is to be hoped that the challenge of state-building, and especially constitution-building, is properly grasped. If that moment comes, I hope that the detailed study of past proposals conducted in this book will be of help to future generations, enabling work on constitutional negotiation and drafting to proceed from a better informed position than might have otherwise been the case, had these previous texts been lost to history.

In the meantime, this book has challenged the view that a written Constitution for Scotland would be a novel, radical or untried idea, or that adopting a Constitution would be a unique or catastrophic break with the British tradition in its global sense. Within the far-flung family descended from the 'Mother of Parliaments', independence is the norm, and written constitutions are the norm too. Examples drawn from Westminster-derived Constitutions around the world have shown that 'Britishness', in a political-constitutional as well as socio-cultural sense, is much bigger and broader than membership of the United Kingdom. Leaving the United Kingdom to establish an independent state would not repudiate all of that heritage – indeed, it could even be seen as a logical extension of it, with Scotland taking the well-worn path from London rule to independence and constitutional democracy that Australia, Canada, India, Malta and many other countries have already taken.

Notes

1. G. Hassan (ed.), *The Modern SNP: From Protest to Power* (Edinburgh: Edinburgh University Press, 2009); J. Mitchell, L. Bennie and R. Johns, *The Scottish National Party: Transition to Power* (Oxford: Oxford University Press, 2012); C. A. McAngus, 'Do stateless-nationalist-regionalist-parties differ from other party types? Comparing organisational reform processes in Plaid Cymru and the Scottish national party', *British Politics* (2 November 2015) <http://www.palgrave-journals.com/bp/journal/vaop/ncurrent/pdf/bp201545a.pdf> (last accessed 8 March 2016).

2. C. A. McAngus, 'Do stateless-nationalist-regionalist-parties differ from other party types?'.
3. W. E. Bulmer, *A Model Constitution for Scotland: Making Democracy Work in an Independent State* (Edinburgh: Luath Press, 2011), p. 15.
4. Scottish Government, 2009, cited in W. E. Bulmer, *A Model Constitution for Scotland*, p. 16.
5. SNP, *A Free Scotland* (2002), p. 4.
6. W. I. Jennings, *The Constitution of Ceylon* (Bombay: Oxford University Press, 1949).
7. This insight is based on my personal observations and conversations with senior members of the Scottish government during my tenure as Research Director of the Constitutional Commission (2009–13).
8. A. Bell, 'Considering a Constitution: a view from a former government insider', in A. Reid and M. Davis (eds), *A Modest Proposal for the Agreement of the People* (Edinburgh: Luath Press, 2014).
9. Y. P. Ghai and J. Cottrell Ghai, *Kenya's Constitution: An Instrument for Change* (Nairobi: Katiba Institute, 2011).
10. W. E. Bulmer, 'Constrained majoritarianism: Westminster constitutionalism in Malta', *Commonwealth and Comparative Politics*, 51/1 (2014), 232–53.
11. G. Austin, *The Indian Constitution, Cornerstone of a Nation*, 2nd edn (Oxford: Oxford University Press, 1999).
12. Constitution of Ireland, Art. 8.
13. A. Seldon, *Trust: How we Lost It and How to Get It Back* (London: Bite Back Publishing, 2010).
14. 'Populist ethical constitutionalism' is the term that best describes the constitutional demands and preferences I encountered in public meetings in Scotland between 2009 and 2013 in my capacity as Research Director of the Constitutional Commission. There was a lot of enthusiasm for a constitution as a means of regulating political behaviour, and, in particular, as a device for enforcing the ethical accountability of governing elites. Because my reflections are based mainly on anecdotal conversations with self-selecting audiences, I have no evidential base from which to make any empirical claims about 'populist ethical constitutionalism'. These reflections did, nevertheless, inspire much of my previous book, *A Constitution for the Common Good: Strengthening Scottish Democracy after the Independence Referendum*, 2nd edn (Edinburgh: Luath Press, 2015), in which – although I do not use the term – some aspects of 'popular ethical constitutionalism' are explored.
15. Thorvaldur Gylfason, *Iceland: Direct Democracy in Action* <https://www.opendemocracy.net/thorvaldur-gylfason/iceland-direct-democracy-in-action> (last accessed 30 June 2016).
16. Interview with Robin McAlpine, Director of Common Weal, 2015.
17. The extent to which a Scottish state could actually live up to these promises, and the degree to which coherence between the 'high-road' of Nordic productivity and welfare and the 'low-road' of Baltic competitiveness could be reconciled, is of course another matter. See M. Keating and M. Harvey, *Small Nations in a Big World: What Scotland can Learn* (Edinburgh: Luath Press, 2014).
18. Scottish Government, 2013.

19. Scottish Government, 2014.
20. Scottish Government, 2014.
21. R. Gargarella, *The Legal Foundations of Inequality: Constitutionalism in the Americas 1776–1860* (Cambridge: Cambridge University Press, 2010); R. Gargarella, *Latin American Constitutionalism 1810–2010: The Engine Room of the Constitution* (New York: Oxford University Press, 2013).
22. R. Gargarella, *The Legal Foundations of Inequality*, pp. 90–152.
23. Ibid. pp. 153–214.
24. Ibid.pp. 9–89.
25. G. L. Negretto, *Making Constitutions: Presidents, Parties and Constitutional Choice in Latin America* (Cambridge: Cambridge University Press, 2013).
26. Ibid. pp. 43–106.
27. H. Kumarasingham, *A Political Legacy of the British Empire: Power and the Parliamentary System in Post-Colonial India and Sri Lanka* (London: I. B Tauris, 2013).
28. P. C. Oliver, *The Constitution of Independence: The Development of Constitutional Theory in Australia, Canada and New Zealand* (Oxford: Oxford University Press, 2005).

CONSTITUTION PREPARED BY THE SCOTTISH PROVISIONAL CONSTITUENT ASSEMBLY, 1962

Note: Section headings are not in the original manuscript. They have been added to help understanding of the text.

I. General Principles

(1) Scotland is a free, independent, democratic nation, the power to rule being vested in the Scottish people and exercised by them through a National Assembly appointed by a free vote of its citizens.

(2) All persons who were domiciled in Scotland at the time of the promulgation of this Constitution shall be citizens of Scotland. Thereafter the acquisition of and loss of Scottish citizenship shall be determined by law, but no person who is a citizen of any other country can be a citizen of Scotland except in cases where the National Assembly by a unanimous resolution shall confer Honorary Citizenship.

(3) Scotland is, in territory, all the mainland, islands and territorial seas which are subject to the jurisdiction of the Scottish Courts. The capital city of Scotland is the City of Edinburgh.

(4) All citizens have freedom of religious belief and worship and there shall be no discrimination on grounds of religion. The national church is the Church of Scotland by law defined in the Act for the Security of the Protestant Religion and Presbyterian Church Government in the Kingdom of Scotland, 1707, and the Articles Declaratory of the Constitution of the Church of Scotland in Matters Spiritual, 1921.

(5) The defence of the territory of the nation, its institutions and general safety, is the duty of every citizen, but no citizen shall bear arms unless called upon and authorised to do so by laws enacted by the National Assembly.

(6) The land and natural resources of the nation shall be fully developed and utilized in the interest of the commonweal. The extent of individual and corporate ownership of land and natural resources shall be limited by law, and all monopolies shall be regulated by the National Assembly.

(7) In the event of the business of a trading, manufacturing, industrial, or any other company domiciled in Scotland being offered for sale, there shall be a right of pre- emption in the National Assembly if the proposed purchaser is a foreign person or concern situated or domiciled furth of Scotland, and provided always that the price offered by the National Assembly shall, in the opinion of independent experts to be summoned, be a fair price.

(8) The State shall protect the basic natural institution of society of which the chief are marriage and the family.

(9) The State shall provide social services for the maintenance of the health, education and general well-being of the people.

(10) The State shall take all possible steps to safeguard the cultural heritage of the nation and shall initiate such measures as are within its power to foster the arts and to promote the full cultural life of the people.

(11) Every citizen shall be liable to pay a share of public expenses in the form of taxes and other dues.

(12) The National Flag is the White Saltire on Azure Blue: the National Badge is the Thistle proper: the Motto is "Nemo me impune lacessit": the Ensign of Public Authority is the Sovereign Achievement (Royal Arms) of Scotland undifferenced: the Great Seal of Scotland shall bear the Sovereign Achievement (Royal Arms) of Scotland undifferenced: the Royal Banner in use in Scotland shall be the tressured Lion Rampant: all as recorded in the Register of Arms by the Lyon King of Arms.

II. Fundamental Rights

(13) The State is not omnipotent, it exists solely to serve the commonweal. At all times, in all its agencies, it shall remain the servant of the citizens and shall be subservient to their fundamental rights as set forth in this Constitution. The State shall not violate the person or the liberty of the individual, nor shall any individual be deprived of personal liberty or property save by due process of law.

(14) All citizens are equal in rights and obligations and are equal before the law. The right of Gaelic-speaking citizens to use their mother tongue before the Courts and the administrative authorities, and to obtain from them all their publications in Gaelic, shall be guaranteed by law.

(15) No citizen shall be compelled against his conscience to render service to the State involving the use of force of arms. Exemption from such service shall be regulated by law.

(16) All citizens shall have the right of freedom of expression and of dissemination of opinion by speech, by writing, and by all visual and auditory media, and the right of free access to information from generally available sources. Freedom of the press, radio, television, the theatre, motion pictures, and all other forms of general communication shall be limited only by law, and for such causes as the law may define.

(17) There shall be no official censorship save in the case of serious emergency under an Emergency Measures Act whose duration shall be limited to a maximum period of 12 months, but subject to renewal by the National Assembly.

(18) All citizens shall have the right of peaceable assembly.

(19) All citizens shall have the right to form associations and societies except where the objects or activities of such associations or societies conflict with the law.

(20) No citizen shall be forced to follow a specific trade or profession or to enter a place of training or a place of work against his or her will, except when deprived of his or her liberty after due process of law. No citizen shall be compelled, as a condition of his right to work, to join, or to abstain from joining, any society, association or combination.

(21) Secrecy of the mail and telecommunications shall be inviolable. Restrictions may be ordered only by law.

(22) Every citizen has the right to leave the country at any time. This right may be restricted only on a warrant issued by a Sheriff.

(23) The home shall not be violated. Searches may be ordered only by a Sheriff or, in the event of danger in delay, by other agents as provided by law, and may be carried out only in the form and manner prescribed by law. The right of the people to be secure in their persons, premises, papers, and effects, against searches and seizures, shall not be violated, except on a warrant issued by a Sheriff.

(24) Every citizen when charged with a breach of the law shall be presumed innocent until his or her guilt has been proven in a court of law.

(25) No citizen shall be detained in custody longer than 48 hours before being brought before a court of law and charged with a breach of the law. The trial of every person who has been charged and detained in prison, or

remanded on bail, must be completed within a period of 110 days from the day on which he or she was committed, except, as heretofore, in case of emergency.

(26) In the event of the infringement of any of the aforementioned fundamental rights, or of any recognised common law right, a citizen can seek redress at law, or by submitting a personal petition to the Commissioner of Commonweal, as provided in Article 65 hereof.

III. *Head of State and the Executive*

(27) The constitutional head of State is the King or Queen, if Queen Regnant, deriving title from the Act of Settlement, 1700, and the Treaty of Union, 1707, hereinafter referred to as the Sovereign.

(28) The Sovereign is proclaimed King or Queen, at Mercat Cross of Edinburgh, on the death or abdication of the reigning Sovereign.

(29) The Sovereign shall be crowned King or Queen of Scots with the Scottish Crown in Edinburgh.

(30) The Sovereign on Coronation shall take an oath to uphold entire the Constitution of the Kingdom of Scotland.

(31) No office of State can be held by any person who is not a citizen of Scotland, except as provided in the Special Provisions of this Constitution.

(32) The Representative of the Sovereign in Scotland shall be the Sovereign's Commissioner and shall be styled the King's or Queen's Commissioner; he or she shall be appointed by the Sovereign on the advice of the Executive Council, provided for in Article 45 hereof, for a term of five years. The appointment of the Sovereign's Commissioner can be terminated, or his or her resignation accepted by the Sovereign, before the full term of office has expired, on the advice of the Executive Council.

(33) The functions of the Sovereign shall be exercised by the King or Queen, or the Sovereign's Commissioner, solely and always on the advice of the Executive Council.

(34) The Sovereign shall summon, prorogue and dissolve the parliaments of the National Assembly.

(35) The Sovereign shall address the National Assembly at the opening of each session of Parliament, and on the invitation of the National Assembly.

(36) The power of pardoning for crime shall reside in the Sovereign, who shall act on the advice of the Commissioner of Commonweal.

(37) The power to appoint ambassadors, to declare war and to make treaties, shall reside in the Sovereign, and shall be exercised solely on the advice of the Executive Council.

(38) The Sovereign, or the Sovereign's Commissioner, shall grant, in Edinburgh, credentials to the diplomatic representatives of Scotland, and shall receive, in Edinburgh, the credentials of the official representatives of other nations accredited to him or her as the Sovereign of Scotland.

(39) The Sovereign, and the Sovereign's Commissioner, shall have official residences in Edinburgh.

(40) The Sovereign shall confer decorations for distinguished services on the advice, or with the consent, of the National Assembly. No rank or title shall be conferred other than that which each office carries with it. The title Lord shall cease to be used in relation to all offices within the nation. No personal or hereditary titles or privileges shall be recognised other than those of Princes and Princesses of the blood royal within the immediate succession. There shall be no party-political honours or decorations. No citizen shall accept rank, title, or privilege from the head of any other State or from the government of any other State without first securing the sanction of the National Assembly. Awards for humane achievements may be awarded and accepted without sanctions.

(41) The chief secretary of State and Head of the Executive Council of the National Assembly shall be styled the Prime Minister. He shall be nominated by the National Assembly and appointed to his office by the Sovereign, who shall also receive his resignation. The Prime Minister at the time of his nomination must be a member of the National Assembly.

(42) The executive and administrative functions of the National Assembly shall be exercised through departments of State. The number, responsibilities and functions of such departments shall be established by law.

(43) Each department of State shall be in the charge of a Secretary of State who shall be appointed and whose resignation shall be received by the Sovereign on the advice of the Prime Minister. Each Secretary must be a member of the National Assembly.

(44) The Prime Minister and Secretaries of State shall be, individually and jointly, responsible to the National Assembly, which shall have the power to call to account and to censure the Prime Minister and any Secretary of State. If a motion of no- confidence in the Executive Council is passed by a majority of the members of the National Assembly, present and voting, the Executive Council shall resign as a body.

(45) The Prime Minister and such Secretaries of State as may be provided for by law – the following always being included, the Secretary of State for Home Affairs, Foreign Affairs, Health and Welfare, Education, Defence, Scientific and Economic Development, and the Treasury – shall form the Executive Council of the National Assembly. The Prime Minister shall preside over the Executive Council.

(46) The Prime Minister, Secretaries of State, and the President of the National Assembly shall receive such renumeration as shall from time to time be provided by Act of the National Assembly.

(47) The Executive Council shall have powers of inquiry and may, with the approval of the National Assembly, appoint special commissions with powers of summons to investigate and report to the National Assembly on matters of general or specific importance. The Prime Minister or any Secretary of State shall not have sole power to appoint any tribunal of investigation or any commission of inquiry of any kind.

(48) The Sovereign, or the Sovereign's Commissioner, shall be informed in general terms by the Prime Minister of the decisions of the Executive Council, but neither of them shall be present at its deliberations.

(49) Bills passed by the National Assembly which have been given the Sovereign's assent, or the assent of the Sovereign's Commissioner on his or her behalf, shall become laws of Scotland; the only Bills which shall not require the Sovereign's assent shall be Bills to amend the Constitution: these having been passed by the National Assembly shall be submitted to a national referendum, as provided for in Article 97 hereof.

IV. *The National Assembly*

(50) The people of Scotland shall exercise legislative power through the National Assembly, whose members shall be styled "Commissioners".

(51) The seat of the National Assembly shall be Edinburgh. In exceptional circumstances, the Assembly may meet in other places in Scotland.

(52) The National Assembly shall be elected by direct universal suffrage by secret ballot, in accordance with the methods and conditions laid down by Acts of the National Assembly.

(53) The system used for elected Commissioners shall be Proportional Representation by the Single Transferable Vote.

(54) The right of voting shall belong to every citizen who has attained 18 years, is of legal capacity and is not a convicted criminal in custody.

(55) The number of Commissioners of the National Assembly shall from time to time be fixed by law, but the total number of Commissioners shall not be fixed at less than one Commissioner for each 25,000 electors. The ratio between the number of Commissioners to be elected at any time for each constituency and the population of each constituency, as ascertained at the last preceding census, shall as far as practicable, be the same throughout the country.

(56) Every candidate for election as a Commissioner of the National Assembly must be a citizen of Scotland over 21 years of age, who has the right to vote and who is not an undischarged bankrupt, or a person who has standing against him or her an unpaid fine for a criminal offence.

(57) The National Assembly is elected for a term of four years, but a General Election may be held before the expiry of the full term, by a decision of the National Assembly on a motion submitted by at least 25 Commissioners and supported by a majority of the members of the National Assembly present and voting. The date of each General Election shall be decided by the National Assembly.

(58) Each duly elected Commissioner to the National Assembly must make and subscribe solemn declaration that he or she will uphold the Constitution before becoming eligible to take his or her seat.

(59) The National Assembly must seat a Commissioner duly elected in accordance with the provisions of the Constitution and the electoral laws, and who makes the declaration of adherence (Art. 58). Each Commissioner shall be bound to conform to such rules of procedure as the National Assembly shall from time to time establish.

(60) A Commissioner cannot be arrested, or cited civilly, or tried, for opinions or comment expressed, or for statements made, or for activities undertaken, in pursuance of his duties within the National Assembly. This immunity does not extend to a Commissioner in breach of criminal law.

(61) A Commissioner can only be deprived of his or her seat during his or her elected term, if convicted of a criminal offence specified in the Rules of the National Assembly.

(62) Each Commissioner on taking his or her seat in the National Assembly shall receive such remuneration and expenses as shall be determined by the National Assembly, which shall organise office accommodation and secretarial services for each Commissioner.

(63)(a) The National Assembly shall exercise the legislative power of the nation in relation to, but not restricted to, the following:-

(i)   The imposition of taxes, duties, customs, and other public charges;

(ii)   The control of the finances of the nation, securing loans on the credit of the nation and appropriate the sums of money necessary to meet the expenditure of the State;

(iii) The determination of the annual appropriation for the Sovereign's Privy Purse and Royal Household, and for the annual honorarium of the Sovereign's Commissioner in Scotland;

(iv) The revision of the list of official salaries and pensions.

(b) It shall have laid before it the complete records of the Executive Council including all documents.

(c) It shall have powers of summons and inquiry in matters of state.

(d) It shall nominate and appoint an Auditor-General who shall, annually, examine the accounts of the State and publish a report thereof, and provide for the organisation of an office wherein such audits can be undertaken.

(e) It shall grant naturalisation and citizenship rights.

(64) The National Assembly shall adhere to the procedures set forth in this Constitution for the making of laws. In a case of serious emergency under an Emergency Measures Act the National Assembly may delegate legislative power to the Executive Council, as in Article 17 hereof.

(65) The National Assembly shall appoint a citizen of legal education, qualification and ability, and of known personal integrity as a Commissioner for Administration, who shall be styled Commissioner of Commonweal, to supervise, on behalf of the National Assembly, all central and local government administration.

The Commissioner of Commonwealth shall be appointed one month after each General Election and shall continue in office until one month after the next General Election, when he shall be eligible for reappointment by the National Assembly for a further term. He shall:

(a) Keep under review the effects on the citizens of the application of laws and statutes;

(b) Receive by petition all complained of injustice and infringements of private and fundamental rights alleged to have been committed by, or caused by the negligence or mistake of, the national or local government authorities, administration, or agencies, or any of their servants, against the petitioner;

(c) Be accorded full powers of investigation, including unreserved access to all records and correspondence, and the right to cite witnesses;

(d) Cause to be brought to Court any case requiring legal judgment, or call on a Government department or local authority to take disciplinary or other appropriate action.

A Deputy Commissioner of Commonwealth, having the same qualities as the Commissioner, may be appointed under the same conditions and for a similar term of office.

The Commissioner of Commonweal shall be accorded the salary of a Judge of the Court of Session and shall be granted an appropriate pension. He shall not hold any office in public or private companies, enterprises, or institutions, except with the consent of a committee which the National Assembly shall instruct to decide on this question.

The Commissioner of Commonweal or the Deputy Commissioner of Commonwealth shall not be removed from office before the expiry of his or her full term except for conduct repugnant to his or her office or for physical or mental incapacity, and then only on a decision of three-quarters of the total membership of the National Assembly.

The duties of the Commissioner of Commonweal shall be laid down in general terms by the National Assembly, but subject to these provisions he or she shall be independent on the National Assembly in the performance of his or her duties.

The Commissioner of Commonweal's jurisdiction shall comprise Secretaries of State, Civil Servants, and persons acting in the service of the State or local government, but shall not include any court of law superior to the courts of local magistrates.

The Commissioner of Commonweal shall present to the National Assembly an Annual Report in which he or she shall give an account of the administration of the affairs of State, and he shall draw the attention of the National Assembly to defects in the working of existing laws and statues. The Report shall be printed and published.

(66) Except when determined by a General Election, the parliamentary sessions of the National Assembly shall commence on the first Tuesday in October and end on the Monday preceding the first Tuesday in the following year. Meetings shall be held regularly during at least eight months of each session. The number and hours of meetings and the dates and duration of the recess shall be determined by the National Assembly and set forth as statutory provisions.

(67) The National Assembly shall be presided over by a President who shall be elected from the Commissioners to the National Assembly at the first meeting of the first parliament after every General Election. The President shall be the constitutional representative of the National Assembly.

He or she shall exercise their office with complete objectivity and impartiality and in accordance with the Rules of Procedure. He or she shall retain their office from the date of their election until the next General Election after which he or she shall be seated as a Commissioner in the National Assembly, without having submitted him or herself to the electorate. He or she shall be eligible for re-election to the office of President.

The President shall be responsible for the effective functioning of the National Assembly and shall exercise domestic authority through a House

Committee, and shall be controller of the administrative officials and employees of the Assembly. A Vice-President shall also be elected to assist the President and to act as his deputy as and when required.

(68) In the first week of each parliamentary session the Sovereign shall open the proceedings of the National Assembly informing it of the general state of the nation and of the legislative programme of the Executive Council.

(69) This speech shall be the subject of a general debate following the withdrawal of the Sovereign.

(70) The President of the National Assembly shall preside over meetings of the Assembly.

(71) Any Commissioner of the Assembly shall be entitled to introduce Bills and other Measures, but the legislative programme and order of business shall be arranged by the President and a Bills Committee of the National Assembly from the Bills and Measures submitted by the Executive Council and by Commissioners.

    In allocating times and priorities, the submissions of the Executive Council shall take precedence, but a quarter of the time of each session must be reserved for the Commissioners' Bills and Measures. Conversely, any balance of time outstanding from the submissions of the Executive Council may be taken up by Commissioners' Bills and Measures.

(72) No Bill or Measure shall be finally passed for Royal Assent until it has been read three times in the National Assembly and passed by a simple majority of the National Assembly.

    After the first reading and before the second all Bills and Measures before the National Assembly may be submitted for scrutiny and comment to the Constitutional Court of the Realm, as provided in Article 84 hereof. The Constitutional Court shall return all Bills and Measures so submitted, along with its comments thereon, not later than ten days from the date of their submission.

    Two-fifths of the Commissioners of the National Assembly present and voting may request the President that the third reading of the Bill or Measures should be deferred for a period of two weeks after the passing of the second reading. This request must be made in writing and signed by the Commissioners making it.

(73) The National Assembly shall lay down its own Rules of Procedure, including rules governing its conduct of business and maintenance of order.

(74) The sessions of the parliaments of the National Assembly shall be conducted in public at all times. Secret sessions can only be held on matters concerning national security and then only by a majority agreement of the Commissioners of the National Assembly. The proceedings of the National

Assembly shall be published verbatim every week, the only exceptions being the minutes of secret sessions; these minutes, however, shall be available on request to all Commissioners of the National Assembly.

(75) Commissioners shall have the right to ask questions of the Prime Minister and any Secretary of State, and, with the approval of the National Assembly, to receive both written and spoken answers.

V. *Judiciary*

(76) Save as hereafter declared the judicial power Scotland shall be exercised in the same Courts with the same jurisdiction and by the same judges, having the same powers, duties, immunity, and privileges, as at the date of promulgation of this Constitution, and except on special cause shewn justice shall always be administered in public.

(77) The shall be created a Council of Judiciary to advise the Sovereign on certain judicial appointments. The Council shall consist of eleven members, five Senators of the College of Justice and five Commissioners of the National Assembly who shall appoint their own Chairman. The Chairman shall not be a member of the legal profession or a Commissioner of the National Assembly or an official or an executive or council member of any political party.

(78) The power to appoint Judges of the Court of Session and Commissioners of Justiciary shall reside in the Sovereign who shall act on the advice of the Council of Judiciary as provided in Article 77 hereof.

(79) The power to appoint Sheriff Principals and Sheriff Substitutes shall reside in the Sovereign, who shall act on the advice of the Council of Justiciary. These judges shall be called respectively "Principal Sheriffs" and "Sheriffs Depute".

(80) The power to appoint Justices of the Peace shall reside in and be exercised by the President of the Court of Session, who shall have the power to remove them for misconduct in their office.

(81) The jurisdiction of the Court of Session shall be exercised in the same manner as at the time of the promulgation of this Constitution and the Court shall have originating and appellate functions, but the decisions of the Inner House shall be final. There shall be created a Court of Criminal Appeal which shall be composed of Commissioners of Justiciary who are not members of the High Court of Justiciary. The decisions of the Court of Criminal Appeal shall be final.

(82) The power of prosecution shall reside exclusively in the Advocate-General and the Solicitor-General and their subordinates, and the right of private prosecution shall be abolished.

(83) The appointment of the Advocate-General and the Solicitor-General shall reside in the Sovereign who shall act on the advice of the Senators of the College of Justice.

(84) There shall be created a Constitutional Court of the Realm. The jurisdiction of the Constitutional Court shall cover:

    (a) All questions of the validity of any law enacted by the National Assembly;
    (b) Any infringement of the Constitution;
    (c) Disputes concerning the constitutional assignment of powers and the exercise of powers within the State.

(85) The Constitutional Court of the Realm shall comprise the Senators of the College of Justice sitting as a collegiate body; seven Senators shall form a quorum.

(86) Any individual citizen or group or association of citizens whether official or unofficial shall have the constitutional right to raise in the Constitutional Court any issue which they believe comes within the competence of the Court.

(87) The jurisdiction of the Court of Session, of the High Court of Justiciary, or any inferior court whatever, shall not extend to the question of the constitutional validity of the law, of or any provision of the law.

(88) Every person appointed to exercise a judicial function under the Constitution shall make and subscribe a declaration that he or she will uphold the Constitution and the law.

(89) All judges shall be independent in the exercise of their judicial functions, and subject only to the Constitution and the law.

(90) No person exercising a judicial function shall be eligible to be a Commissioner of the National Assembly, or to hold other office or position of emolument.

(91) Judges of the Court of Session, Commissioners of Judiciary and Sheriffs, shall not be removed from office except for conduct repugnant to their office, or for physical and mental incapacity, and then only by an address from the National Assembly assented to by three quarters of the Commissioners of the National Assembly.

VI. Local Government

(92) The National Assembly shall grant to Local Authorities certain rights and powers to make and publish local by-laws and to levy local rates and taxes, and to manage their own affairs. All such rights and powers shall be

safeguarded by law, but all by- laws and levies shall be subject to the scrutiny and sanction of the National Assembly.

(93) The areas and functions of Local Authorities shall be defined by statue in such a manner as to provide local bodies with as much power and initiative as is practicable within the Constitution.

VII. *Transitional Provisions and Amendments*

(94) During the first four years after the promulgation of this Constitution persons over 21 years of age who were born and educated in Scotland but who are domiciled furth of Scotland shall be eligible for appointment to office in the service of the State, provided that they take up residence and become domiciled in Scotland immediately on appointment to such office. Such persons on appointment shall, along with their dependents, become citizens of Scotland.

(95) During the first year after the promulgation of this Constitution persons over 21 years of age who were born and educated in Scotland, but who are domiciled furth of Scotland may stand for election as Commissioners of the National Assembly at the first general election to be held after the promulgation of this Constitution, provided that they have taken up residence and domiciled in Scotland. On being nominated for election such persons and their dependents shall become citizens of Scotland.

(96) During the first decade after the promulgation of this Constitution it shall be the duty of successive National Assemblies to apply in any *casus improvisus* the law which has hitherto applied, and as early as possible to introduce a measure for the remedying of the defect. It shall furthermore be the duty of successive National Assemblies to appoint a Commission on the Constitution to make recommendations for correcting discernible defects.

(97) The Articles of this Constitution can be amended, whether by modification, addition, or repeal, only in accordance with the following provisions:

(a) Each proposal for an amendment shall be initiated in the National Assembly as a Bill and shall be published in print;
(b) Such a Bill having been passed by a two-thirds majority of the total membership of the National Assembly shall be submitted by Referendum to the decision of the electorate, in accordance with the laws governing the conduct of a Referendum which shall be passed by the National Assembly;
(c) Each proposal for amendment to this Constitution which is submitted by Referendum to the decision of the electorate shall be held to have been approved by the electorate, if, upon having been submitted, a simple majority of votes cast at such a Referendum shall have been cast in favour of its enactment into law;
(d) Every such Bill shall be entitled, "A Bill to Amend the Constitution";

(e) A Bill containing a proposal for the amendment of this Constitution having been passed by the National Assembly and approved by the electorate in a Referendum in accordance with the provisions of this Article shall become a part of the Constitution.

CONSTITUTION PREPARED BY THE SCOTTISH NATIONAL PARTY (2002) ('MACCORMICK DRAFT')

Article I – Constitution and People

(1) The rights of the people of Scotland to self-determination and to sovereignty over the territory and natural resources of Scotland are absolute and shall be limited only by such agreements as may be freely entered into by it with other nations or states or international organisations for the purpose of furthering international co-operation, trade, and world peace.

(2) These rights shall be exercised in accordance with this Constitution, which shall be the supreme law of the land, and which may be amended only in accordance with provisions as to amendment hereinafter stated; all rights and obligations of European Union membership shall also be recognised; the extent of Scotland's rights to territorial waters and natural resources beyond territorial waters shall be determined according to international law.

(3) The Territory of Scotland comprises all those areas over which the Court of Session and High Court of Justiciary have exercised jurisdiction since the time of, and in virtue of, the ratification of the Articles of Union of 1707, and all the territorial waters appertaining thereto under international law at the time at which this Constitution comes into force, and the sovereignty of the Scottish state extends over all such rights in relation to exploitation of the resources of the sea, the sea bed and the sub soil thereof beyond the limit of territorial waters as are enjoyed and exercised by states under international law at the time at which this Constitution comes into effect; and for the future, the extent of the territorial waters and of such other rights shall be determined in accordance with the relevant provisions of the law of nations for the time being.

(4) (a) Every person whose principal place of residence is in Scotland at the date at which this Constitution comes into force shall be a citizen of Scotland, and shall remain so until such time, if any, as he or she shall renounce such citizenship.

(b) Every person whose place of birth was in Scotland or either of whose parents was born in Scotland, being a person who is alive at the date at which this Constitution comes into force, shall be a citizen of Scotland, and shall remain so until such time, if any, as he or she shall renounce citizenship.

(c) As soon as is reasonably possible after the date at which this Constitution shall come into force, the Parliament of Scotland shall enact legislation making further provision as to citizenship, which shall inter alia prescribe:

    (i)   What formal steps shall be required to constitute voluntary renunciation of citizenship;

    (ii)   What conditions and procedures shall be necessary to acquisition of Scottish citizenship by naturalisation; and

    (iii) What future provision shall be made as to acquisition of Scottish citizenship by birth or by marriage – provided that no law may be passed whereby any person who is or at any time becomes a Scottish citizen may be deprived of that citizenship save by a voluntary act of renunciation, which may include, but only if and insofar as Parliament shall so prescribe by legislation, acquisition of or voluntary continuation in the exercise of, citizenship of any other state or states; nor may any law concerning the acquisition of citizenship be discriminatory on any such ground as sex, race, colour, religion, personal beliefs, abilities, status, or sexual orientation.

(d) Adopted children shall for purposes of citizenship be treated as though they had been born to their adoptive parents.

(e) All persons whose principal place of residence is in Scotland at the date at which this Constitution comes into force shall have the right to continue in residence in Scotland, and to return to residence in Scotland after any period or periods of absence, whether they exercise or renounce their rights to Scottish citizenship; and all children under the age of eighteen years whose parents' principal residence is in Scotland at the date at which this Constitution comes into force shall have the same rights to residence and to citizenship as though they had been resident in Scotland at that date. No law may be passed under which any person's existing right of residence may be extinguished by any means other than voluntary renunciation.

Article II – Head of State and Executive

(1) The Head of State shall be Queen Elizabeth and her successors as determined by the law of Scotland, acting in right of Scotland.

(2) During any period of absence of the Monarch from Scotland, the Chancellor of Scotland (the elected Presiding Officer of Parliament) shall act as Head of State.

(3) The Head of State shall be responsible for the exercise of all lawful governmental functions in Scotland, excepting functions expressly delegated to Ministers or other public authorities. The Head of State shall exercise such functions only upon the advice of his or her Ministers who shall be chosen from among the Members of, and who shall be directly answerable to, the Parliament of Scotland, and who shall be selected with a view to their ability to command and retain the confidence of Parliament, and whose appointment shall be confirmed by Parliament.

(4) The residual powers of the Executive in Scotland at the date at which this Constitution comes into force shall be identical with the prerogatives of the Crown existing in the United Kingdom of Great Britain and Northern Ireland according to the law of Scotland immediately prior to that time, with the exception of any right, power or liberty or immunity belonging to the prerogative of the Crown which would be inconsistent with the provisions of this Constitution. Acts of the Parliament of Scotland shall override the residual powers of the Executive in any case of inconsistency.

(5) The Head of State shall appoint as Prime Minister whichever person being a Member of the Parliament of Scotland is elected by Parliament to serve in that office, or in default of such election, whichever person being a Member of Parliament is in the opinion of the Head of State best able to command the confidence of Parliament.

(6) The number of persons holding office as, or receiving payment as Ministers in Scotland shall not at any time be greater than one-fifth of the number of the whole membership of the Parliament of Scotland.

(7) No Act passed by the Parliament of Scotland for the levying of any form of general taxation payable in Scotland may remain in force for a period longer than eighteen months after the date upon which such Act came into force.

(8) No public money shall be spent for any purpose save as authorised by or under Acts of the Parliament of Scotland.

Article III – Legislature

(1) Subject to the provisions of this Constitution, legislative power shall be vested exclusively in the Parliament of Scotland, and in any person or body to whom Parliament shall expressly delegate the power to make subordinate legislation within some defined sphere of competence. Subject to detailed provisions to be made by Parliament concerning any matters of procedure in relation to subordinate legislation, no regulation made or order made by way of subordinate legislation may take effect as law until it has been laid before Parliament, approved by Parliament and published in such form as will reasonably bring it to the attention of the public in general or such section of the public as is directly affected by the provisions in question. Parliament shall

elect its own Presiding Officer and shall under his or her direction regulate its own procedures in accordance with the provisions of this Constitution. The Presiding Officer of Parliament shall hold the office of Chancellor of Scotland.

(2) With the exception of any rules of law inconsistent with this Constitution, every rule of law which is in force in Scotland at the date at which this Constitution comes into force shall remain in force until such time, if any, as it is repealed or amended by Act of Parliament or other competent legislative act or by desuetude (notorious contrary custom).

(3) The Parliament of Scotland shall be a single-chamber Parliament, and shall be composed of the persons lawfully elected to serve therein. All citizens of Scotland and all persons permanently resident in Scotland of the age of sixteen years and over shall (subject to any lawful exceptions hereto) have the right to vote in Parliamentary and local government elections and in referenda; elections to Parliament shall be conducted by a system of proportional representation so as to secure a fair reflection of the composition of Scottish society, both in general and with particular regard to party preference and to geographical diversity.

(4) The Parliament of Scotland shall enact laws making detailed provisions for all matters concerned with the conduct of elections.

(5) The term of each Parliament shall be four years, save in the cases prescribed in Articles III.6 and III.7 below, and the date for each General Election shall be appointed by proclamation of the Head of State to take place on a day not more than thirty days earlier nor more than thirty days later than the fourth anniversary of the preceding General Election. If any vacancy arises in the membership of Parliament at any time up to four months earlier than the end of the term of the Parliament, such a vacancy shall be filled by by-election for the remaining part of the term.

(6) If at any time Parliament is unable to agree on a Government, in the sense that no person can be found who is able to command its confidence as Prime Minister, the Head of State may dissolve Parliament and by Proclamation appoint a date for the holding of a General Election to take place within one month of such a situation arising; and during the intervening period the Head of State may appoint an interim Prime Minister and Government. The Parliament of Scotland elected at such a General Election shall serve for the remainder of the unexpired term of the Parliament so dissolved.

(7) Parliament shall in time of war have power by resolution to extend its term for a period not exceeding one year.

(8) No treaty or binding international agreement of any kind shall be of any effect unless and until it is confirmed either by a resolution of Parliament, or by enabling legislation to the extent that it purports to affect any person's legal

rights or duties. Every such treaty or agreement shall be valid and effective for all purposes and shall constitute valid law within Scotland, provided that no treaty which is inconsistent with the provisions of this Constitution shall take effect unless and until it is confirmed by the normal process of Constitutional amendment.

(9) No declaration of war or conclusion of peace shall be made by the Head of State save in conformity with the terms of any resolution passed by Parliament.

(10) The Parliament of Scotland shall from time to time by resolution make provisions as to the procedures required for the passing Acts of Parliament and all such Acts as are passed in accordance with these procedures shall be submitted to the Head of State for signification of Assent, and upon signification of such Assent such Acts shall take effect as laws; but the following shall normally be required elements in any procedure adopted by Parliament:

(a) The first stage of legislation shall be publication of a Proposed Measure which shall be debated in principle by Parliament, and if approved by a majority of those voting, shall be carried forward to the second stage.

(b) The second stage shall be consideration of such a proposed measure by a Committee of Parliament; the committee may during such period of time as is prescribed by resolution of the Parliament conduct hearings to which representations may be made by or on behalf of all persons or groups of persons interested in the subject matter of the proposed measure. The Committee may recommend amendments to the proposed measure and shall report thereon to Parliament.

(c) The third stage shall be consideration by Parliament of the Report by the Committee, and Parliament shall adopt or reject amendments recommended by the Committee, or further amend the proposed measure as it sees fit.

(d) The fourth stage shall be a vote by Parliament to enact or not enact the proposed measure in the form adopted in conclusion of the third stage.

(e) In the case of any proposed measure which the Presiding Officer of the Parliament of Scotland certifies as concerning solely or mainly the raising or the spending of national revenues, the proposed measure may be submitted for Assent by the Head of State as soon as it shall have passed the fourth stage by the vote of a majority of members of Parliament present and voting.

(f) In the case of any proposed measure not so certified by the Presiding Officer the proposed measure may be submitted in like manner for Assent unless within ten days a resolution is supported by the vote of two fifths of the whole membership of Parliament requiring that adoption of the proposed measure be deferred; any such resolution moved within the prescribed period of ten days shall take precedence over other business in Parliament, and a vote on the resolution shall be taken within the prescribed period.

(g) In any case in which such a resolution is passed, the proposed measure may be reconsidered by Parliament in the manner appropriate to the fourth stage at any date not less than twelve months and not more than eighteen months after the date of such resolution, and if the proposed measure is then enacted by the votes of a majority of the members present and voting it may forthwith be submitted for Assent by the Head of State.

(h) If such a resolution as is mentioned in sub-section (f) above is passed, the Parliament shall have power by resolution of a majority of those present and voting to submit the proposed measure as a whole to a National Referendum, which shall concern only the question whether to adopt or not adopt the proposed measure as a whole, if a majority of the electors voting in such a referendum votes in favour of adoption of the proposed measure it shall forthwith be submitted to the Head of State for Assent.

(11) All proceedings of the Parliament of Scotland or of any of its committees shall be held in public, except as provided in Section 12.

(12) The Parliament of Scotland and its members shall enjoy such privileges and immunities as are essential to the free unimpeded and democratic conduct of the affairs of the nation. The Standing Orders of Parliament may include provision as to exclusion of members of the public and the holding of proceedings in private where necessary to uphold the values enshrined in this constitution.

Article IV – Local Government

(1) Local government shall be guaranteed genuine autonomy and freedom from interference by central government (including ministers) within the areas entrusted by law to local authorities.

(2) Parliament will have the power to legislate generally for local government, and in particular to legislate concerning the composition, areas of authority, and financial and taxing powers of local authorities, but the exercise by a local authority of any power conferred on it by law shall not be subject to direct or indirect interference or overriding by any decision of the central government.

(3) The Islands authorities as presently constituted shall continue to enjoy all such special powers as they have at present, and legislation shall not be passed which derogates from their powers or varies their territorial jurisdiction save if this is confirmed by a majority vote of the islanders within the islands concerned.

(4) A fair system of proportional representation, similar to the system for parliamentary elections, shall apply in all local government elections.

Article V – Judiciary

(1) The Supreme Courts in Scotland shall be the Court of Session and the High Court of Justiciary as constituted by law, and with the jurisdiction pertaining respectively thereto, at the time at which this constitution comes into force. There shall be no appeal to any other Tribunal from decisions of either Court on any matter which falls within its jurisdiction. All appeals to or within either Court on such matters shall be determined in accordance with the law in force at the time at which this constitution comes into force, which may for the future be amended according to the ordinary process of legislation.

(2) Any question arising in any litigation whatsoever concerning the provisions of this Constitution shall, in the event of an appeal, be referred to the Court of Session sitting as a Court of not fewer than seven judges, and the decision of any such question by the Court shall be final and binding for all purposes. In interpreting the Constitution, the Court of Session shall not be bound to follow its own precedents.

(3) Senators of the College of Justice and the Lords Commissioners of Justiciary shall be independent of the executive and the legislature. The Head of State shall make appointments to the offices of Senator of the College of Justice, Lord Commissioner of Justiciary, Lord President of the Court of Session, Lord Justice General and Lord Justice Clerk upon the advice of a Commission on Judicial Appointments comprising the Lord Advocate, the Presiding Officer of the Parliament of Scotland, a Senator of the College of Justice elected by the whole body of Senators, and two eminent and impartial persons elected to serve for a term of ten years by the Parliament. Judicial appointments shall be terminable only by resignation, or on the achievement of the statutory retiring age, or on grounds of permanent incapacity by reason of ill health, or by order of the Head of State upon receipt of a resolution passed by two thirds of the whole membership of the Parliament calling for the dismissal of a judge on grounds of stated misconduct.

(4) So far as is consistent with the provisions of this Constitution:

(a) The Court of Session and High Court of Justiciary shall continue to have power to make Acts of Sederunt and Acts of Adjournal in the same manner and form and concerning the same subjects as they have power to do on the day on which this Constitution comes into force; and

(b) Parliament shall have power to legislate by ordinary process of legislation on all matters concerning the administration of justice in Scotland.

(c) The Sheriff Court and all Courts or tribunals of inferior or local or otherwise limited jurisdiction shall continue in existence as provided for by laws in force on the day on which this Constitution comes into force; save that the power to advise on appointments to the office of

Sheriff or Sheriff Principal shall be transferred to the Commission on Judicial Appointments, laws on any subjects concerning such Courts or tribunals may be passed by ordinary process of legislation.

Article VI – Fundamental Rights and Liberties

(1) (a) The following provisions shall have effect for the purpose of guaranteeing the fundamental rights and liberties of all Scottish Citizens and of all persons for the time being within the jurisdiction of any Scottish Court; the rights and liberties guaranteed shall be enjoyed by all persons without discrimination on any grounds such as sex, race, colour, religion, personal beliefs, abilities, status or sexual orientation; there shall be no limitation upon their exercise save such as is necessary to prevent or penalise actings by any person or group of persons calculated to infringe or destroy the rights and liberties of other persons or groups, or forcibly to subvert the constitutional order which establishes and guarantees those rights and liberties and, subject to the last mentioned qualification, no law may be passed which abrogates or derogates from the guaranteed rights and liberties, unless it shall be passed by way of a constitutional amendment in accordance with Article VII of this Constitution; every person shall be granted by a competent court a full and adequate and speedy remedy for any infringement whatsoever of his or her guaranteed rights and liberties; where the rights upheld in this Article have equivalent rights in the European Convention of Human Rights and Fundamental Liberties, they are at least as extensive as those rights; a court or tribunal in determining the rights upheld in this Article must have regard to the jurisprudence of the European Court of Human Rights.

(b) None of the rights guaranteed in this Article of the Constitution shall be subjected to any restriction or limitation other than as expressly provided, nor shall any such restriction or limitation be applied for any purpose other than that expressly prescribed.

(2) (a) Every person has the right to life. No person shall be condemned to death or executed, saving only that provision may be made in law for the death penalty in respect of acts committed in time of war or of imminent threat of war; such penalty shall be applied only in the instances laid down in the law and in accordance with its provisions.

(b) If any person's death occurs as a result of another person's acting in a manner which is permitted by law and which is no more than necessary;

 (i)   To defend a person or persons from unlawful violence;
 (ii) To effect a lawful arrest or to prevent the escape of a person lawfully detained. The action so taken shall not be rendered unlawful by the fact that death has result from it.

(3) No person shall be subjected to torture, or to inhuman or degrading treatment or punishment.

(4) No person shall be held in slavery or servitude, nor shall any person be required to perform forced or compulsory labour. For the purposes of this article "forced or compulsory labour" shall not include:

(a) Any work required to be done in the ordinary course of detention imposed according to the provisions of paragraph 5 of this Article or during conditional release from such detention;

(b) Any service of a military character or, in case of conscientious objectors in countries where they are recognised, service exacted instead of compulsory military service;

(c) Any service exacted in case of an emergency or calamity threatening the life or wellbeing of the community;

(d) Any work or service which forms part of normal civic obligations.

(5) (a) Every person has the right to personal liberty and security, and accordingly no person shall be deprived of liberty save in the following cases and in accordance with the procedures prescribed by the law of Scotland:

(i) In the case of his or her lawful detention in accordance with the sentence passed by a competent Court upon his or her conviction of an offence;

(ii) In the case of his or her lawful arrest or detention for non-compliance with the lawful order of a court;

(iii) In the case of his or her lawful arrest or detention upon reasonable suspicion of having committed, or being engaged in the commission of, or being about to commit, a criminal offence under the law of Scotland;

(iv) In the case of detention of a person under the age of sixteen years by lawful order for the purpose of his or her educational supervision or personal welfare;

(v) In case of the lawful detention of a person who is, or is reasonably believed to be, of unsound mind;

(vi) In case of the lawful detention of a person for the purpose of preventing the spread of an infectious disease;

(vii) In the case of the lawful arrest of a person to prevent his or her unlawfully entering Scotland, or of a person against whom lawful action is being taken with a view to deportation or extradition.

(b) Every person who is arrested or detained shall be informed, as soon as is possible in the circumstances of the case, in a language which he or she understands, of the reason for his or her arrest or detention and of any charge which is to be laid against him or her; he or she shall be entitled to inform a member of his or her family of his or her whereabouts and of the stated reason for his or her detention, and shall be entitled as soon as possible to consult a legal practitioner.

(c) Every person who is arrested or detained in accordance with paragraph 5(a)(iii) shall, wherever it is practicable to do so, be brought before a competent court not later than the first lawful day after being taken into custody, such day not being a public or local holiday: failing which, he or she shall be brought before a competent court as soon as is possible thereafter.

(d) Every person who has been arrested or detained in accordance with paragraph 5(a)(iii) shall be brought to trial as soon as is possible; no person who has been committed for trial of any offence shall be detained in custody for more than one hundred and ten days from the date of such committal, except in so far as the High Court of Justiciary shall have, and shall in any case have exercised, power to grant extension of that period on any grounds which may be provided for in legislation for the time being in force; every person who has been committed for trial shall be set at liberty and declared forever free from all question or process for the crime for which he or she was committed, unless he or she has been brought to trial and the trial concluded within the aforesaid period of one hundred and ten days, subject to any lawful extension granted by the High Court of Justiciary.

(e) Every person who has been deprived of liberty by arrest or detention has the right to petition the Court of Session or High Court of Justiciary for liberation, and shall be liberated by order of the Court as soon as is practicable in the circumstances of the case unless such deprivation of liberty is proven to be lawful; if a person so deprived of liberty is for any reason unable to take proceedings on his or her own behalf any other person who can show good cause for so doing may petition the Court in his or her name to test the lawfulness of any such detention.

(6) (a) Every person has the right to fair and public judicial proceedings to determine any question raised by proper process of law concerning his or her legal rights or obligations, or any criminal charge against him or her. Every such question or charge shall be heard and determined by the competent court or tribunal established by competent court or tribunal established by law, and judgment shall be pronounced publicly, except if, or in so far as, the law permits a court of tribunal to exclude members of the public from part of such proceedings or to prohibit publication of reports concerning part of such proceedings on all or any of the following grounds:

(i)   The protection of national security;
(ii)   The prevention of disorder in court;
(iii)   The protection of children or young people;
(iv)   The protection of the personal privacy of the parties;
(v)   The protection of the interests of justice in circumstances in which publicity would inevitably cause serious prejudice to the fair determination of an issue.

(b) Every person charged with a criminal offence shall be presumed innocent until proved guilty according to law.

(c) Every person charged with a criminal offence has the following rights:

- (i) To be informed in detail, as soon as is possible in the circumstances of the case, and in a language which he or she understands, of the charge which is made against him or her;
- (ii) To have adequate time and facilities for preparing a defence to the charge;
- (iii) To defend himself or herself in person or through a legal practitioner of his or her own choosing;
- (iv) To such financial assistance as is necessary in the light of his or her means to secure adequate legal assistance if desired;
- (v) To examine or have examined witnesses against him or her and to obtain the attendance and examination of witnesses on his or her behalf in the same conditions as witnesses against him or her;
- (vi) to have all proceedings in court connected with the charge against him or her translated by a competent interpreter into the language which he or she best understands, if that language is not the language of the Court;
- (vii) to be informed in a language which he or she understands of the provisions of this paragraph of this Article of the Constitution, before the commencement of the trial.

(7) No person shall be convicted of any criminal offence save in respect of an act or omission which, at the date of its commission, constituted a criminal offence under the law of Scotland or the law of nations, nor shall any penalty be imposed which is heavier than the maximum permitted under the law of Scotland at that date.

(8) (a) Everyone has the right to respect for privacy in his or her personal affairs, family life, home, and correspondence.
- (b) Every interference with personal privacy in these respects shall be unlawful unless it is proven to be in accordance with provisions of the law which are necessary;

- (i) for the protection of national security;
- (ii) for public safety;
- (iii) for the prevention of crime or civil disorder;
- (iv) for the protection of public health; or
- (v) for the protection of the fundamental rights or freedoms of other persons and every person who suffers unlawful interference with his or her personal privacy shall be entitled to an adequate civil remedy therefore.

(9) (a) Every person has the right to freedom of thought and of conscience and to the free confession and the practice of religion.
- (b) A person's freedom in the practice of religion shall not be restricted by law save to such an extent, if any, as is necessary for the protection

of public order or public health or for the protection of the rights and freedoms of others.

(10) Every person shall have the right of access to governmental information save on a restricted range of matters in which secrecy or confidentiality is authorised or required by law and in the public interest.

(11)(a) Every person has the right to freedom of opinion and of the expression of opinion, including the right to impart and receive information and ideas freely to and from any other person or persons whatsoever, except in so far as the law may restrict or penalise the expressing of opinion or the transmission of information so far as is necessary for any of the following purposes:

    (i)   the protection of national security or public safety;
    (ii)   the prevention of crime;
    (iii) the prevention of incitement to hatred on any grounds such as sex, race, colour, abilities, religion, personal beliefs or status;
    (iv) for the protection of public health;
    (v)   for preventing the public display of obscene or indecent materials;
    (vi) for the protection of individuals' rights and reputations;
    (vii) for the protection of information given and received in confidence;
    (viii) for protection of the Parliament and Courts of Law from acts of contempt.

  (b) The foregoing provision shall not be interpreted as invalidating laws regulating the licensing of broadcast transmissions or cinemas, theatres and other like places of public resort.

(12) Every person has the right to freedom of peaceful assembly and to freedom of association with others for all lawful purposes including the right to form and to join trade unions for the protection of his or her interests: the right to freedom of assembly and of association shall be subject only to such restrictions as are prescribed by law and are necessary for any of the following purposes:

    (i)   the protection of national security or public safety;
    (ii)   the prevention of crime or civil disorder;
    (iii) the protection of public health;
    (iv) the protection of the fundamental rights of individuals.

But provision (i) above does not apply to the right to form and join trade unions.

(13) Men and women of marriageable age have the right to marry and to found a family, in accordance with the law of Scotland.

(14) Every person has the right to hold private property, and to the peaceful enjoyment of his or her property; no laws may be passed which limit, restrict or

abrogate the right to acquire or retain private property except in cases in which the Parliament determines that the needs of the community clearly require to be given precedence over the rights of individuals; and all laws which sanction measures of expropriation shall make provision for fair compensation.

(15)(a) Every person has the right to work and to pursue freely any profession or vocation subject only to such requirements as to minimum qualifications as may be prescribed by or in accordance with the law.

(b) Every person in employment has the right to conditions of work which are fair and which respect the dignity of the person in the sense implied by this Article of this Constitution; in particular, everyone has the right to safe and healthy conditions of work, as determined by legislation concerning health and safety at work.

(c) Every person who is unable to work by reason of age or physical or mental disability or infirmity, or by reason of family responsibilities, or because suitable employment is unavailable, has a right to be provided with reasonable alternative means of subsistence to be determined in accordance with law; in particular, persons who have reached the age of retirement as prescribed by law shall, in terms prescribed by law, have the right to pensions sufficient to maintain the dignity and independence of elderly people in the general social and climatic conditions prevailing in Scotland.

(16) Every person has the right to freedom of movement within Scotland, including the right of access to hills, mountains, waterways and open countryside, except in cases in which unrestricted access is likely to cause substantial interference with agriculture, forestry or fishing, and subject to any provisions of the law which are necessary:

(i)   for the protection of national security or public safety;
(ii)   for the protection of public health;
(iii)   for the protection of the physical environment.

(17) Every person who is over the age of sixteen years, who is not presently in detention in accordance with law as being a person of unsound mind, who is a citizen of Scotland or whose principal place of residence is in Scotland, shall have the right to vote, and to present himself or herself as a candidate, in elections to membership of the Parliament of Scotland or (subject to such further requirements as to residence as may be prescribed by law) to any local authority. This right shall be exercised in accordance with the law for the time being in force concerning electoral procedures and regulating proper electoral practices; restrictions of the right to vote on grounds of citizenship may be established by ordinary process of legislation.

(18) All forms of monopoly or of restrictive trade practice shall be unlawful except in so far as they are expressly permitted by or under laws in force at the time at which this Constitution comes into force, or subsequently enacted by the Parliament of Scotland.

(19) For all purposes, every person has the right to use any of Scotland's three official languages, Gaelic, Scots or English.

(20) Everyone has a right to housing. Parliament shall be responsible for ensuring by legislation that no person is involuntarily deprived of adequate shelter and living accommodation.

(21) Everyone has the right to the provision of reasonable health care to secure wellbeing and human dignity within an acceptable level of overall cost and subject to prevailing conditions of medical practice. Parliament shall be responsible for securing by legislation that health services are properly maintained and are available on fair terms to all persons.

(22) Everyone has the right to education for the optimal development of their abilities and potentialities within an acceptable level of overall cost and subject to prevailing conditions of educational practice; Parliament shall be responsible for securing by legislation that educational services are properly maintained at nursery, primary, secondary and post-school levels and are available on fair terms to all persons.

(23) Nothing in paragraphs 10, 11, 13, 14 or 16 of this Article of the Constitution shall have the effect of invalidating legislation by the Parliament of Scotland, which imposes restrictions on the political activities of aliens.

(24) The Parliament of Scotland may enact legislation providing for the restriction of the application of this Article of the Constitution during times of war or other grave public emergency, but such legislation must contain provision for approval by resolution passed with the support of not less than three-fifths of the whole membership of Parliament of any declaration by the Government of a state of emergency within two weeks thereof, and for renewal of such approval no less frequently than three months from the date of any prior resolution approving of such a declaration; and such legislation may not authorise any derogation from paragraph 2 of this Article, except in respect of deaths arising from lawful acts of war, or from paragraphs 3, 4 and 7 of this Article of the Constitution.

Article VII – Amendment to the Constitution

This Constitution, including this Article of this Constitution, may be amended only by the following procedure: The passing of a proposed measure at its third stage by a majority of three-fifths of the whole membership of the Parliament of Scotland followed, within a period of between two and six months, reference to the proposed measure to a National Referendum in which a majority of those voting shall have voted for the proposed measure.

C

SCOTTISH INDEPENDENCE BILL (DRAFT INTERIM CONSTITUTION), 2014

An Act of the Scottish Parliament to provide for Scotland to become an independent State; to provide an interim constitution for Scotland to have effect from independence; to provide for the establishment of a Constitutional Convention to draw up a permanent constitution for Scotland; and for connected purposes.

PART 1

INDEPENDENCE

1 Independence

(1) On Independence Day, Scotland becomes an independent State under the constitution set out in Part 2 of this Act.

(2) "Independence Day" is a day to be specified by a resolution of the Scottish Parliament.

(3) From Independence Day, and subject to the constitution –

(a) the Scottish Parliament has full competence to make and modify the law of Scotland,
(b) the Scottish Government assumes full responsibility for the government of Scotland.

PART 2

CONSTITUTION

Sovereignty

2 Sovereignty of the people

In Scotland, the people are sovereign.

3   The nature of the people's sovereignty

(1) In Scotland, the people have the sovereign right to self-determination and to choose freely the form in which their State is to be constituted and how they are to be governed.

(2) All State power and authority accordingly derives from, and is subject to, the sovereign will of the people, and those exercising State power and authority are accountable for it to the people.

(3) The sovereign will of the people is expressed in the constitution and, in accordance with the constitution and laws made under it, through the people's elected representatives, at referendums and by other means provided by law.

(4) The sovereign will of the people is limited only by the constitution and by the obligations flowing from international agreements to which Scotland is or becomes a party on the people's behalf, in accordance with the constitution and international law.

4   Interim constitution for Scotland

(1) Until a written constitution for the State is agreed by or on behalf of the people of Scotland in accordance with section 33, this Part is to have effect as the constitution for Scotland.

(2) References in this Act to "the constitution" are references to this Part.

The State

5   Name of the State

(1) The name of the State, by which it is to be known formally, is Scotland.

(2) Scotland may enter into international agreements, and become a member of international organisations, in that name.

6   The territory of Scotland

In accordance with international law, the territory of Scotland continues to consist of all the land, islands, internal waters and territorial sea that formed the territory of Scotland immediately before Independence Day.

7   Form of State and government

(1) Scotland is an independent, constitutional monarchy.

(2) The form of government in Scotland is a parliamentary democracy.

8   National flag and anthem

(1) The national flag of Scotland continues to be the Saltire or Saint Andrew's Cross.

(2) The Scottish Parliament may choose, as it sees fit, a national anthem for Scotland.

Head of State

9   Head of State

(1) Her Majesty Queen Elizabeth is to be Head of State, as Queen.

(2) Her Majesty is to be succeeded as Head of State (and as Queen or, as they case may be, King) by Her heirs and successors to the Crown according to law.

(3) Her Majesty, and Her successor to the Crown, continue to enjoy all the rights, powers and privileges which, according to law, attached to the Crown in Scotland immediately before Independence Day.

(4) Subsection (3) is subject to –

    (a) the constitution, and
    (b) provision made by Act of the Scottish Parliament.

Legislature

10   Legislature

(1) Legislative power to make and modify the law continues to be vested in the Scottish Parliament.

(2) The Parliament's power is subject to the constitution.

Executive

11   Executive

(1) Executive power to administer and govern continues to be vested in the Scottish Government.

(2) The Government's power is subject to the constitution.

State accountability

12   State accountability to the people

(1) The Scottish Parliament and its members, as the elected representatives of the people, are accountable to the people.

(2) The Scottish Government and its members are accountable to the Scottish Parliament and, through the Parliament as their elected representatives, to the people.

Juridical

13 Independence of the judiciary

All members of the judiciary are to be independent, and free from any external influence or control, in carrying out their judicial functions.

14 Supreme Court

(1) The Court of Session is the final court of appeal in civil matters.

(2) The High Court of Justiciary is the final court of appeal in criminal matters.

(3) Each of those Courts is, within its respective area of competence, the Supreme Court of Scotland.

(4) Accordingly, no appeal lies against the decisions of the Supreme Court to any other court or tribunal, and the decisions of the Supreme Court are not subject to review by any other court or tribunal.

(5) This section does not affect the jurisdiction of the Court of Justice of the European Union, the European Court of Human Rights or any other court or tribunal established under an international agreement to which Scotland is a party.

15 The rule of law

(1) The principle of the rule of law continues to apply in Scotland.

(2) Every person is accordingly subject to, and must act in accordance with, that principle.

The civil service

16 The Scottish civil service

(1) There is to be a Scottish civil service.

(2) All members of the Scottish civil service are to act with integrity, honesty, objectivity and impartiality.

(3 Further provision about the Scottish civil service is to be made by Act of the Scottish Parliament.

Local government

17 Local government

(1) There is to continue to be local government in Scotland.

(2) Local government is to be administered by local councils which have autonomy over the carrying out of their functions.

(3) Each local council is to represent and promote the interests of the people living within the local area.

(4) The members of each local council are to be elected in accordance with law –

(a) directly by people living within the local area,
(b) at elections to be held at intervals of not more than 5 years.

(5) In this section, "the local area" means the area for which the council is the local council.

Citizenship

18   Scottish citizenship

(1) The following people automatically hold Scottish citizenship, namely –

(a) all those who, immediately before Independence Day, hold British citizenship and either –

(i)   are habitually resident in Scotland at that time, or
(ii) are not habitually resident in Scotland at that time but were born in Scotland,

(b) any person born in Scotland on after Independence Day if either of the person's parent, at the time of the person's birth –

(i)   holds Scottish citizenship, or
(ii) has indefinite leave to remain in Scotland, and

(c) any person born outside Scotland on or after Independence Day if –

(i)   either of the person's parents, at the time of the person's birth, hold Scottish citizenship, and
(ii) the person's birth is registered in Scotland.

(2) The following people are entitled to claim Scottish citizenship according to the prescribed procedures, namely –

(a) any person born in Scotland on or after Independence Day if either of the person's parents meets the prescribed requirements,
(b) any person with –

(i)   a prescribed connection by descent with a person holding Scottish citizenship, or
(ii) any other prescribed connection with Scotland.

(3) A person holding Scottish citizenship may also hold other nationalities or citizenships at the same time.

(4) Further provision about entitlement to Scottish citizenship is to be made by Act of the Scottish Parliament, and "prescribed" means prescribed by or under such an Act.

(5) Such an Act may, in particular, include provision supplementing, qualifying or modifying the provision in this section.

International relations

19 International relations and foreign policy

In conducting its international relations and in determining its foreign policy, Scotland will –

  (a) observe, and promote respect for, international law,
  (b) promote Scotland's values and best interests,
  (c) promote international peace, justice and security,
  (d) promote friendly relations among States and nations.

20 International organisations

The Scottish Government may take whatever steps it considers appropriate to secure that Scotland maintains membership of any international organization.

21 Ratification of international agreements

(1) International agreements to which Scotland becomes a signatory are not to be ratified on behalf of Scotland, or otherwise to bind Scotland, unless –

  (a) the Scottish Government has laid a copy of the agreement before the Scottish Parliament, and
  (b) the Parliament has approved the agreement in accordance with such procedures as the Parliament may determine.

(2) That does not apply to any international agreement ratified in relation to Scotland before Independence Day and by which Scotland, as an independent State, continues to be bound on or after Independence Day in accordance with international law.

22 Incorporation of international agreements

(1) International agreements to which Scotland is a party do not by themselves have direct effect in Scots law.

(2) Such agreements take direct effect in Scots law only to the extent provided by Act of the Scottish Parliament.

Nuclear disarmament

23 Nuclear disarmament

The Scottish Government must pursue negotiations with a view to securing –

  (a) nuclear disarmament in accordance with international law, and
  (b) the safe and expeditious removal from the territory of Scotland of nuclear weapons based there.

Europe

24 Incorporation of European law

(1) Directly effective EU law forms part of Scots law.

(2) Scots law is of no effect so far as it is inconsistent with EU law.

(3) In this section –

   (a) "EU law" means –

   (i) all those rights, powers, liabilities, obligations and restrictions from time to time created or arising by or under the EU Treaties, and

   (ii) all those remedies and procedures from time to time provided for by or under those Treaties,

   (b) EU law is directly effective if, in accordance with EU Treaties, it is to be given legal effect or used in Scotland without further enactment.

25 European citizenship

A person holding Scottish citizenship is also, in accordance with Article 20.1 of the Treaty on the Functioning of the European Union, a citizen of the European Union.

Rights

26 Respect for human rights

(1) Every person has the rights and fundamental freedoms set out in the European Convention on Human Rights.

(2) Scots law is of no effect so far as it is incompatible with those rights and fundamental freedoms.

(3) The Scottish Government and public authorities must, in carrying out their functions, respect and comply with those rights and freedoms.

27 References to the European Convention on Human Rights

(1) The references in section 26 to the rights and fundamental freedoms set out in the European Convention on Human Rights are to the rights and fundamental freedoms set out in –

   (a) Articles 2 to 12 and 14 of the Convention,
   (b) Articles 1 to 3 of the First Protocol to the Convention, agreed at Paris on 20 March 1952,
   (c) Article 1 of the Thirteenth Protocol to the Convention, agreed at Vilnius on 3 May 2001, as read with Articles 16 to 18 of the Convention.

242] *Constituting Scotland*

(2) Those rights and freedoms have effect for the purposes of this Act as they have effect for the time being in relation to Scotland.

(3) In this section, "the Convention" means the Convention for the Protection of Human Rights and Fundamental Freedoms, agreed by the Council of Europe at Rome on 4 November 1950.

28 Equality

(1) Every person in Scotland is equal before the law and has equal entitlement to its protection and benefit.

(2) Every person is entitled to be treated –

    (a) with respect regardless of status or personal characteristics,
    (b) without unfair discrimination on the basis of personal characteristics.

(3) The Scottish Government and public authorities must, in carrying out their functions, seek to promote and secure equality of opportunity for every person in Scotland regardless of personal characteristics.

(4) In this section, the references to personal characteristics include (as well as other characteristics) –

    (a) age,
    (b) disability,
    (c) gender reassignment,
    (d) marriage or civil partnership,
    (e) pregnancy or maternity,
    (f) race,
    (g) religion or belief,
    (h) sex,
    (i) sexual orientation.

29 Children's wellbeing

(1) The Scottish Government and public authorities must, in carrying out their functions, seek to safeguard, support and promote the wellbeing of the children of Scotland.

(2) In subsection (1), "children" are people who have not attained the age of 18 years.

Island communities

30 Island communities

The Scottish Government must, in carrying out its functions, take account of the particular needs of island communities, having special regard to the distinctive geographical characteristics of each of the areas inhabited by those communities.

Environmental matters

31 The environment

(1) Every person is entitled to live in a healthy environment.

(2) Accordingly, and in recognition of the importance of the environment to the people of Scotland, the Scottish Government and public authorities must, in carrying out their functions, seek to protect and enhance the quality of the environment.

(3) In particular, they must seek to promote –

    (a) the conservation of biodiversity,
    (b) measures to tackle climate change.

32 Natural resources

  Scotland's natural resources are to be used in a manner which is –

    (a) best calculated to be sustainable, and
    (b) of economic, social, environmental or other benefit to the people of Scotland.

Permanent constitution

33 Provision for a permanent constitution

(1) The Scottish Parliament must, as soon as possible after Independence Day, make provision by Act of the Parliament for the establishment of an independent Constitutional Convention to be charged with the task of drawing up a written constitution for agreement by or on behalf of the people of Scotland.

(2) The Act must include provision for the Convention to be established, and to begin its task, as soon as possible after the Act is enacted.

(3) The Act must also include provision about –

    (a) the membership of the Convention,
    (b) the funding of, and administrative support for, the Convention,
    (c) the time by which the Convention is to complete its task,
    (d) the procedures and processes to be followed by the Convention in carrying out its task,
    (e) the procedure by which the written constitution prepared by the Convention is to be agreed by or on behalf of the people,
    (f) the dissolution of the Convention on the completion of its task.

(4) The Convention is "independent" if it, and its members and staff, are free from the direction or control of –

    (a) the Scottish Government or any of its members, and

    (b) the Scottish Parliament or any of its members.

PART 3

TRANSITIONAL AND CONSEQUENTIAL

34   Continuity of laws

(1) The laws that are in effect in Scotland immediately before Independence Day are to continue to have effect on and after Independence Day unless and until they are –

    (a) repealed or modified by Act of the Scottish Parliament or subordinate legislation, or

    (b) otherwise modified by operation of law.

(2) That is subject to the constitution.

(3) The laws referred to include any law, whether contained in a rule of law, an Act of the Scottish Parliament, an Act of the Parliament of the United Kingdom, an Act of the Parliaments of Scotland passed before or in 1707, subordinate legislation, a prerogative instrument or any other instrument or document having the effect of law.

35   Repeal of the Act of Union

The Union with England Act 1707 is repealed.

PART 4

GENERAL

36   Commencement

(1) This section and sections 1, 18, 20, 34 and 37 come into force on the day after Royal Assent.

(2) Other provisions of this Act come into force on Independence Day.

37   Short title

The short title of this Act is the Scottish Independence Act 2015.

BIBLIOGRAPHY

Ackerman, B., *The Future of Liberal Revolution* (New Haven, CT: Yale University Press, 1992).

Ackerman, B., 'The new separation of powers', *Harvard Law Review*, 113/3 (2000), 633–729.

Adams, J. [1776], *Thoughts on Government*, <http://press-pubs.uchicago.edu/founders/documents/v1ch4s5.html> (last accessed 10 March 2011).

Adams, J. C. and P. Barile, *The Government of Republican Italy*, 3rd edn (Boston: Houghton-Mifflin, 1972).

Alexander, R., *The Voice of the People: A Constitution for Tomorrow* (London: Weidenfeld and Nicolson, 1997).

Ágh, A., *The Politics of Central Europe* (London: Sage, 1998).

Andeweg, R. B. and G. A. Irwin, *Governance and Politics of the Netherlands*, 3rd edn (Basingstoke: Palgrave Macmillan, 2009).

Arrow, K. J., 'A difficulty in the concept of social welfare', *Journal of Political Economy*, 58/4 (1950), 328–46.

Arrowood, C. F., *The Powers of the Crown in Scotland, being a translation, with notes and an Introductory Essay, of George Buchanan's 'De jure regni apud scotos'* (Austin: University of Texas Press, 1949).

Arter, D., *The Scottish Parliament: A Scandinavian-Style Assembly?* (London: Frank Cass, 2004).

Arter, D., *Democracy in Scandinavia: Consensual, Majoritarian or Mixed?* (Manchester: Manchester University Press, 2006).

Ashdown, P., 'Beyond Westminster', Williamson Memorial Lecture, Stirling University, 15 April 1994.

Aughey, A., 'The wager of devolution and the challenge to Britishness', *Political Quarterly*, 78 (2009), 136–48.

Austin, G., *The Indian Constitution: Cornerstone of a Nation*, 2nd edn (Oxford: Oxford University Press, 1999).

Avril, P., *Politics in France*, trans. J. Ross (London: Penguin Books, 1969).

Bache, I. and M. Flinders, 'Multi-level governance and the study of the British state', *Public Policy and Administration*, 19/1 (2004), 31–51.

Bagehot, W. [1867], *The English Constitution* (London: Fontana, 1963).

Bell, A., 'Considering a Constitution: a view from a former government insider', in A. Reid and M. Davis (eds), *A Modest Proposal for the Agreement of the People* (Edinburgh: Luath Press, 2014).

Bellamy, R. P., *Political Constitutionalism: A Republican Defence of the Constitutionality of Democracy* (Cambridge: Cambridge University Press, 2007).

Bennie, L. G. and A. Clark, 'Towards moderate pluralism: Scotland's post-devolution party system 1999–2002', *British Elections and Parties Review*, 13 (2003), 134–55.

Bergman, T., 'Formation rules and minority government', *European Journal of Political Research*, 23/1 (1993), 55–66.

Bergman, T., W. Müller, K. Strøm and M. Blombren, 'Democratic delegation and accountability: cross-national patterns', in K. Strøm, W. C. Müller and T. Bergman (eds), *Delegation and Accountability in Parliamentary Democracies*, Comparative Politics (Oxford: Oxford University Press, 2003), pp. 109–220.

Bergman, T., 'Sweden: From separation of power to parliamentary supremacy – and back again?', in K. Strøm, W. C. Müller and T. Bergman (eds), *Delegation and Accountability in Parliamentary Democracies*, Comparative Politics (Oxford: Oxford University Press, 2003), pp. 594–619.

Birch, A., *The British System of Government* (London: Allen and Unwin, 1967).

Blackburn, R. and R. Plant, 'Introduction', in R. Blackburn and R. Plant (eds), *Constitutional Reform: The Labour Government's Constitutional Reform Agenda* (Harlow: Addison Wesley Longman, 1999).

Blokker, P., *New Democracies in Crisis? A Comparative Constitutional Study of the Czech Republic, Hungary, Poland, Romania and Slovakia* (London: Routledge, 2013).

Bobbio, N. and M. Viroli, *The Idea of the Republic* (Cambridge and Oxford: Polity Press, 2003).

Böckenförde, M., *Constitutional Amendment Procedures* (Stockholm: International Institute for Democracy and Electoral Assistance, 2014).

Böckenförde, M., N. Hedling and W. Wahiu, *A Practical Guide to Constitution Building* (Stockholm: International Institute for Democracy and Electoral Assistance, 2011).

Bogdanor, V., '*The Monarchy and the Constitution*' (Oxford: Oxford University Press, 1997).

Bonney, N., 'Scottish independence, state religion and the monarchy', *Political Quarterly*, 83/2 (2012), 360–7.

Bonney, N. and B. Morris, 'Tuvalu and you: the monarch, the United Kingdom and the realms', *Political Quarterly*, 83/2 (2012), 368–73.

Bort, E., R. McAlpine and G. Morgan, *The Silent Crisis: Failure and Revival in Local Democracy in Scotland* (Glasgow: Jimmy Reid Foundation., 2012).

Boulanger, C., '"Is it a dictatorship and a police state yet?" Scheppele and Halmai on current Hungarian constitutional politics', *Verfassungsblog* (11 July 2012), <http://verfassungsblog.de/dictatorship-police-state/> (last accessed 1 August 2012).

Bradley, J. M., 'Political, religious and cultural identities: the undercurrents of Scottish football', *Politics*, 17/1 (1997), 25–32.

Brazier, R., *Constitutional Reform* (Alderley: Clarendon Press, 1991).

Brezezinski, M., *The Struggle for Constitutionalism in Poland* (Basingstoke: Macmillan, 2000).

Brierley, P., *UK Church Statistics, 2005–2015* (Tonbridge: ADBC Publishers, 2011).

Brownlie, I. and G. S. Goodwill-Gill, *Basic Documents on Human Rights*, 4th edn (Oxford: Oxford University Press, 2002).

Bruce, S., T. Glendinning, I. Paterson and M. Rosie, 'Religious discrimination in Scotland: fact or myth?', *Ethnic and Racial Studies*, 28/1 (2005), 151–68.

Brzezinski, M., *The Struggle for Constitutionalism in Poland* (Basingstoke: Macmillan Press, 2000).

Bulmer, W. E., 'An analysis of the Scottish National Party's Draft Constitution for Scotland', *Parliamentary Affairs*, 64/4 (2011), 674–93.

Bulmer, W. E., 'Minority veto referendums: an alternative to bicameralism', *Politics*, 31/3 (2011), 107–120.

Bulmer, W. E., *A Model Constitution for Scotland: Making Democracy Work in an Independent State* (Edinburgh: Luath Press, 2011).

Bulmer, W. E., *What is a Constitution? Principles and Concepts* (Stockholm: International Institute for Democracy and Electoral Assistance, 2014).

Bulmer, W. E., 'The emergent Scottish constitutional tradition: Scottish, Nordic and Global influences', in K. P. Muller (ed.), *Scotland 2014 and Beyond – Coming of Age and Loss of Innocence* (Frankfurt am Main: Peter Lang, 2014), pp. 201–24.

Bulmer, W. E., 'Constrained majoritarianism: Westminster constitutionalism in Malta', *Commonwealth and Comparative Politics*, 51/1 (2014), pp. 232–53.

Bulmer, W. E., 'Exclusionary constitutionalism: developments in Chile and Hungary', in S. Bisarya (ed.), *Annual Review of Constitution Building Processes, 2014* (Stockholm: International Institute for Democracy and Electoral Assistance, 2015), pp. 47–56.

Bulmer, W. E. and B. Mkangi, *Constitutional Change as a Response to Inter-Communal Violence: Kenya 2007–2010* (Stockholm: International Institute for Democracy and Electoral Assistance, forthcoming).

Bulsara, H. and B. Kissane, 'Arend Lijphart and the transformation of Irish democracy', *West European Politics*, 32/1 (2009), 172–195.

Burton, J. H., *The History of Scotland, From Agricola's Invasion to the Extinction of the Last Jacobite Insurrection* (Edinburgh and London: William Blackwood, 1901).

Campbell, P., *French Electoral Systems and Elections since 1789* (London: Faber and Faber, 1958).

Campbell, T., K. D. Ewing and A. Tomkins (eds), *The Legal Protection of Human Rights: Essays* (Oxford: Oxford University Press, 2011).

Cappelletti, M., 'Judicial review in comparative perspective', *California Law Review*, 58/5 (1970), 1017–53.

Casey, J., *Constitutional Law in Ireland* (London: Sweet and Maxwell, 1992).

Castle, M. and R. Taras, *Democracy in Poland*, 2nd edn (Oxford: Westview Press, 2002).

Charter, D., 'Grand Duke Henri of Luxembourg opposes euthanasia and loses power', *The Times*, 4 December 2008.

Choudhry, S., *The Migration of Constitutional Ideas* (Cambridge: Cambridge University Press, 2006).

Choudhry, S., 'Bridging comparative politics and comparative constitutional law', in S. Choudhry (ed.), *Constitutional Design for Divided Societies* (Oxford: Oxford University Press, 2008).

Choudhry, S., 'Bills of Rights as instruments of nation building in multinational states: the Canadian *Charter* and Quebec nationalism', in J. B. Kelly and C. P. Manfredi (eds), *Contested Constitutionalism: Reflections on the Canadian Charter of Rights and Freedoms* (Vancouver and Toronto: UBC Press, 2009).

Chubb, B., *Cabinet Government in Ireland* (Dublin: Institute of Public Administration, 1974).

Chubb, B., *The Government and Politics of Ireland*, 3rd edn (London: Longman, 1992).

Church of Scotland Special Commission on the Purposes of Economic Activity, *A Right Relationship With Money* (Edinburgh: Church of Scotland, 2012).

Coakley, J., 'Selecting a prime minister: the Irish experience', *Parliamentary Affairs*, 37/1 (1984), 403–17.

Collins, N., 'Parliamentary democracy in Ireland', *Parliamentary Affairs*, 57/3 (2004), 601–12.

Colomer, J., 'It's parties that choose electoral systems (or, Duverger's laws upside down)', *Political Studies*, 53/1 (2005), 1–21.

Commonwealth Secretariat, *Harare Declaration* (1991).

Commonwealth Secretariat, *Latimer House Guidelines* (1998).

Commonwealth Secretariat, *Principles on the Accountability of and the Relationship between the Three Branches of Government* (2003).

Conley, F., *General Elections Today*, 2nd edn (Manchester: Manchester University Press, 1994).

Constant, B., 'Principles of politics applicable to all representative governments', in B. Fontana (ed.), *Constant: Political Writings* (Cambridge: Cambridge University Press, 1988), pp. 171–305.

Council of Europe (nd), *Explanatory Report on the European Charter of Local Self Government ETS No. 122*, <http://conventions.coe.int/treaty/en/Reports/Html/122.htm> (last accessed 18 May 2012).

Council of Europe, *European Charter of Local Self Government*, 1985, <http://conventions.coe.int/Treaty/EN/Treaties/Html/122.htm> (last accessed 18 May 2012).

Cowan, E. J., *For Freedom Alone: The Declaration of Arbroath* (Edinburgh: Birlinn, 2008).

Craig, C., 'Constituting Scotland', *Irish Review*, 28 (Winter 2001), 1–27.

Crewe, I. and A. King, *SDP: The Birth, Life and Death of the Social Democratic Party* (Oxford: Oxford University Press, 1995).

Curtice, J. and R. Ormston, 'Is Scotland more left-wing than England?', *ScotCen Special Edition*, no. 42 (5 December 2011).

Dagger, R., *Civic Virtues: Rights, Citizenship and Republican Liberalism* (Oxford: Oxford University Press, 1997).

Darling, A., Speech given at *The Times Conference on the Future of the Union*, Royal Society of Edinburgh, Friday, 2 March 2012.

De Gaulle, C., 'The Bayeux manifesto [1946]', in A. Lijphart (ed.), *Parliamentary versus Presidential Government*, Oxford Readings in Politics and Government (Oxford: Oxford University Press 1992), pp. 139–41.

De Merieux, M., 'The codification of constitutional conventions in the Commonwealth Caribbean constitutions', *International and Comparative Law Quarterly*, 3/2 (1982), 263–77.

De Smith, S. A., 'Westminster's export models: the legal framework of responsible government', *Journal of Commonwealth Political Studies*, 1/1 (1961), 2–16.

De Tocqueville, A., *L'Ancien Regime*, trans. M. W. Patterson (Oxford: Basil Blackwell, 1962).

De Winter, L. and P. Dumont, 'Belgium: delegation and accountability under partitocratic rule', in K. Strøm, W. C. Müller and T. Bergman (eds), *Delegation and Accountability in Parliamentary Democracies* (Oxford: Oxford University Press, 2003), ch. 6, pp. 253–80.

Dicey, A. V. [1914], *Introduction to the Study of the Law of the Constitution*, 8th edn (Indianapolis: Liberty Fund, 1982).

Dierickx, G., 'Christian democracy and its ideological rivals', in D. Hanley (ed.), *Christian Democracy in Europe: A Comparative Perspective* (London: Pinter 1994), pp. 15–30.

Dudley Edwards, O. (ed.), *A Claim of Right for Scotland* (Edinburgh: Polygon, 1989).

Duverger, M., *Political Parties: Their Organization and Activities in the Modern State*, 3rd edn (London: Methuen, 1964).

Economist, 'Harper goes prorogue', *The Economist*, 7 January 2010.

Economist, 'Orbán and the wind from the east', *The Economist*, 14 November 2011.

Elder, N. C. M., *The Government in Sweden: The Executive at Work* (Oxford and New York: Pergamon Press, 1970).

Elgie, R. and P. Fitzgerald, 'The President and the Taoiseach', in J. Coakley and M. Gallagher (eds), *Politics in the Republic of Ireland*, 4th edn (Abingdon: Routledge, 2007), ch. 11, pp. 305–27.

Elkins, Z., T. Ginsburg and J. Melton, *The Endurance of National Constitutions* (Cambridge: Cambridge University Press, 2009).

Elster, J., 'Constitutionmaking in Eastern Europe: rebuilding the boat in the open sea', *Public Administration*, 71/1–2 (1993), 169–217.

Emy, H. V. (1978), *The Politics of Australian Democracy: Fundamentals in Dispute*, 2nd edn (South Melbourne: Macmillan, 1978).

Eskridge, W. N. Jr and J. Ferejohn, '*A Republic of Statutes: The New American Constitution*' (New Haven, CT: Yale University Press, 2010).

Findlay, P. J., *Contribution to the Constitutional Committee*, second draft, 1968, SNP Archives, National Library of Scotland, A/C No. 10090/98.

Finlayson, A. (2008) 'Politics as an argument about the common good', in S. White and D. Leighton (eds), *Building a Citizen Society: The Emerging Politics of Republican Democracy* (London: Lawrence and Wishart, 2008).

Finer, S. E., *Five Constitutions: Contrasts and Comparisons* (Harmondsworth, Middlesex: Penguin Books, 1979).

Fitzmaurice, J., *Politics in Denmark* (London: Hurst, 1981).

Fitzmaurice, J., *The Politics of Belgium: Crisis and Compromise in a Plural Society*, 2nd edn (London: Hurst, 1988).

Flinders, M., 'Majoritarian democracy in Britain: New Labour and the constitution', *West European Politics*, 28/1 (2005), 61–93.

Gallagher, M., 'The constitution and the judiciary', in J. Coakley and M. Gallagher (eds), *Politics in the Republic of Ireland,* 4th edn (Abingdon: Routledge, 2007), ch. 3, pp. 72–102.

Gallagher, M. (2007), 'Parliament', in J. Coakley and M. Gallagher (eds), *Politics in the Republic of Ireland*, 4th edn (Abingdon: Routledge, 2007), ch. 8, pp. 211–41.

Gallagher, M., 'The Oireachtas: president and parliament', in J. Coakley and M. Gallagher (eds), *Politics in the Republic of Ireland*, 5th edn (Abingdon: Routledge, 2010), ch. 7, pp. 198–229.

Gallagher, M., 'The changing constitution', in J. Coakley and M. Gallagher (eds), *Politics in the Republic of Ireland*, 5th edn (Abingdon: Routledge, 2010), ch. 3, pp. 72–108.

Gamble, A., 'The constitutional revolution in the United Kingdom', *Journal of Federalism*, 36/1 (2006), pp. 19–36.

Gargarella, R., *The Legal Foundations of Inequality: Constitutionalism in the Americas 1776–1860*, Cambridge Studies in the Theory of Democracy (Cambridge: Cambridge University Press, 2010).

Gargarella, R., *Latin American Constitutionalism 1810–2010: The Engine Room of the Constitution* (New York: Oxford University Press, 2013).

General Register Office for Scotland, 'Mid-2011 population estimates for Scotland', <http://www.gro-scotland.gov.uk/files2/stats/population-estimates/mid-2011/j22829703.htm (last accessed 1 September 2012).

General Register Office for Scotland, 'Life expectancy for administrative areas within Scotland,2005–2007',<http://www.gro-scotland.gov.uk/files1/stats/life-expectancy-for-administrative-areas-within-scotland-2005-2007/j1009104.htm#f1> (last accessed 1 September 2012).

Gerring, J. and S. Thacker, *A Centripetal Theory of Democratic Governance* (Cambridge: Cambridge University Press, 2008).

Geyer, A., *Ideology in America: Challenges to Faith* (Louisville, KY: Westminster John Knox Press, 1997).

Ghai, Y. P. and J. Cottrell Ghai, *Kenya's Constitution: An Instrument for Change.* (Nairobi: Katiba Institute, 2011).

Ginsburg, T., *Judicial Review in New Democracies: Constitutional Courts in Asian Cases* (Cambridge: Cambridge University Press, 2003).

Ginsburg, T. and A. Simpser (eds), *Constitutions in Authoritarian Regimes* (Cambridge: Cambridge University Press, 2013).

Glover, M. and R. Hazell, 'Introduction: forecasting constitutional futures', in R. Hazell (ed.), *Constitutional Futures Revised: Britain's Constitution to 2020* (Basingstoke: Palgrave Macmillan, 2008).

Goldsworthy, J., 'Questioning the migration of constitutional ideas: rights, constitutionalism and the limits of convergence', in S. Choudhry (ed.), *The Migration of Constitutional Ideas* (Cambridge: Cambridge University Press, 2006), pp. 115–41.

Gordon, S., *Controlling the State: Constitutionalism from Ancient Athens to Today* (Cambridge, MA: Harvard University Press, 2002).

Grant, A., *Independence and Nationhood: Scotland 1306–1469* (Edinburgh: Edinburgh University Press, 1984).

Gray, J., *Liberalism* (Milton Keynes: Open University Press, 1986).

Grayling, A. C., *Towards the Light: The Story of the Struggles for Liberty and Rights that made the Modern West* (London: Bloomsbury Publishing, 2007).

Greer, S., *The European Convention on Human Rights: Achievements, Problems and Prospects*, Cambridge Studies in European Law and Policy (Cambridge: Cambridge University Press, 2006).

Grey, T. C., 'The constitution as scripture', *Stanford Law Review*, 37/1 (1984), 1–24.

Griffith, J. A. G., 'The political constitution', *Modern Law Review*, 42/1 (1979), 1–21.

Gruijters, J. P. A. (1992) 'The case for a directly elected prime minister in the Netherlands', in A. Lijphart (ed.), *Parliamentary versus Presidential Government* (Oxford: Oxford University Press, 1992), ch. 27, pp. 191–93.

Hall, P. A. and R. C. R. Taylor, 'Political science and the three new institutionalisms', *Political Studies*, XLIV (1996), 936–57.

Hart, G., *Restoration of the Republic: The Jeffersonian Ideal in 21st Century America* (Oxford: Oxford University Press, 2002).

Hassan, G. (ed.), *The Modern SNP: From Protest to Power* (Edinburgh: Edinburgh University Press, 2009).

Hassan, G., 'The "forward march" of Scottish nationalism and the end of Britain as we know it', *Renewal: A Journal of Social Democracy*, 19/2 (2011).

Hassan, G. and P. Lynch, *The Almanac of Scottish Politics* (London: Politicos, 2001).

Hassan, G., *Caledonian Dreaming: The Quest for a Different Scotland* (Edinburgh: Luath Press, 2014).

Hatchard, J. and P. Slinn, *Parliamentary Supremacy and Judicial Independence: A Commonwealth Approach* (London: Cavendish Publishing, 1999).

Hazell, R., 'Conclusion: where will the Westminster model end up?' in R. Hazell (ed.), *Constitutional Futures Revised: Britain's Constitution to 2020* (Basingstoke: Palgrave Macmillan, 2008).

Hazell, R., *The Political Rights of Constitutional Reform*, Stevenson Lecture at the University of Glasgow, 2 November 2010.

Headlam-Morley, A., *The New Democratic Constitutions of Europe: A Comparative Study of Post-War European Constitutions With Special Reference to Germany, Czechoslovakia, Poland, Finland, the Kingdom of the Serbs, Croats and Slovenes and the Baltic States* (London: Oxford University Press, 1928).

Hearn, J., *Claiming Scotland: National Identity and Liberal Culture* (Edinburgh: Edinburgh University Press, 2000).

Henderson, D., *Supplementary Evidence Submitted to the Commission on the Constitution*, 1970, SNP Archives, National Library of Scotland 10090/98.

Henderson, G. D., *Presbyterianism* (Aberdeen: Aberdeen University Press, 1954).

Henderson, G. D., *The Church of Scotland: A Short History*, (Edinburgh: Church of Scotland Youth Committee, 1958).

Himsworth, C. M. G. and C. M. O'Neill, *Scotland's Constitution: Law and Practice* (Haywards Heath: Bloomsbury Professional, 2009).

Himsworth, C. M. G., 'Human rights at the interface of state and sub-state: the case of Scotland', in T. Campbell, K. D. Ewing and A. Tomkins (eds), *The Legal Protection of Human Rights: Sceptical Essays* (Oxford: Oxford University Press, 2011).

Hirschl, R., *Towards Juristocracy: The Origins and Consequences of the New Constitutionalism* (Cambridge, MA: Harvard University Press, 2004).

Hirschl, R., 'The question of case selection in comparative constitutional law', *American Journal of Comparative Law*, 52 (2005), 125–56.

Hirschl, R., *Constitutional Theocracy* (Cambridge, MA: Harvard University Press, 2010).

Holmberg, E. and N. Stjernquist, *The Constitution of Sweden* (Stockholm: Swedish Riksdag, 1995).

Holmstrom, B., 'The judicialization of politics in Sweden', *International Political Science Review/Revue internationale de science politique*, 15/2 (1994), pp. 153–64.

Honohan, I., *Civic Republicanism* (London: Routledge, 2002).

Höpfl, H. (ed.), *Luther and Calvin on Secular Authority*, Cambridge Texts in the History of Political Thought (Cambridge: Cambridge University Press, 1991).

Horowitz, D., 'Democracy in divided societies', *Journal of Democracy*, 4/4 (1993), 18–38.

Hutchins, K., 'Modelling democracy', *Global Society*, 12/2 (1998), 159–75.

Irvine, D., 'Parliamentary sovereignty and judicial independence: keynote address', in J. Hatchard and P. Slinn, *Parliamentary Supremacy and Judicial Independence: A Commonwealth Approach* (London: Cavendish Publishing, 1999), 29–34.

Jackson, B., 'The moderniser: Alex Salmond's journey', *Renewal: A Journal of Social Democracy*, 20/1 (2012).

Jägerskiöld, S., 'Administrative law', in S. Ströholm (ed.), *An Introduction to Swedish Law*, 2nd edn (Stockholm: Norstedt, 1988).

Jennings, W. I., *The Constitution of Ceylon* (Bombay: Oxford University Press, 1949).

Jennings, W. I., *The Approach to Self-Government* (Cambridge: Cambridge University Press, 1958).

Jones, B. and D. Kavanagh, *British Politics Today* (Manchester: Manchester University Press, 1979).

Judge, D., *Political Institutions in the United Kingdom* (Oxford: Oxford University Press, 2005).

Kaldelis, A., *The Byzantine Republic: People and Power in New Rome* (Cambridge, MA: Harvard University Press, 2015).

Kane, J. and H. Patapan, *The Democratic Leader: How Democracy Defines, Empowers and Limits its Leaders* (Oxford, Oxford University Press, 2012).

Keating, M., 'Parliamentary behaviour as a test of Scottish integration into the United Kingdom', *Legislative Studies Quarterly*, 3/3 (1978), 409–30.

Keating, M., 'Stateless nation-building: Quebec, Catalonia and Scotland in the changing state system', *Nations and Nationalism*, 3/4 (1997), 689–717.

Keating, M., 'Reforging the Union: devolution and constitutional change in the United Kingdom', *Publius*, 28/1, 'The State of American Federalism, 1997–1998' (Winter, 1998), 217–34.

Keating, M., 'Introduction', in M. Keating (ed.), *Scottish Social Democracy: Progressive Ideas for Public Policy* (Brussels: Peter Lang, 2007).

Keating, M., 'The strange death of unionist Scotland', *Government and Opposition*, 45/3 (2010), 365–85.

Keating, M. and M. Harvey, *Small Nations in a Big World: What Scotland can Learn* (Edinburgh: Luath Press, 2014).

Keating, M., L. Stevenson, P. Cairney and K. Taylor, 'Does devolution make a difference? Legislative output and policy divergence in Scotland', *Journal of Legislative Studies*, 9/3 (2003), 110–39.

Kekic, L., 'Democracy index 2010: democracy in retreat' (London: Economist Intelligence Unit, 2010).

Kellas, J. G., *The Scottish Political System*, 4th edn (Cambridge: Cambridge University Press, 1989).

Kellas, J. G., 'Nationalism and ethnic conflict: the contribution of political science to political accommodation', *Studies in East European Thought: Nationalism and Social Science*, 46/1/2 (1994), 105–17.

Kelly, E., 'Challenging sectarianism in Scotland: the prism of racism', *Scottish Affairs*, 42 (Winter 2003), XX.

Kelly, J. B. and C. P. Manfedi, 'Should we cheer? Contested constitutionalism and the Canadian Charter of Rights and Freedoms', in J. B. Kelly and C. P. Manfredi (eds), *Constested Constitutionalism: Reflections on the Canadian Charter of Rights and Freedoms* (Vancouver and Toronto: UBC Press, 2009).

Kennedy, H., *Just Law: The Changing Face of Justice – And Why It Matters To Us All* (London: Chatto and Windus, 2004).

Kersbergen, K. van, 'The distinctiveness of Christian democracy', in D. Hanley (ed.), *Christian Democracy in Europe: A Comparative Perspective* (London: Pinter, 1994), pp. 31–50.

Khosla, M., *The Indian Constitutions* (New Delhi: Oxford University Press India, 2012).

King, A., *Does the United Kingdom still have a Constitution?* Hamlyn Lecture Series, no. 52 (London: Sweet and Maxwell, 2001).

Knapp, A. and V. Wright, *The Government and Politics of France*, 5tth edn (Abdingdon: Routledge, 2006).

Kohn, L., *The Constitution of the Irish Free State* (London: Allen and Unwin, 1932).

Kumarasingham, H., *A Political Legacy of the British Empire: Power and the Parliamentary System in Post-Colonial India and Sri Lanka* (London: I. B Tauris, 2013).

Kuyper, A. [1898], *Lectures on Calvinism* (New York: Cosimo Classsics, 2007).

Lafon, J. L., 'France', in C. N. Tate and T. Vallinder (eds), *The Global Expansion of Judicial Power* (New York: New York University Press, 1995).

Lane, J.-E., *Constitutions and Political Theory* (Manchester: Manchester University Press, 1996).

Larson, T. and H. Bäck, *Governing and Governance in Sweden* (Stockholm: Swedish Institute, 2008).

Law, D. S. and M. Versteeg, 'The evolution and ideology of global constitutionalism', *California Law Review*, 99 (2011), 1163–254.

Law, D. S. and M. Versteeg, 'The declining influence of the United States Constitution', *New York University Law Review*, 87 (2012), 762–858.

Lerner, H., *Making Constitutions in Deeply Divided Societies* (Cambridge: Cambridge University Press, 2011).

Lefebvre, E., *The Citizen Burgher: The Belgian Constitution of 1831*, discussion paper presented at Zentrum für Europäische Rechtspolitik, Bremen, 1997.

Leicester, G., 'Scotland', in Robert Hazell (ed.), *The State and the Nations: The First Year of Devolution in the United Kingdom* (Exeter: Imprint Academic, 2000), pp. 13–36.

Leith, M., 'Governance and identity in a devolved Scotland', *Parliamentary Affairs*, 63/2 (2010), 286–301.

Levinson, S., 'Do constitutions have a point?: reflections on "Parchment Barriers" and preambles', in E. F. Paul, F. D. Miller Jr and J. Paul, *What Should Constitutions Do?* (Cambridge: Cambridge University Press, 2011), ch. 6.

Lijphart, A., *Patterns of Democracy: Government Forms and Performance in Thirty-Six Countries* (New Haven, CT: Yale University Press, 1999).

Lijphart, A., 'Constitutional design for divided societies', *Journal of Democracy,* 15/2 (2004), 96–109.

Lipset, S. M. and S. Rokkan, *Party Systems and Voter Alignments: Cross-National Perspectives* (New York: Free Press, 1967).

Lindström, E., *The Swedish Parliamentary System: How Responsibilities are Divided and Decisions are Made* (Stockholm: Swedish Institute, 1982).

Little, G., 'Scotland and parliamentary sovereignty', *Legal Studies*, 24/4 (2004), 540–67.

Longley, C., 'Government and the common good', in N. Spencer and J. Chaplin (eds), *God and Government* (London: SPCK, 2009), ch. 7.

Low, D. A., 'Introduction: the Westminster model', in *Constitutional Heads and Political Crises: Commonwealth Episodes, 1945–85* (Basingstoke: Macmillan, 1988).

Lutz, D., *Principles of Constitutional Design* (Cambridge: Cambridge University Press, 2006).

Lynch, P., *Scottish Government and Politics* (Edinburgh: Edinburgh University Press, 2001).

Lynch, P., *SNP: The History of the Scottish National Party* (Cardiff: Welsh Academic Press, 2002).

Lynch, P., 'From social democracy back to no ideology: the Scottish National Party and ideological change in a multi-level electoral setting', *Regional and Federal Studies*, 19/4-4 (2009), 619–37.

McAngus, C. A, 'Do stateless-nationalist-regionalist-parties differ from other party types? Comparing organisational reform processes in Plaid Cymru and the Scottish national party', *British Politics* (2 November 2015) <http://www.palgrave-journals.com/bp/journal/vaop/ncurrent/pdf/bp201545a.pdf> (last accessed 8 March 2016).

MacAskill, K., *Building a Nation: Post Devolution Nationalism in Scotland* (Edinburgh, Luath Press, 2004).

McConnell, A., *Scottish Local Government* (Edinburgh: Edinburgh University Press, 2004).

McCormick, J., *Understanding the European Union: A Concise Introduction*, 4th edn (Basingstoke: Palgrave Macmillan, 2008).

MacCormick, N., 'An idea for a Scottish constitution', in W. Finnie, C. M. G. Himsworth and N. Walker (eds), *Edinburgh Essays in Public Law* (Edinburgh: Edinburgh University Press, 1991), pp. 159–81.

MacCormick, N., 'Is there a constitutional path to Scottish independence?', *Parliamentary Affairs*, 53/4 (2000), 721–36.

MacCormick, N., personal communication (interview), 2008.

McCrone, D., *Understanding Scotland: The Sociology of a Nation*, 2nd edn (London: Routledge, 2001).

McCrone, D., *Explaining Scotland: Does the Exception Prove the Rule*, address given to Arts and Humanities Research Council Postgraduate Conference, University of Strathclyde, 19 April 2008, transcript by Institute of Governance, Edinburgh.

McDunphy, M., *The President of Ireland: His Powers, Functions and Duties* (Dublin: Browne and Nolan, 1945).

McIlroy, D., 'The role of government in classical Christian political thought', in N. Spencer and J. Chaplin (eds), *God and Government* (London: SPCK, 2009), ch. 4.

Mackie, J. D., *A History of Scotland*, 2nd edn (New York: Hippocrene Books, 1978).

MacKinnon, J., *The Constitutional History of Scotland: From Early Times to the Reformation* (Harlow: Longmans, Green, 1924).

MacLeod, D. and M. Russell, *Grasping the Thistle* (Glendaruel: Argyll Publishing, 2006).

Macy, J. and J. W. Gannaway, *Comparative Free Government* (New York: Macmillan, 1915).

Mandel, M., 'Legal politics Italian style', in C. N. Tate and T. Vallinder (eds), *The Global Expansion of Judicial Power* (New York: New York University Press, 1995).

Mandle, J. R., 'British Caribbean economic history: an interpretation', in F. W. Knight and C. A. Palmer (eds), *The Modern Caribbean* (Chapel Hill, NC: University of North Carolina Press, 1989).

Manin, B., *The Principles of Representative Government* (Cambridge: Cambridge University Press, 1997).

Manning, M., 'Ireland', in D. Butler and A. Ranney (eds), *Referendums* (Washington, DC: American Enterprise Institute for Public Policy Research, 1978), pp. 204–6.

Manow, P. *In the King's Shadow: The Political Anatomy of Democratic Representation* (Cambridge: Polity Press, 2010).

Marquand, D., *The New Reckoning: Capitalism, States and Citizens* (Cambridge and Oxford: Polity Press, 1997).

Maynor, J. W., *Republicanism in the Modern World* (Cambridge and Oxford: Polity Press, 2003).

Medhurst, K., 'Spain's evolutionary pathway from dictatorship to democracy', *West European Politics*, 7/2 (1984), 30–50.

Meston, M. C., 'Scots law today', in M. C. Meston, W. D. H. Sellar and T. M. Cooper, *The Scottish Legal Tradition* (Edinburgh: Saltire Society, 1991).

Mill, J. S. [1861], 'Considerations on representative government', in H. B. Acton (ed.), *J. S. Mill: Utilitarianism, On Liberty and Considerations on Representative Government* (London: Dent, 1972).

Misner, P., 'Christian Democratic social policy: precedents for third-way thinking', in T. Kselman and J. A. Buttigieg (eds), *European Christian Democracy: Historical Legacies and Comparative Perspectives* (Notre Dame, IN: University of Notre Dame Press, 2003).

Mitchell, J., 'The narcissism of small differences: Scotland and Westminster', *Parliamentary Affairs*, 63 (2010), 98–116.

Mitchell, J., R. Johns and L. Bennie, 'Who are the SNP members?', in G. Hassan (ed.), *The Modern SNP: From Protest to Power* (Edinburgh: Edinburgh University Press, 2009), ch. 6.

Mitchell, J., L. Bennie and R. Johns, *The Scottish National Party: Transition to Power* (Oxford: Oxford University Press, 2012).

Mitchell, P., 'Ireland: "O What a Tangled Web" – delegation, accountability and executive power', in K. Strøm, W. C. Müller and T. Bergman (eds), *Delegation and Accountability in Parliamentary Democracies*, Comparative Politics (Oxford: Oxford University Press, 2003), ch. 13, pp. 418–45.

Moffat, R. (ed.), *Scotland's Constitution* (Glasgow: Moffat Press, 1993).

Möllers, C., '"We are (afraid of) the people": constituent power in German constitutionalism', in M. Loughlin and N. Walker (eds), *The Paradox of Constitutionalism: Constituent Power and Constitutional Form* (Oxford: Oxford University Press, 2007), ch. 5.

Montgomery, P., 'Belgian king, unable to sign abortion law, takes day off', *New York Times*, 5 April 1990.

Moos, M., 'Don Luigi Sturzo: Christian Democrat', *American Political Science Review*, 9/2 (1945), 278.

Morgan, D. G., 'Selection of superior judges in Ireland', paper from the conference on Judicial Reform: Function, Appointment and Structure, held by the Centre for Public Law, University of Cambridge, on 4 October 2003.

Moreno, L., 'Scotland, Catalonia, Europeanization and the "Moreno question"', *Scottish Affairs*, 54/1 (Winter 2006), 1–21.

Murphy, W. F., *Constitutional Democracy: Creating and Maintaining a Just Political Order* (Baltimore: Johns Hopkins University Press, 2007).

Murray, C. and R. Simeon, 'Recognition without empowerment: minorities in a democratic South Africa', *International Journal of Constitutional Law*, 5/4 (2007), 699–729.

Myers, A. R., *Parliaments and Estates in Europe to 1789* (London: Thames and Hudson, 1975).

Negretto, G. L., *Making Constitutions: Presidents, Parties and Constitutional Choice in Latin America* (Cambridge: Cambridge University Press, 2013).

Norton, P., 'Playing by the rules: the constraining hand of parliamentary procedure', *Journal of Legislative Studies*, 7/3 (2001), 13–33.

Nothomb, C. F., *Principes de Démocratie : Le modèle de la Belgique fédérale.* (Louvain-la-Neuve: Duculot SA, 1994).

Nyman, O., 'Some basic features of Swedish constitutional law', in S. Ströholm (ed.), *An Introduction to Swedish Law*, 2nd edn (Stockholm: Norstedt, 1988).

O'Brien, D., *The Constitutional Systems of the Commonwealth Caribbean: A Contextual Analysis*, Constitutional Systems of the World (Oxford: Hart Publishing, 2014).

Olivier, P. (1999) 'Parliamentary sovereignty and "judge-made" law; judicial review of legislation', in J. Hatchard and P. Slinn, *Parliamentary Supremacy and Judicial Independence: A Commonwealth Approach* (London: Cavendish Publishing, 1999),pp. 53–58.

Ordeshook, P. C., 'Constitutions for new democracies: reflections of turmoil or agents of stability?', *Public Choice*, 90 (1997), 55–72.

Osur J., *The Great Controversy: A Story of Abortion, the Church and Constitution-Making in Kenya* (Nairobi: Zeus Media, 2011).

O'Toole, F., *Enough is Enough: How to Build a New Republic* (London:Faber and Faber, 2011).

Paine, T. [1791], 'The rights of man', in M. Foot and I. Kramnick (eds), *The Thomas Paine Reader* (London: Penguin Classics, 1987).

Pallarés, F., J. Ramon Montero and F. José Llera, 'Non-state-wide parties in Spain: an attitudinal study of nationalism and regionalism', *Publius*, 27/4, Toward Federal Democracy in Spain (Autumn 1997), pp. 135–69.

Palmer, G. and M. S. R. Palmer, *Bridled Power: New Zealand's Constitution and Government*, 4th edn (Melbourne: Oxford University Press, 2004).

Palmer, M. S. R., 'Using constitutional realism to identify the *complete* constitution: lessons from an unwritten constitution', *American Journal of Comparative Law*, 54/3 (2006), 587–636.

Paterson, L., A. Brown, J. Curtice, K. Hinds, D. McCrone, A. Park, K. Sproston and P. Surridge, *New Scotland, New Politics?* (Edinburgh: Edinburgh University Press, 2001).

Pettit, P., *Republicanism: A Theory of Freedom and Government* (Oxford: Oxford University Press, 1997).

Pettit, P., *A Theory of Freedom: From the Psychology to the Politics of Agency* (Cambridge and Oxford: Polity Press, 2001).

Pickles, D., *France: the Fourth Republic* (London: Methuen, 1955).

Pickles, D., *The Fifth French Republic: Institutions and Politics* (London: Methuen University Paperbacks, 1965).

Plischke, E., *Contemporary Government of Germany* (London: George Allen and Unwin, 1964).

Pocock, J. A. G., *The Machiavellian Moment: Florentine Political Thought and the Atlantic Republican Tradition* (Princeton, NJ: Princeton University Press, 1975).

Pontuso, J. F., *Václav Havel: Civic Responsibility in the Postmodern Age*, 20th Century Political Thinkers (Rowman and Littlefield Publishers, 2004).

Qvortrup, M., *A Comparative Study of Referendums: Government by the People* (Manchester: Manchester University Press, 2005).

Ramsey, M., *What's Wrong With Liberalism: A Radical Critique of Liberal Political Philosophy* (Leicester: Leicester University Press, 1997).

Reid, G., 'The fourth principle: sharing power with the people of Scotland', in B. Crick and A. Lockyer (eds), *Active Citizenship: What Could it Achieve and How?* (Edinburgh: Edinburgh University Press, 2010).

Reilly, B., 'Electoral systems for divided societies', *Journal of Democracy*, 13/2 (April 2002), 156–70.

Rhodes, R. A. W., *Understanding Governance: Policy Networks, Governance, Reflexivity and Accountability* (Buckingham: Open University Press, 1997).

Richards, S. G., *Introduction to British Government* (London and Basingstoke: Macmillan Press, 1978).

Riker, W., 'The justification of bicameralism', *International Political Science Review*, 12/1 (1992), 101–16.

Robbins, C. (ed.), *Two English Republican Tracts* (Cambridge: Cambridge University Press, 1969).

Roberts, G. K., *German Politics Today* (Manchester: Manchester University Press, 2000).

Robertson, J. (ed.), *Andrew Fletcher: Political Works*, Cambridge Texts in the History of Political Thought (Cambridge: Cambridge University Press, 1997).

Rosie, M. and R. Bond, 'Social democratic Scotland?', in M. Keating (ed.), *Scottish Social Democracy: Progressive Ideas for Public Policy* (Brussels: P.I.E. Peter Lang SA, 2007).

Rosen, K., 'Judicial review: old and new', *Yale Law Journal*, 81/7 (1972), 1411–20.

Rudd, N., *Cicero: The Republic and The Laws* (Oxford: Oxford World's Classics, 1998).

Russell, M., 'What are second chambers for?', *Parliamentary Affairs*, 54 (2001), 442–58.

Russell, P. H., 'The *Charter* and Canadian democracy', in J. B. Kelly and C. P. Manfredi (eds), *Constested Constitutionalism: Reflections on the Canadian Charter of Rights and Freedoms* (Vancouver and Toronto: UBC Press, 2009).

Saalfield, T., 'The United Kingdom: still a single chain of command? The hollowing out of the Westminster model', in K. Strøm, W. C. Müller and T. Bergman (eds), *Delegation and Accountability in Parliamentary Democracies*, Comparative Politics (Oxford: Oxford University Press, 2003), pp. 620–48.

Sabine, G. H. and S. B. Smith, 'Cicero: on the commonwealth', Library of the Liberal Arts (New York: Macmillan, 1976).

Sajó, A., *Limiting Government: An Introduction to Constitutionalism* (Budapest: Central European University Press, 1999).

Sap, J. W., *The Queen, the Populists and the Others: New Dutch Politics Explained for Foreigners* (Amsterdam: VU University Press, 2010).

Sammut, J., personal communication, 2009.

Sampford, C. J. G., 'Recognise and declare: an Australian experiment in codifying constitutional conventions', *Oxford Journal of Legal Studies*, 7/3 (Winter 1987), 369–420.

Sanders, D., 'Behaviouralism', in D. Marsh and G. Stoker (eds), *Theory and Methods in Political Science*, 2nd edn (Basingstoke: Palgrave Macmillan, 2002), ch. 2, pp. 45–64.

Sant, M., *Proposals for a Constitutional Reform Agenda in Malta: Why the Constitution of Malta requires Updating* (Saarbrücken: VDM Verlag Dr. Müller, 2010).

Sartori, G., *Parties and Party Systems: A Framework for Analysis* (Cambridge: Cambridge University Press, 1976).

Sartori, G., *Comparative Constitutional Engineering: An Inquiry into Structures, Incentives and Outcomes*, 2nd edn (Basingstoke: Macmillan Press, 1997).

Saunders, C., *The Constitution of Australia: A Contextual Analysis*, Constitutional Systems of the World (Oxford and Portland, Oregon: Hart Publishing, 2011).

Seldon, A., *Trust: How we Lost It and How to Get It Back* (London: Bite Back Publishing, 2010).

Scotsman, 'The Scottish parliament, adjourned on 25th March 1707, is hereby reconvened', *The Scotsman*, 13 May 1999.

Scotsman, 'Catholic church moves into pole position', *The Scotsman*, Saturday, 24 May 2008, <http://www.scotsman.com/news/catholic_church_moves_into_pole_position_1_1433537> (last accessed 24 February 2012).

Scottish Government, *Analysis of Ethnicity in the 2001 Census – Summary Report*, 2004 <http://www.scotland.gov.uk/Publications/2004/02/18876/32939> (last accessed 23 February 2012).

Scottish Government, *Analysis of Religion in the 2001 Census – Summary Report*, 2005, <http://scotland.gov.uk/Publications/2005/02/20757/53568> (last accessed 9 March 2012).

Scottish Office, *Shaping Scotland's Parliament: Report of the Consultative Steering*

Group on the Scottish Parliament, presented to the Secretary of State for Scotland December 1998, Edinburgh, Scottish Office.

Scottish Parliament, 'The Presiding Officer', <http://www.scottish.parliament.uk/abouttheparliament/22008.aspx> (last accessed 9 September 2012).

Siaroff, A., 'Varieties of parliamentarianism in the advanced industrial democracies', *International Political Science Review/Revue international de science politique,* 24/4 (October 2003), 445–64.

Singh, M. P., *V. N. Shukla's Constitution of India,* 12th edn (Lucknow: Eastern Book Company, 2013).

Sinnott, R., 'The rules of the electoral game', in J. Coakley and M. Gallagher (eds), *Politics in the Republic of Ireland,* 4th edn (Abingdon: Routledge, 2007), pp. 105–34.

Shell, D., *Does Scotland Need a Senate?,* Stevenson Lecture on Citizenship, University of Glasgow, 2012.

Shephard, M. and P. Cairney, 'The impact of the Scottish Parliament in amending executive legislation', *Political Studies,* 53/2 (2005), 303–19.

Skinner, Q., *Liberty Before Liberalism* (Cambridge: Cambridge University Press, 1998).

Smith, A. D., *Nationalism and Modernism* (Abingdon: Routledge, 1998).

Smith Commission, *Report of the Smith Commission for Further Devolution of Powers to the Scottish Parliament,* 27 November 2014 <http://www.smith-commission.scot/wp-content/uploads/2014/11/The_Smith_Commission_Report-1.pdf> (last accessed 12 November 2015).

SNP, *The Parliament and Constitution of an Independent Scotland* (Edinburgh: SNP, 1997).

SNP, *A Free Scotland* (Edinburgh: SNP, 2002).

SNP, *Constitution of the Scottish National Party* (Edinburgh: SNP, 2009).

Spotts, F. and T. Weiser, *Italy: A Difficult Democracy* (Cambridge: Cambridge University Press, 1986).

Stepan, A., J. J. Linz and J. F. Minoves, 'Democratic parliamentary monarchies', *Journal of Democracy,* 25/2 (2014), 35–51.

Steinbeis, M. (2011) 'Europeas letztes Aufgebot', *Welt Online,* 7 January 2012 <http://www.welt.de/print/die_welt/kultur/article13802809/Europas-letztes-Aufgebot.html> (last accessed 20 January 2012).

Steven, M., 'The place of religion in devolved Scottish politics: an interest group analysis of the Church of Scotland and Scottish Catholic Church', *Scottish Affairs,* 58/1 (Winter 2007), 56–110.

Stjernquist, N., 'Judicial review and the rule of law: comparing the United States and Sweden', *Policy Studies Journal,* 19/1 (1990), 106–15.

Stone Sweet, A., 'Constitutional courts and parliamentary democracy', *West European Politics,* 25/1 (2002), 77–100.

Storrar, W., *Scottish Identity: A Christian Vision* (Haddington: Handsel Press, 1990).

Strøm, K., W. C. Müller and T. Bergman (eds), *Delegation and Accountability in Parliamentary Democracies* (Oxford: Oxford University Press, 2003).

Strøm, K. and H. M. Narud (2003) 'Norway: virtual parlamentarism', in K. Strøm, W. C. Müller and T. Bergman (eds), *Delegation and Accountability in Parliamentary Democracies* (Oxford: Oxford University Press, 2003), ch. 17, pp. 523–52.

Strömholm S. (ed.), *An Introduction to Swedish Law*, 2nd edn (Stockholm: Norstedt, 1988).

Sunkin, M., 'The United Kingdom', in C. N. Tate and T. Vallinder (eds), *The Global Expansion of Judicial Power* (New York: New York University Press, 1995).

Sunstein, C., 'Designing democracy: what constitutions do' (Oxford: Oxford University Press, 2002).

Sunstein, C., *The Second Bill of Rights: FDR's Unfinished Revolution* (New York: Basic Books, 2004).

Swift-MacNeill, J. G., 'Thoughts on the Constitution of the Irish Free State', *Journal of Comparative Legislation and International Law*, 5/3 (1923), 52–62.

Taagepera, R., 'The size of national assemblies', *Social Science Research*, 1 (December 1972), 385–400.

Tangelder, J. D., 'Reformed reflections: Canada's social charter', 1990 <http://www.reformedreflections.ca/cultural-political/can-soc-charter.html> (last accessed 2 February 2016).

Tate, C. N. and T. Vallinder (eds), *The Global Expansion of Judicial Power* (New York: New York University Press, 1995).

Taylor, G., 'Two refusals of royal assent in Victoria', *Sydney Law Review*, 29 (2007), 85–130.

Ten Kate, J. and P. J. Van Koppen, 'The Netherlands: toward a form of judicial review', in C. N. Tate and T. Vallinder (eds), *The Global Expansion of Judicial Power* (New York: New York University Press, 1995).

Tesón, F. R., 'The Liberal constitution and foreign affairs', in E. F. Paul, F. D. Miller Jr and J. Paul (eds), *What Should Constitutions Do?* (Cambridge: Cambridge University Press, 2011).

Thiébault, J.-L. (2003) 'France: delegation and accountability in the Fifth Republic', in K. Strøm, W. C. Müller and T. Bergman (eds), *Delegation and Accountability in Parliamentary Democracies* (Oxford: Oxford University Press, 2003), pp. 325–46.

Thornhill, C., *A Sociology of Constitutions: Constitutions and State Legitimacy in Socio-Historical Perspective* (Cambridge: Cambridge University Press, 2011).

Timmermans, A. and R. B. Andeweg, 'The Netherlands: rules and mores in delegation and accountability relationships', in K. Strøm, W. C. Müller and T. Bergman (eds), *Delegation and Accountability in Parliamentary Democracies* (Oxford: Oxford University Press, 2003), pp. 498–522.

Tomkins, A., *Our Republican Constitution* (Oxford: Hart Publishing, 2005).

Tomkins, A., 'Republican constitutionalism and constitutional reform', in S. White and D. Leighton (eds), *Building a Citizen Society: The Emerging Politics of Republican Democracy* (London: Lawrence and Wishart, 2008), ch. 3, pp. 33–43.

Turp, D., 'L'avant-projet de loi sur la souveraineté: texte annoté', *L'Action nationale*, LXXXV/8 (October 1995), 52–77.

Valinder, T., 'When the courts go marching in', in C. N. Tate and T. Vallinder (eds), *The Global Expansion of Judicial Power* (NY and London: New York University Press, 1995).

Van Loon, R. J. and M. S. Whittington, *The Canadian Political System: Environment, Structure and Process* (Toronto: McGraw-Hill Ryerson, 1987).

Viroli, M., *Republicanism*, trans. A. Shugaar (New York: Hill and Wang, 2002).

Ward, A. J., 'Exporting the British constitution: responsible government in New

Zealand, Canada, Australia and Ireland', *Journal of Commonwealth and Comparative Politics*, 25/1 (1987), 3–25.

Webber, J., *The Constitution of Canada: A Contextual Analysis*, Constitutional Systems of the World (Oxford: Hart Publishing, 2015).

Weinrib, L. E., 'The postwar paradigm and American exceptionalism', in S. Choudhry, *Migration of Constitutional Ideas* (Cambridge: Cambridge University Press, 2006).

Wilks-Heeg, S. and S. Weir, *The Unspoken Constitution*, Democratic Audit, 2009 <http://www.opendemocracy.net/files/unspoken_constitution.pdf accessed> (last accessed 5 January 2012).

Williams, P., *Politics in Post-War France: Parties and the Constitution in the Fourth Republic* (London: Longmans, Green, 1958).

Wilson, G., 'The Westminster model in comparative perspective', in I. Budge and D. McKay, *Developing Democracy: Comparative Research in Honour of J. F. P. Blondel* (London: Sage, 1994).

Wolf-Phillips, L., 'Post-independence constitutional change in the Commonwealth', *Political Studies*, 18/1 (1970), 18–42.

Wormald, J., *Court, Kirk and Community: Scotland 1470–1625* (Edinburgh: Edinburgh University Press, 1981).

Wright, K., *'Expressing and Exercising Scottish Sovereignty'*, Open Democracy, 30 November 2009 <http://www.opendemocracy.net/ourkingdom/canon-kenyon-wright/expressing-and-exercising-scottish-sovereignty> (last accessed 3 January 2012).

Wright, K., Submission to UK Constitutional and Political Reform Select Committee, 2012.

Wright, O., 'Ministers plot end to Civil Service neutrality', *The Independent*, London, 1 August 2012.

Zifcak, R. and R. Eckersley, 'The constitution and democracy in Victoria: Westminster on trial', *Australian Journal of Political Science*, 36/1 (2001), 61–80.

Ziller, J., 'European models of government: towards a patchwork of missing pieces', *Parliamentary Affairs*, 54/1 (2001), 102–19.

INDEX

EU representative:
Easy Access System Europe
Mustamäe tee 50, 10621 Tallinn, Estonia
Gpsr.requests@easproject.com

www.ingramcontent.com/pod-product-compliance
Lightning Source LLC
Chambersburg PA
CBHW061239220326
41599CB00028B/5484